Applications of ATILA FEM software to smart materials

Related titles:

Advanced piezoelectric materials
(ISBN 978-1-84569-534-7)

Ultrasonic transducers
(ISBN 978-1-84569-989-5)

MEMS for automotive and aerospace applications
(ISBN 978-0-85709-118-5)

Details of these books and a complete list of titles from Woodhead Publishing can be obtained by:

- visiting our web site at www.woodheadpublishing.com
- contacting Customer Services (e-mail: sales@woodheadpublishing.com; fax: +44 (0) 1223 832819; tel.: +44 (0) 1223 499140 ext. 130; address: Woodhead Publishing Limited, 80, High Street, Sawston, Cambridge CB22 3HJ, UK)
- in North America, contacting our US office (e-mail: usmarketing@ woodheadpublishing.com; tel.: (215) 928 9112; address: Woodhead Publishing, 1518 Walnut Street, Suite 1100, Philadelphia, PA 19102-3406, USA

If you would like e-versions of our content, please visit our online platform: www.woodheadpublishingonline.com. Please recommend it to your librarian so that everyone in your institution can benefit from the wealth of content on the site.

We are always happy to receive suggestions for new books from potential editors. To enquire about contributing to our Electronic and Optical Materials series, please send your name, contact address and details of the topic/s you are interested in to laura.pugh@woodheadpublishing.com. We look forward to hearing from you.

The Woodhead team responsible for publishing this book:
Commissioning Editor: Laura Pugh
Publications Co-ordinator: Steven Mathews
Project Editor: Sarah Lynch
Editorial and Production Manager: Mary Campbell
Production Editor: Richard Fairclough
Cover Designer: Terry Callanan

Woodhead Publishing Series in Electronic and Optical Materials:
Number 31

Applications of ATILA FEM software to smart materials

Case studies in designing devices

Edited by

Kenji Uchino and Jean-Claude Debus

WP

WOODHEAD
PUBLISHING

Oxford   Cambridge   Philadelphia   New Delhi

Published by Woodhead Publishing Limited,
80 High Street, Sawston, Cambridge CB22 3HJ, UK
www.woodheadpublishing.com
www.woodheadpublishingonline.com

Woodhead Publishing, 1518 Walnut Street, Suite 1100, Philadelphia,
PA 19102-3406, USA

Woodhead Publishing India Private Limited, G-2, Vardaan House, 7/28 Ansari Road,
Daryaganj, New Delhi – 110002, India
www.woodheadpublishingindia.com

First published 2013, Woodhead Publishing Limited

British Library Cataloguing in Publication Data
A catalogue record for this book is available from the British Library.

Library of Congress Control Number: 2012949972

ISBN 978-0-85709-065-2 (print)
ISBN 978-0-85709-631-9 (online)
ISSN 2050-1501 Woodhead Publishing Series in Electronic and Optical Materials (print)
ISSN 2050-151X Woodhead Publishing Series in Electronic and Optical Materials (online)

The publisher's policy is to use permanent paper from mills that operate a sustainable
forestry policy, and which has been manufactured from pulp which is processed using acid-
free and elemental chlorine-free practices. Furthermore, the publisher ensures that the text
paper and cover board used have met acceptable environmental accreditation standards.

Typeset by Replika Press Pvt Ltd, India
Printed by Lightning Source

Contents

Contributor contact details

(* = main contact)

Editor and Chapters 1 and 3

Dr Kenji Uchino
Office of Naval Research
ONR Global-Asia
7-23-17 Roppongi, Minato-ku
Tokyo 106-0032
Japan

and

135 Materials Research Laboratory
  Building
The Pennsylvania State University
University Park, PA 16802
USA

E-mail: kenjiuchino@psu.edu;
        kenjiuchino@mmech.com

Editor and Chapters 2, 4, 5, 11, 12 and 13

Dr Jean-Claude Debus
ISEN Lille
Institut Supérieur de l'Electronique
  et du Numérique
41 Boulevard Vauban
59046 Lille cedex
France

E-mail: Jean-Claude.Debus@isen.fr

Chapter 6

Dr Seungho Park
Micromechatronics Inc.
200 Innovation Blvd. Suite 155
State College, PA 16803
USA

E-mail: sxp953@gmail.com

Chapter 7

Dr Seok-Jin Yoon
Future Convergence Technology
    Research Division
Korea Institute of Science and
    Technology
Korea

E-mail: sjyoon@kist.re.kr

Chapters 8 and 9

Dr Anne-Christine Hladky-Hennion
IEMN
ISEN Lille
UMR 8520 CNRS
41 Boulevard Vauban
59046 Lille
France

E-mail: anne-christine.hladky@isen.fr

Chapter 10

Dr Alain Loussert*
ISEN Brest
Acoustic Department
C.S. 42807
29228 Brest Cedex 2
France

E-mail: alain.loussert@isen.fr

Dr Jean-Claude Debus
ISEN Lille
Acoustic Department
41 Boulevard Vauban
59046 Lille Cedex
France

Dr Gérard Vanderborck
Thales Underwater Systems SAS
Acoustic Department
525 route des Dolines
BP 157
06903 Sophia Antipolis Cedex
France

Woodhead Publishing Series in Electronic and Optical Materials

Part I

Introduction to the ATILA finite element method (FEM) software

1

Overview of the ATILA finite element method (FEM) software code

K. UCHINO, The Pennsylvania State University, USA

DOI: 10.1533/9780857096319.1.3

Abstract: The finite element method and its application to smart transducer systems are introduced in this chapter. The fundamentals of finite element analysis are introduced first. Then, the section 'Defining the equations for the problem' treats how to integrate the piezoelectric constitutive equations, and 'Application of the finite element method' describes the meshing. The last section 'FEM simulation examples' introduces six cases; multilayer actuator, Π-type linear ultrasonic motor, windmill ultrasonic motor, metal tube ultrasonic motor, piezoelectric transformer, and 'cymbal' underwater transducer, which includes most of the basic capabilities of ATILA FEM code.

Key words: finite element method, piezoelectric constitutive equation, node, shape function, variational principle, discretization, parent element, assembly.

1.1 An introduction to finite element analysis

Consider the piezoelectric domain Ω pictured in Fig. 1.1, within which the displacement field, **u**, and electric potential field, ϕ, are to be determined. The **u** and ϕ fields satisfy a set of differential equations that represent the

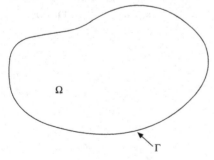

1.1 Schematic representation of the problem domain Ω with boundary Γ.

A part of this chapter is based on and cited from the ATILA User Manual authored by Dr Philippe Bouchilloux (Currently Heptagon, Singapore) with his permission.

physics of the continuum problem considered. Boundary conditions are usually imposed on the domain's boundary, Γ, to complete the definition of the problem.

The finite element method is an approximation technique for finding solution functions.[1] The method consists of subdividing the domain Ω into sub-domains, or finite elements, as illustrated in Fig. 1.2. These finite elements are interconnected at a finite number of points, or nodes, along their peripheries. The ensemble of finite elements defines the problem mesh. Note that because the subdivision of Ω into finite elements is arbitrary, there is not a unique mesh for a given problem.

Within each finite element, the displacement and electric potential fields are uniquely defined by the values they assume at the element nodes. This is achieved by a process of interpolation or weighing in which shape functions are associated with the element. By combining, or assembling, these local definitions throughout the whole mesh, we obtain a trial function for Ω that depends only on the nodal values of $\mathbf{u}$ and ϕ and that is 'piecewise' defined over all the interconnected elementary domains. Unlike the domain Ω, these elementary domains may have a simple geometric shape and homogeneous composition.

We will show in the following sections how this trial function is evaluated in terms of the variation principle to produce a system of linear equations whose unknowns are the nodal values of $\mathbf{u}$ and ϕ.[2]

1.2   Defining the equations for the problem

1.2.1   The constitutive and equilibrium equations

The constitutive relations for piezoelectric media may be derived in terms of their associated thermodynamic potentials.[3,4] Assuming the strain, x, and electric field, E, are independent variables, the basic equations of state for the converse and direct piezoelectric effects are written:

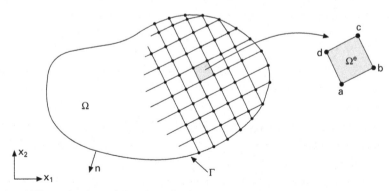

1.2 Discretization of the domain Ω.

$$\begin{cases} X_{ij} = c^{E}_{ijkl} x_{kl} - e_{kij} E_k \\ D_i = e_{ikl} x_{kl} + \chi^{x}_{ij} E_j \end{cases} \quad [1.1]$$

The quantities c^E (elastic stiffness at constant electric field), e (piezoelectric stress coefficients), and χ^x (dielectric susceptibility at constant strain) are assumed to be constant, which is reasonable for piezoelectric materials subjected to small deformations and moderate electric fields. Furthermore, no distinction is made between isothermal and adiabatic constants.

On the domain, Ω, and its boundary, Γ, (where the normal is directed outward from the domain), the fundamental dynamic relation must be verified:

$$\rho \frac{\partial^2 \mathbf{u}_i}{\partial t^2} = \frac{\partial \mathbf{X}_{ij}}{\partial r_j} \quad [1.2]$$

where $\mathbf{u}$ is the displacement vector, ρ the mass density of the material, t the time, $\mathbf{X}$ the stress tensor, and $\mathbf{r} = <r_1\ r_2\ r_3>$, a unit vector in the Cartesian coordinate system.

When no macroscopic charges are present in the medium, Gauss' theorem imposes for the electric displacement vector, $\mathbf{D}$:

$$\frac{\partial D_i}{\partial r_i} = 0 \quad [1.3]$$

Considering small deformations, the strain tensor, $\mathbf{x}$, is written as:

$$x_{kl} = \frac{1}{2}\left(\frac{\partial u_k}{\partial r_l} + \frac{\partial u_l}{\partial r_k} \right) \quad [1.4]$$

Assuming electrostatic conditions, the electrostatic potential, ϕ, is related to the electric field $\mathbf{E}$ by

$$\mathbf{E} = -\operatorname{grad} \phi \quad [1.5]$$

or, equivalently

$$E_i = -\frac{\partial \phi}{\partial r_i} \quad [1.6]$$

Using Equations [1.2], [1.3] and [1.6] in combination with Equation [1.1] yields:

$$\begin{cases} -\rho \omega^2 u_i = \dfrac{\partial}{\partial r_j}(c^{E}_{ijkl} x_{kl} - e_{kij} E_k) \\[2mm] \dfrac{\partial}{\partial r_j}(e_{ikl} x_{kl} + \chi^{x}_{ij} E_j) = 0 \end{cases} \quad [1.7]$$

1.2.2   Boundary conditions

Mechanical and electrical boundary conditions complete the definition of the problem.

The mechanical conditions are as follows:

- The Dirichlet condition on the displacement field, **u**, is given by:

$$u_i = u_i^o \qquad [1.8]$$

  where **u**^{o} is a known vector. For convenience, we name the ensemble of surface elements subjected to this condition S_u.
- The Neumann condition on the stress field, **X**, is given by:

$$X_{ij} \cdot n_j = f_i^o \qquad [1.9]$$

  where **n** is the vector normal to Γ, directed outward, and **f**^{o} is a known vector. For convenience, we name the ensemble of surface elements subjected to this condition S_X.

The electrical conditions are as follows:

- The conditions for the excitation of the electric field between those surfaces of the piezoelectric material that are not covered with an electrode and are, therefore, free of surface charges is given by:

$$D_i \cdot n_i = 0 \qquad [1.10]$$

  where **n** is the vector normal to the surface. For convenience, we name the ensemble of surface elements subjected to this condition S_σ. Note that with the condition in Equation [1.9], we assume that the electric field outside Ω is negligible, which is easily verified for piezoelectric ceramics.
- When considering the conditions for the potential and excitation of the electric field between those surfaces of the piezoelectric material that are covered with electrodes, we assume that there are p electrodes in the system. The potential on the whole surface of the pth electrode is:

$$\phi = \phi_p \qquad [1.11]$$

  The charge on that electrode is:

$$-\iint_{S_p} D_i n_i dS_p = Q_p \qquad [1.12]$$

In some cases, the potential is used, and in others it is the charge. In the former case, ϕ_p is known and Equation [1.11] is used to determine Q_p. In the latter case, Q_p is known and Equation [1.10] is used to determine ϕ. Finally, in order to define the origin of the potentials, it is necessary to impose the condition that the potential at one of the electrodes be zero ($\phi_o = 0$).

1.2.3   The variational principle

The variational principle identifies a scalar quantity Π, typically named the functional, which is defined by an integral expression involving the unknown function, **w**, and its derivatives over the domain Ω and its boundary Γ. The solution to the continuum problem is a function **w** such that

$$\delta\Pi = 0 \qquad [1.13]$$

Π is said to be stationary with respect to small changes in **w**, δ**w**. When the variational principle is applied, the solution can be approximated in an integral form that is suitable for finite element analysis. In general, the matrices derived from the variational principle are always symmetric.

Equation [1.7] and the boundary conditions expressed by Equations [1.8] to [1.12] allow us to define the so-called Euler equations to which the variational principle is applied such that a functional of the following form is defined that is stationary with respect to small variations in **w**.

$$\Pi = \iiint_{\Omega} \frac{1}{2}\,(x_{ij}c^{E}_{ijkl}x_{kl} - \rho\omega^2 u_i^2)\,d\Omega$$

$$- \iint_{S_u} (u_i - u_i^{o})n_j(c^{E}_{ijkl}x_{kl} - e_{kij}E_k)dS_u$$

$$- \iiint_{\Omega} \frac{1}{2}\,(2x_{kl}e_{ikl}E_i + E_i\chi^{x}_{ij}E_j)\,d\Omega - \iint_{S_x} f_i u_i dS_x$$

$$- \sum_{p=0}^{M} \iint_{S_p} (\phi - \phi_p)n_i(e_{ikl}x_{kl} + \chi^{x}_{ij}E_j)\,dS_p + \sum_{p=0}^{P} \phi_p Q_p \qquad [1.14]$$

Note that the first term of this expression for Π represents the Lagrangian of the mechanical state. Satisfying the stationary condition for Π implies that all the conditions described by Equations [1.7] through [1.12] are satisfied.

1.3   Application of the finite element method (FEM)

1.3.1   Discretization of the domain

The domain Ω is divided into sub-domains Ω^e, or finite elements (Fig. 1.2), such that:

$$\Omega = \sum_{e} \Omega^e \qquad [1.15]$$

Common finite elements available for discretizing the domain are shown in Fig. 1.3. As a result of the discretization, the functional Π can then be written as:

$$\Pi = \sum_{e} \Pi^e \qquad [1.16]$$

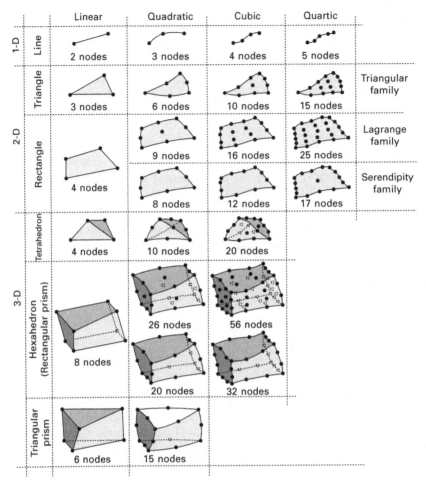

1.3 Common finite elements.

Note that the term Π^e contains only volume integral terms if the element Ω^e is inside the domain Ω. Elements having a boundary coincident with Γ will have a term Π^e that contains both volume and surface integrals.

1.3.2   Shape functions

The finite element method, being an approximation process, will result in the determination of an approximate solution of the form

$$\mathbf{w} \approx \hat{\mathbf{w}} = \sum \mathbf{N}_i \, \mathbf{a}_i \qquad\qquad [1.17]$$

where the $\mathbf{N}_i$ are shape functions prescribed in terms of independent variables (such as coordinates) and the $\mathbf{a}_i$ are nodal parameters, known or unknown.

The shape functions must guarantee the continuity of the geometry between elements. Moreover, to ensure convergence, it is necessary that the shape functions be at least C^m continuous if derivatives of the mth degree exist in the integral form. This condition is automatically met if the shape functions are polynomials complete to the mth order.

The construction of shape functions for an element Ω^e, defined by n nodes, usually requires that if N_i is the shape function for node i, then $N_i = 1$ at node i, and $N_i = 0$ at the other nodes. Also, for any point $\mathbf{p}$ in Ω^e we must have

$$\sum_1^n N_i(\mathbf{p}) = 1 \qquad [1.18]$$

Polynomials are commonly used to construct shape functions. For instance a Lagrange polynomial

$$N_i(\xi) = \prod_{\substack{k=1 \\ k \neq 1}}^n \frac{\xi_k - \xi}{\xi_k - \xi_i} \qquad [1.19]$$

can be used at node i of a one-dimensional element containing n nodes (see Fig. 1.4). It verifies the following conditions.

$$\begin{cases} N_i(\xi_i) = 1 \\ N_i(\xi_{k \neq 1}) = 0 \\ \sum_1^n N_i(\xi) = 1 \end{cases} \qquad [1.20]$$

For the four-node rectangular element of Fig. 1.5, we can write the four shape functions as:

$$N(\xi, \eta) = N_i(\xi) N_j(\eta) \qquad [1.21]$$

where i and j indicate the row and column of the node in the element and i, j = 1, 2. The conditions described by Equation [1.20] can be verified for

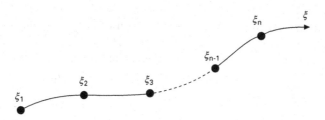

1.4 A generalized n-node linear element.

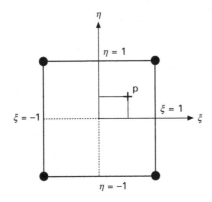

1.5 An example of a four-node quadrilateral element.

these functions. Finally, the position of any point p with coordinates (ξ, η) in the element is given by:

$$
\begin{bmatrix} \xi \\ \eta \end{bmatrix} = \left\langle \left(\frac{1}{4}\right)[(-1) + \xi][(-1) + \eta] \left(-\frac{1}{4}\right)[(1) + \xi][(-1) + \eta] \right.
$$

$$
\left. \left(-\frac{1}{4}\right)[(-1) + \xi][(1) + \eta] \left(\frac{1}{4}\right)[(1) + \xi][(1) + \eta] \right\rangle \begin{bmatrix} -1 & -1 \\ 1 & -1 \\ -1 & 1 \\ 1 & 1 \end{bmatrix}
$$

$$[1.22]$$

In most cases, the same shape functions are used to describe the element geometry and to represent the solution $\hat{\mathbf{w}}$.

1.3.3 Parent elements

In order to better represent the actual geometry, it is generally useful to use curvilinear finite elements for the discretization of Ω. These elements are then mapped into parent finite elements (Fig. 1.6) in order to facilitate the computation of Π^e.

An isoparametric representation is commonly used to perform the mapping of the actual elements into the reference elements. Consider a volume element Ω^e of the domain Ω defined by n nodes. The position vector $\mathbf{R}$ of a point p of Ω^e can be written as a function of parameters ξ, η, and ζ:

$$\xi \rightarrow \mathbf{R} = \mathbf{R}(\xi) \qquad\qquad [1.23]$$

which is the same as:

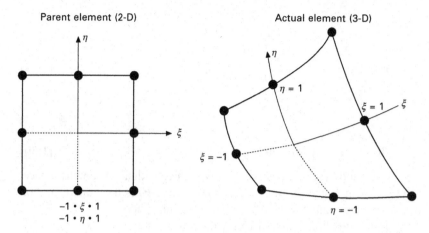

1.6 An example of a parent element for an eight-node quadrilateral element.

$$\mathbf{R} = \begin{Bmatrix} x \\ y \\ z \end{Bmatrix} = \begin{Bmatrix} x(\xi, \eta, \zeta) \\ y(\xi, \eta, \zeta) \\ z(\xi, \eta, \zeta) \end{Bmatrix} \tag{1.24}$$

The finite element representation can be written in the following form:

$$\begin{aligned}
x &= \mathbf{N}(\xi, \eta, \zeta)\, \mathbf{x_n} \\
y &= \mathbf{N}(\xi, \eta, \zeta)\, \mathbf{y_n} \\
z &= \mathbf{N}(\xi, \eta, \zeta)\, \mathbf{z_n}
\end{aligned} \tag{1.25}$$

where:

$$\begin{aligned}
\mathbf{x_n} &= \langle x_1\ x_2\ \dots\ x_n \rangle \\
\mathbf{y_n} &= \langle y_1\ y_2\ \dots\ y_n \rangle \\
\mathbf{z_n} &= \langle z_1\ z_2\ \dots\ z_n \rangle \\
\mathbf{N} &= \langle N_1\ N_2\ \dots\ N_n \rangle
\end{aligned} \tag{1.26}$$

The scalars x_i, y_i, and z_i represent the Cartesian coordinates at node i and N_i is the shape function at node i. A differential element at point p is thus defined by:

$$d\mathbf{R} = \mathbf{F}_\xi = d\xi \tag{1.27}$$

and

$$\frac{\partial}{\partial \xi} = \mathbf{F}_\xi^x \frac{\partial}{\partial \mathbf{R}} = \mathbf{J} \frac{\partial}{\partial \mathbf{R}} \tag{1.28}$$

where:

$$\mathbf{F}_\xi = \begin{bmatrix} x_{,\xi} & x_{,\eta} & x_{,\zeta} \\ y_{,\xi} & y_{,\eta} & y_{,\zeta} \\ z_{,\xi} & z_{,\eta} & z_{,\zeta} \end{bmatrix} = [\mathbf{a}_1 \ \mathbf{a}_2 \ \mathbf{a}_3] \tag{1.29}$$

and

$$d\mathbf{R} = \mathbf{a}_1 d\xi + \mathbf{a}_2 \, d\eta + \mathbf{a}_3 \, d\zeta \tag{1.30}$$

Vectors $\mathbf{a}_1, \mathbf{a}_2$, and $\mathbf{a}_3$ are the base vectors associated with the parametric space, $\mathbf{J}$ is the Jacobian matrix of the transformation, and $\mathbf{F}_\xi$ is the transformation matrix from the parametric space to the Cartesian space.

From Equations [1.27] and [1.28], we obtain:

$$d\xi = \mathbf{F}_\xi^{-1} d\mathbf{R} \tag{1.31}$$

and

$$\frac{\partial}{\partial \mathbf{R}} = \mathbf{J}^{-1} \frac{\partial}{\partial \xi} = \mathbf{j} \frac{\partial}{\partial \xi} \tag{1.32}$$

A volume element is defined by

$$d\mathrm{V} = |(d\mathbf{x} \wedge d\mathbf{y}) \cdot d\mathbf{z}| \tag{1.33}$$

which, in Cartesian space, is $d\mathrm{V} = d\mathbf{x} \, d\mathbf{y} \, d\mathbf{z}$, and in parametric space:

$$d\mathrm{V} = |(\mathbf{a}_1 d\xi \wedge \mathbf{a}_2 d\eta) \cdot \mathbf{a}_3 d\zeta| \tag{1.34}$$

which is the same as

$$d\mathrm{V} = J d\xi d\eta d\zeta \tag{1.35}$$

where : $J = |det \, \mathbf{J}|$

Therefore, the quantity Π^e can be expressed in parametric space as

$$\int_{\Omega^e} (\ldots) d\mathbf{x} d\mathbf{y} \, d\mathbf{z} = \int_{\Omega^{\text{parent}}} (\ldots) J \, d\xi \, d\eta \, d\zeta \tag{1.36}$$

which allows the computation of each element to be performed on the parent element rather than on the real element.

1.3.4   Discretization of the variational form

We now write the solution functions for the piezoelectric problem in terms of the shape functions. For each element Ω^e defined by n nodes, the electric field is obtained from Equation [1.6] and can be written in the form:

$$\mathbf{E} = - \mathbf{B}_\phi^e \Phi \tag{1.37}$$

where Φ is the vector associated with the nodal values of the electrostatic potential:

$$\mathbf{B}_\phi^e = [\mathbf{B}_{\phi1}^e \quad \mathbf{B}_{\phi2}^e \quad \ldots \quad \mathbf{B}_{\phi n}^e] \tag{1.38}$$

and

$$\mathbf{B}_{\phi i}^e = \begin{bmatrix} \dfrac{\partial N_i^e}{\partial x} \\[2ex] \dfrac{\partial N_i^e}{\partial y} \\[2ex] \dfrac{\partial N_i^e}{\partial z} \end{bmatrix} \tag{1.39}$$

The terms $\mathbf{B}_{\phi i}^e$ are the first spatial derivatives of the shape functions. Similarly, for each Ω^e the strain tensor defined by Equation [1.4] becomes

$$\mathbf{x} = -\mathbf{B}_u^e \mathbf{U} \tag{1.40}$$

where $\mathbf{U}$ is the vector of the nodal values of the displacement:

$$\mathbf{B}_u^e = [\mathbf{B}_{u1}^e \quad \mathbf{B}_{u2}^e \ldots \mathbf{B}_{un}^e] \tag{1.41}$$

and

$$\mathbf{B}_{ui}^e = \begin{bmatrix} \dfrac{\partial N_i^e}{\partial x} & 0 & 0 \\[2ex] 0 & \dfrac{\partial N_i^e}{\partial y} & 0 \\[2ex] 0 & 0 & \dfrac{\partial N_i^e}{\partial z} \\[2ex] 0 & \dfrac{\partial N_i^e}{\partial z} & \dfrac{\partial N_i^e}{\partial y} \\[2ex] \dfrac{\partial N_i^e}{\partial z} & 0 & \dfrac{\partial N_i^e}{\partial x} \\[2ex] \dfrac{\partial N_i^e}{\partial y} & \dfrac{\partial N_i^e}{\partial x} & 0 \end{bmatrix} \tag{1.42}$$

Consequently, Equation [1.1] becomes:

$$\begin{cases} \mathbf{X} = c^E \mathbf{B}_u^e \mathbf{U} + e^x \mathbf{B}_\phi^e \Phi \\ D = e \mathbf{B}_u^e \mathbf{U} + \chi^x \mathbf{B}_\phi^e \Phi \end{cases} \tag{1.43}$$

Finally, we can rewrite the functional Π^e on the element, as

$$\Pi^e = \frac{1}{2} \iiint_{\Omega^e} U^{e^X} (B_u^{e^X} c^E B_u^e - \rho\omega^2 N^{e^X} N^e) U^e d\Omega^e$$

$$+ \iiint_{\Omega^e} U^{e^X} B_u^{e^X} e B_\phi^e \Phi^e d\Omega^e$$

$$- \frac{1}{2} \iiint_{\Omega^e} \Phi^{e^X} B_\phi^{e^X} \chi^x B_\phi^e \Phi^e d\Omega^e$$

$$- \iint_{s_X^e} U^{e^X} N^{e^X} f \, dS_X^e + \sum_{p=0}^{p} \phi_p Q_p \qquad [1.44]$$

After integrating the shape function matrices and their derivatives, we can write:

$$\Pi^e = \frac{1}{2} U^{e^X} (K_{uu}^e - \omega^2 M^e) U^e + U^{e^X} K_{u\phi}^e \Phi^e$$

$$+ \frac{1}{2} \phi^{e^X} K_{\phi\phi}^e \Phi^e - U^{e^X} F^e + \sum_{p=0}^{p} \phi_p Q_p \qquad [1.45]$$

where

$$K_{uu}^e = \iiint_{\Omega^e} B_u^{e^X} c^E B_u^e d\Omega^e$$

$$M^e = \iiint_{\Omega^e} \rho\omega^2 N^{e^X} N^e d\Omega^e$$

$$K_{\phi u}^e = \iiint_{\Omega^e} B_u^{e^X} e B_\phi^e d\Omega^e \qquad [1.46]$$

$$K_{\phi\phi}^e = - \iiint_{\Omega^e} B_\phi^{e^X} \chi^x B_\phi^e d\Omega^e$$

$$F^e = \iint_{s_X^e} N^{e^X} f d S_X^e$$

and K_{uu}^e, $K_{\phi u}^e$, and $K_{\phi\phi}^e$ are the elastic, piezoelectric and dielectric susceptibility matrices, and M^e is the consistent mass matrix.

1.3.5   Assembly

The matrices in Equation [1.46] must be rearranged for the whole domain Ω by a process called assembly. From this process, we obtain the following matrices:

$$K_{uu} = \sum_e K_{uu}^e$$

$$M = \sum_e M^e$$

$$K_{\phi u} = \sum_e K_{\phi u}^e \qquad [1.47]$$

$$K_{\phi\phi} = \sum_e K_{\phi\phi}^e$$

$$F = \sum_e F^e$$

The application of the variational principle implies the minimization of the functional Π with respect to variations of the nodal values $\mathbf{U}$ and $\mathbf{\Phi}$. Therefore:

$$\frac{\partial \Pi}{\partial u_i} = 0 \quad \forall \, i \qquad\qquad [1.48]$$

and

$$\frac{\partial \Pi}{\partial \phi_j} = 0 \quad \forall \, j \qquad\qquad [1.49]$$

Making use of Equations [1.45] and [1.16], and applying the stationary condition to Π, we obtain:

$$\begin{bmatrix} K_{uu} - \omega^2 M & K_{u\phi} \\ K_{u\phi}^{X} & K_{\phi\phi} \end{bmatrix} \begin{bmatrix} U \\ \Phi \end{bmatrix} = \begin{bmatrix} F \\ -Q \end{bmatrix} \qquad\qquad [1.50]$$

The vector for the nodal charges, $\mathbf{Q}$, is such that for all nodes i that belong to an electrode p with potential ϕ_p, the sum of the charges Q_i is equal to ϕ_p. For all other nodes j that do not belong to an electrode, $Q_j = 0$.

1.3.6   Computation

Specific integration, diagonalization and elimination techniques are employed to solve the system (Equation [1.50]) on a computer. A full description of these techniques is a topic that extends well beyond the scope of this text and thus will not be presented here. The matrix in Equation [1.50] may be adapted for a variety of different analyses, such as the static, modal, harmonic, and transient types:

- static analysis:

$$\begin{bmatrix} K_{uu} & K_{u\phi} \\ K_{u\phi}^{X} & K_{\phi\phi} \end{bmatrix} \begin{bmatrix} U \\ \Phi \end{bmatrix} = \begin{bmatrix} F \\ -Q \end{bmatrix} \qquad\qquad [1.51]$$

- modal analysis:

$$\begin{bmatrix} K_{uu} - \omega^2 M & K_{u\phi} \\ K_{u\phi}^{X} & K_{\phi\phi} \end{bmatrix} \begin{bmatrix} U \\ \Phi \end{bmatrix} = \begin{bmatrix} 0 \\ -Q \end{bmatrix} \qquad\qquad [1.52]$$

- harmonic analysis

$$\begin{bmatrix} K_{uu} - \omega^2 M & K_{u\phi} \\ K_{u\phi}^{X} & K_{\phi\phi} \end{bmatrix} \begin{bmatrix} U \\ \Phi \end{bmatrix} = \begin{bmatrix} F \\ -Q \end{bmatrix} \qquad\qquad [1.53]$$

• transient analysis

$$
\begin{bmatrix} M & 0 \\ 0 & 0 \end{bmatrix} \begin{bmatrix} \ddot{U} \\ \ddot{\Phi} \end{bmatrix} + \frac{1}{\omega_0} \begin{bmatrix} K'_{uu} & K'_{u\phi} \\ K'^X_{u\phi} & K'_{\phi\phi} \end{bmatrix} \begin{bmatrix} \dot{U} \\ \dot{\Phi} \end{bmatrix} + \begin{bmatrix} K_{uu} & K_{u\phi} \\ K^X_{u\phi} & K_{\phi\phi} \end{bmatrix} \begin{bmatrix} U \\ \Phi \end{bmatrix} = \begin{bmatrix} F \\ -Q \end{bmatrix}
$$ [1.54]

1.4   Finite element method (FEM) simulation examples

Application examples of the finite element method ATILA to piezoelectric actuators and transducers are introduced in this chapter, including multilayer actuators, Π-type linear, 'windmill', metal tube ultrasonic motors, piezoelectric transformers and 'Cymbal' underwater transducers.

1.4.1   Multilayer actuator

As shown in Fig. 1.7, a multilayer piezoelectric actuator is composed of active and inactive areas, corresponding to the electrode-overlapped and -unoverlapped portions. Accordingly, concentration of electric field and stress is expected around the internal electrode edges.

Plates I and II (between pages 194 and 195) are the 2D calculation results with ATILA under pseudo-DC drive in an eight-layered multilayer actuator in terms of the potential distribution and stress concentration around the internal electrode edges. The maximum tensile stress should be lower than the fracture strength of this PZT ceramic.

1.4.2   Π-type linear ultrasonic motor

Using a Longitudinal 1st-Bending 4th (L1-B4) coupled mode linear motor as illustrated in Fig. 1.8, we can learn how to optimize the motor dimensions.[5] Figure 1.9 shows the dependence of the L 1 mode and B 4 mode resonance frequencies on the thickness of the elastic bar around 2.8 mm. The L1 mode

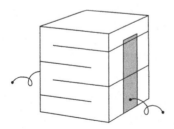

1.7 Multilayer piezoelectric actuator with an interdigital electrode pattern.

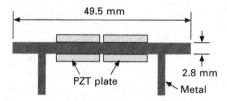

49.5 mm

2.8 mm

PZT plate

Metal

1.8 Dimensions of a π-shaped linear motor optimally determined by the finite element analysis (FEM): the bimorph type.

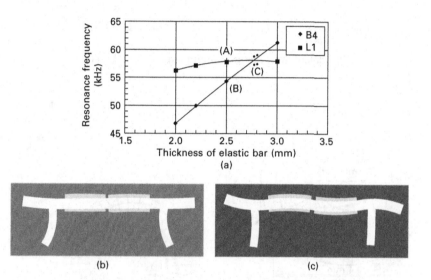

(a)

(b)   (c)

1.9 (a) Dependence of the L1 and B4 resonance frequencies on the thickness of the elastic bar around 2.8 mm. Driving at point (A) or at (B) corresponds to a symmetrical wagging or an up-down action. Driving at (C) provides a horse-trotting motion. The animations show the (b) wagging and (c) up-down actions.

resonance frequency is rather insensitive to the bar thickness, while the B4 mode frequency varies significantly with the thickness. When the thickness is 2.5 mm, driving at a point (A) provides a symmetrical large leg wagging motion, while driving at (B) provides a leg up-down action. Neither can provide the motor movement. When the thickness is adjusted to 2.8 mm, driving at a point (C), which superposes L1 and B4 modes simultaneously, we observe a horse-trotting mode with a 90° phase lag between two leg wagging motions, which must be the optimized condition.

Figure 1.10 compares the ATILA calculation and experimental results for a brass motor. The optimum bar thicknesses are 2.75 mm and 2.80 mm, respectively, which differs only less than 2%.

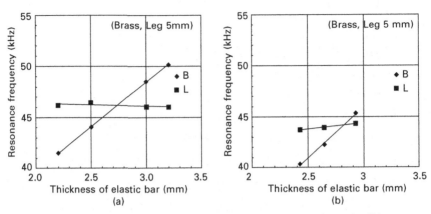

1.10 ATILA calculation results (a) and experimental results (b).

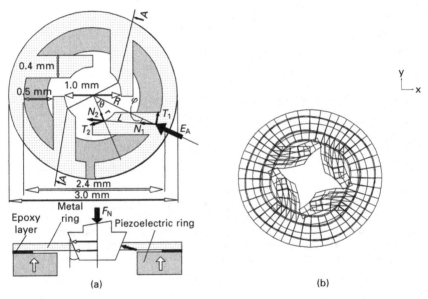

1.11 (a) Windmill motor illustration, and (b) a metal ring/finger coupled vibration mode.

1.4.3   Windmill ultrasonic motor

Figure 1.11(a) illustrates the 'Windmill' motor structure, and Fig. 1.11(b) shows the corresponding metal ring/finger coupled vibration mode (radial-bending coupling), calculated by ATILA (axisymmetrical 2D calculation).[6] Note that when the radial and bonding vibration modes are synchronized, the motion seems to be a grasping-twisting action of four fingers.

1.4.4 Metal tube ultrasonic motor

A metal tube motor is composed of two PZT rectangular plates bonded on a metal tube, as depicted in Fig. 1.12.[7] Due to this asymmetric configuration of the two PZT plates, the resonance frequencies of the two orthogonal bending modes along x′ and y′ deviate slightly. Thus, driving the motor at the intermediate frequency exhibits a superposed vibration, like a hula-hoop mode, because of 90° phase lag between the above two split modes. Exciting either X or Y plate generates counter-clockwise or clockwise wobbling motion of the metal tube, respectively (see the ATILA calculation in Fig. 1.13. Time sequence is from top to bottom). Refer to the next chapter for the design optimization of the metal tube motor.

The ATILA software can calculate the stator vibration under mechanically free or forced condition, but without coupling another software which treats the surface friction model, we cannot calculate the motor characteristics (speed, torque, etc.).

1.4.5 Piezoelectric transformer

Disk type transformers have advantages over the rectangular plate Rosen type because of the usage of k_p, instead of k_{31} ($k_p > k_{31}$). One of the disk types shown in Fig. 1.14 particularly exhibits enhanced step-up voltage ratio more than 300 under zero load, because the curved electrode configuration excites k_{15} mode superposing on k_p mode (note again that $k_{15} > k_p$).[8] Furthermore, usage of curved electrodes reduces the stress concentration, which can be calculated by the ATILA.[1] Figure 1.15 demonstrates higher order vibration modes and the calculated potential distribution.

The most recent version of ATILA can simulate step-up/down voltage ratio even under a certain electrical load condition.

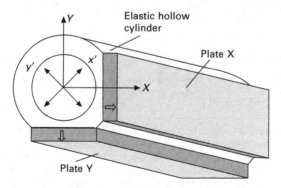

1.12 Structure of a metal tube motor. Two PZT plates are bonded asymmetrically on a metal tube.

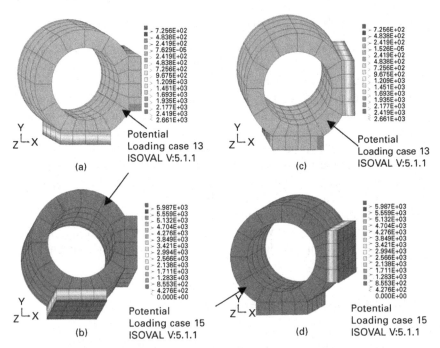

1.13 (a, b) Top view of orthogonal bending mode shapes when plate X was excited (Time sequence: a → b): (c, d) Bending mode shapes when plate Y was excited (Time sequence: c → d). X or Y plate excitation generates counter-clockwise or clockwise rotation.

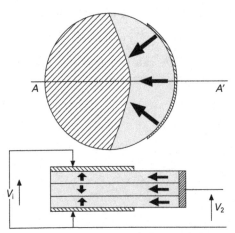

1.14 Disk shape piezoelectric transformer with crescent curved electrodes (Penn State). Different from the conventional Rosen-type, the circular shape (k_p) enhances the energy conversion rate and voltage step-up ratio. Also the curved electrode contour excites local shear mode (k_{15}), which further enhances the voltage step-up ratio more than 300. 25 mm diameter, 1 mm thick PZT disk can generate 10 W or higher, so that this three-layer transformer can be applied to the small laptop computer AC/DC adaptor.

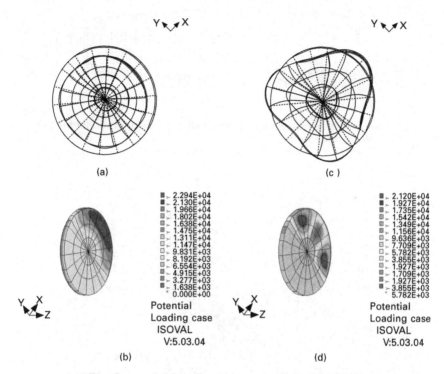

1.15 The first and third vibration modes ((a) and (c)) of a crescent electrode type disk transformer, and their corresponding voltage distribution calculation by ATILA ((b) and (d)). Without load (open circuit).

We demonstrated lighting up the 4W CCFL directly by 500V using a single disk sample (25 mm in diameter and 1 mm in thickness) without using an additional booster coil.

1.4.6   'Cymbal' underwater transducer

A 'cymbal' (Fig. 1.16(a)) is a sort of displacement amplifier, and also fits well with water in view of its relatively low acoustic impedance. Figures 1.16(b) and 1.17 exhibit mesh structures of the cymbal and surrounding water, respectively. Figure 1.18 shows an alternative mesh structure, structured to minimize the node numbers, leading to reduced calculation time.

In this textbook, with using the ATILA-Light education version, the reader is recommended to learn the most effective structured mesh in order to simulate the device with the minimum node number.

Figure 1.19 compares the resulting ATILA simulation and the experimental result in terms of transmitting voltage response as a function of operating

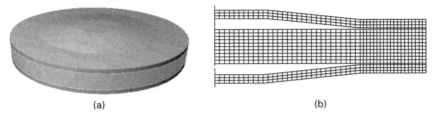

1.16 Cymbal appearance (a) and a half cross-section model for the ATILA calculation (b).

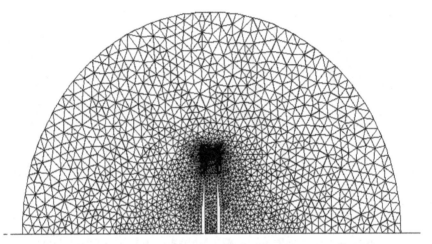

1.17 Automatically generated mesh for water surrounding the Cymbal transducer.

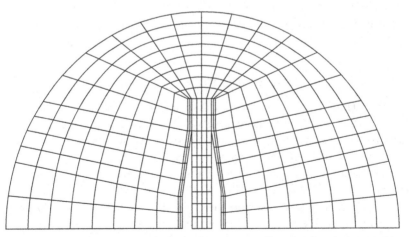

1.18 Structured mesh for water surrounding the Cymbal transducer, taking into account the symmetry.

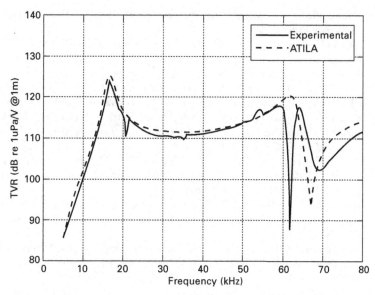

1.19 Comparison of the ATILA simulation and the experimental result in terms of transmitting voltage response (TVR) as a function of frequency.

frequency. A sharp dip of the transmitted voltage response (TVR) signal around 65 kHz is also successfully traced.[9]

1.5   Conclusion

The finite element method and its application to smart transducer systems were introduced in this chapter. The fundamentals of finite element analysis were introduced in Section 1.1. Then, Section 1.2 'Defining the equations for the problem' treated how to integrate the piezoelectric constitutive equations, and Section 1.3 'Application of the finite element method' describes the meshing. Section 1.4 'FEM simulation examples' introduced six cases; multilayer actuator, Π-type linear ultrasonic motor, windmill ultrasonic motor, metal tube ultrasonic motor, piezoelectric transformer, and 'cymbal' underwater transducer, which includes most of the basic capabilities of ATILA FEM code. Based on the fundamental knowledge in this chapter, you will learn advanced techniques of ATILA in the following chapters.

1.6   References

1.   Olgierd Cecil Zienkiewicz, *The Finite Element Method* – 3rd expanded and revised edn, ISBN 0-07-084072-5, McGraw-Hill Book Company (UK) Limited (1977).
2.   Jean-Noël Decarpigny, Application de la Méthode des Eléments Finis à l'Etude de Transducteurs Piézoélectriques, Doctoral Thesis, ISEN, Lille, France (1984).

3. Takuro Ikeda, *Fundamentals of Piezoelectricity*, ISBN: 0-19-856339-6, Oxford University Press (1990).
4. Bertrand Dubus, Jean-Claude Debus and Jocelyne Coutte, Modélisation de Matériaux Piézoélectriques et Electrostrictifs par la Méthode des Eléments Finis, *Revue Européenne des Eléments Finis*, Vol. 8, No. 5–6, pp. 581–606 (1999).
5. T.-Y. Kim, B.-J. Kim, T.-G. Park, M.-H. Kim and K. Uchino, 'Design and Driving Characteristics of Ultrasonic Linear Motor,' *Ferroelectrics*, **263**, 113–118 (2001).
6. B. Koc. P. Bouchilloux and K. Uchino, 'Piezoelectric Micromotor Using A Metal-Ceramic Composite Structure,' *IEEE Ultrasonic, Ferroelectrics, and Frequency Control Trans.*, **47** (4), 836–843 (2000).
7. B. Koc, S. Cagatay and K. Uchino, 'A Piezoelectric Motor Using Two Orthogonal Bending Modes of a Hollow Cylinder,' *IEEE Ultrasonic, Ferroelectric, Frequency Control Trans.*, **49**(4), 495–500 (2002).
8. B. Koc and K. Uchino, 'A Disk Type Piezoelectric Transformer with Crescent Shape Input Electrodes,' *Proc. Piezoelectric Materials: Adv. in Sci. Tech. and Appl.*, p. 375–382 (2000).
9. J. Zhang, W. J. Hughes, P. Bouchilloux, R. J. Meyer Jr., K. Uchino and R. E. Newnham, 'A Class V Flextensional Transducer: The Cymbal,' *Ultrasonics*, **37**, 387–393 (1999).

2

The capabilities of the new version of ATILA

J-C. DEBUS, ISEN Lille, France

DOI: 10.1533/9780857096319.1.25

Abstract: The aim of this chapter is to compare the new version of ATILA (ATILA++) with the previous one. In Section 2.3, the new developments in the pre- and post-processor are presented. Then in Section 2.5, a time comparison is made from several examples. With a first example which is a 3D electromechanical structure, the CPU and real times are compared for the computation of the 10 resonance and anti-resonance frequencies and for a harmonic analysis of 30 frequencies. The second example concerns a fluid harmonic analysis with 30 frequencies of a piezoelectric transducer. A thermal harmonic analysis is performed on a piezoelectric cylinder. Using the same cylinder, a transient analysis is carried with 100 time steps. For each analysis, the CPU and real times are presented and a comparison is made between the two versions.

Key words: finite-element, analysis, modal, harmonic, transient, transducer.

2.1   Introduction

ATILA is a finite element code that has been specifically developed to help in the design of sonar transducers, but it can also be used for all types of transducers[1] (industrial machining, cleaning, welding, nondestructive testing, acoustic imaging, actuators) or for passive structures. Its working domain is one of small and linear strains. It permits the static, modal, harmonic and transient analyses of unloaded elastic, piezoelectric, magnetostrictive or electrostrictive structures. It also enables the harmonic and transient analyses of radiating elastic or piezoelectric structures (in any fluid, water or air, for example) and modal or harmonic analysis of periodic structures with 1D, 2D or 3D periodicity. Moreover, it can perform analyses of axisymmetrical, 2D or 3D structures. Depending upon the problem, it provides: the displacement field, the nodal plane positions, the stress field, near-field and far-field pressures, transmitting voltage response, directivity patterns and the electrical impedance. Its ability to describe the behaviour of different transducers (Tonpilz transducers, double headmass, axisymmetrical length expanders, free-flooded rings, flextensional transducers, bender-bars, cylindrical and trilaminar hydrophones) and the accuracy of the results have been checked by modelling many different structures and comparing numerical and experimental results. Most results have been described in numerous reports, papers and articles; some of them are listed in reference 2.

ATILA is the result of many years of research, the first thesis was the start of this code with J. N. Decarpigny[2]; more than 20 PhD theses have contributed to the development of the ATILA code.

ATILA is mainly written in standard FORTRAN 77, except for some system interfacing written in C. It comprises more than 220 000 lines of code (including 4 000 lines of C code). It has been carefully designed to be easily portable on almost all platforms. It was developed on an IBM 370 series mainframe (VM/CMS), it is maintained at ISEN on IBM-PC compatible computers (64-bit applications under Windows 98, Windows NT, Windows 2000, Windows XP and Linux) or Apple computers.

2.2   The new version of ATILA

A newer version of ATILA with new solvers that result in significantly faster computing times is proposed. A finite element calculation process solves systems of equations. In ATILA, according to the type of analysis, three different solvers are used: LU or Cholesky decomposition procedure for static and harmonic analysis, Lanczos algorithm for modal analysis, and central difference, Newmark's, or Wilson's methods for transient analysis. The main improvement is reduction of the filling of sparse matrices generated by the analysis. A skyline storing scheme is used and consists in storing elements of the matrix in such a way that most of the zero elements are not stored. This reduces the amount of memory used to store matrices as well as reducing the number of calculations during the factorization process. The skyline storing scheme when used together with a direct solving procedure is well suited for FEM calculations. This is because FEM calculations generate sparse matrices with a symmetric structure and also because the skyline structure is preserved during the LU factorization. However, this method implies extra calculations mostly during the factorization process and this storage scheme has only a clear advantage over using fully populated matrices if these matrices are strongly sparse. It is possible to greatly reduce the amount of stored data by using programs for producing fill reducing orderings. Many algorithms presented in the literature seem to give better results than the ones currently implemented in ATILA. Note that if these algorithms could improve the calculation speed in ATILA in the case of harmonic and transient analysis, they will not be very efficient if eigenfrequencies of a transducer are to be found. Transducer models use coupled electric-mechanical-fluid equations. Electric constitutive relationships generate null entries in the mass matrix. Hence the mass matrix cannot be easily factorized using a gauss elimination procedure. Currently, a static condensation of electric equations is used in ATILA. It consists in eliminating electric equations using the electro-mechanical coupling equations. This significantly increases the amount of storage because the structure of the matrix is changed and this makes reordering algorithms inefficient. There are two ways to solve this problem either by changing the storage scheme or reorganizing the way electric equations are accounted for.

Many other storage schemes are presented in the literature. For most of these, they are very efficient if used together with an incremental solving procedure. As discussed above we think that the direct solving procedure is very adequate due to the symmetric structure of matrices involved in FEM calculations.

In order to reorganize the way data are managed in the code, it is interesting to note that we are generally looking for the natural mode of the structure. Hence it is not necessary to hold electric equations during the eigenmode calculation – they must be accounted for during the factorization procedure. The new method is to organize equations in order to take into account the null entries in the mass matrix during the matrix factorization by eliminating electric equations during the eigenmode calculations. Using this method, it is possible to keep the symmetric sparse structure of the matrix and then efficiently use the ordering procedure to reduce the matrix filling. For the new version of ATILA called ATILA++, the used language is the C++.

2.3   Pre- and post-processor GiD

GiD[3], developed by CIMNE, in Spain, is a universal, adaptive and user-friendly pre- and post-processor for numerical simulations in science and engineering. It has been designed to cover all the common needs in the numerical simulations field from pre- to post-processing: geometrical modelling, effective definition of analysis data, mesh generation, transfer data to analysis software and visualization of results.

GiD is an effective and easy-to-use geometric user interface. The GiD/ATILA interface supports the functions for applying boundary conditions (mechanical, electrical, thermal and magnetic) to the structure as well as defining materials. A material database of standard materials is included. Post-processing functions are numerous and varied: geometry and mesh visualization (including cuts), deformation, contour lines and colour maps, vectors, grids, animations, stress field, near-field and far-field pressures, transmitting voltage response, directivity patterns, electrical impedance. The ATILA code architecture[4] is shown in Fig. 2.1.

2.4   New capacities in ATILA/GiD

2.4.1   Pre-processor

In the data menu, among the modifications, some icons have been altered to obtain a better choice of device analysis. Figure 2.2 displays the use of parallel

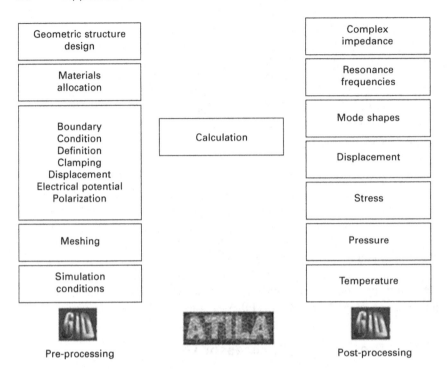

Geometric structure design		Complex impedance
Materials allocation		Resonance frequencies
Boundary Condition Definition Clamping Displacement Electrical potential Polarization	Calculation	Mode shapes
		Displacement
		Stress
Meshing		Pressure
Simulation conditions		Temperature

Pre-processing   ATILA   Post-processing

2.1 ATILA code architecture.

impedances for a piezoelectric ceramic. Up to three parallel impedances can be defined with resistors, inductors and capacitors. The initial surface or the line displacement and pressure can be imposed (Fig. 2.3).

With the material icon (Fig. 2.4), more items are proposed like the thin elastic patch, thin elastic piezo patch, elastic and anisotropic shell. When the thickness of a piece is very thin, a thin elastic patch can be used, it is a membrane element (Fig. 2.5). The thin piezo patch is used to model a macro fiber composite (MFC), the spacing between the fiber is defined. For example, Fig. 2.6 shows a clamped beam with a MFC patch. The contour fill of the z-displacement is displayed in Fig. 2.7. Figure 2.8 shows the elastic shell icon for a multilayer shell; with this icon, the number of layers can be given and for each layer, the thickness and the principal direction of the anisotropy are given as well. The elastic anisotropy properties are defined with the icon in Fig. 2.9. Figure 2.10 displays the contour fill of the z-displacement for a clamped multilayer beam. This beam has four layers of E-glass material, respectively, the orientation angles are 0°, 45°, −45° and 0°.

With the problem data item, an eigenvalue shift can be defined (Fig. 2.11); with this value, the eigenvalues before this value are not computed. For example, Fig. 2.12 displays a 3D flextensional transducer; the eigenvalues before 500 Hz will be not computed.

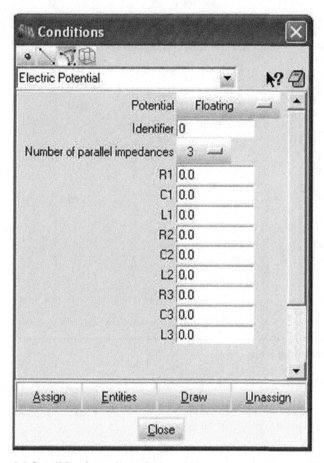

2.2 Condition icon: impedance.

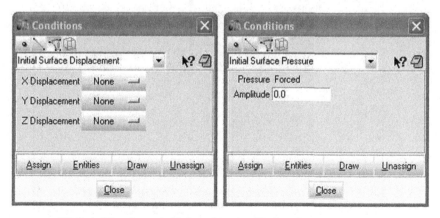

2.3 Condition icon: initial surface or displacement.

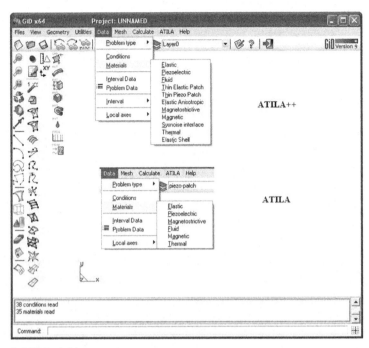

2.4 Material icon.

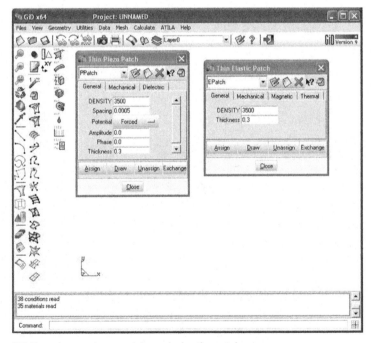

2.5 New icon: piezo patch and elastic patch.

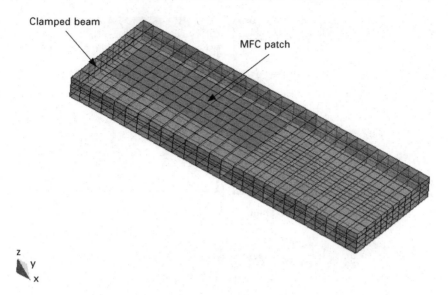

2.6 Clamped beam with a MFC patch.

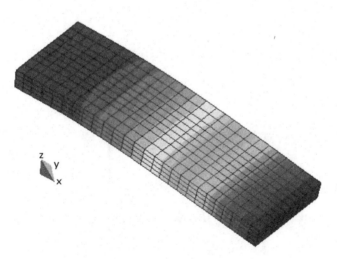

2.7 Contour fill of z-displacement.

2.4.2   Post-processor

Some modifications are shown in Plates III and IV (between pages 194 and 195), respectively, illustrating the contour fill of the strain and the contour of the far-field pressure.

2.8 New icon: elastic shell.

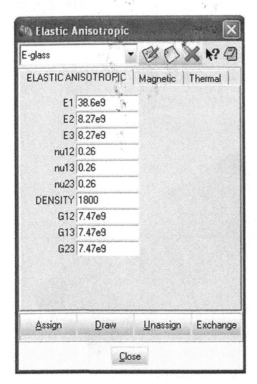

2.9 New icon: elastic anisotropy.

2.5   Time comparison between ATILA and ATILA++

The important amelioration of the new version is the speed of the computation. With these examples, several analyses have been performed and the computing times have been compared between the ATILA and ATILA++ versions.

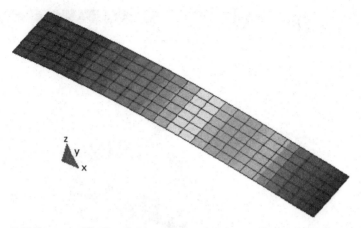

2.10 Contour fill of z-displacement of a clamped multilayer beam.

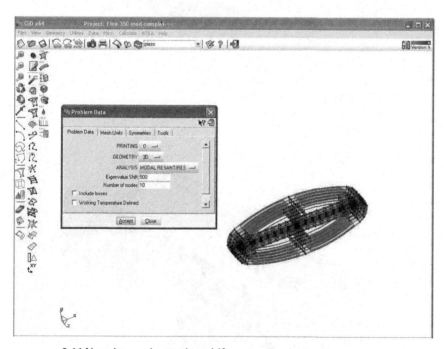

2.11 New item: eigenvalue shift.

2.5.1   Piezoelectric structure in air

The first structure tested for comparison is a 3D clamped structure with a piezoelectric plate and stacks in air (Fig. 2.13). The columns of Table 2.1 show, for seven different computations, respectively, the number of degrees of freedom, of nodes, and of elastic and piezoelectric elements. The last

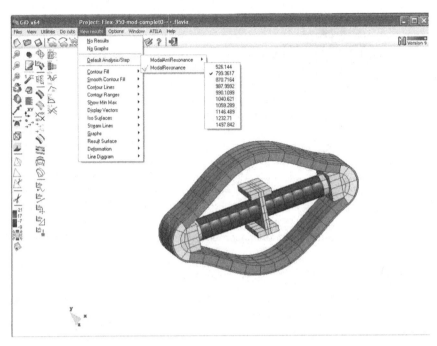

2.12 Modal resonance.

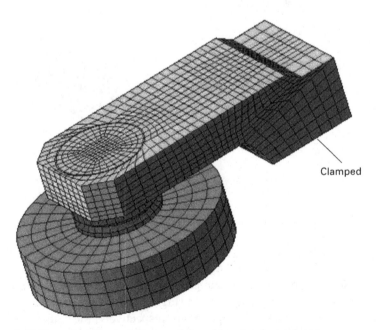

2.13 Piezoelectric structure-modal and harmonic analyses.

Table 2.1 Characteristics of the structure model

Degrees of freedom	Nodes	Elements		Blocks	
		Elastic	Piezoelectric	Modal	Harmonic
5 671	1 958	316	16	3	4
10 625	3 749	670	16	6	9
22 433	7 866	1 534	16	16	28
35 248	12 241	2 338	126	47	71
45 689	15 864	3 092	162	74	106
58 092	19 707	4 004	196	137	169
67 205	23 320	4 648	234	159	219

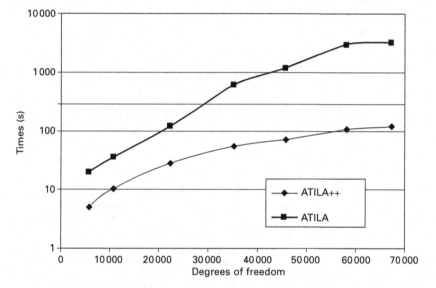

2.14 CPU time from a modal analysis for the structure.

two columns display the number of storage blocks used with the ATILA version, respectively, for modal and harmonic analyses. Figures 2.14 and 2.15 compare, respectively; the CPU and real times from a modal analysis versus the number of degrees of freedom, with 10 resonance and anti-resonance frequencies; the values of CPU and real times are shown on Table 2.2. The ratio of the computing real time between the ATILA and ATILA++ versions reaches 150. The results for a harmonic analysis with 30 frequencies are shown in Table 2.3 and in Figs 2.16 and 2.17. The real time ratio is near 100. Then, the last mesh for this structure has given 63 574 nodes, 13 802 elements and 186 486 degrees of freedom. The modal analysis has only been performed with ATILA++; the duration of the CPU time for 10 resonance frequencies is 340 s. Because of the size of the mesh, a computation with ATILA was not possible.

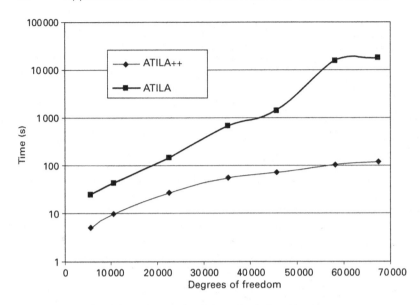

2.15 Real time from a modal analysis for the structure.

Table 2.2 CPU and real times of the modal analysis

Degrees of freedom	CPU time (s)		Real time (s)	
	ATILA++	ATILA	ATILA++	ATILA
5671	5	20	5	25
10625	10	36	10	45
22433	28	120	28	145
35248	55	595	55	671
45689	72	1153	72	1398
58092	105	2927	105	15235
67205	120	3226	120	17952

Table 2.3 CPU and real times of the harmonic analysis

Degrees of freedom	CPU time (s)		Real time (s)	
	ATILA++	ATILA	ATILA++	ATILA
5675	8	106	8	146
10621	15	312	15	355
22429	90	1720	90	2026
35248	182	6711	182	7782
45689	240	12022	240	17681
58092	340	23109	340	35124
67201	603	34084	603	55476

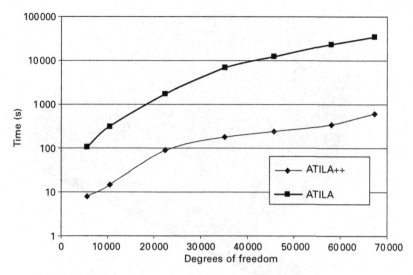

2.16 CPU time from a harmonic analysis for the structure.

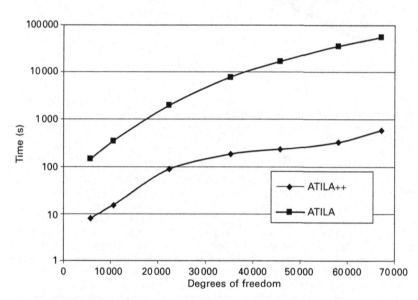

2.17 Real time from a harmonic analysis for the structure.

2.5.2 Piezoelectric transducer in fluid

The second example concerns a piezoelectric transducer in water (Fig. 2.18). The characteristics of the numerical model are summed up in Table 2.4. The results of the CPU and real times are displayed in Table 2.5 and in Figs 2.19 and 2.20. The real time ratio is near 130. Another modelling has been

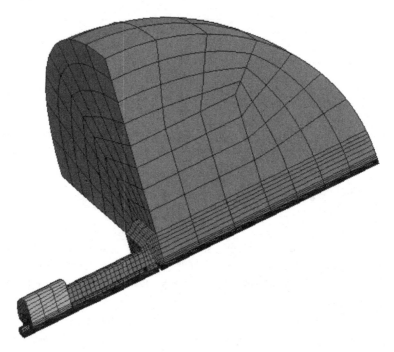

2.18 Piezoelectric transducer in water.

Table 2.4 Characteristics of the transducer model

Degrees of freedom	Nodes	Elements			Blocks	
		Elastic	Piezoelectric	Fluid	Damper	Harmonic
6 453	3 090	276	48	228	52	5
10 240	4 877	400	96	380	60	8
17 633	8 278	750	144	696	99	21
28 212	12 776	1 312	192	1 104	144	37
40 574	17 313	1 872	432	1 216	168	83
66 172	27 169	3 200	768	1 680	208	187

Table 2.5 CPU and real times of the fluid harmonic analysis

Degrees of freedom	CPU time (s)		Real time (s)	
	ATILA++	ATILA	ATILA++	ATILA
6 453	9	166	12	237
10 240	15	254	20	343
17 633	36	1 121	44	1 326
28 212	60	2 310	71	2 744
40 574	125	8 738	140	13 672
66 175	273	27 014	299	38 052

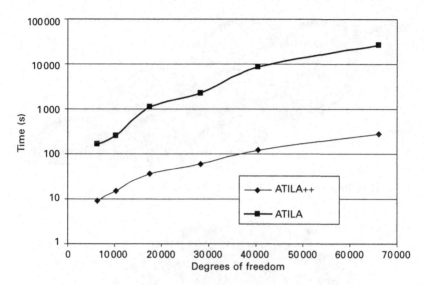

2.19 CPU time from a harmonic analysis for the transducer.

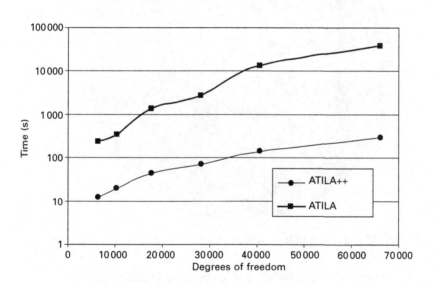

2.20 Real time from a harmonic analysis for the transducer.

performed to test the performance of the new version. This model is a cymbal transducer array. Figure 2.21 shows the array with nine cymbal transducers. The fluid mesh is presented in Fig. 2.22. The model is represented by 174 051 nodes, 183 304 elements and 232 850 degrees of freedom. The CPU time for a harmonic analysis with 151 frequencies is 6 720 s.

2.21 Deformed mesh of the cymbal array.

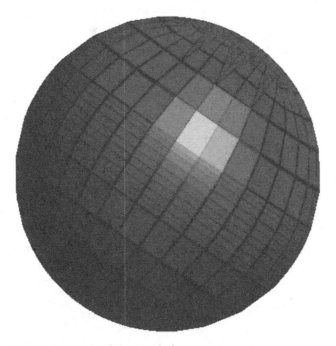

2.22 Fluid mesh of the cymbal array.

2.5.3   Thermal harmonic analysis of a piezoelectric cylinder

The last structure is a piezoelectric cylinder with three symmetry planes; only one eighth of the structure is modelled (Fig. 2.23). A thermal analysis with 30 frequencies is performed to compare the computing times between the two versions of ATILA. The characteristics of the numerical model are shown in Table 2.6 and the results are displayed in Table 2.7 and in Figs 2.24 and 2.25. The higher real time ratio is 286. A new modelling has permitted

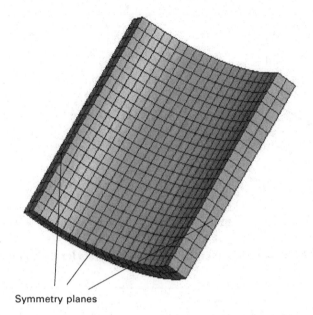

Symmetry planes

2.23 Piezoelectric cylinder.

Table 2.6 Characteristics of the cylinder model

Degrees of freedom	Nodes	Elements		Blocks	
		Piezoelectric	Convection	Harmonic	Thermal
4636	1265	200	220	4	1
10976	2901	480	504	9	1
18076	4725	800	840	26	1
27058	7069	1320	940	52	2
36874	9557	1800	1260	68	3
54984	14167	2700	1890	162	6

Table 2.7 CPU and real times of the thermal harmonic analysis

Degrees of freedom	CPU time (s)		Real time (s)	
	ATILA++	ATILA	ATILA++	ATILA
4636	17	167	25	489
10976	42	514	58	1802
18080	68	2466	93	8384
27102	145	5966	182	19675
36874	208	8186	255	30736
54984	364	30160	438	125205

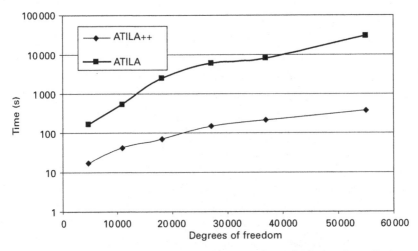

2.24 CPU time from a thermal harmonic analysis for the cylinder.

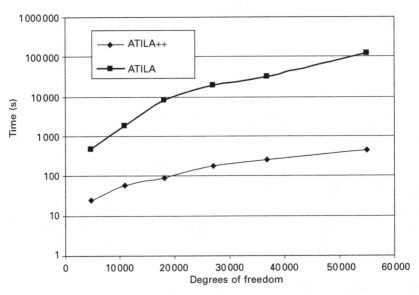

2.25 Real time from a thermal harmonic analysis for the cylinder.

to test the new version with a large mesh, 39 744 nodes, 8 100 elements and 155 786 degrees of freedom. The CPU time for this thermal harmonic analysis with 30 frequencies is 2 220 s.

2.5.4　Transient analysis of a piezoelectric cylinder

With the same structure as previously, a transient analysis is performed, 100 time steps are computed using a direct integration method with the Newmark method. Figures 2.26 and 2.27 display, respectively, the CPU and real times between the two versions of the ATILA code. The characteristics of the numerical model are shown in Table 2.8. Table 2.9 displays the results of the computation. The time ratios are 15. The same cylinder has been analyzed with a new mesh realized with 39 744 nodes, 8 100 elements and 155 786 degrees of freedom, the CPU time for the new version is 650 s.

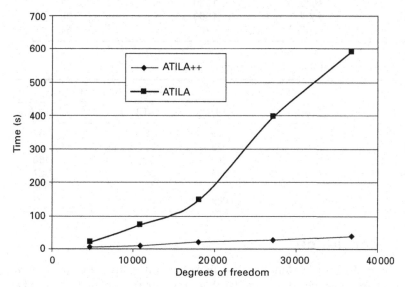

2.26 CPU time from a transient analysis for the cylinder.

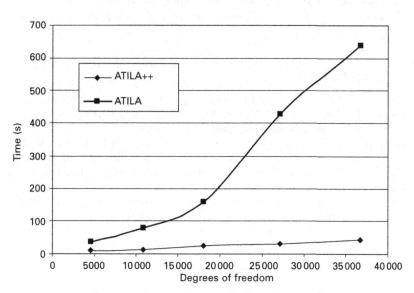

2.27 Real time from a transient analysis for the cylinder.

Table 2.8 Characteristics of the cylinder model

Degrees of freedom	Nodes	Elements (piezoelectric)	Blocks (transient)
4636	1265	200	2
10908	2901	480	6
18076	4725	800	11
27076	7069	1320	25
36764	9557	1800	36
54984	14167	2700	64

Table 2.9 CPU and real times of the transient analysis

Degrees of freedom	CPU time (s)		Real time (s)	
	ATILA++	ATILA	ATILA++	ATILA
4636	7	20	8	37
10908	10	73	11	81
18076	21	147	24	160
27076	26	394	30	427
36764	38	591	43	638
54984	81	1099	90	1208

2.6   Conclusion

From these different examples, the new version ATILA++ displays a significant improvement for a modal, harmonic or transient analysis. The time ratio between the two versions is very important. With this new version, the size of the mesh can be bigger than 200 000 elements with a reasonable CPU time.

2.7   References

1.   'ATILA Finite-Element Code for Piezoelectric and Magentostrictive Transducer and Actuator Modelling', Version 5.2.2, User Manual September 2002, Institut Supérieur de l'Electronique et du Numérique, Acoustics Laboratory
2.   Decarpigny J. N., 'Application de la méthode des éléments finis à l'étude des transducteurs piézoélectriques' (Application of the Finite Element Method to the Modeling of Piezoelectric Transducers), Thèse de Doctorat d'Etat, Université des Sciences et Techniques de Lille (1984).
3.   GID, The Personal Pre And Post Processor, International Center for Numerical Methods in Engineering, Barcelona, Spain, http://gid.cimne.upc.es.
4.   Meyer R. J., 'Finite Element Analysis of Ultrasonic Probe', Code Comparison Workshop and Tutorial, Ultrasonics Industry Association, Cambridge MA, April 2010.

3

Loss integration in ATILA software

K. UCHINO, The Pennsylvania State University, USA

DOI: 10.1533/9780857096319.1.45

Abstract: Finite element analysis can be applied to smart structures with piezoelectric or magnetostrictive materials rather successfully when neither the applying electric field nor the generating AC strain is very large and when the linear relation can be supposed in the strain vs electric field or the strain vs stress. However, further improvement in the FEM algorithm is required for high field or high power drive of the piezoelectric system, where nonlinear and hysteretic characteristics should be taken into account, as well as heat generation. In this chapter, we will discuss the high power issues. There are three hysteresis loss components for piezoelectric vibrators, i.e., dielectric, elastic and piezoelectric losses. Mechanical quality factors play a significant role in the loss study of piezoelectrics, and they are basically related to all dielectric, elastic and piezoelectric loss factors. Besides, a higher quality factor at the antiresonance is usually observed in the PZT based experiments, in comparison with that at the resonance. ATILA is the unique software for adopting dielectric, elastic and piezoelectric losses separately to calculate the impedance/admittance curve.

Key words: piezoelectrics, magnetostrictor, loss mechanism, hysteresis, resonance, antiresonance, piezoelectric loss, heat generation.

3.1 Introduction: nonlinear and hysteresis characteristics

The key factor to the miniaturization of piezoelectric devices is the power density, which is limited by material's inherent losses that stem from the microscopic domain dynamics, resulting in the heat generation.[1-3] Therefore, to advance the power level of piezoelectric devices it is necessary to clarify the loss phenomenology and mechanism. Hysteresis losses in piezoelectrics are considered to have three types in general: dielectric, elastic, and piezoelectric losses.[4-7] Further, each loss can be classified into intensive or extensive factors upon the boundary conditions.[8,9] The dielectric and elastic loss factors are commonly reported by researchers and companies, while so far little attention has been paid to the piezoelectric loss factor.[10] However, relatively large piezoelectric loss factors were reported in the previous study.[11]

Ferroelectric materials tend to exhibit *nonlinear* and *hysteretic* characteristics in the relationships of polarization vs electric field, strain vs electric field, and strain vs stress. Nonlinearity is inevitable for ferroelectrics, because ferroelectricity is originated from the nonlinear characteristics of the atomic

45

lattice elastic properties. To the contrary, the hysteretic behavior is primarily originated from the domain reorientation. The situation is illustrated in Fig. 3.1.

The hysteresis is simulated in the FEM as an intensive loss factor: dielectric loss tan δ', elastic loss tan ϕ' and piezoelectric loss tan θ'. However, it is notable that the hysteresis curve due to this sort of loss factor is elliptic, which is different from the actual hysteresis. Also, note that the value of the loss factor should be less than 10% (or 0.1) in theory. The treatment for large hysteresis, such as a butterfly-shape strain curve, has not been established yet.

Also, note that the loss factors should have tensor properties similar to the real parameters. For example, there are 10 independent parameters in a PZT ceramic; elastic compliances, $s_{11}^E, s_{12}^E, s_{13}^E, s_{33}^E, s_{44}^E$; piezoelectric constants, d_{33}, d_{31}, d_{15}; and dielectric constants $\varepsilon_{11}^X/\varepsilon_0$, $\varepsilon_{33}^X/\varepsilon_0$. Accordingly, there must be 10 loss tensor components; that is, 20 loss components taking into account intensive and extensive losses.

ATILA is the unique software for adopting dielectric, elastic and piezoelectric losses separately to calculate the impedance/admittance curve. At present only three loss factors, dielectric loss tan δ', elastic loss tan ϕ' and piezoelectric loss tan θ' can be integrated in the calculation in the ATILA software (that is, isotropic).

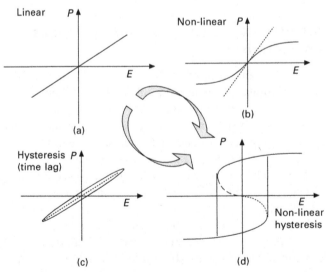

3.1 The relationship of polarization versus electric field in a linear material (a), in a nonlinear material (b), in a hysteretic material (c) or in an actual material (d).

3.1.1   Elastic nonlinearity

Elastic nonlinearity provides theoretically asymmetric (or skewed) impedance or strain spectrum under frequency sweep.[12] With increasing further electric field level, *jump* and *hysteresis* during rising and falling frequency are observed experimentally, as illustrated in Figs 3.2 and 3.3. The PZN-PT single crystal is known as a very high electromechanical coupling material, but its significant nonlinearity is also noticeable. With an increase in the drive

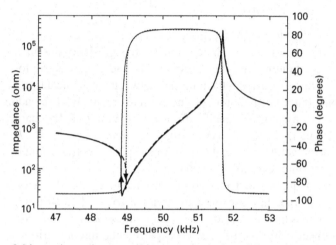

3.2 Impedance jump and hysteresis during rising and falling frequency around the electromechanical resonance point (observed under a relatively large electric field in a doped $Pb(Zn_{1/3}Nb_{2/3})O_3$-$PbTiO_3$ single crystal).

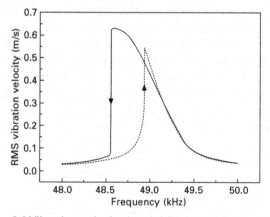

3.3 Vibration velocity (strain) jump and hysteresis during rising and falling frequency around the electromechanical resonance point (observed under a relatively large electric field in a doped $Pb(Zn_{1/3}Nb_{2/3})O_3$-$PbTiO_3$ single crystal).

electric field level, the material becomes stiffer, and also with an increase in the stress, the material becomes stiffer. This nonlinearity introduces the hysteresis phenomenon with drive frequency in the impedance and the strain spectrum.

The Standard ATILA cannot provide this sort of asymmetric impedance spectrum at present, because no information is put on the elastic nonlinearity of PZTs.

3.1.2   Loss anisotropy

The methodology to obtain the three loss factors in piezoelectric ceramics is explained in this section. There are three hysteresis loss components for piezoelectric vibrators, i.e., dielectric, elastic and piezoelectric losses. The equations were derived about the relations between mechanical quality factors and all contributing loss factors by the complex analysis of the admittance/impedance expressions for specific piezoelectric vibrators. By characterizing mechanical quality factors and coupling coefficients in k_{31}, k_t, k_{33}, k_p, and k_{15} modes, 20 loss factors can be obtained for the piezoelectric ceramic material with ∞mm or 6mm crystal symmetry.

Mechanical quality factors play a significant role in the loss study of piezoelectrics, and they are basically related to all dielectric, elastic and piezoelectric loss factors. Besides, a higher quality factor at the antiresonance is usually observed in the PZT based experiments, in comparison with that at the resonance.[13–15] However, the previous theory without considering the piezoelectric loss could not explain the deviation of the resonance quality factor Q_A and antiresonance quality factor Q_B explicitly. The IEEE Standard only provided the method to derive Q_A based on the equivalent circuit, and assumed that the resonance quality factor is equal to the antiresonance quality factor from a similar traditional thought.[16]

In this section, the equations for piezoelectric quality factors are provided with regard to three loss factors and other material properties. The difference of Q_A and Q_B is explained by the results. Within the study we focused on ferroelectric ceramics with ∞mm or 6mm crystal symmetry, exemplified by the conventional lead zirconate titanate (PZT) ceramics with uniform distribution of the fine grains. To cover 20 material property parameters, k_{31}, k_t, k_{33}, k_p, and k_{15} vibration modes are analyzed. Then the methodology to derive loss factors is proposed, based on the theoretical equations. By characterizing quality factors and other parameters 20 loss factors can be obtained. The loss characterization methodology is applied on PZT ceramic APC 850. All the real and imaginary material properties are obtained, and the orientation dependence of the loss factors is accordingly discussed.

Derivations of quality factors

Complex parameters are integrated to express the hysteresis losses in piezoelectrics.[17] We use $\tan\delta'$, $\tan\phi'$ and $\tan\theta'$ to represent 'intensive' dielectric, elastic and piezoelectric loss factors, respectively. The 'extensive' loss factors are given by corresponding notations without prime. The definitions are given by

$$\varepsilon^{T*} = \varepsilon^{T}(1 - j \tan \delta') \tag{3.1}$$

$$s^{E*} = s^{E}(1 - j \tan \phi') \tag{3.2}$$

$$d^{*} = d(1 - j \tan \theta') \tag{3.3}$$

$$\beta^{s*} = \beta^{s}(1 + j \tan \delta) \tag{3.4}$$

$$c^{D*} = c^{D}(1 + j \tan \phi) \tag{3.5}$$

$$h^{*} = h(1 + j \tan \theta) \tag{3.6}$$

Here j is the imaginary notation, ε^{T} the dielectric constant under constant stress, β^{S} the inverse dielectric constant under constant strain, s^{E} the elastic compliance under constant electric field, c^{D} the elastic stiffness under constant electric displacement, d the piezoelectric constant, and h the inverse piezoelectric charge constant.

From the view point of the physics, an intensive property is a physical property of a system that does not depend on the system size or the amount of material in the system, while the extensive property is directly proportional to the size or amount. In addition, state variables are extensive and field variables are intensive.[18,19] As for the loss factors, intensive loss corresponds to the boundary conditions of constant stress T or electric field E, while extensive loss is attributed to the boundary conditions of constant strain S or electric displacement D. Here T and E are intensive parameters, and S and D are extensive properties.

Note that the phenomenological equations only hold when the piezoelectric sample works in the linear region and the loss is treated as a perturbation. In practice, the theoretical equations derived in this way are accurate for the cases where the loss factors are less than 0.1. Then we derived the mechanical quality factors of ferroelectric ceramics in k_{31}, k_t, k_{33}, k_p, and k_{15} vibration modes. Each Q_A or Q_B equation is derived from the complex impedance/admittance expression of the specific mode based on the 3 dB definition as shown in Fig. 3.4, utilizing the first order approximation. The derivation method and details can be found in our previous publications.[20,21]

The geometries for the vibration modes are shown in Fig. 3.5. There are dimension requirements for each mode, according to the standard.[16] Notice that there are two configurations of k_{15} shear samples. The thickness shear mode ($L \gg t$) corresponds to the constant induction condition, and the length

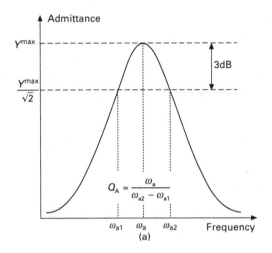

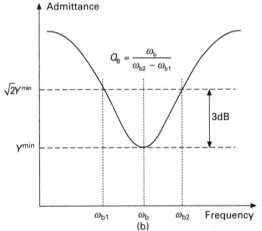

3.4 Definitions of quality factors at (a) resonance and (b) antiresonance.

shear mode ($L \ll t$) has the constant electric field condition. The quality factor equations for different vibration modes are shown as follows:

k_{31} mode:

$$Q_{A,31} = \frac{1}{\tan\phi'_{11}} \tag{3.7}$$

$$\frac{1}{Q_{B,31}} = \frac{1}{Q_{A,31}} - \frac{2}{1 + \left(\dfrac{1}{k_{31}} - k_{31}\right)^2 \Omega_B^2} (2 \tan \theta'_{31} - \tan \delta'_{33} - \tan\phi'_{11}) \tag{3.8}$$

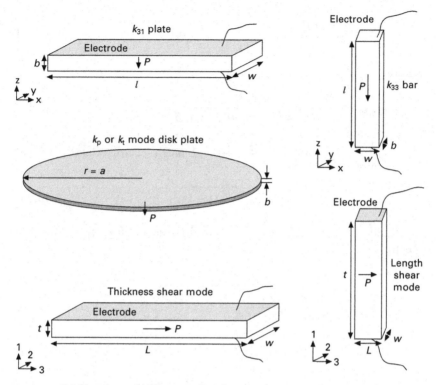

3.5 Sketches of different vibration modes.

Here $\tan\delta'_{33}$, $\tan\phi'_{11}$ and $\tan\theta'_{31}$ are intensive loss factors for ε^T_{33} and s^E_{11} and d_{31}, respectively. The k_{31} mode is under the constant E and T condition, so the intensive loss factors are included. Ω_B is the parameter proportional to the antiresonance frequency ω_B, and ρ is the density:

$$\Omega_B = \frac{\omega_B l}{2}\sqrt{\rho s^E_{11}}$$

[3.9]

k_t mode:

$$Q_{B,t} = \frac{1}{\tan\phi_{33}}$$

[3.10]

$$\frac{1}{Q_{A,t}} = \frac{1}{Q_{B,t}} + \frac{2}{k_t^2 - 1 + \Omega_A^2/k_t^2}(\tan\delta_{33} + \tan\phi_{33} - 2\tan\theta_{33})$$

[3.11]

Here $\tan\delta_{33}$, $\tan\phi_{33}$ and $\tan\theta_{33}$ are loss factors for ε^S_{33}, c^D_{33} and h_{33}, respectively. To the contrary, k_{33} mode has the constant D and S condition and the extensive losses are included. The parameter Ω_A is proportional to the resonance frequency ω_A:

$$\Omega_A = \frac{\omega_A b}{2} \sqrt{\frac{\rho}{c_{33}^D}} \tag{3.12}$$

k_{33} mode:

$$Q_{B,33} = \frac{1 - k_{33}^2}{\tan \phi_{33}' - k_{33}^2 (2 \tan \theta_{33}' - \tan \delta_{33}')} \tag{3.13}$$

$$\frac{1}{Q_{A,33}} = \frac{1}{Q_{B,33}} + \frac{2}{k_{33}^2 - 1 + \Omega_A^2 / k_{33}^2} (2 \tan \theta_{33}' - \tan \delta_{33}' - \tan \phi_{33}') \tag{3.14}$$

$$\Omega_A = \frac{\omega_A l}{2} \sqrt{\rho s_{33}^D} = \frac{\omega_A l}{2} \sqrt{\rho s_{33}^E (1 - k_{33}^2)} \tag{3.15}$$

In this mode $\tan \delta_{33}'$, $\tan \phi_{33}'$ and $\tan \theta_{33}'$ are loss factors for ε_{33}^T, s_{33}^E and d_{33}, respectively.

k_p mode:

$$Q_{A,p} = \frac{\alpha_{11} - \alpha_{12}}{\alpha_{11} \tan \phi_{11}' - \alpha_{12} \tan \phi_{12}'} \tag{3.16}$$

$$\alpha_{11} = \frac{1 + \sigma^2}{1 - \sigma^2} \Omega_A^2 - (1 - \sigma)^2 \tag{3.17}$$

$$\alpha_{12} = 2\sigma \left[\frac{\sigma}{1 - \sigma^2} \Omega_A^2 + (1 - \sigma) \right] \tag{3.18}$$

For the disk, σ is the Poisson's ratio, $\tan \phi_{12}'$ the loss factor for s_{12}^E, and Ω_A the parameter proportional to the resonance frequency:

$$\sigma = -s_{12}^E / s_{11}^E \tag{3.19}$$

$$\Omega_A = \frac{\omega_A a}{v^P} \tag{3.20}$$

$$v^P = \sqrt{\frac{c_{11}^P}{\rho}} = \sqrt{\frac{1}{\rho s_{11}^E} \frac{1}{1 - \sigma^2}} \tag{3.21}$$

The equation for $Q_{B,p}$, a complicated expression, is neglected here, since it does not affect the methodology of loss characterization. The only material property characterized in k_p mode is s_{12}^E, which is already covered by $Q_{A,p}$.

k_{15} mode (constant E – length shear mode):

$$Q_{A,15}^E = \frac{1}{\tan \phi_{55}'} \tag{3.22}$$

$$\frac{1}{Q^E_{B,15}} = \frac{1}{Q^E_{A,15}} - \frac{2}{1 + \left(\dfrac{1}{k_{15}} - k_{15}\right)^2 \Omega^2_B} (2\tan\theta'_{15} - \tan\delta'_{11} - \tan\phi'_{55})$$

[3.23]

$$\Omega_B = \frac{\omega_B L}{2} \sqrt{\rho s^E_{55}}$$ [3.24]

Here $\tan\delta'_{11}$, $\tan\phi'_{55}$ and $\tan\theta'_{15}$ are loss factors for ε^T_{11}, s^E_{55} and d_{15}, respectively.

k_{15} mode (constant D – thickness shear mode):

$$Q^D_{B,15} = \frac{1}{\tan\phi_{55}}$$ [3.25]

$$\frac{1}{Q^D_{A,15}} = \frac{1}{Q^D_{B,15}} + \frac{2}{k^2_{15} - 1 + \Omega^2_A/k^2_{15}} (\tan\theta_{11} + \tan\delta_{55} - 2\tan\theta_{15})$$ [3.26]

$$\Omega_A = \frac{\omega_A t}{2} \sqrt{\frac{\rho}{c^D_{55}}}$$ [3.27]

Here $\tan\delta_{11}$, $\tan\phi_{55}$ and $\tan\theta_{15}$ are loss factors for ε^S_{11}, c^D_{55} and h_{15}, respectively.

From the quality factor equations, we can find the deviation of Q_A and Q_B which comes from the loss factors. For example, in k_{31} mode the key factor to determine whether Q_B is larger than Q_A is the term $(2\tan\theta' - \tan\delta' - \tan\phi')$. This term should be positive to get the higher Q_B that matches the experimental results, which means the piezoelectric loss factor $\tan\theta'$ is significant and should have relatively large value.

Loss anisotropy in PZT

In the experiment, a Agilent 4294A Precision Impedance Analyzer was utilized for the impedance measurements. The loss characterization methodology was applied on the soft PZT based piezoelectric ceramic APC 850 (American Piezo Ceramic International Ltd., Mackeyville, PA, USA), following the procedures explained above. The dimensions of different modes are given by: k_{31} mode – $20 \times 4 \times 1$ mm; k_{33} mode – $20 \times 4 \times 4$ mm; k_t and k_p mode disk – diameter 25 mm, thickness 1 mm; thickness shear mode – $18 \times 18 \times 1$ mm; length shear mode – $1 \times 18 \times 18$ mm. Initially the real material properties were characterized, which are listed in Table 3.1. Then all the 20 loss factors were measured and derived as shown in Table 3.2.

Four points are summarized upon the data as follows:

Table 3.1 The real-part of the material properties of APC 850

s (10^{-12} m^2/N)

s_{11}^E	s_{12}^E	s_{13}^E	s_{33}^E	s_{55}^E
16.46	−5.27	−7.58	18.48	47.57

c (10^{+10} N/m^2)

c_{11}^D	c_{12}^D	c_{13}^D	c_{33}^D	c_{55}^D
12.83	8.24	7.51	16.37	4.62

ε

ε_{33}^T	ε_{11}^T	ε_{33}^S	ε_{11}^S
2075	1834	988	835

d (10^{-12} C/N or m/V)			h (10^{+8} N/C or V/m)		
d_{31}	d_{33}	d_{15}	h_{31}	h_{33}	h_{15}
−196	416	649	−5.10	21.94	18.44

Table 3.2 The loss factors of APC 850 with experimental uncertainties

	$\tan\phi'_{11}$	$\tan\phi'_{12}$	$\tan\phi'_{13}$	$\tan\phi'_{33}$	$\tan\phi'_{55}$	
Result	0.01096	0.0095	0.01507	0.01325	0.0233	
Uncertainty	0.00007	0.0003	0.00034	0.00033	0.0022	
Relative	0.6%	3.2%	2.2%	2.5%	9.6%	
	$\tan\phi_{11}$	$\tan\phi_{12}$	$\tan\phi_{13}$	$\tan\phi_{33}$	$\tan\phi_{55}$	
Result	0.0105	0.0104	0.0076	0.00433	0.0149	
Uncertainty	0.0018	0.0028	0.0013	0.00008	0.0003	
Relative	17%	28%	17%	1.7%	2.1%	
	$\tan\delta'_{33}$	$\tan\delta'_{11}$	$\tan\delta_{33}$	$\tan\delta_{11}$		
Result	0.0143	0.0176	0.0058	0.0092		
Uncertainty	0.0002	0.0004	0.0011	0.0023		
Relative	1.4%	2.3%	20%	25%		
	$\tan\theta'_{31}$	$\tan\theta'_{33}$	$\tan\theta'_{15}$	$\tan\theta_{31}$	$\tan\theta_{33}$	$\tan\theta_{15}$
Result	0.0184	0.0178	0.0296	0.0133	0.0004	0.0024
Uncertainty	0.0006	0.0004	0.0026	0.0081	0.0004	0.0013
Relative	3.2%	2.1%	8.8%	61%	100%	57%

1. The piezoelectric loss factors are not negligible, and play a significant role in the loss behavior. In fact the piezoelectric loss factor is the reason for the higher mechanical quality factor at the antiresonance.
2. Compared to extensive losses, intensive losses seem to have larger values.

3. Theoretically there are two $\tan\delta_{33}$ with different expressions, but in practice the factor in 31 mode and the one in 33 mode are almost same.
4. Loss anisotropy can be summarized as follows: elastic losses, $\tan\phi'_{11}$ < $\tan\phi'_{33}$, $\tan\phi_{11}$ < $\tan\phi_{33}$; piezoelectric losses, $\tan\theta'_{31}$ > $\tan\theta'_{33}$, $\tan\theta_{31}$ < $\tan\theta_{33}$. This loss relationship conversion is very intriguing from the microscopic domain dynamics.

According to the data all the loss factors obtained here are much less than 0.1, which satisfies the requirement that the loss could be treated as a perturbation. Therefore, the methodology is effective and accurate enough from the viewpoint of the theory. Note that the error analysis is also included in the results. The result of each parameter is the mean value of several samples with the same condition. The experimental measurement errors or uncertainties were obtained by the standard deviations. For the derived parameters, the error propagation was computed using the software GUM Workbench Professional Version 2.4 (Metrodata GmbH, Germany). Some of the loss factors have quite large uncertainties due to the error propagations during the derivations, especially the extensive piezoelectric losses $\tan\theta_{31}$, $\tan\theta_{33}$ and $\tan\theta_{15}$. The methodology will be improved in the future using some alternative measurements or derivations to reduce these errors.

3.1.3   ATILA simulation

To verify the analytical solutions, we employed the finite element method (FEM) software ATILA (Ver. 5.2.4) commercialized by ISEN (Institute Superieure de l'Electronique et du Numerique, Lille, France) and distributed by Micromechatronics Inc. (State College, PA, USA), which has the capability to apply three intensive loss factors (dielectric, elastic and piezoelectric losses). The limitation of the software is that the loss anisotropy is not included in the present version, and the loss factors are therefore, the same for all directions.

In the simulation, a typical hard lead zirconate titanate ceramic (PZT-8) was used. For this material, $\tan\phi' = 0.001$, $\tan\delta' = 0.004$, and different $\tan\theta'$ values were selected.[21] The dimensions for k_{31} and k_{33} analysis are $20 \times 3 \times 1$ mm^3 and $2 \times 2 \times 20$ mm^3, respectively. The mesh conditions are shown in Fig. 3.6. In simulations Q_A or Q_B can be obtained around the resonance or antiresonance peak. As shown in Fig. 3.7, the simulation results match the calculations well. Further in both k_{31} and k_{33} modes when $2\tan\theta' = \tan\delta' + \tan\phi' = 0.005$, $Q_A = Q_B$; when $2\tan\theta' < \tan\delta' + \tan\phi'$, $Q_A > Q_B$; when $2\tan\theta' > \tan\delta' + \tan\phi'$, $Q_A < Q_B$. This conclusion is consistent with Eqs. [3.7] and [3.8]. It should be noted that $(2\tan\theta' - \tan\delta' - \tan\phi') = -(2\tan\theta - \tan\delta - \tan\phi)$. In experiments, Q_B usually has larger value than Q_A in either k_{31} or k_{33} mode, which indicates a relatively high intensive piezoelectric loss factor.

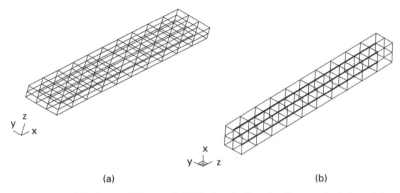

3.6 Mesh conditions of FEM simulation for k_{31} mode (a) and k_{33} mode (b).

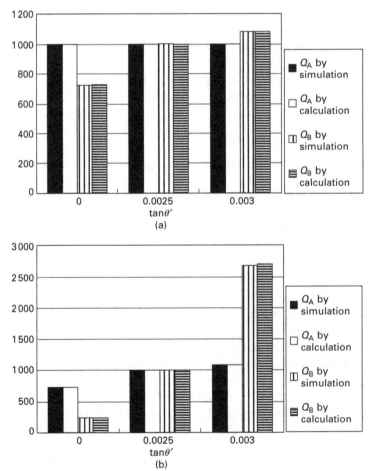

3.7 Quality factors derived by simulation and analytical calculation for k_{31} mode (a) and k_{33} mode (b).

3.2   Heat generation

With increasing the drive voltage, the hysteretic property is accompanied inevitably by heat generation from the piezoelectric material. Heat generation in various types of PZT-based actuators has been studied under a relatively large electric field applied (1 kV/mm or more) at an off-resonance frequency, and a simple analytical method was established to evaluate the temperature rise, which is very useful for the design of piezoelectric high-power actuators.

Zheng *et al.* reported the heat generation from various sizes of multilayer type piezoelectric ceramic actuators.[22] Figure 3.8 shows the temperature change with time in the actuators when driven at 3 kV/mm and 300 Hz, and Fig. 3.9 plots the saturated temperature as a function of V_e/A, where V_e is the effective volume (electrode overlapped part) and A is the surface area. This linear relation is reasonable because the volume V_e generates the heat and this heat is dissipated through the area A. Thus, if we need to suppress the temperature rise, a small V_e/A design is preferred.

According to the law of energy conservation, the rate of heat storage in the piezoelectric resulting from heat generation and dissipation effects can be expressed as

$$q_g - q_{out} = V_{\rho c} \, (dT/dt) \qquad [3.28]$$

assuming uniform temperature distribution in the sample. V, ρ, c are total volume, density and specific heat, respectively. The heat generation is considered to be caused by losses. Thus, the rate of heat generation (q_g) in the piezoelectric can be expressed as

$$q_g = u f V_e \qquad [3.29]$$

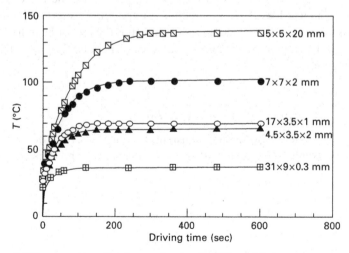

3.8 Temperature rise for various soft PZT multilayer actuators while driven at 300 Hz and 3 kV/mm.

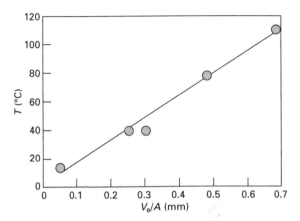

3.9 Temperature rise vs V_e/A (3 kV/mm, 300 Hz), where V_e is the effective volume generating the heat and A is the surface area dissipating the heat.

where u is the loss of the sample per driving cycle per unit volume, f, the driving frequency, and V_e is the effective volume where the ceramic is activated. According to the measuring condition, this u corresponds to the intensive dielectric loss w_e, which consists of the extensive dielectric loss $\tan \delta$ and the electro-mechanical and piezoelectric combined loss ($\tan\phi - 2 \tan\theta$):

$$u = w_e = \pi \, \varepsilon^X \varepsilon_0 \, E_0^2 \tan \delta'$$
$$= [1/(1 - k^2)][\tan \delta + k^2(\tan \phi - 2 \tan \theta)] \, \pi \, \varepsilon^X \varepsilon_0 \, E_0^2 \qquad [3.30]$$

Note that we do not need to add w_{em} explicitly, because the corresponding electromechanical loss is already included implicitly in w_e.

When we neglect the conduction heat transfer, the rate of heat dissipation (q_{out}) from the sample is the sum of the rates of heat flow by radiation (q_r) and convection (q_c):

$$q_{out} = q_r + q_c$$
$$= \sigma e A(T^4 - T_0^4) + h_c \, A(T - T_0) \qquad [3.31]$$

where σ is the Stefan-Boltzmann constant, e is the emissivity of the sample, h_c is the average convective heat transfer coefficient, and A is the sample surface area.

Thus, Eq. [3.28] can be written in the form:

$$u f V - A \, k(T) \, (T - T_0) = V \rho \, c \, (dT/dt) \qquad [3.32]$$

where

$$k(T) = \sigma e(T^2 + T_0^2)(T + T_0) + h_c \qquad [3.33]$$

is defined as the overall heat transfer coefficient. If we assume that $k(T)$ is relatively insensitive to temperature change, the solution to Eq. [3.32] for the piezoelectric sample temperature is given as a function of time (t):

$$T - T_0 = [u f V_e / k(T) A] [1 - e^{-t/\tau}] \qquad [3.34]$$

where the time constant τ is expressed as

$$\tau = \rho c V / k(T) A \qquad [3.35]$$

Figure 3.10(a) and (b) show the dependence of $k(T)$ on applied electric field and frequency. Since $k(T)$ is not really constant, we can calculate the total loss u of the piezoelectric more precisely through Eq. [3.34]. The calculated results are shown in Table 3.3. The experimental data of P-E hysteresis losses under a stress-free condition are also listed for comparison. It is seen that the P-E hysteresis intensive loss agrees well with the total loss contributing to the heat generation under an off-resonance drive.

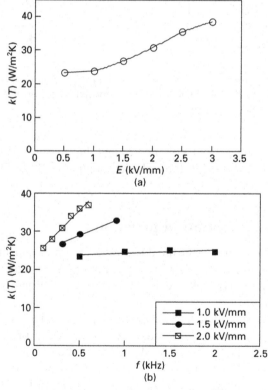

3.10 Overall heat transfer coefficient $k(T)$ as a function of applied electric field (400 Hz) (a) and frequency (b) (data from the actuator with dimensions of 7 mm × 7 mm × 2 mm).

Table 3.3 Loss and overall heat transfer coefficient for PZT multilayer samples (E = 3 kV/mm, f = 300 Hz)

Actuator	4.5 × 3.5 × 2 mm	7 × 7 × 2 mm	17 × 3.5 × 1 mm
Total loss ($\times 10^3$J/m^3) $$u = \frac{\rho cv}{fv_e}\left(\frac{dT}{dt}\right)_{t \to 0}$$	19.2	19.9	19.7
P-E hysteresis loss ($\times 10^3$J/m^3)	18.5	17.8	17.4
$k(T)$ (W/m^{2}K)	38.4	39.2	34.1

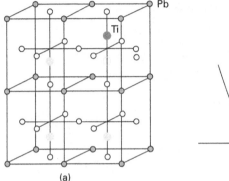 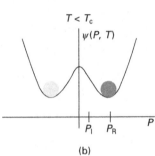

(a)   (b)

3.11 (a) PbTiO$_3$ crystal lattice model – there are two potential minima for the Ti ion position and (b) double-well model, showing the two potential minima.

Temperature rise in the piezoelectric device and the successive property change should be included in the future calculation process of the FEM for smart transducer system.

3.3   Hysteresis estimation program

With using a statistical treatment of the domain reversal mechanism, there are various computer simulation trials in polarization (P-E), magnetization (M-H) and strain (x-X) curves. We review here the calculation algorithm proposed by R. C. Smith.[23]

We adopt here the so-called mesoscopic model to treat ferroelectric, ferromagnetic and ferroelastic materials. Let us consider primarily a ferroelectric such as PbTiO$_3$, the crystallographic structure of which is illustrated in Fig. 3.11(a). There are basically two potential minima for the Ti ion position, so that we can assume the double well model in Fig. 3.11(b).

Introducing the Helmholtz energy (temperature stability of polarization) for this double-well polarization model at a finite temperature T:

$$\psi(P, T) = U - ST = \frac{\Phi_0 N}{4V} [1 - (P/P_s)^2]$$

$$+ \frac{TkN}{2VP_s} \left[P \ln\left(\frac{P + P_s}{P_s - P}\right) + P_s \ln(1 - (P/P_s)^2) \right] \qquad [3.36]$$

we obtain the following relationship:

$$\psi(P) = \begin{cases} \frac{\eta}{2}(P \pm P_R)^2, & |P| \geq P_1 \\ \frac{\eta}{2}(P_1 - P_R)\left[\frac{P^2}{P_1} - P_R\right], & |P| < P_1 \end{cases} \qquad [3.37]$$

Then, we introduce the Gibbs energy for a ferroelectric:

$$G(E, P, T) = \psi(P, T) - EP \text{ (ferroelectric)} \qquad [3.38]$$

The Gibbs energy curves for various electric fields are depicted in Fig. 3.12.

In order to introduce the temperature fluctuation of the polarization more explicitly, *Boltzmann probability* is introduced (refer to Fig. 3.13):

$$\mu(G) = Ce^{-GV/kT} \Rightarrow p_{+-} = \sqrt{\frac{kT}{2\pi m V^{2/3}}} \cdot \frac{e^{-G(E.P_0(T),T)V/kT}}{\int_{P_0}^{\infty} e^{-G(E,P,T)V/kT} dP} \qquad [3.39]$$

By taking the evolution relations:

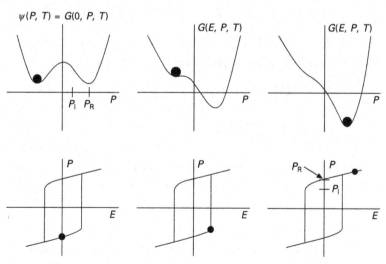

3.12 Gibbs energy curves for various electric field *E* levels.

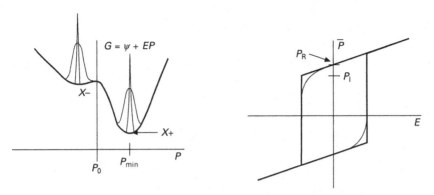

3.13 Introduction of Boltzmann probability to realize the rounded hysteresis curve in the polarization and electric field relation.

$$\frac{dx_+}{dt} = -p_{+-}\,x_+ + p_{-+}\,x_-,\; \frac{dx_-}{dt} = -p_{-+}\,x_- + p_{+-}\,x_+ \qquad [3.40]$$

we finally obtain the polarization under a uniform lattice

$$\bar{P} = x_+\,\langle P_+\rangle + x_-\,\langle P_-\rangle \qquad [3.41]$$

where

$$\langle P_+\rangle = \int_{P_0}^{\infty} P\mu(G)dP \qquad [3.42]$$

The Gibbs energy for a ferromagnetic and a ferroelastic can be obtained in a similar fashion:

$$G(H, M, T) = \psi(M, T) - \mu_0 HM \text{ (ferromagnetic)}$$

$$G(\sigma, \varepsilon, T) = \psi(\varepsilon, T) - \sigma\varepsilon \qquad [3.43]$$

Then, the average magnetization can be obtained as

$$\bar{M} = x_+\langle M_+\rangle + x_-\langle M_-\rangle \qquad [3.44]$$

$$\langle M_+\rangle = \int_{M_0}^{\infty} M\mu(G)dM \qquad [3.45]$$

Finally, Fig. 3.14 demonstrates the *P-E*, *M-H* and *x-X* hysteresis curves for PZT 5A piezoelectric, Terfenol-D magnetostrictive and NiTi film shape memory materials, respectively. Notice that the hysteresis curve starting from any intermediate external parameter (*E*, *H* or *X*) exhibits a reasonable agreement with the experimental curves.

We will seek the combination of this hysteresis estimation program with ATILA FEM software in the future, in order to introduce the nonlinear and

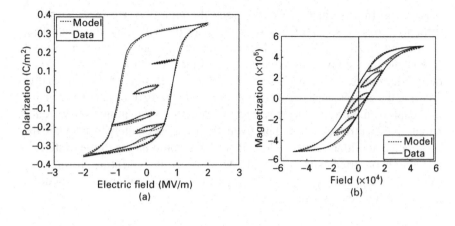

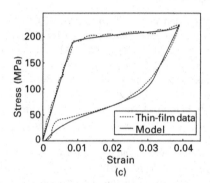

3.14 Hysteresis curves obtained from the mesoscopic approach in comparison with the experimental data: (a) polarization vs electric field in piezoelectric PZT 5A (b) magnetization vs magnetic field in magnetostrictive Terfenol-D and (c) strain vs stress in shape memory NiTi film.[23]

hysteretic behavior in the vibration calculation, as well as the heat generation evaluation.

3.4   Conclusion

Finite element analysis can be applied to smart structures with piezoelectric or magnetostrictive materials rather successfully when neither the applying electric field nor the generating AC strain is very large and when the linear relation can be supposed in the strain vs electric field or the strain vs stress. However, further improvement in the FEM algorithm is required for high field or high power drive of the piezoelectric system, where nonlinear and hysteretic characteristics should be taken into account, as well as heat generation. In this chapter, we discussed the high power issues. There are three hysteresis loss components for piezoelectric vibrators, i.e., dielectric, elastic and piezoelectric losses. Mechanical quality factors play a significant role in the loss study of piezoelectrics, and they are basically related to all dielectric, elastic and piezoelectric loss factors. Besides, a higher quality factor at the antiresonance is usually observed in the PZT-based experiments, in comparison with that at the resonance. ATILA is the unique software for adopting dielectric, elastic and piezoelectric losses separately to calculate the impedance/admittance curve. We will seek the combination of the hysteresis estimation program with ATILA FEM software in the future, in order to introduce the nonlinear and hysteretic behavior in the vibration calculation, as well as the heat generation evaluation.

3.5   References

1. S. Hirose, M. Aoyagi, and Y. Tomikawa, Dielectric loss in a piezoelectric ceramic transducer under high-power operation: increase of dielectric loss and its influence on transducer efficiency. *Jpn. J. Appl. Phys.* **32**, 2418–2421 (1993).
2. S. Tashiro, M. Ikehiro, and H. Igarashi, Influence of temperature rise and vibration level on electromechanical properties of high-power piezoelectric ceramics. *Jpn. J. Appl. Phys.* **36**, 3004–3009 (1997).
3. S. Zhang, R. Xia, L. Lebrun, D. Anderson, and T. R. Shrout, Piezoelectric materials for high power, high temperature applications. *Mater. Lett.* **59**(27), 3471–3475 (2005).
4. G. E. Martin, Dielectric, elastic, and piezoelectric losses in piezoelectric materials. *Proc. Ultrason. Symp.* Milwaukee, 613–617 (1974).
5. R. Holland, Representations of the dielectric, elastic, and piezoelectric losses by complex coefficients. *IEEE Trans. Sonics Ultrason.* **14**(1), 18–20 (1967).
6. S. Sherrit, H. D. Wiederick, B. K. Mukherjee, Non-iterative evaluation of the real and imaginary material constants of piezoelectric resonators. *Ferroelectrics* **134**, 111–119 (1992).
7. J. G. Smits, Iterative method for accurate determination of the real and imaginary parts of the material coefficients of piezoelectric ceramics. *IEEE Trans. Sonics Ultrason.* **23**(6), 393–401 (1976).
8. K. Uchino, J. H. Zheng, Y. H. Chen, X. H. Du, J. Ryu, Y. Gao, S. Ural, S. Priya, and S. Hirose, Loss mechanisms and high power piezoelectrics. *J. Mater. Sci.* **41**(1), 217–228 (2006).
9. K. Uchino and S. Hirose, Loss mechanisms in piezoelectrics: how to measure different losses separately. *IEEE Trans. Ultrason. Ferroelectr. Freq. Control* **48**, 307–321 (2001).
10. T. Ikeda, *Fundamentals of Piezoelectric Materials Science* (Ohmsha, Tokyo, 1984).
11. X. Du, Q. Wang, and K. Uchino, Accurate determination of complex materials coefficients of piezoelectric resonators. *IEEE Trans. Ultrason. Ferroelectr. Freq. Control* **50**, 312–320 (2003).
12. N. Aurella, D. Guyomar, C. Richard, P. Gonrard and L. Eyraud, *Ultrasonics*, **34**, 187–191 (1996).

13. S. O. Ural, S. Tuncdemir, Y. Zhuang, and K. Uchino, Development of a high power piezoelectric characterization system and its application for resonance/ antiresonance mode characterization. *Jpn. J. Appl. Phys.* **48**, 056509 (2009).

14. S. Hirose, M. Aoyagi, Y. Tomikawa, S. Takahashi, and K. Uchino, High power characteristics at antiresonance frequency of piezoelectric transducers. *Ultrasonics* **34**, 213–217 (1996).

15. A. V. Mezheritsky, Efficiency of excitation of piezoceramic transducers at antiresonance frequency. *IEEE Trans. Ultrason. Ferroelectr. Freq. Control* **49**(4), 484–494 (2002).

16. *ANSI/IEEE Std 176-1987 IEEE Standard on Piezoelectricity* (Institute of Electrical and Electronics Engineers, New York, 1987).

17. G. Arlt and H. Dederichs, Complex elastic, dielectric and piezoelectric constants by domain wall damping in ferroelectric ceramics. *Ferroelectrics* **29**, 47–50 (1980).

18. H. B. Callen, *Thermodynamics and an Introduction to Themostatistics 2nd edition* (John Wiley & Sons, New York, 1985).

19. G. N. Lewis and M. Randall, *Thermodynamics 2nd edition* (McGraw-Hill, New York, 1961).

20. Y. Zhuang, S. O. Ural, A. Rajapurkar, S. Tuncdemir, A. Amin, and K. Uchino, Derivation of piezoelectric losses from admittance spectra. *Jpn. J. Appl. Phys.* **48**, 041401 (2009).

21. Y. Zhuang, S. O. Ural, S. Tuncdemir, A. Amin, and K. Uchino, Analysis on loss anisotropy of piezoelectrics with ∞ mm crystal symmetry. *Jpn. J. Appl. Phys.* **49**, 021503 (2010).

22. J. Zheng, S. Takahashi, S. Yoshikawa, K. Uchino and J. W. C. de Vries, Heat generation in multilayer piezoelectric actuators. *J. Amer. Ceram. Soc.*, **79**, 3193–3198 (1996).

23. R. C. Smith, *Smart Materials Systems: Model Development* (Society of Industrial and Applied Mathematics, Philadelphia, 2005).

Part II

Case studies of finite element modelling using ATILA

4

Finite element analysis of flexural vibration of orthogonally stiffened cylindrical shells with ATILA

J-C. DEBUS, ISEN Lille, France

DOI: 10.1533/9780857096319.2.69

Abstract: The vibration and sound radiation of structures, like plates or shells stiffened by frames or ribs, is a problem of interest in the analysis of aircraft and marine structures. If the ribs are uniformly spaced, then the composite structure is spatially periodic. Many authors have proposed solutions for stiffened infinite shells with simple shapes. But, when the shape is more complicated, such as for a submarine or an aircraft, the numerical methods are not appropriate and the finite element method seems justified with finite element characterizing the stiffeners. In this chapter, from the theory of shells with the complicating effects of anisotropy due to the stiffeners, one finite element is presented. After, the presentation of the boundary conditions on the shell, a first validation will be realized on circular cylindrical shells having tranverse stiffeners. The modes of vibration obtained from the new shell element are compared with analytical and experimental results. The second validation concerns an elastic target with a stiffened shell. The comparison is made between the use of the new shell element and a 3D analysis.

Key words: finite element, shell theory, vibration, shell boundary conditions.

4.1   Introduction

Cylindrical shells are the principal structural element of various marine and airborne structures. These structures are often stiffened by frames or ribs. Calculation of the sound scattering properties of stiffened circular shapes is difficult. Much research has focused on the acoustic radiation from a stiffened infinite shell with a simple shape[1-6]. But, when the shape is more complicated like for a submarine or an aircraft, the numerical methods are not appropriate and the finite element method seems justified with finite element characterizing the stiffeners.

The results of the computation from a fluid-structure coupling of a stiffened shell must be close to the reality. Particularly, the elements in the model must take into account the parameters characterizing the elasticity.

From the theory of shells with the complicating effects of anisotropy due to the stiffeners, one finite element will be developed. The validation of this

69

element will be performed in comparison with an analytical solution and experimental results.

4.2   Shell formulation

To analyze a stiffened shell, circumferential rings can be combined with the shell but these rings have an offset with the mean axis shell. Many researchers have proposed such elements in the case of plane vibration[7,8] or in 3D[9]. This type of element is not convenient because it increases the number of degrees of freedom (+6) to the degrees of freedom of the shell element. The number of degrees of freedom for a submarine structure is very large; it is better to create a finite element taking into account the effective rigidity of the ring-stiffener.

From the theory of orthotropic shells, several other researchers have proposed analytical methods to take into account the orthogonal stiffeners[10–20]. Between the different methods, the method proposed by Nelson et al.[12] has been chosen. The ring can have a T shape and this method can take into account the flexural inertia and the offset of the ring.

4.2.1   Stiffness constant of the shell

Hooke's law-orthotropy

In the classical theory of small displacements of thin shells with the assumption made by Love-Kirchhoff[21], for an orthotropic shell, the stress-strain equations (Hooke's law) are:

$$\varepsilon_\alpha = \frac{1}{E_\alpha}(\sigma_\alpha - \upsilon_\alpha \sigma_\beta)$$

$$\varepsilon_\beta = \frac{1}{E_\beta}(\sigma_\beta - \upsilon_\beta \sigma_\alpha)$$

$$\varepsilon_{\alpha\beta} = \frac{\tau_{\alpha\beta}}{G} \qquad\qquad\qquad [4.1]$$

where E_α et E_β are the longitudinal elasticity modulus in the α and β directions (Fig. 4.1), G is the shear modulus and υ_α and υ_β are the Poisson ratios in the same axes.

The force resultants acting on the faces perpendicular to the α and β axes can be expressed as:

$$\begin{Bmatrix} N_\alpha \\ N_{\alpha\beta} \end{Bmatrix} = \int_{-h/2}^{h/2} \begin{Bmatrix} \sigma_\alpha \\ \sigma_{\alpha\beta} \end{Bmatrix}\left(1 + \frac{z}{R_\beta}\right)dz$$

$$\begin{Bmatrix} N_\beta \\ N_{\beta\alpha} \end{Bmatrix} = \int_{-h/2}^{h/2} \begin{Bmatrix} \sigma_\beta \\ \sigma_{\beta\alpha} \end{Bmatrix}\left(1 + \frac{z}{R_\alpha}\right)dz \qquad\qquad [4.2]$$

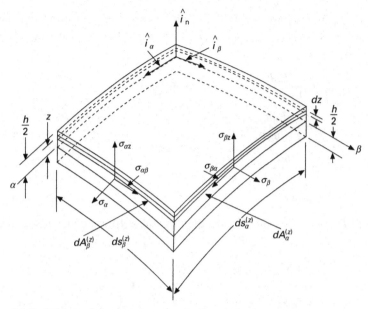

4.1 Definition of the stresses in shell coordinates.

where R_α and R_β are the curvatures of the α curves and the β curves and h is the thickness of the shell.

The moment resultants are given by:

$$\begin{Bmatrix} M_\alpha \\ M_{\alpha\beta} \end{Bmatrix} = \int_{-h/2}^{h/2} \begin{Bmatrix} \sigma_\alpha \\ \sigma_{\alpha\beta} \end{Bmatrix} \left(1 + \frac{z}{R_\beta} \right) z\,dz$$

$$\begin{Bmatrix} M_\beta \\ M_{\beta\alpha} \end{Bmatrix} = \int_{-h/2}^{h/2} \begin{Bmatrix} \sigma_\beta \\ \sigma_{\beta\alpha} \end{Bmatrix} \left(1 + \frac{z}{R_\alpha} \right) z\,dz$$

$$[4.3]$$

Stiffness constants in the shell

Substituting Eq. [4.1] into the generalized force resultant integrals of the shell theory of Eqs [4.2] and [4.3] (neglecting z/R_α and z/R_β) yields:

$$N_\alpha = C_{11}\varepsilon_\alpha + C_{12}\varepsilon_\beta$$

$$N_\beta = C_{12}\varepsilon_\alpha + C_{22}\varepsilon_\beta$$

$$N_{\alpha\beta} = N_{\beta\alpha} = C_{66}\varepsilon_{\alpha\beta}$$

$$M_\alpha = D_{11}\kappa_\alpha + D_{12}\kappa_\beta$$

$$M_\beta = D_{12}\kappa_\alpha + D_{22}\kappa_\beta$$

$$M_{\alpha\beta} = M_{\beta\alpha} = D_{66}\tau_{\alpha\beta}$$

$$[4.4]$$

where κ_α and κ_β are the mid-surface changes in curvature, $\tau_{\alpha\beta}$ the mid-surface twist and C_{11}, C_{12}, C_{22} and C_{66} are the extensional stiffness constants defined by:

$$C_{11} = \frac{E_\alpha h}{1 - v_\alpha v_\beta}$$

$$C_{22} = \frac{E_\beta h}{1 - v_\alpha v_\beta}$$

$$C_{12} = \frac{v_\alpha E_\beta h}{1 - v_\alpha v_\beta} = \frac{v_\beta E_\alpha h}{1 - v_\alpha v_\beta}$$

$$C_{66} = Gh$$

[4.5]

where D_{11}, D_{12}, D_{22} and D_{66} are the flexural stiffness constants defined by:

$$D_{11} = \frac{E_\alpha h^3}{12(1 - v_\alpha v_\beta)}$$

$$D_{22} = \frac{E_\beta h^3}{12(1 - v_\alpha v_\beta)}$$

$$D_{12} = \frac{v_\alpha E_\beta h^3}{12(1 - v_\alpha v_\beta)} = \frac{v_\beta E_\alpha h^3}{12(1 - v_\alpha v_\beta)}$$

$$D_{66} = \frac{Gh^3}{12}$$

[4.6]

4.2.2 Stiffness constant of the stiffened shell

The shell is stiffened by rings having the same material as the shell (Fig. 4.2), E and v being respectively the modulus of elasticity and the Poisson ratio. The equivalent orthotropic extensional stiffness constants are defined[12] as:

$$C_{11} = \frac{Eh}{1 - v^2}$$

$$C_{12} = vC_{11}$$

$$C_{22} = \frac{1}{L_{Rx}} \left(EA_F + \frac{EhL_{Rx}}{1 - v^2} \right)$$

$$C_{66} = \frac{(1 - v)C_{11}}{2}$$

[4.7]

and the equivalent orthotropic flexural stiffness constants are defined as:

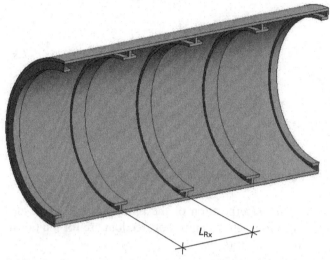

4.2 Repeating section of a ring of a cylindrical shell.

$$D_{11} = \frac{Eh^3}{12(1 - v^2)}$$

$$D_{22} = vD_{11}$$

$$D_{22} = \frac{1}{L_{Rx}}\left(EI_{F\beta} + \frac{EI_{SS}}{1 - v^2}\right)$$ [4.8]

$$D_{66} = \frac{(1 - v)D_{11}}{2}$$

with

$$I_{F\beta} = I_F + A_F(Y_F + h - r_\beta)^2$$

$$r_\beta = \frac{A_F(Y_F + h) + 0{,}75L_{Rx}h^2/2}{A_F + 0{,}75L_{RX}h}$$ [4.9]

$$I_{SS} = 0{,}75L_{Rx}h^3/12 + 0{,}75L_{Rx}h(r_\beta - h/2)^2$$

where A_F is the cross-sectional area of the rings, L_{Rx} is the length of the repeating section, I_F and I_{SS} are the area moments of the inertia of the ring about the own centroidal axis, I_{Sx} is the area moment of inertia of rings and skin, respectively, h is the skin thickness, and Y_F is the distance from the centroidal axis of the ring to the underside of the skin.

4.3   Stiffened shell finite element

The stiffened shell finite element is an eight-node quadrilateral thin shell element. It is plane and enables facet shell modelling (Fig. 4.3). This element

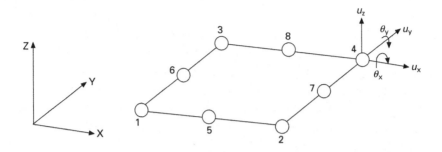

4.3 Eight-node quadrilateral thin shell element.

is equivalent to the superposition of the plane-stress element and the flat plate element. The five active degrees of freedom are for the translation u_x, u_y, u_z and for the rotation θ_x, θ_y.

Eq. (4.4) can be written as:

$$\{N\} = [C]\{\varepsilon\}$$
$$\{M\} = [D]\{\kappa\}$$

[4.10]

The element deformation vector for the stretching and the bending are, respectively:

$$\{\varepsilon^e\} = \lfloor B_\varepsilon^e \rfloor \{U^e\}$$
$$\{\kappa^e\} = [B_\kappa^e]\{\theta^e\}$$

[4.11]

The elementary membrane and bending rigidity matrices are, respectively:

$$[K_m^e] = \int_{D^e} [B_\varepsilon^e]^T [C][B_\varepsilon^e]dD^e$$
$$[K_b^e] = \int_{D^e} [B_\kappa^e]^T [D][B_\kappa^e]dD^e$$

[4.12]

The geometry entry parameters are defined as (Fig. 4.4):

h: thickness of the shell, L_{RX}: length of the repeating section, *a*: width of the flange of the stiffener, *b*: thickness of the web of the stiffene, *c*: depth of the stiffener and *d*: thickness of the flange of the stiffener.

4.4   Validation

4.4.1   Boundary conditions for symmetry and anti-symmetry

For a numerical analysis of a 3D structure, particularly a cylindrical shell, it is convenient to use symmetry and anti-symmetry boundary conditions.

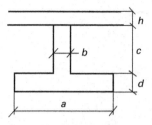

4.4 Stiffener geometry.

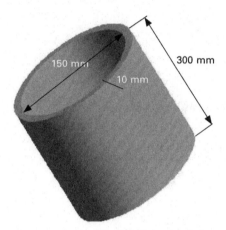

4.5 Geometry of the aluminium tube.

This use can be interesting to obtain very fast and good precision to get, for example, the resonant frequencies of a structure. The example for these boundary conditions is an aluminium tube having an internal diameter of 150 mm, a length of 300 mm and a thickness of 10 mm (Fig. 4.5). A modal analysis will be performed.

Boundary conditions in a global coordinate system

To study the boundary conditions in a global coordinate system, 1/8th of the tube is cut out (Fig. 4.6). To obtain the resonant frequencies of the entire tube, several boundary conditions will be applied to the model.

On each face, a boundary condition will be applied to obtain a symmetry condition (S) or an anti-symmetry condition (A). The faces S_1, S_2 and S_3 are, respectively, parallel to xOy, yOz and zOx (Fig. 4.6). The boundary conditions concern the u_x, u_y and u_z displacements on each face. Tables 4.1 and 4.2 show, respectively, the symmetry and anti-symmetry boundary conditions. So, to obtain the frequencies for the entire tube, 1/8th of the tube

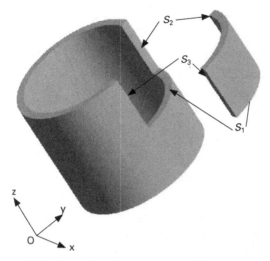

4.6 Definition of the boundary condition faces of the tube.

Table 4.1 Symmetry boundary conditions

	u_x	u_y	u_z
S_1 (xOy)			0
S_2 (yOz)	0		
S_3 (zOx)		0	

Table 4.2 Anti-symmetry boundary conditions

	u_x	u_y	u_z
S_1 (xOy)	0	0	
S_2 (yOz)		0	0
S_3 (zOx)	0		0

is analyzed with the followed boundary combinations on the S_1, S_2 and S_3 faces: SSS, SAA, SSA or SAS, ASS, ASA or AAS and AAA.

Table 4.3 compares the results obtained for the entire tube with those obtained for 1/8th of the tube (Table 4.3). For the entire tube, the first frequency (1 025.1 Hz) is the 7th frequency because this model has no boundary condition, so, six rigid body modes exist corresponding to the six degrees of freedom.

For example, Fig. 4.7 shows the first mode of the entire tube (1 025.1 Hz) corresponding to the first mode of 1/8th of the tube (1 029.9 Hz). Figure 4.8 shows the 12th mode of the entire tube (3 877.3 Hz) corresponding to the 2nd SAS mode of 1/8th of the tube (1 029.9 Hz). The dashed line is the rested structure.

Table 4.3 Resonant frequencies of the aluminium tube

Entire tube		Boundary condition	1/8 tube	
Frequency no	Frequency (Hz)		Frequency no	Frequency (Hz)
1	1 025.1	SSS	1	1 029.9
2	1 025.1	SAA	1	1 029.9
3	1 129.3	AAA	1	1 134.5
4	1 129.3	ASS	1	1 134.5
5	2 863.3	SSA	1	2 881.1
6	2 863.3	SAS	1	2 881.1
7	3 008.2	AAS	1	3 027.0
8	3 008.2	ASA	1	3 027.0
9	3 209.6	SSS	2	3 213.0
10	3 209.6	SAA	2	3 212.9
11	3 877.3	SSA	2	3 893.5
12	3 877.3	SAS	2	3 893.5
13	5 151.8	AAA	2	5 151.9
14	5 401.3	SSS	3	5 452.3
15	5 404.7	SAA	3	5 443.8
16	5 475.6	SSA	3	5 476.6
17	5 475.6	SAS	3	5 476.6
18	5 555.3	AAA	3	5 599.7
19	5 559.4	ASS	2	5 608.7
20	5 667.4	AAS	2	5 689.8
21	5 667.4	ASA	2	5 689.8
22	5 777.7	ASS	3	5 788.7
23	5 777.7	AAA	4	5 788.6
24	6 231.0	SAA	4	6 271.4
25	6 234.8	SSS	4	6 279.7
26	6 267.1	AAS	4	6 267.7
27	6 267.1	ASA	4	6 267.7
28	7 526.9	AAA	5	7 574.1
29	7 528.4	ASS	4	7 576.3
30	7 792.1	SSS	5	7 792.2

Boundary conditions in a local coordinate system

Symmetry and anti-symmetry boundary conditions in a local coordinate system can also be defined. For example, on the S_4 face located at 60° with the OX axis (Fig. 4.9), if a symmetry or anti-symmetry boundary condition is applied, respectively, the boundary conditions in the O_{xyz} local axis system are $u_y = 0$ or $u_x = 0$ and $u_z = 0$.

As an application, to perform a modal analysis for 1/12th of the tube corresponding to an angle of 60° (Fig. 4.9), with an anti-symmetrical condition on S_1 (XOY global axis) face, a symmetry condition on S_4 (local XOZ axis) face and a anti-symmetry condition on S_3 (ZOX global axis) face, the boundary conditions are on the S_1 face, $u_x = u_y = 0$, u_y (local) = 0 on S_4 face and $u_x = u_z = 0$ on S_3 face.

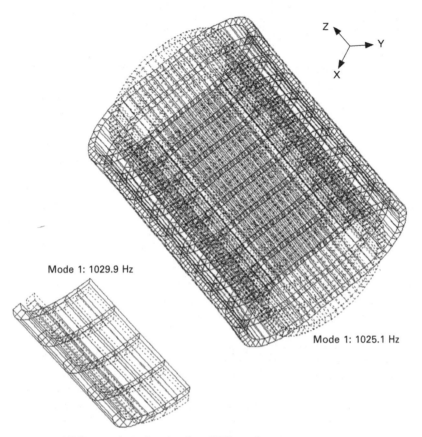

Mode 1: 1029.9 Hz

Mode 1: 1025.1 Hz

4.7 Comparison for the first SSS mode.

The first mode (Fig. 4.10) of 1/12th of the tube (3 013.3 Hz) with the ASS boundary conditions corresponds to the first mode of 1/8th of the tube (3 027.0 Hz) with the AAS boundary conditions (Table 4.3) and to the 8th mode of the entire tube (3 008.2 Hz).

4.4.2   Circular cylindrical shell

The validation is obtained for an aluminium shell (Fig. 4.11) having an internal diameter of 97.79 mm and a length of 394.5 mm. The shell thickness is 16.51 mm and the stiffeners have a width of 3.175 mm, a depth of 5.33 mm, and spacing of 19.05 mm. This shell is supported by shear diaphragms.

Mesh of the shell and boundary conditions

To validate the element of the stiffened shell, the aluminium tube is modelled with three symmetry or anti-symmetry boundary conditions (Fig. 4.12).

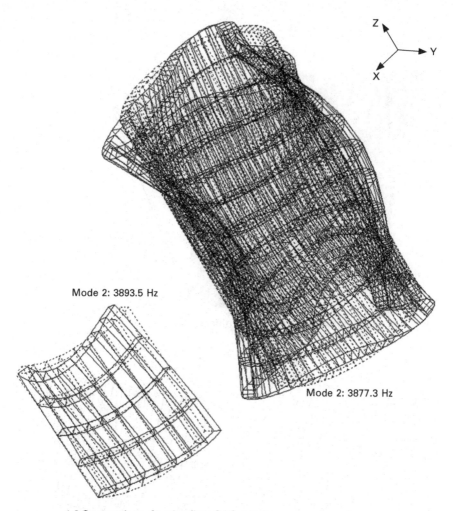

4.8 Comparison for the first SAS mode.

The mesh is made of 20 elements along the longitudinal x axis and eight elements along the curve axis. With these symmetry planes, only 1/8th of the shell is modelled.

On the BD line where the diaphragm is, the boundary conditions are $u_y = u_z = 0$. For the other AB, AC or CD lines, respectively, for the ZOX, YOZ or XOY planes, the boundary conditions are shown in Table 4.4.

Results

The numerical results have been compared with the experimental[16] and different analytic results[12,18,20]. In Table 4.5, n is the number of circumferential

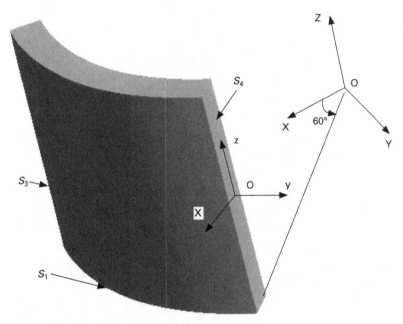

4.9 Definition of the local coordinate system.

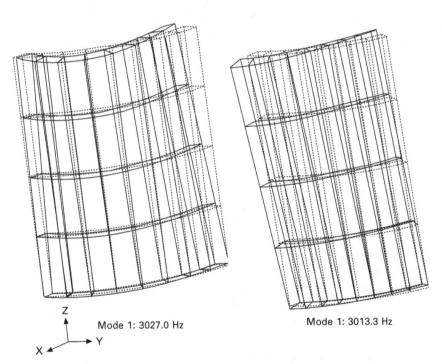

Mode 1: 3027.0 Hz   Mode 1: 3013.3 Hz

4.10 Results for the first mode of 1/8th and 1/12th of the tube.

4.11 Model test of stiffened shell.[17]

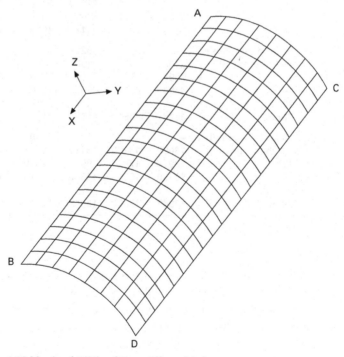

4.12 Mesh of 1/8th of the stiffened tube.

Table 4.4 Symmetry and anti-symmetry conditions of the tube

Plane	Symmetry					Anti-symmetry				
	u_x	u_y	u_z	θ_x	θ_y	u_x	u_y	u_z	θ_x	θ_y
XOY			0	0		0	0			0
YOZ	0				0		0	0	0	
ZOX		0		0		0		0		0

Table 4.5 Lowest frequencies (Hz) for a ring-stiffened shell supported by shear diaphragms

Number of circumferential waves (n)	Reference	Number of axial nodes (m)				
		1	2	3	4	5
2	16 (experimental)	1530	2040	3200	4440	6200
	16 (theoretical)	1530	2100	3330	4860	6480
	12	1529	2112	3266	4608	5932
	18	1413	2447	4030	5668	7188
	20	1660	2270	3500	4960	6420
	Shell	**1532**	**2101**	**3156**	**4408**	**5670**
3	16 (experimental)	4080	4090	4520	5000	5700
	16 (theoretical)	4230	4320	4500	5040	5760
	12	4170	4234	4472	4933	5576
	18	3537	3731	7261	5094	6090
	20	4500	4590	4850	5360	6070
	Shell	**4198**	**4281**	**4514**	**4958**	**5567**
4	16 (experimental)	–	–	7520	7800	7920
	16 (theoretical)	8100	8100	8190	8280	–
	12	7994	8000	8055	8179	8395
	18	6700	6772	6957	7296	7787
	20	–	–	8520	8680	8950
	Shell	**8026**	**8050**	**8129**	**8258**	**8484**
5	16 (experimental)	–	–	–	11400	–
	16 (theoretical)	13050	13100	13140	13230	–
	12	12928	12930	19946	12990	–
	18	10730	10783	10892	11079	11357
	20	–	–	–	–	–
	Shell	**12967**	**12980**	**13010**	**13071**	**13171**

waves (n = 2, 3, 4, 5) (Fig. 4.13) and m is the number of axial nodes (m = 1 to 5). In Table 4.5, experimental results are given by reference 16. The results obtained from the numerical analysis are close to the experimental results and similar to the analytic ones. Figures 4.14 to 4.17 show the modal deformation at 1 532, 4 281, 8 129 and 13 071 Hz frequencies corresponding to different nodal patterns.

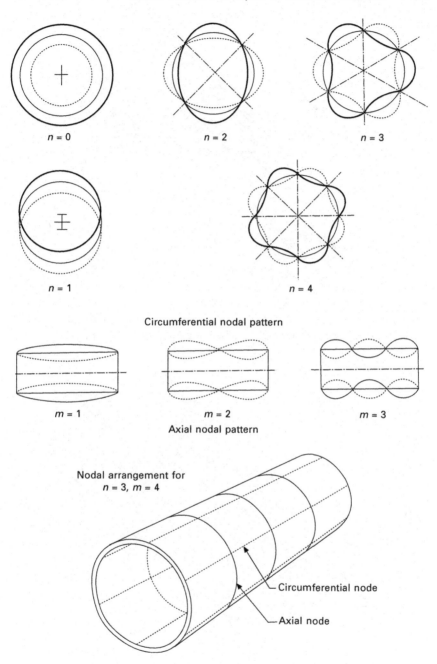

4.13 Nodal patterns for circular cylindrical shells supported at both end by shear diaphragms.

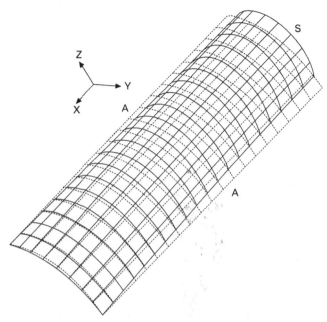

4.14 Deformed shape of the shell at a 1532 Hz frequency, $m = 1$, $n = 2$.

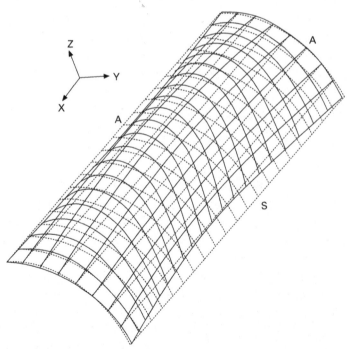

4.15 Deformed shape of the shell at a 4281 Hz frequency, $m = 2$, $n = 3$.

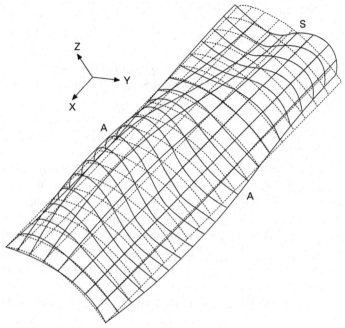

4.16 Deformed shape of the shell at a 8129 Hz frequency, *m* = 3, *n* = 4.

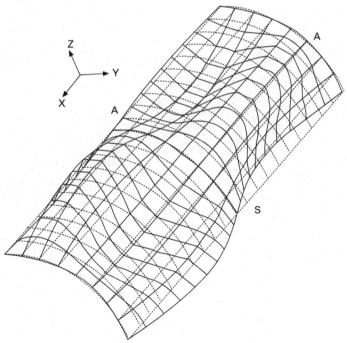

4.17 Deformed shape of the shell at a 13 071 Hz frequency, *m* = 4, *n* = 5.

4.3.3   Stiffened shell of elastic target

As a second application, an elastic target with a stiffened shell is modelled. It is a steel cylinder with an internal diameter of 2 m, a length of 10 m, a shell thickness of 5 mm and is closed by two hemispheres. The stiffeners have a T shape and are spaced out by 0.5 m; their dimensions are shown on Fig. 4.18.

Modal analysis of the elastic target

In Fig. 4.19, the mesh of 1/8th of the shell is shown. Only 1/8th of the structure has been modelled from the three symmetry planes. The cylindrical part has been meshed with 12 × 12 elements; the same mesh has been used for the hemispherical part. Comparing the results obtained with stiffened shell elements, a 3D mesh has been formed (Fig. 4.20), the mesh of the stiffeners is shown Fig. 4.18. To take into account the effect of the girders on the cylinder, the same analysis has been performed on the structure without stiffeners.

In Table 4.6, the 10 first resonant frequencies are given. The first column

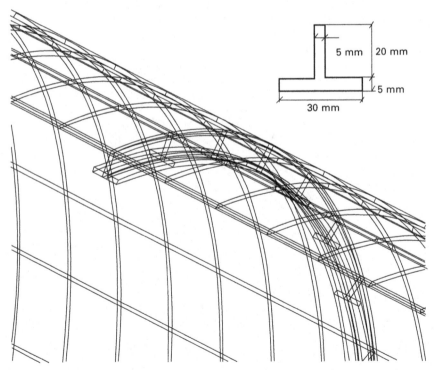

4.18 Stiffener dimensions and stiffener meshing.

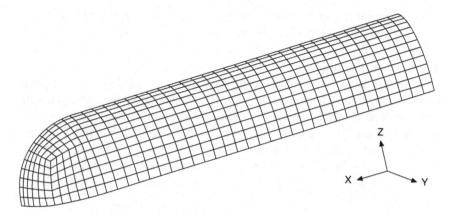

4.19 Mesh of the stiffened target with three symmetry planes.

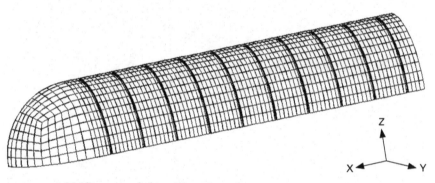

4.20 3D mesh of the stiffened target.

Table 4.6 Ten first resonant frequencies of the stiffened target

Frequency no	Stiffened shell (Hz)	3D (Hz)	Shell with no stiffener (Hz)
1	18.3	20.0	15.5
2	68.7	74.0	18.9
3	77.2	84.0	44.5
4	101	110	
5	113	121	
6	163	173	43.1
7	164	175	48.2
8	169	181	68.4
9	171	182	175
10	183	209	

shows the frequencies of the shell with the stiffened shell element, the
second with the 3D analysis and the last with the shell with no stiffener.
The comparison between these two first models is quite good. For the last

column, except for the first mode, the results for the mode are different due to the effect of the stiffeners. With the same mesh, the number of degrees of freedom is 7 116 with the shell elements and 35 768 with the 3D elements; this difference is large.

Figures 4.21 to 4.23 display, respectively, the first mode of the structure with the stiffened shell element, the 3D analysis and the shell without stiffener. The results are good in comparison to the first two analyses. For the last analysis, the frequency is lower because the shell has no stiffener.

The second mode of the structure with the stiffened shell element is shown in Figs 4.24 to 4.26. The results are good in comparison to the stiffened shell and 3D analysis. The mode for the shell without stiffener is similar to the

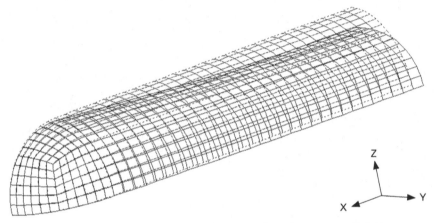

4.21 First resonant frequency of the stiffened target at 18.3 Hz frequency –stiffened shell mesh.

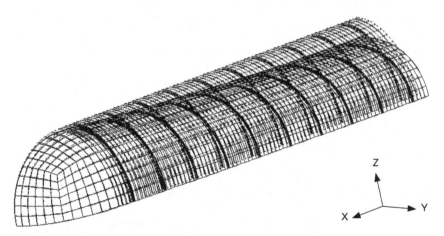

4.22 First resonant frequency of the stiffened target at 20.0 Hz frequency – 3D mesh.

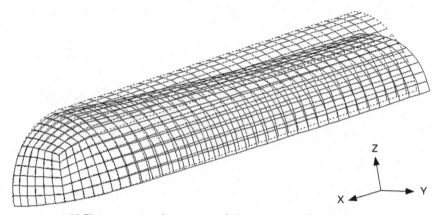

4.23 First resonant frequency of the target at 15.5 Hz frequency – shell mesh.

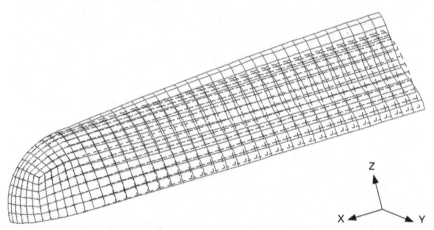

4.24 Second resonant frequency of the stiffened target at 68.7 Hz frequency – shell mesh.

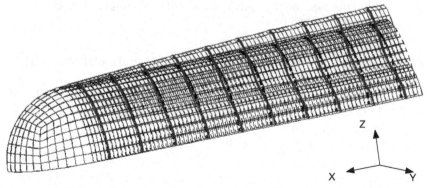

4.25 Second resonant frequency of the stiffened target at 74.0 Hz frequency – 3D mesh.

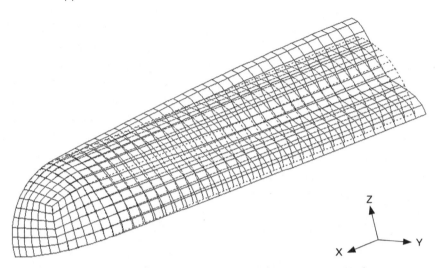

4.26 Second resonant frequency of the target at 18.9 Hz frequency – shell mesh.

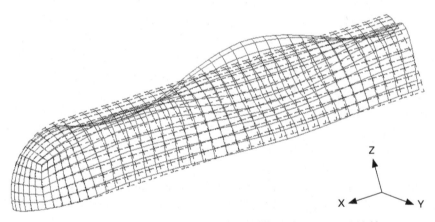

4.27 Fifth resonant frequency of the stiffened target at 113 Hz frequency – shell mesh.

previous one but the frequency is very different from the other frequencies because the effect of the stiffener is important.

For the fifth resonant frequency, the results are good for the stiffened shell and 3D analysis (Figs 4.27 and 4.28); when the shell has no stiffener, this mode does not exist.

The last figures display the sixth resonant frequency – the results are also good; the shapes for Figs 4.29 to 4.31 are similar but the value of the frequency of the shell without stiffener is much lower than the two other values.

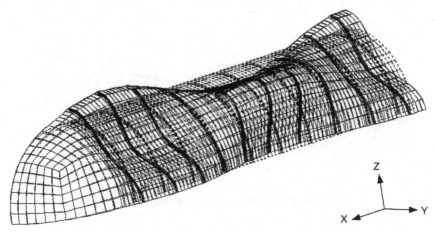

4.28 Fifth resonant frequency of the stiffened target at 121 Hz frequency – 3D mesh.

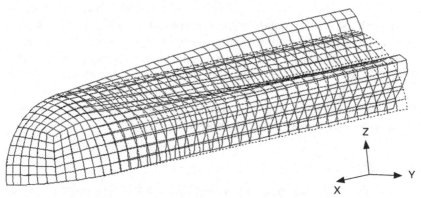

4.29 Sixth resonant frequency of the stiffened target at 163 Hz frequency – 3D mesh.

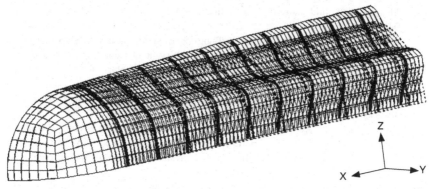

4.30 Sixth resonant frequency of the stiffened target at 173 Hz frequency – 3D mesh.

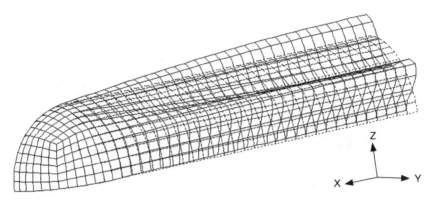

4.31 Sixth resonant frequency of the target at 43.1 Hz frequency – shell mesh.

4.5 Conclusion

To analyze structures such as a submarine or an aircraft, when the shape is complicated, the models require numerical methods to be appropriate. These structures are often stiffened by frames or ribs. The proposed solution uses a finite element method which takes into account the parameters characterizing the elasticity of the stiffeners. Several examples such as a stiffened cylinder or a stiffened shell of elastic target have shown the interest of this solution. Then, with an example of a 3D cylinder, the use of symmetry and anti-symmetry boundary conditions are shown.

4.6 References

1. Tran Van Nhieu 'Scattering from slender bodies at high Frequency', *J. Acoust. Soc. Am.* 89, 1991.
2. Laulagnes B., Gugader J. L. 'Sound radiation by finite cylindrical ring stiffened shells', *J S V* 138(2), 173–191, 1990.
3. Moser P. J. 'Sound scattering from a finite cylinder with ribs', *J. Acoust. Soc. Am.* 94(6) 3342–3351, 1993.
4. Mattei P. O. 'Rayonnement acoustique d'une coque cylindrique infinie périodiquement raidie, immergée dans un fluide lourd et subissant des contraintes localisées' *Colloque à Physique*, colloque C4, tome 51, 403–406, 1990.
5. Dubus B., Veksler N. D., Lavie A. 'Acoustic wave scattering from a composed shell reinforced by a simple rib: characteristic of peripheral waves', *Ultrasonics* 38, 838–841, 2000.
6. Burroughs C. B. 'Acoustic radiation from fluid-loaded infinite circular cylinders with doubly periodic ring supports', *J. Acoust. Soc. Am.* 75(3), 715–723, 1984.
7. Davis R., Henshell R. D., Warburton G. B. 'Constant curvature beam finite elements for in plane-vibration', *JSV* 25 561–576, 1972.
8. Litewka P., Rakowski J. 'An efficient curved beam finite element', *IJNME*, 40, 2669–2652 1997.

9. Davis R., Henshell R. D., Warburton G. B. 'Curved beam finite element for coupled bending and torsional vibration', *I. J. Earthquake Eng. Struct. Dyn.* 1, 1965–1975, 1972.

10. Digiovani P. R., Dugundji J. 'Vibrations of freely-supported orthotropic cylindrical shells under internal pressure', *AFOSR. Sci. Rept* AFOSR 65-0640, February 1965.

11. Mikulas M., Mcelman J. A. 'On free vibrations of eccentrically stiffened cylindrical shells and flat plates', NASA-TN-D-3010, September 1965.

12. Nelson H. C., B. Zapotowski B., Berstein M. 'Vibration analysis of orthogonally stiffened circular fuselage and comparison with experiment', *Proc. Inst. Aero. Sci. Natl.* Specialist Meeting on Dynamics and Aeroelasticity, 77–87, November 1958.

13. Resnick B., Dugundji J. 'Effects of orthotropicity, boundary conditions, and eccentricity on the vibrations of cylindrical shells', *AFOSR. Sci. Rept* Vol. AFOSR 66-2821, November 1966.

14. Das Y. C. 'Vibrations of orthotropic cylindrical shells', *Appl. Sci. Res. Ser. A*, 12, 4/5, 317–326, 1964.

15. Dong S. B. 'Free vibration of laminated orthotropic cylindrical shells', *J. Acoust. Soc. Am.* 44 (3), 1628–1635, December 1968.

16. Hoppmann W. H. 'Some characteristics of the flexural vibrations of orthogonally stiffened cylindrical shells', *J. Acoust. Soc. Am.* 30 (1), 77–82, January 1958.

17. Hoppmann W. H. 'Flexural vibrations of orthogonally stiffened cylindrical shells', 9th *Congress Inter. Mecan. Appl. Univ. Bruxelles*, Vol. 7, 225–237, 1957.

18. Hu W. C. L., Wah T. 'Vibrations of ring- stiffened cylindrical shells – an exact method', Tech. Rept. No 7, Contract NASr-94(06), Southwest Res. Inst., October 1966.

19. Wah T., Hu W. C. L. 'Vibration analysis of stiffened cylindrical including inter-ring motion', *J. Acoust. Soc. Am.* 43 (5), 1005–1016, May 1968.

20. Geers T. L. 'Vibration 'An approximate method for analyzing the vibrations of stiffened plates and shells', AD 646 353, Nov. 1966.

21. Love A. E. H. *A Treatise on the Mathematical Theory of Elasticity* 1st edn, Cambridge University Press, 1892; 4th edn Dover Publishers Inc. (New York), 1944.

5

Utilization of piezoelectric polarization in ATILA: usual to original

J-C. DEBUS, ISEN Lille, France

DOI: 10.1533/9780857096319.2.94

Abstract: This chapter provides the utilization of piezoelectric polarization. In smart structures, the polarization and the electric field are not necessarily parallel to each other. However, applying an electric field in a particular direction may change the behaviour of the device. Sections 5.3 to 5.5 present the utilization of Cartesian polarization with different electric fields on a PZT cube and on a PZT ring to compare analytical and numerical (ATILA) solutions. On the same ring with a cylindrical polarization, analytical and numerical results are compared. In Section 5.6, using original polarization, two new designs of PZT actuator are studied. The first device consists of an open ring of piezoelectric material polarized in the thickness direction. Under an appropriate electrical field applied in the poling direction and/or the radial direction, the ring behaves as a spring having rectangular torsion behaviour. The second device consists of a simple stripe actuator with an original polarization. This actuator can be used as a flexing actuator similar to a bilaminar transducer. For these two actuators, numerical results obtained with the ATILA code and analytical results are compared with experimental findings.

Key words: piezoelectricity, polarization, actuator, piezoelectric ring.

5.1   Introduction

The finite element code ATILA has been specifically developed to aid in the design of all types of transducers. The design of these transducers is closely associated with the use of piezoelectric ceramics. The aim of this chapter is to explain the utilization of the polarization in a ceramic for different poling axes. Two simple devices will be modelized and the results will be compared between the ATILA and analytical analysis. First, a cartesian polarization, in cartesian coordinates, will be applied on a cube for, successively, X, Y and Z poled axes and different field axis. Then, on a ring, with a poled axial, in cylindrical coordinates, an axial, radial and tangential field will be analyzed. With the same device, with a poled cylindrical, the same fields previously mentioned will be applied on this ring.

94

5.2   Piezoelectric effect

5.2.1   Definition of stress and strain

For an elementary parallelepiped (Fig. 5.1), the components of the stress tensor are:

$$[T_{ij}] = \begin{bmatrix} T_{11} & T_{12} & T_{13} \\ T_{21} & T_{22} & T_{23} \\ T_{31} & T_{32} & T_{33} \end{bmatrix} \qquad\qquad [5.1a]$$

or in engineering calculations the stress matrix $[T]$ is:

$$[T] = \begin{bmatrix} T_1 & T_6 & T_5 \\ T_6 & T_2 & T_4 \\ T_5 & T_4 & T_3 \end{bmatrix} \qquad\qquad [5.1b]$$

For a slight deformation, letting x_1, x_2, x_3 be the coordinate axes and u_1, u_2, u_3 be the displacement components along these coordinate directions, respectively, the components for an infinitesimal strain are (Fig. 5.2):

$$S_{11} = \frac{\partial u_1}{\partial x_1} \quad S_{22} = \frac{\partial u_2}{\partial x_2} \quad S_{33} = \frac{\partial u_3}{\partial x_3} \quad S_{21} = S_{12} = \frac{1}{2}\left(\frac{\partial u_2}{\partial x_1} + \frac{\partial u_1}{\partial x_2}\right)$$

$$S_{31} = S_{13} = \frac{1}{2}\left(\frac{\partial u_3}{\partial x_1} + \frac{\partial u_1}{\partial x_3}\right) \quad S_{32} = S_{23} = \frac{1}{2}\left(\frac{\partial u_3}{\partial x_2} + \frac{\partial u_2}{\partial x_3}\right) \qquad [5.2a]$$

in engineering application, the strain tensor components can be written as:

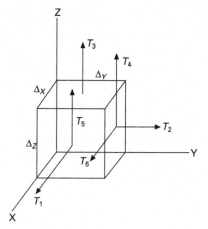

5.1 Definition of the stress components on the faces of a parallelepiped.

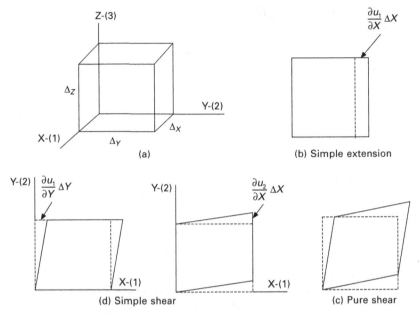

5.2 Definition of the strain components on the faces of a parallelepiped.

$$S_{11} = S_1 \quad 2S_{32} = 2S_{23} = S_4$$
$$S_{22} = S_2 \quad 2S_{13} = 2S_{31} = S_5 \qquad [5.2b]$$
$$S_{33} = S_3 \quad 2S_{12} = 2S_{21} = S_6$$

In this case, the strain matrix $[S]$ is defined as:

$$[S] = \begin{bmatrix} S_1 & S_6 & S_5 \\ S_6 & S_2 & S_4 \\ S_5 & S_4 & S_3 \end{bmatrix} \qquad [5.3]$$

5.2.2   Piezoelectric relations

Neglecting the magnetic and pyroelectric effects, when the stress $\{T\}$ and the electric field $\{E\}$ are independent, the piezoelectric equation for the strain $\{S\}$ and the electric deformation $\{D\}$ in matrix form are[1-6]:

$$\{S\} = [s^E]\{T\} + [d]^T \{E\}$$
$$\{D\} = [d]\{T\} + [\varepsilon^T]\{E\} \qquad [5.4]$$

where $[s^E]$ is the the elastic compliance matrix at electric field constant,

$[d]$ is the piezoelectric matrix at strain constant and $[\varepsilon^T]$ is the dielectric permittivity matrix at strain constant.

For a piezoelectric ceramic where the z-axis is the poled axis, Eq. [5.4] becomes:

$$S_1 = s_{11}^E T_1 + s_{12}^E T_2 + s_{13}^E T_3 + d_{31}E_3$$

$$S_2 = s_{12}^E T_1 + s_{22}^E T_2 + s_{13}^E T_3 + d_{31}E_3$$

$$S_3 = s_{13}^E T_1 + s_{13}^E T_2 + s_{33}^E T_3 + d_{31}E_3$$

$$S_4 = s_{44}^E T_4 + d_{15}E_2$$

$$S_5 = s_{44}^E T_5 + d_{15}E_1$$

$$S_6 = s_{66}^E T_6$$

[5.5]

In this case the poled axis is the 3-axis, the piezoelectric matrix $[d]$ is defined as:

$$[d] = \begin{bmatrix} 0 & 0 & 0 & 0 & d_{15} & 0 \\ 0 & 0 & 0 & d_{15} & 0 & 0 \\ d_{31} & d_{31} & d_{33} & & & \end{bmatrix}$$

[5.6]

5.3   Utilization of the Cartesian polarization: Cartesian coordinates

5.3.1   Definition of Euler angles

The polarization is homogeneous in the ceramic and the natural axes OX_1, OX_2 and OX_3 are defined with respect to the global axis O_x, O_y and O_z. If the OX_3 axis is the poled axis, the transformation O_{xyz} into $OX_3X_1X_2$ is realized by three Euler angles α, β and γ (Fig. 5.3a–c).

5.3.2   Piezoelectric equations in Cartesian coordinates

The piezoelectric equations (Eq. [5.5]), if all stresses are zero, become:

$$S_{11} = S_1 = d_{31}E_3$$

$$S_{22} = S_2 = d_{31}E_3$$

$$S_{33} = S_3 = d_{33}E_3$$

$$2S_{32} = S_4 = d_{15}E_2$$

$$2S_{13} = S_5 = d_{15}E_1$$

$$2S_{12} = S_6 = 0$$

[5.7]

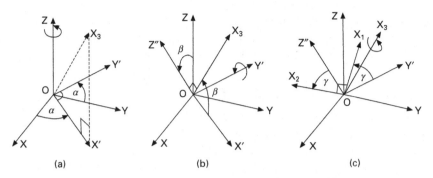

5.3 Definition of the Euler angles ($\alpha > 0$, $\beta > 0$, $\gamma > 0$).

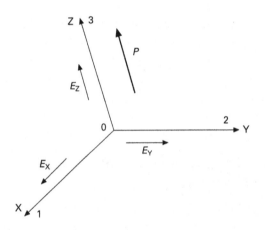

5.4 Definition of the axis for a poled Z-axis.

When the poled axis is the Z-axis (Fig. 5.4), Eq. [5.7] can be written as:

$$S_{XX} = d_{31}E_Z$$
$$S_{YY} = d_{31}E_Z$$
$$S_{ZZ} = d_{33}E_Z$$
$$2S_{YZ} = d_{15}E_Y \tag{5.8}$$
$$2S_{XZ} = d_{15}E_Y$$
$$2S_{XY} = S_6 = 0$$

Then, the strain-displacement relations (Eq. [5.2a]) become:

$$S_{XX} = \frac{\partial U_X}{\partial X}$$

$$S_{YY} = \frac{\partial U_Y}{\partial Y}$$

$$S_{ZZ} = \frac{\partial U_Z}{\partial Z}$$

$$2S_{ZY} = \frac{\partial U_Z}{\partial Y} + \frac{\partial U_Y}{\partial Z}$$

$$2S_{ZX} = \frac{\partial U_Z}{\partial X} + \frac{\partial U_X}{\partial Z}$$

$$2S_{XY} = \frac{\partial U_X}{\partial Y} + \frac{\partial U_Y}{\partial X}$$

[5.9]

5.3.3   Cube with a Cartesian polarization

The first example is a cube with a dimension of 1 mm. The used material is a PZT4 ceramic whose properties are:

$$[S^E] = \begin{bmatrix} 1.23 & -0.405 & -0.531 & 0 & 0 & 0 \\ -0.405 & 1.23 & -0.531 & 0 & 0 & 0 \\ -0.531 & -0.531 & 1.55 & 0 & 0 & 0 \\ 0 & 0 & 0 & 3.90 & & \\ 0 & 0 & 0 & 0 & 3.90 & \\ 0 & 0 & 0 & & & 3.27 \end{bmatrix} (10^{-11} \mathrm{m}^2/\mathrm{N})$$

$$[d] = \begin{bmatrix} 0 & 0 & 0 & 0 & -4.96 & 0 \\ 0 & 0 & 0 & -4.96 & 0 & 0 \\ -1.23 & -1.23 & 2.89 & 0 & 0 & 0 \end{bmatrix} (10^{-10} \mathrm{C/N})$$

$$[\varepsilon^T] = \begin{bmatrix} 1.306 & 0 & 0 \\ 0 & 1.306 & 0 \\ 0 & 0 & 1.151 \end{bmatrix} (10^{-8} \mathrm{m/F})$$

[5.10]

The mesh is shown in Fig. 5.5. The boundary conditions are $U_X = 0$, $U_Y = 0$ and $U_Z = 0$, respectively on the P_1, P_2 and P_3 planes (Fig. 5.6).

In this example, the X axis is the poled axis (Fig. 5.7) and the 3-axis is parallel to the X-axis (Fig. 5.8). The relations in Eq. [5.2a] become:

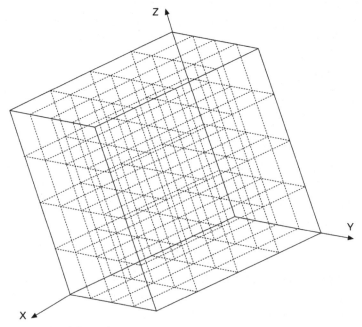

5.5 Mesh of the cube.

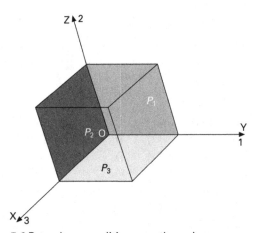

5.6 Boundary conditions on the cube.

$$S_{11} = S_1 = d_{31}E_3 \quad \text{or} \quad S_{YY} = d_{31}E_X$$
$$S_{22} = S_2 = d_{31}E_3 \quad \text{or} \quad S_{ZZ} = d_{31}E_X$$
$$S_{33} = S_3 = d_{33}E_3 \quad \text{or} \quad S_{XX} = d_{33}E_X$$
$$2S_{32} = S_4 = d_{15}E_2 \quad \text{or} \quad 2S_{ZX} = d_{15}E_Z \qquad [5.11]$$
$$2S_{13} = S_5 = d_{15}E_1 \quad \text{or} \quad 2S_{XY} = d_{15}E_Y$$
$$2S_{12} = S_6 = 0 \quad \text{or} \quad 2S_{ZY} = 0$$

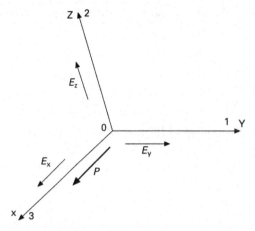

5.7 Poled X-axis.

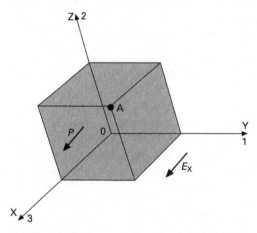

5.8 Electric field parallel to the poled X-axis.

Electric field parallel to the poled axis

If the electric field is parallel to the pole axis (X-axis) (Fig. 5.8), the relations in Eq. [5.11] are simplified as:

$$S_{YY} = d_{31}E_X$$
$$S_{ZZ} = d_{31}E_X$$
$$S_{XX} = d_{33}E_X$$
$$2S_{ZX} = 0 \hspace{3cm} [5.12]$$
$$2S_{XY} = 0$$
$$2S_{ZY} = 0$$

With the Eqs [5.9] and [5.12], the S_{XX} and S_{YY} deformations can be written as:

$$S_{XX} = d_{33}E_X = \frac{\partial U_X}{\partial X} = \frac{dU_X}{dX}$$

$$S_{YY} = d_{31}E_X = \frac{\partial U_Y}{\partial Y} = \frac{dU_Y}{dY}$$

[5.13]

Then, the U_X and U_Y displacements of the cube are:

$$U_X = d_{33}\left(-\frac{dV}{dX}\right)X$$

$$U_Y = U_Z = d_{31}\left(-\frac{dV}{dX}\right)X$$

[5.14]

If V, the applied potential, is equal to 1 V and c is the size of the cube equal to 1 mm, the components of the displacement of the 'A' node are:

$$U_X^A = d_{33}\left(-\frac{V}{c}\right)c = 2.89 \; 10^{-10} \frac{1}{c}c = 2.89 \; 10^{-10} \text{ m}$$

$$U_Y^A = U_Z^A = d_{31}\left(-\frac{V}{c}\right)c = -1.23 \; 10^{-10} \frac{1}{c}c = -1.23 \; 10^{-10} \text{ m}$$

Due to the unit electric field, the U_X and U_Y displacements correspond to the values of the piezoelectric constants d_{33} and d_{31}, respectively.

The comparison between the numerical (ATILA) and the analytical results is perfect (Table 5.1). The deformation of the cube is shown in Fig. 5.9. In plate V (between pages 194 and 195), the potential profile is displayed.

Electric field parallel to the Y-axis

For this application, the electric field is parallel to the Y-axis (Fig. 5.11), the relations in Eq. [5.11] become:

Table 5.1 Displacements of the 'A' node of the cube (10^{-10} m)

	Analytical	ATILA
U_X	2.89	2.89
U_Y	1.23	1.23
U_Z	1.23	1.23

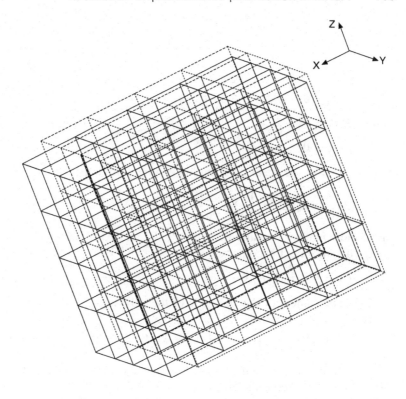

5.9 Deformation of the cube.

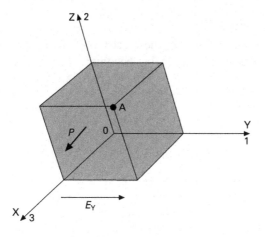

5.10 Electric field parallel to the Y-axis.

$$S_{YY} = 0$$

$$S_{ZZ} = 0$$

$$S_{XX} = 0$$

$$2S_{ZX} = 0 \qquad\qquad\qquad [5.15]$$

$$2S_{XY} = d_{15}E_Y$$

$$2S_{ZY} = 0$$

From Eq. [5.15], the shear deformation can be written as:

$$2S_{XY} = d_{15}E_Y = \frac{\partial U_X}{\partial Y} + \frac{\partial U_Y}{\partial X} \qquad\qquad [5.16]$$

Due to the boundary conditions on the P1, P2 and P3 planes, $U_X = U_Z = 0$. The U_Y displacement becomes:

$$U_Y = f(X) = d_{15}E_Y X \qquad\qquad\qquad [5.17]$$

The U_Y displacement of the 'A' node of the cube is:

$$U_Y^A = d_{15}\left(-\frac{dV}{dX}\right)c = d_{15}\frac{1}{c}c = 4.96\ 10^{-10}\ \text{m} \qquad [5.18]$$

Due to the unit electric field, the U_Y displacement corresponds to the value of the piezoelectric constants d_{15}.

The comparison between the numerical (ATILA) and the analytical results is exact (Table 5.2). The deformation of the cube is shown in Fig. 5.11. In plate VI (between pages 194 and 195), the potential profile is displayed.

Electric field parallel to the Z-axis

For the last application with this cube, the electric field is parallel to the Z-axis (Fig. 5.12), the relations in Eq. [5.11] become:

Table 5.2 Displacements of the 'A' node of the cube (10^{-10} m)

	Analytical	ATILA
U_X	0	-1.55×10^{-14}
U_Y	4.96	4.96
U_Z	0	-1.38×10^{-13}

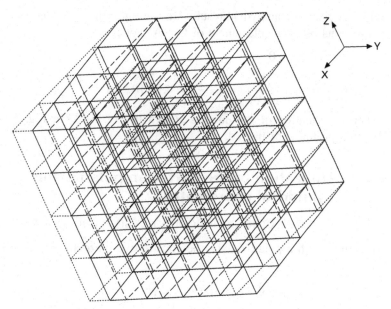

5.11 Deformation of the cube.

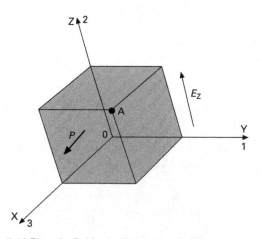

5.12 Electric field parallel to the Z-axis.

$$S_{YY} = 0$$
$$S_{ZZ} = 0$$
$$S_{XX} = 0$$
$$2S_{ZX} = d_{15}E_z$$ [5.19]
$$2S_{XY} = 0$$
$$2S_{ZY} = 0$$

The numerical and analytical results are similar to the previous results. The components of the displacement of the 'A' node are:

$$U_X = U_Y = 0$$

$$U_Z^A = d_{15}\left(-\frac{dV}{dX}\right)c = d_{15}\frac{1}{c}c = 4.96\ 10^{-10}\text{m}$$ [5.20]

The deformation of the cube is shown in Fig. 5.13. In Fig. 5.14, the potential profile is displayed.

5.4   Utilization of the Cartesian polarization: cylindrical coordinates

5.4.1   Piezoelectric equations in cylindrical coordinates

For a ring, with a poled Z-axis, the constitutive piezoelectric relations are (Fig. 5.15):

$$S_{rr} = s_{11}^E T_{rr} + s_{12}^E T_{\theta\theta} + s_{13}^E T_{ZZ} + d_{31}E_Z$$
$$S_{\theta\theta} = s_{12}^E T_{rr} + s_{11}^E T_{\theta\theta} + s_{13}^E T_{ZZ} + d_{31}E_Z$$
$$S_{ZZ} = s_{13}^E T_{rr} + s_{13}^E T_{\theta\theta} + s_{33}^E T_{ZZ} + d_{33}E_Z$$
$$2S_{Z\theta} = s_{44}^E T_{Z\theta} + d_{15}E_\theta$$ [5.21]
$$2S_{rZ} = s_{44}^E T_{rZ} + d_{15}E_r$$
$$2S_{r\theta} = s_{66}^E T_{r\theta}$$

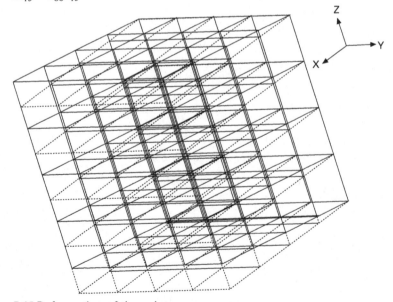

5.13 Deformation of the cube.

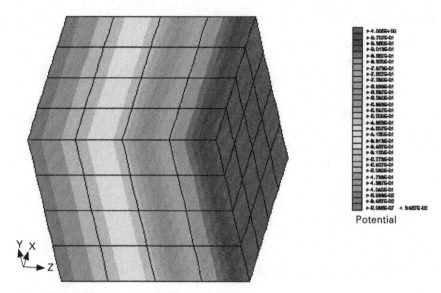

5.14 Potential profile in the cube.

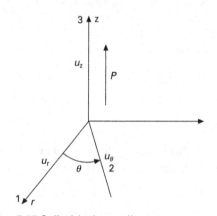

5.15 Cylindrical coordinates.

The piezoelectric equations (Eq. [5.21]), if all stresses are zero, become:

$$S_{rr} = d_{31}E_Z$$
$$S_{\theta\theta} = d_{31}E_Z$$
$$S_{ZZ} = d_{33}E_Z$$
$$2S_{Z\theta} = d_{15}E_\theta$$
$$2S_{rZ} = d_{15}E_r$$
$$2S_{r\theta} = 0$$

[5.22]

In cylindrical coordinates, the strain-displacement relations are:

$$S_{rr} = \frac{\partial U_r}{\partial r}$$

$$S_{\theta\theta} = \frac{1}{r}\frac{\partial U_\theta}{\partial \theta} + \frac{U_r}{r}$$

$$S_{zz} = \frac{\partial U_z}{\partial z}$$

$$2S_{\theta z} = \frac{1}{r}\frac{\partial U_z}{\partial \theta} + \frac{\partial U_\theta}{\partial Z}$$

$$2S_{rz} = \frac{\partial U_r}{\partial Z} + \frac{\partial U_z}{\partial r}$$

$$2S_{r\theta} = \frac{\partial U_\theta}{\partial r} - \frac{U_\theta}{r} + \frac{1}{r}\frac{\partial U_r}{\partial \theta}$$

[5.23]

5.4.2 Ring with an axial polarization

The second example is a piezoelectric ring having an inner (R_i) and outer (R_o) radius of 1 cm and 1.4 cm, respectively, and a thickness (t) of 0.1 cm (Fig. 5.16). The numerical model has two symmetry planes P_1 (XOZ) and P_2 (YOZ) with $U_Y = 0$ and $U_X = 0$ as the boundary conditions on P_1 (XOZ) and P_2 (YOZ), respectively. $U_Z = 0$ on the P_3 (XOY) plane. On the L_1 line, the boundary conditions are $U_X = U_Y = U_Z = 0$. In Fig. 5.16, a quarter of the ring is presented and analyzed with $\theta_0 = \pi/2$.

Electric field parallel to the Z-axis

For this analysis, the boundary conditions are the defined boundaries on the P_1, P_2 and P_3 planes (Fig. 5.16). With the electric field being parallel to the

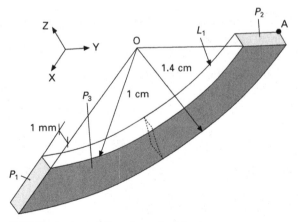

5.16 Geometry of the piezoelectric ring.

Z-axis (Fig. 5.17), Eq. [5.22] becomes:

$$S_{rr} = d_{31}E_Z$$

$$S_{\theta\theta} = d_{31}E_Z$$

$$S_{ZZ} = d_{33}E_Z$$

$$2S_{Z\theta} = 0 \hspace{3cm} [5.24]$$

$$2S_{rZ} = 0$$

$$2S_{r\theta} = 0$$

With the Eqs [5.23] and [5.24], the radial and axial deformations can be written as:

$$\frac{\partial U_r}{\partial r} = \frac{dU_r}{dr} = Srr = d_{31}E_Z$$

$$\frac{\partial U_Z}{\partial Z} = \frac{dU_Z}{dZ} = SZ = d_{33}E_Z \hspace{2cm} [5.25]$$

Then, the radial and axial displacements of the ring are:

$$U_r = d_{31}\left(-\frac{dV}{dz}\right)r = -d_{31}\frac{V}{t}r$$

$$U_Z = d_{33}\left(-\frac{dV}{dz}\right)Z \hspace{3cm} [5.26]$$

with V, the applied potential, equal to 1 V and t, the ring thickness, equal to 0.1 cm, the radial and axial displacements of the 'A' node of the ring are:

$$U_r^A = d_{31}\left(-\frac{dV}{dZ}\right)R_o = -1.23\ 10^{-10}\left(\frac{1}{10^{-3}}\right)1.4\ 10^{-2} = -1.722\ 10^{-9}m$$

$$U_z^A = d_{33}\left(-\frac{dV}{dZ}\right)t = 2.89\ 10^{-10}\left(\frac{1}{10^{-3}}\right)10^{-3} = 2.89\ 10^{-9}m$$

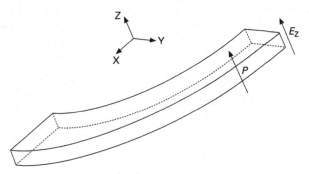

5.17 Electric field parallel to the poled Z-axis.

The comparison between the numerical (ATILA) and the analytical results is exact (Table 5.3). The deformation of the ring is shown in Fig. 5.18. In Fig. 5.19, the potential profile is displayed.

Radial electric field

For this analysis, the boundary conditions are the defined boundaries on the P_1, P_2 planes and the L_1 line (Fig. 5.16). With the electric field being parallel to the Z-axis (Fig. 5.20), Eqs [5.22] and [5.23] become:

Table 5.3 Displacements of the 'A' node of the ring (10^{-10} m)

	Analytical	ATILA
U_r	−17.2	−17.2
U_z	2.89	2.89

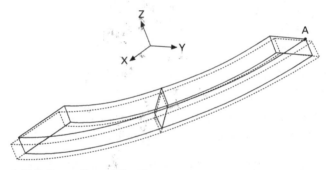

5.18 Deformation of the ring.

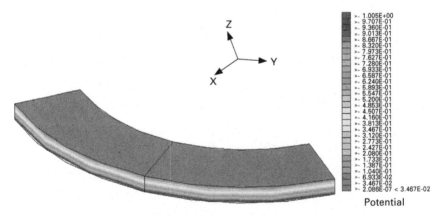

```
>- 1.005E+00
>- 9.707E-01
>- 9.360E-01
>- 9.013E-01
>- 8.667E-01
>- 8.320E-01
>- 7.973E-01
>- 7.627E-01
>- 7.280E-01
>- 6.933E-01
>- 6.587E-01
>- 6.240E-01
>- 5.893E-01
>- 5.547E-01
>- 5.200E-01
>- 4.853E-01
>- 4.507E-01
>- 4.160E-01
>- 3.813E-01
>- 3.467E-01
>- 3.120E-01
>- 2.773E-01
>- 2.427E-01
>- 2.080E-01
>- 1.733E-01
>- 1.387E-01
>- 1.040E-01
>- 6.933E-02
>- 3.467E-02
>- 2.086E-07 < 3.467E-02
```
Potential

5.19 Potential profile in the ring.

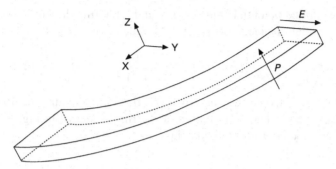

5.20 Radial electric field.

$$S_{rr} = 0$$

$$S_{\theta\theta} = 0$$

$$S_{ZZ} = 0$$

$$2S_{Z\theta} = 0 \qquad\qquad [5.27]$$

$$2S_{rZ} = d_{15}E_r$$

$$2S_{r\theta} = 0$$

$$\frac{\partial U_r}{\partial r} = 0$$

$$\frac{1}{r}\frac{\partial U_\theta}{\partial \theta} + \frac{U_r}{r} = 0$$

$$\frac{\partial U_z}{\partial z} = 0$$

$$\frac{1}{r}\frac{\partial U_z}{\partial \theta} + \frac{\partial U_\theta}{\partial Z} = 0 \qquad\qquad [5.28]$$

$$\frac{\partial U_r}{\partial Z} + \frac{\partial U_z}{\partial r} = d_{15}E_r$$

$$\frac{\partial U_\theta}{\partial r} - \frac{U_\theta}{r} + \frac{1}{r}\frac{\partial U_r}{\partial \theta} = 0$$

With the boundary conditions, U_θ is equal to 0 and from the 2nd equation of [5.28], U_r is also equal to 0. From the 5th equation of [5.28], the U_z deformation is:

$$\frac{\partial U_z}{\partial r} = \frac{dU_z}{dr} = d_{15}E_r \qquad\qquad [5.29]$$

Then, the axial displacement of the ring:

$$U_z = d_{15}\left(-\frac{dV}{dr}\right)Z \qquad\qquad [5.30]$$

with V, the applied potential, equal to 1 V and t, the ring thickness, equal to 0.1 cm, the radial displacement of the 'A' node of the ring is:

$$U_z = d_{15}\left(-\frac{V}{R_o - R_i}\right)t = 4.96 \ 10^{-10}\left(\frac{1}{0.4 \ 10^{-2}}\right)0.4 \ 10^{-2} = 4.96 \ 10^{-10} \text{ m}$$

The comparison between the numerical (ATILA) and the analytical results is exact (Table 5.4). The deformation of the ring is shown in Fig. 5.21. In Fig. 5.22, the potential profile is displayed.

Table 5.4 Displacements of the 'A' node of the ring (10^{-10} m)

	Analytical	ATILA
U_r	0	-1.52×10^{-12}
U_z	4.96	4.96

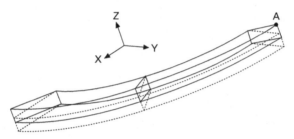

5.21 Deformation of the ring.

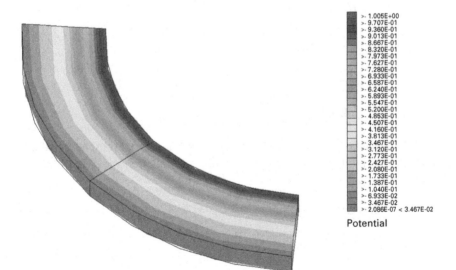

>- 1.005E+00
>- 9.707E-01
>- 9.360E-01
>- 9.013E-01
>- 8.667E-01
>- 8.320E-01
>- 7.973E-01
>- 7.627E-01
>- 7.280E-01
>- 6.933E-01
>- 6.587E-01
>- 6.240E-01
>- 5.893E-01
>- 5.547E-01
>- 5.200E-01
>- 4.853E-01
>- 4.507E-01
>- 4.160E-01
>- 3.813E-01
>- 3.467E-01
>- 3.120E-01
>- 2.773E-01
>- 2.427E-01
>- 2.080E-01
>- 1.733E-01
>- 1.387E-01
>- 1.040E-01
>- 6.933E-02
>- 3.467E-02
>- 2.086E-07 < 3.467E-02

Potential

5.22 Potential profile in the ring.

Circumferential electric field

When the electric field is circumferential, the boundary conditions are $U_X = U_Y = U_Z = 0$ on the P_1 plane. With the electric field being circumferential (Fig. 5.23), Eqs [5.22] and [5.23] become:

$$S_{rr} = 0$$

$$S_{\theta\theta} = 0$$

$$S_{ZZ} = 0$$

$$2S_{Z\theta} = d_{15}E_\theta \qquad\qquad [5.31]$$

$$2S_{rZ} = 0$$

$$2S_{r\theta} = 0$$

$$\frac{\partial U_r}{\partial r} = 0$$

$$\frac{1}{r}\frac{\partial U_\theta}{\partial \theta} + \frac{U_r}{r} = 0$$

$$\frac{\partial U_z}{\partial z} = 0$$

$$\frac{1}{r}\frac{\partial U_z}{\partial \theta} + \frac{\partial U_\theta}{\partial Z} = d_{15}E_\theta \qquad\qquad [5.32]$$

$$\frac{\partial U_r}{\partial Z} + \frac{\partial U_z}{\partial r} = 0$$

$$\frac{\partial U_\theta}{\partial r} - \frac{U_\theta}{r} + \frac{1}{r}\frac{\partial U_r}{\partial \theta} = 0$$

From Eq. [5.32], U_r and U_θ are equal to 0, the 4th equation of [5.32] becomes:

$$\frac{\partial U_z}{\partial \theta} = \frac{dU_z}{d\theta} = rd_{15}E_\theta = rd_{15}\frac{dV}{rd\theta} \qquad\qquad [5.33]$$

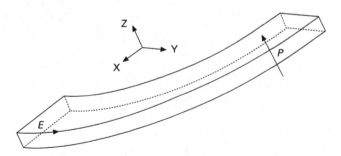

5.23 Circumferential electric field.

The electric field, being a constant value, is defined as:

$$\frac{dV}{rd\theta} = \frac{V}{r\theta_0}$$ [5.34]

with V, the applied potential, equal to 1 V at $\theta = 0$, the U_z deformation can be written as:

$$U_z = d15 \frac{V}{\theta_0} \theta$$ [5.35]

the axial displacement of the 'A' node of the ring is, with $\theta_0 = \pi/2$:

$$U_z = d_{15}V = 4.96 \ 10^{-10} \ m$$

The comparison between the numerical (ATILA) and the analytical results is exact (Table 5.5). The deformation of the ring is shown in Fig. 5.18. In Fig. 5.19, the potential profile is displayed.

The comparison between the numerical (ATILA) and the analytical results is exact (Table 5.4). The deformation of the ring is shown in Fig. 5.24. In Fig. 5.25, the potential profile is displayed.

Table 5.5 Displacements of the 'A' node of the ring (10^{-10} m)

	Analytical	ATILA
U_r	0	-7.65×10^{-12}
U_θ	0	-6.27×10^{-12}
U_z	4.96	4.96

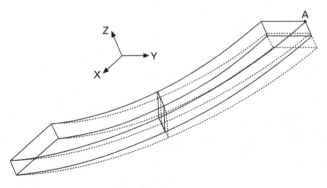

5.24 Deformation of the ring.

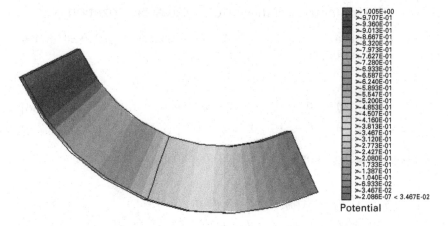

Potential

5.25 Potential profile in the ring.

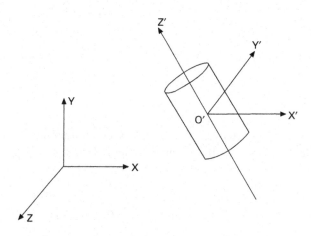

5.26 Definition of the O'X'Y'Z' system for the cylindrical polarization.

5.5   Utilization of the cylindrical polarization: cylindrical coordinates

5.5.1   Definition of the cylindrical polarization

In ATILA code, the polarization is radial depending on the Z-axis (Fig. 5.26). The Z-axis can be modified with the use of Euler angles. In this case the polarization is radial with respect to a given O'Z' axis. A O'X'Y'Z' system that contains the O'Z' axis must specify the O' coordinates (X_0, Y_0, Z_0) and the Euler angles $(\alpha, \beta$ and $\gamma)$ that transform the OXYZ global system into the O'X'Y'Z' system.

5.5.2   Piezoelectric relations for a radial polarization

In case of a radial polarisation, the polarisation axis is the X'-axis, the piezoelectric matrix $[d]$ (Eq. [5.6]) becomes:

$$[d] = \begin{bmatrix} d_{33} & d_{31} & d_{31} & 0 & 0 & 0 \\ 0 & 0 & 0 & 0 & 0 & d_{15} \\ 0 & 0 & 0 & 0 & d_{15} & 0 \end{bmatrix} \qquad [5.36]$$

The piezoelectric relations in cylindrical coordinates for a radial polarization are:

$$\begin{aligned}
S_{rr} &= s_{33}^E T_{rr} + s_{13}^E T_{\theta\theta} + s_{13}^E T_{ZZ} + d_{33}E_r \\
S_{\theta\theta} &= s_{13}^E T_{rr} + s_{11}^E T_{\theta\theta} + s_{12}^E T_{ZZ} + d_{31}E_r \\
S_{ZZ} &= s_{13}^E T_{rr} + s_{12}^E T_{\theta\theta} + s_{11}^E T_{ZZ} + d_{31}E_r \\
2S_{Z\theta} &= s_{66}^E T_{Z\theta} \\
2S_{rZ} &= s_{44}^E T_{rZ} + d_{15}E_Z \\
2S_{r\theta} &= s_{44}^E T_{r\theta} + d_{15}E_\theta
\end{aligned} \qquad [5.37]$$

Tangential electric field

The electric field is tangential and the boundary conditions are $U_X = U_Y = U_Z = 0$ on the P_1 plane. With this electric field (Fig. 5.27), Eq. [5.21] becomes:

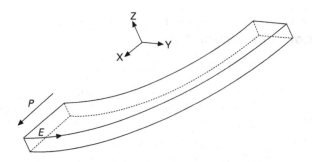

5.27 Tangential electric field.

$$S_{rr} = s_{33}^E T_{rr} + s_{13}^E T_{\theta\theta} + s_{13}^E T_{ZZ}$$

$$S_{\theta\theta} = s_{13}^E T_{rr} + s_{11}^E T_{\theta\theta} + s_{12}^E T_{ZZ}$$

$$S_{ZZ} = s_{13}^E T_{rr} + s_{12}^E T_{\theta\theta} + s_{11}^E T_{ZZ}$$

$$2S_{z\theta} = s_{66}^E T_{z\theta}$$ [5.38]

$$2S_{rz} = s_{44}^E T_{rz}$$

$$2S_{r\theta} = s_{44}^E T_{r\theta} + d_{15}E_\theta$$

With these boundary conditions, the stresses are neglected, Eq. [5.23] can be written as:

$$\frac{\partial U_r}{\partial r} = 0$$

$$\frac{1}{r}\frac{\partial U_\theta}{\partial \theta} + \frac{U_r}{r} = 0$$

$$\frac{\partial U_z}{\partial z} = 0$$

$$\frac{1}{r}\frac{\partial U_z}{\partial \theta} + \frac{\partial U_\theta}{\partial z} = 0$$ [5.39]

$$\frac{\partial U_r}{\partial z} + \frac{\partial U_z}{\partial r} = 0$$

$$\frac{\partial U_\theta}{\partial r} - \frac{U_\theta}{r} + \frac{1}{r}\frac{\partial U_r}{\partial \theta} = d_{15}E_\theta$$

With the first equation of [5.39], the radial displacement is defined as:

$$U_r = f_1(\theta, z) + C_1 = -\frac{\partial U_\theta}{\partial \theta}$$ [5.40]

The second equation can be written as:

$$\frac{\partial U_\theta}{\partial \theta} + U_r = 0$$ [5.41]

Then U_θ is a function of θ.

The axial displacement can be obtained with the third equation of [5.39] as:

$$U_z = f_2(\theta, r) + C_2$$ [5.42]

With the fifth equation, Eq. [5.40] becomes:

$$U_r = f_1(\theta) + C_1 = -\frac{\partial U_\theta}{\partial \theta}$$ [5.43]

the last equation can be written as:

$$-U_\theta + \frac{\partial U_r}{\partial \theta} = rd_{15}E_\theta = -U_\theta - \frac{\partial^2 U_\theta}{\partial \theta^2} \qquad [5.44]$$

The circumferential and radial displacements are:

$$U_\theta = A \cos \theta + B \sin \theta - rd_{15}E_\theta \qquad [5.45]$$

$$U_r = A \sin \theta - B \cos \theta \qquad [5.46]$$

where the electric field is:

$$E_\theta = -\frac{2V}{r\pi} \qquad [5.47]$$

With the boundary conditions, $U_r = U_\theta = 0$ at $\theta = 0$, the displacements can be written as:

$$U_\theta = -\frac{2V}{\pi} d_{15}(1 - \cos\theta)$$
$$\qquad\qquad\qquad\qquad [5.48]$$
$$U_r = -\frac{2V}{\pi} d_{15} \sin\theta$$

with V, the applied potential, equal to 1 V, the displacements of the 'A' node of the ring are:

$$U_\theta = U_r = -\frac{2}{\pi} 4.96 \ 10^{-10} = -3.1576 \ 10^{-10}\text{m}$$

The comparison between the numerical (ATILA) and the analytical results is good (Table 5.6). The deformation of the ring is shown in Fig. 5.28. In Fig. 5.29, the potential profile is displayed.

Axial electric field

The boundary conditions are the defined boundaries on the P_1, P_2 planes and L_1 line (Fig. 5.16). The electric field being axial (Fig. 5.30), Eq. [5.22] becomes:

Table 5.6 Displacements of the 'A' node of the ring (10^{-10} m)

	Analytical	ATILA
U_r	−3.16	−3.13
U_θ	−3.16	−3.13

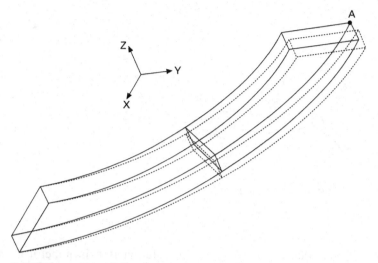

5.28 Deformation of the ring.

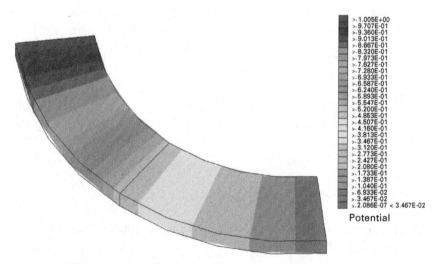

Potential

5.29 Potential profile in the ring.

$$S_{rr} = s_{33}^E T_{rr} + s_{13}^E T_{\theta\theta} + s_{13}^E T_{zz}$$
$$S_{\theta\theta} = s_{13}^E T_{rr} + s_{11}^E T_{\theta\theta} + s_{12}^E T_{zz}$$
$$S_{zz} = s_{13}^E T_{rr} + s_{12}^E T_{\theta\theta} + s_{11}^E T_{zz}$$
$$2S_{z\theta} = s_{66}^E T_{z\theta}$$
$$2S_{rz} = s_{44}^E T_{rz} + d_{15}E_z$$
$$2S_{r\theta} = s_{44}^E T_{r\theta}$$

[5.49]

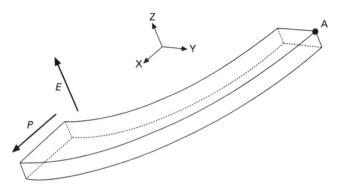

5.30 Axial electric field.

With these boundary conditions, the solution is axisymmetrical and the stresses are neglected, then Eq. [5.23] can be written as:

$$\frac{\partial U_r}{\partial r} = 0$$

$$\frac{1}{r}\frac{\partial U_\theta}{\partial \theta} + \frac{U_r}{r} = 0$$

$$\frac{\partial U_z}{\partial z} = 0$$

$$\frac{1}{r}\frac{\partial U_z}{\partial \theta} + \frac{\partial U_\theta}{\partial z} = 0$$ [5.50]

$$\frac{\partial U_r}{\partial z} + \frac{\partial U_z}{\partial r} = d_{15}E_z$$

$$\frac{\partial U_\theta}{\partial r} - \frac{U_\theta}{r} + \frac{1}{r}\frac{\partial U_r}{\partial \theta} = 0$$

With the two first equations of [5.50], $U_r = 0$ and with the third and the fifth equations, the axial displacement is:

$$U_z = f(r) + C_1 = rd_{15}E_z + C_1$$ [5.51]

At $r = r_i$, $U_z(r_i) = 0$, the constant C_1 is defined as:

$$C_1 = -r_i d_{15}E_z$$ [5.52]

The axial displacement is:

$$U_z = (r - r_i)\, d_{15}E_z$$ [5.53]

where the electric field $E_z = -V/t$
with V, the applied potential , equal to 1 V, the displacement of the 'A' node of the ring is:

$$U_z(r_e) = (r_e - r_i)\, 4.9610^{-10}\left(-\frac{1}{0.1^{10-2}}\right) = 1.984\ 10^{-9}\,\text{m}$$

The analytical result given by ATILA is 1.987^{10-9} m.

The comparison between the numerical (ATILA) and the analytical results is good. The deformation of the ring is shown in Fig. 5.31. In Fig. 5.32, the potential profile is displayed.

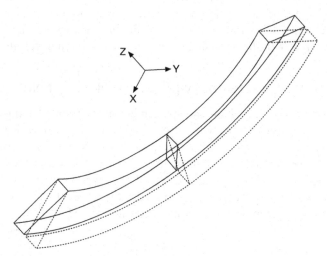

5.31 Deformation of the ring.

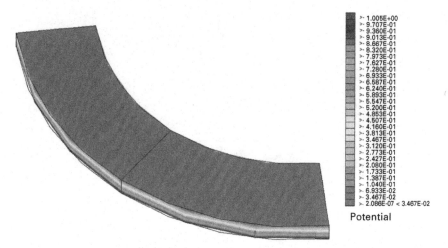

5.32 Potential profile in the ring.

5.6   Original polarization

A new design of PZT actuators is proposed to obtain, under an appropriate electric field, a large displacement with a simple design. The two devices proposed in this part are of a classical shape such as a ring and a stripe. The first device is a ring having a cut in the rectangular area. This actuator behaves like a spring having torsion behaviour.

In the first part, several electrical fields will be applied in the spring with several directions of poling. An analytical solution will be developed and compared with the numerical results. A solution to obtain an efficient actuator will be proposed. Some experimental results will be compared.

In the second part, a simple stripe actuator will be analysed with an original electrical configuration to obtain a flexing behaviour. The results will be compared with the analytical results and experimental results.

5.6.1   Open ring actuator with simple electric field

The aim of this study is to obtain a displacement of the ring behaving like a spring, so several polarizations with different applied electrical fields will be performed to produce a maximum z displacement at the end of the ring.

The ring to be studied is presented in Fig. 5.33. The geometry of this structure is defined as: S_1 is a fixed end, S_2 is the free end, r the mean radius, l is the width and h the thickness. S_3 to S_6 are the areas of the electrodes. For each case, a numerical analysis has been performed with the ATILA code.

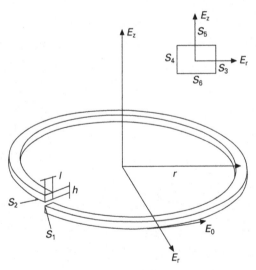

5.33 Geometrical characteristics of a cylindrical ring.

The poling direction along the ring axis and the radial axis will be analyzed, the tangential direction will not be studied because it is not possible to perform such a polarization.

Polarization along the ring axis direction (z axis)

Axial electric field

The first case is an applied field along the ring axis direction (z axis) with two electrodes on the faces S_5 and S_6 ($E_r = 0$ and $E_\theta = 0$). In Fig. 5.34, the major displacement is along the r axis. This ring has an extension behaviour, the result is not satisfactory.

Radial electric field

The second case is an applied field along the radial direction with electrodes on the S_3 and S_4 faces. The ring has a shear behaviour (d_{15}) (Fig. 5.35); the maximum displacement is reached for $\theta = \pi$. This configuration is not acceptable.

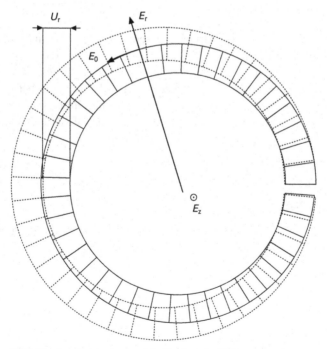

5.34 Strained structure with E_z electric field.

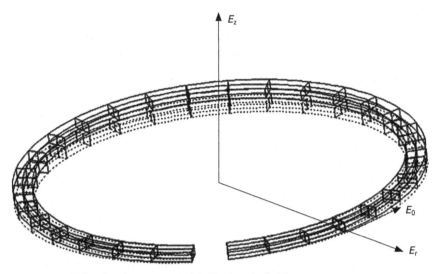

5.35 Strained structure with E_r electric field.

Tangential electric field

The last case is when the field is tangential; we can observe a good behaviour for this application (Fig. 5.36). The z displacement is linear with t. This result can be compared with an analytical solution (Eq. [5.35]).

To validate this case, a comparison between an analytical and numerical solution has been performed on a PZT ring having an inner radius of 19mm, an outer radius of 21 mm, a width $l = 1$ mm and a thickness $h = 2$ mm. The applied voltage is equal to 2 V. There is a good agreement between the analytical result and the numerical result. For the maximum displacement, the difference is 0.5%. Table 5.7 displays the analytical and numerical displacements.

Polarization along the radial direction

Radial electric field

The electrodes are on the faces S_3 and S_4. In Fig. 5.37, the major displacement is tangential. This ring has an extension behaviour, the result is not in good agreement.

Tangential electric field

The electrodes are on faces S_1 and S_2. The strained structure is shown in Fig. 5.38; the axial displacement is negligible.

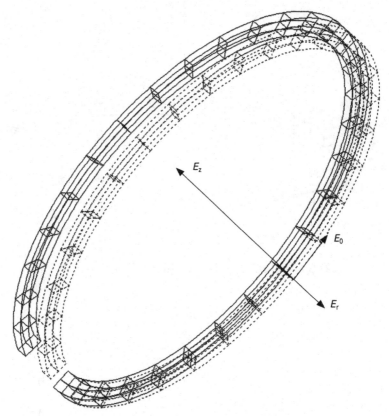

5.36 Strained structure with tangential electric field.

Table 5.7 Analytical/numerical comparison

θ (radians)	Numerical (10^{-10} m)	Analytical (10^{-10} m)
$\pi/5$	0.992	0.640
$2\pi/5$	1.86	0.480
$3\pi/5$	2.98	1.47
$4\pi/5$	3.97	3.04
π	4.96	4.97
$6\pi/5$	5.95	6.88
$7\pi/5$	7.07	8.44
$8\pi/5$	7.94	9.44
$9\pi/5$	8.93	9.86
2π	9.97	9.92

Axial electric field

In this case, faces S_5 and S_6 are the electrodes; the results are the same as given on page 123 (Radial electric field) (Fig. 5.39). The axial is maximum at $\theta = \pi$; this configuration is not satisfactory.

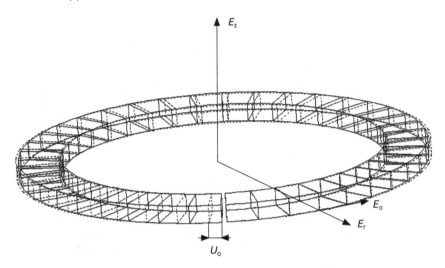

5.37 Strained structure with E_r electric field.

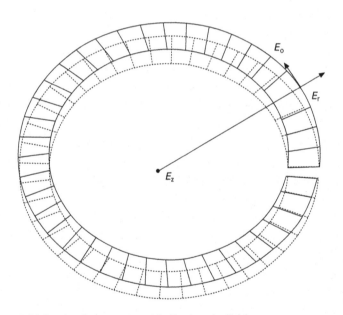

5.38 Strained structure with E_θ electric field.

The first conclusion is that the ring must be a shear behaviour (d_{15} coefficient), so the polarization and field axis can have the same direction. The second conclusion is that a polarization along the tangential or radial direction is not appropriate. So, the only proposal is an axial direction with tangential electric field.

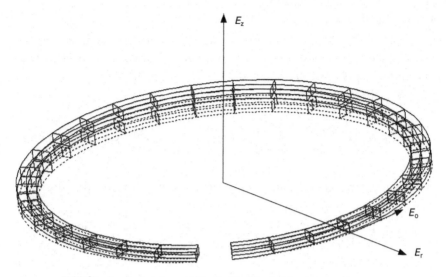

5.39 Strained structure with E_z electric field.

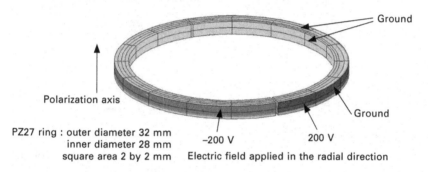

5.40 Mesh of a ring with a combined electric field.

5.6.2   Open ring actuator with combined electric fields

Description of the ring

With the previous case, it is not easy to obtain a good result so the solution is to create a shear behaviour in the ring. The proposed solution here is to obtain an original electric field in the ring. This PZT ring has an inner radius of 19 mm, an outer radius of 21 mm, a width $l = 1$ mm and a thickness $h = 2$ mm. In Fig. 5.40, the poling direction is the z direction and the electric field is applied in the radial direction. One half of the outer area of the ring is 200 V and the other one is – 200V. The other areas are grounded. The result of the ATILA simulation is 23.5 mm (Fig. 5.40).

Analytical solution

Assuming the ring is submitted to an equivalent torque, an analytical formula has been obtained to describe the deflexion of the spring[7] (Fig. 5.41) where $\bar{r}$ is the mean radius of the ring and $2a \times 2b$ is cross area. The shear stress in the ring is:

$$T_5(r, z) = \frac{16\theta a}{S_{44}^E \pi^2} \sum_{n=1,3,5}^{\infty} \frac{1}{n^2} (-1)^{(n-1)/2} \left\{ 1 - \frac{ch\,\dfrac{n\pi z}{2a}}{ch\,\dfrac{n\pi b}{2a}} \right\} \sin \frac{n\pi r}{2a} \qquad [5.54]$$

The mean value can be obtained by integration in the area of the ring as:

$$\bar{T}_5 = \frac{1}{a}\frac{1}{2b} \frac{16\theta a}{S_{44}^E \pi^2} \sum_{n=1,3,5}^{\infty} \frac{1}{n^2} (-1)^{(n-1)/2} \int_0^a \int_{-b}^b \left\{ 1 - \frac{ch\,\dfrac{n\pi z}{2a}}{ch\,\dfrac{n\pi b}{2a}} \right\} \sin \frac{n\pi r}{2a}\, dz dr$$

$$[5.55]$$

The mean stress in the ring due to a unit angle of twist is defined as:

$$\bar{T}_5 = \frac{32\theta a}{S_{44}^E \pi^3} \sum_{n=1,3,5} (-1)^{(n-1)/2} \left(\frac{1}{n^3} - \frac{2a}{n^4 \pi b} \tanh \frac{n\pi b}{2a} \right) = \frac{2a\theta}{S_{44}^E} \delta \qquad [5.56]$$

where

$$\delta = \frac{16}{\pi^3} \sum_{n=1,3,5} (-1)^{(n-1)/2} \left(\frac{1}{n^3} - \frac{2a}{n^4 \pi b} \tanh \frac{n\pi b}{2a} \right) \qquad [5.57]$$

The total angle of twist is:

$$\phi = \bar{r}\ell = 2\pi \bar{r}\theta \qquad [5.58]$$

The total displacement of the ring is:

$$\Delta = \bar{r}\phi \qquad [5.59]$$

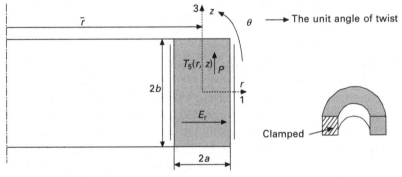

5.41 Behaviour of the ring.

With Eqs [5.50] and [5.56], the mean shear stress can be written as:

$$\overline{T_5} = -\frac{d_{15}E_r}{S_{44}^E} = \frac{2a\theta}{S_{44}^E}\,\delta \qquad [5.60]$$

The total displacement of the ring, from Eqs [5.58] to [5.60] is:

$$\Delta = \frac{\pi}{\delta}\left(\frac{\overline{r}}{2a}\right)^2 d_{15}V \qquad [5.61]$$

The numerical results for the displacement of the ring is 20.2 μm.

Experimental results

Experiments have been performed[8] on the ring (Fig. 5.42). The measured displacements have been obtained by superposition of the views from an electronic microscope (Fig. 5.43). Figure 5.44 displays the displacement of the ring versus the applied potential. For an applied potential of 200 V, the obtained displacement of the ring is 31 μm.

Numerical results

To perform a numerical analysis with the ATILA code, a mesh of the structure has been realized as displayed in Fig. 5.41. The strained structure of the ring is displayed in Fig. 5.45. The dashed lines are the rested structure, the full

5.42 View of the experimental analysis.

5.43 View of rested and deformed ring.

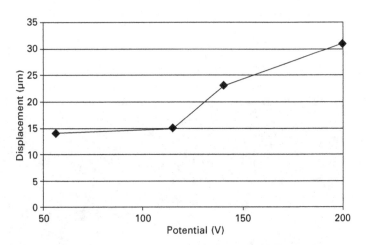

5.44 Displacement of the ring versus the applied potential.

lines are the deformed structure. The total displacement of the ring is 23.5 μm. Table 5.8 compares the numerical, analytical and experimental results of the displacement of the ring.

Conclusion

The static displacement, in the thickness direction, obtained with such an actuator is more than one hundred times the displacement obtained with a

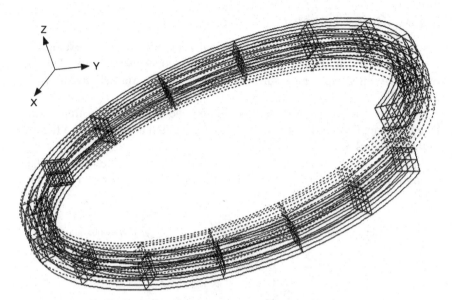

5.45 Strained structure of the ring.

Table 5.8 Comparison of the displacement of the ring

Δ	Numerical	Analytical	Experimental
μm	23.5	20.0	31.0

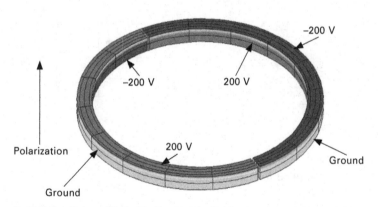

5.46 Potential profile with E_z electric field.

standard piezoelectric ring. Numerical and analytical results are then compared with experimental findings and a very good agreement is obtained. This concept can be extended for a multi-spire ring. Then under an appropriate electric field applied in the poling direction and a radial direction (Fig. 5.46), the numerical displacement is 41 μm, twice the previous value.

5.6.3   Stripe actuator

The second design is a bar with an original applied field. As an example, a clamped bar is defined in Fig. 5.47; the electroded surfaces are divided into two parts with a gap. These surfaces produce an electric field as shown in Fig. 5.48.

The behaviour of this structure is like the one of a bilaminar transducer. Due to the applied field in the bar, a torque is created and produces a flexure in the bar (Fig. 5.49).

In Fig. 5.50, the result is obtained with the ATILA code. This bar has a length L of 30 mm, a width b of 10 mm and a thickness t of 1 mm. The

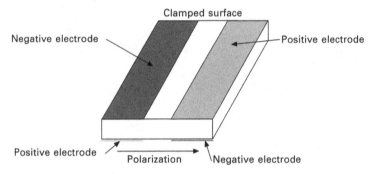

5.47 Electroded surfaces of the stripe actuator.

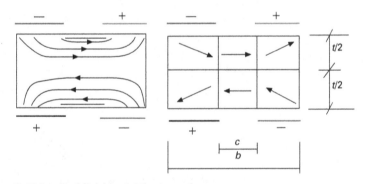

5.48 Applied field in the rectangular area.

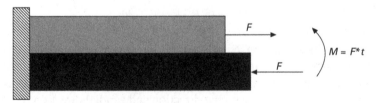

5.49 Behaviour of the bar.

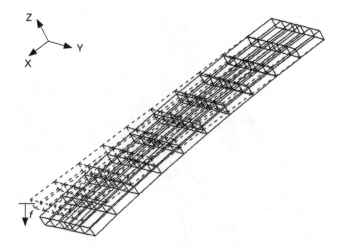

Z

Y

X

5.50 Static analysis of the stripe actuator.

gap between the electrodes is 2 mm. The material is PZT5A ceramic; the maximum displacement f at the free end is 1.70×10^{-8} m/V.

An analytical result has been developed and been compared with the numerical result. The formula for the deflexion at the end of the bar is:

$$f = \frac{3}{2} d_{31} \left(\frac{2t}{b} \right) \left(\frac{L}{2t} \right)^2 V \qquad [5.62]$$

For 1 V, the analytical result is 2.31×10^{-8}m. A 30% difference is due to the difficulty to take the field value in the bar into account.

Another result has been obtained for a free bar having a length of 27.5 mm, a width of 9.96 mm and a thickness of 0.68 mm. The gap between the electrodes is 1.02 mm (Fig. 5.51). A modal analysis has been performed. The first frequency with the numerical result is 3 157 Hz. This result is very good compared to the experimental result (3 201 Hz) (Fig. 5.52).

5.7   Conclusion

With these examples, when applying an electric field in a particular direction, it is easy to understand the behaviour of piezoelectric devices. With a simple design, it is possible under an original applied field to obtain a good result, which is useful to microactuator applications. The concept of an open ring can be extended for a multispire ring. It is quite straightforward with the ATILA code to simulate and design new actuators. Any shape can be designed to obtain, for example, a large displacement such as an helimorph structure.

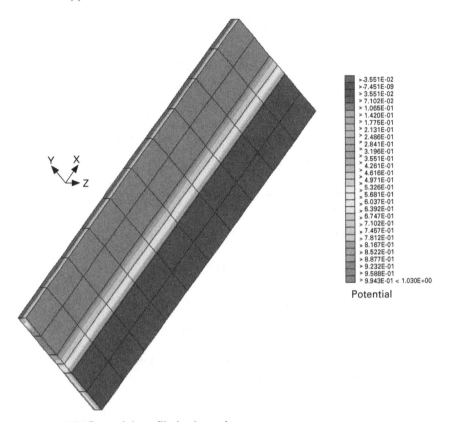

	>-3.551E-02
	>-7.451E-09
	> 3.551E-02
	> 7.102E-02
	> 1.065E-01
	> 1.420E-01
	> 1.775E-01
	> 2.131E-01
	> 2.486E-01
	> 2.841E-01
	> 3.196E-01
	> 3.551E-01
	> 4.261E-01
	> 4.616E-01
	> 4.971E-01
	> 5.326E-01
	> 5.681E-01
	> 6.037E-01
	> 6.392E-01
	> 6.747E-01
	> 7.102E-01
	> 7.457E-01
	> 7.812E-01
	> 8.167E-01
	> 8.522E-01
	> 8.877E-01
	> 9.232E-01
	> 9.588E-01
	> 9.943E-01 < 1.030E+00

Potential

5.51 Potential profile in the stripe actuator.

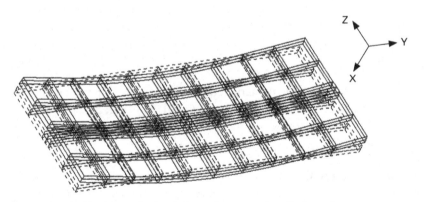

5.52 Modal analysis of the stripe actuator: first mode.

5.8   References

1.   Wilson O. B., *An Introduction to the Theory and Design of Sonar Transducers*, Peninsula Publishing, Los Altos, CA, 1988.

2. Berlincourt D., 'Piezoelectric crystals and ceramics'. In *Ultrasonic Material*, O. E. Mattiat (Ed) Plenum, New York, 1971.
3. Mason W. P., *Piezoelectric Crystals and Their Appplications to Ultrasonics*, Van Nostrand, New York, 1950.
4. Cady W. G., *Piezoelectricity* Vol. 1, Dover, New York, 1964.
5. Jaffe B., Cook W.R., Jaffe H., *Piezoelectric Ceramics*, Academic Press, New York, 1971.
6. Brissaud M., *Materiaux Piézoélectriques, Caracrérisation, Modélisation et Vibration*, Presses Polytechniques et Universitaires Romandes, 2007.
7. Timoshenko, S. P. and Goodier, J. N., *Theory of* Elasticity, 3rd edition, McGraw-Hill, New York, 1970.
8. Debus J. C., Granger C., Evrard P., 'Electromechanical actuators used with an original polarization', 7th CanSmart Meeting International Workshop Smart Materials and Structures, Montreal, October 2004.

6

Time domain analysis of piezoelectric devices with the transient module in ATILA

S-H. PARK, Micromechatronics Inc., USA

DOI: 10.1533/9780857096319.2.136

Abstract: This chapter describes time domain analysis capabilities of ATILA which might be useful in evaluating acoustic wave propagation and reflection by transducers, transient signal response of sensors, and overshoot and ringing behaviors for actuators. Three examples from different application fields were selected to show how time domain analysis can be achieved in ATILA, focusing on an analytical approach in simulation modeling, decisions based on transient module parameters, and interpretation of time domain results.

Key words: time domain, transient analysis, impulse driving, custom waveform.

6.1   Introduction

A time domain analysis with the finite element analysis tool, ATILA, is an observation of an electromechanical system in the flow of time and it is differentiated from a harmonic analysis that simulates the system in a frequency domain. The harmonic analysis can provide information on resonance mode, displacement, stress, and fluid pressure, however it is mainly frequency based data and its time sequence analysis is limited to a single cycle of one frequency, e.g. 1kHz = 0.001 sec. ATILA has a solver, which is called the transient module, that can precisely analyze time-domain-based issues. This chapter provides different case studies, such as propagation, overshoot, and ringing control of actuators and acoustic signal generation and detection of transducers. Additionally, a custom transient analysis method that enables use of any kind of user defined waveform is also introduced.

The ATILA transient (time-domain) solver can be set to use any of the following integration methods: central difference, Newmark, or Wilson-θ. These types of analyses can be applied to elastic structures excited by external forces and/or displacements, piezoelectric and/or magnetostrictive structures excited by external forces, displacements and/or potentials radiating piezoelectric and/or magnetostrictive structures excited by external forces, displacements and/or potentials. For these analyses, the excitation function can be a step, pulse, sine, or any other function defined by a user. Material losses can be taken into account in this analysis and results include displacements, stresses, pressures, electrical potential, and acoustic radiation quantities.

6.1.1   Transient module applications

Time domain analysis can provide transient response of a system to be analyzed and it is useful in understanding flow of both electrical and mechanical energies, such as structural change of a system, wave propagation, and electric potential generated by external excitations. Since ATILA was originally developed for underwater transducer applications, the initial goal of this module was to simulate acoustic wave propagation and reflection through a fluid medium to detect an object. This process includes excitation of a transducer, propagation of an acoustic signal, scattering at the target, propagation of the returning wave, and sensing of the reflected signal. Consequently, the module can be used for analysis of other similar applications such as sensors, accelerometers, and non-destructive testing.

The transient module can also be used for applications that do not need signal propagation across a medium, such as actuators and energy harvesting devices. When an electromechanical system is excited by external electric or mechanical energy, there can be overshoot and ringing effects which are observable only in the transient analysis. This information can be very useful in understanding behavior of a device and optimizing its structure and operation conditions.

6.1.2   The devices to be modeled

Three transient analysis case studies are described in this chapter with details. The first example is an underwater transducer to show basic transient analysis techniques and acoustic wave propagation in ATILA. The second example is a transient electrical energy generation with piezoelectric disk under pulse impact. And the last one is an overshoot and ringing control of an actuator by changing an applied electric signal waveform. This case study will also describe how to implement user-defined excitation signals into ATILA.

A transducer for acoustic signal generation and detection

A well-known Langevin transducer is selected as an example device for 2D underwater acoustic wave propagation and reflective signal detection. 2D axis symmetry was used along the x-axis so the structure has a fluid hemisphere on the aluminum head mass side. Detailed dimensions for the Langevin transducer are shown in Fig. 6.1. Two piezoelectric disks are polarized in an opposite direction so the input electrode can be shared in the middle. Aluminum head mass and steel tail mass are sandwiching the disks

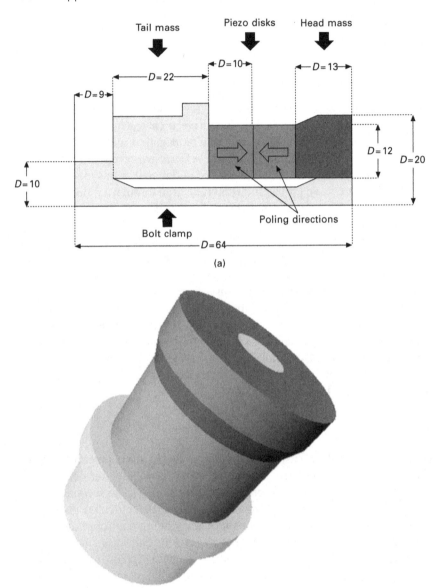

6.1 Langevin transducer with detailed dimensions (a) designed from GiD pre-processor in 2D and (b) automatically generated 3D view in ATILA supervisor.

through the bolt clamp. The transducer will be driven with a pulse wave to send an acoustic signal toward the fluid domain and reflected responses by an object will be sensed.

A piezoelectric disk under shock impact

The second example is a piezoelectric disk under an impulse shock and observation of the electric signal output in terms of time, as shown in Fig. 6.2. This case can be applied to pressure sensors, accelerometers, and energy harvesting device analysis. The bottom of the disk is clamped in the thickness direction to assume the disk is on a table. Downward pressure of 10 MPa is applied on the top surface of the disk with the shock duration of 5 μsec. In this example, three steps of the ATILA-GiD calculation will be described to show basic ATILA code file modification technique.

An actuator driven by a controlled input signal

A bimorph actuator that has PZT and brass layers is completely clamped on one side by a clamping structure is the third transient example, as shown in Fig. 6.3. Initially, 1 V-peak forced potential and ground conditions will be applied to the top and bottom surfaces of the PZT layer, which is the same as in the normal conditioning process with the harmonic module. Later, this portion will be modified from the ATILA code file (project.ati) to integrate user defined wave forms into the simulation set. Overshoot and ringing behaviors of the actuator will be controlled by adjusting rise and fall times of the input waveform which can be easily generated from Microsoft Excel.

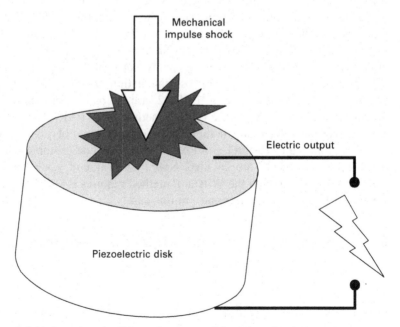

6.2 A piezoelectric disk under external impulse shock pressure.

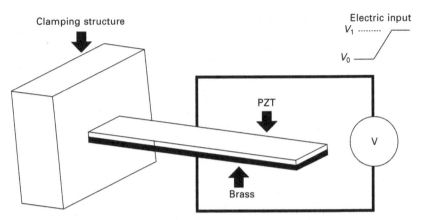

6.3 A bimorph piezoelectric actuator with a customized waveform excitation.

6.2 Key design issues and parameters

ATILA provides five main transient functions as shown in Fig. 6.4 (a). Sinusoidal, DC biased sinusoidal, constant, pulse, and external waveforms are the ones that can be applied as an electrical potential condition in the transient module. Amplitude, frequency and duration for the pulse are the parameters that can be defined by users for these waveforms. Figure 6.4 (b) shows transient module parameters when 'Transient' is selected in the 'Analysis' option in the 'Problem Data' window. 'Number of Steps' decides how many steps will be calculated based on 'Delta T', 'NS', and 'NSKIP'. 'Delta T' is the time gap between measurement points and NS is increment of the step, while NSKIP decides how many steps will be skipped each step. 'FL' parameter is a frequency for loss calculation and inverse of 'Delta T' is generally used. 'PARA1' and 'PARA2' are the parameters that are used for transient calculations. In the Central method, both PARA1 and PARA2 are ignored. The Newmark method has two parameters of γ and β which are corresponding to PARA1 and PARA2. This method is stable when $\gamma \geq 0.5$ and $\beta \geq (0.5 + \gamma)^2/4$ are satisfied. Note that a value of $\gamma > \frac{1}{2}$ introduces a numerical damping and the Wilson θ method requires PARA1 larger than 1.366 and PARA2 is not necessary in this case.

6.3 Step-by-step use of ATILA transient module

6.3.1 Transducer: acoustic signal propagation and reflection

Figure 6.5 shows the overall simulation concept and structure of the transient example for acoustic signal propagation and reflection with a Langevin

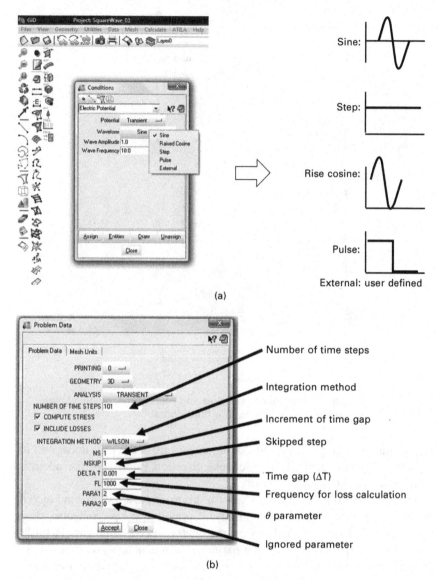

(a)

(b)

6.4 Transient module parameters (a) transient potential boundary conditions and (b) the transient parameters in the 'Problem Data' menu.

transducer. A fluid domain with water is placed as a quarter-circle and is in contact with the head mass of the transducer. Since 2D axis symmetry option is used, it will act like a water hemisphere is interfaced with the transducer. A radiating boundary condition needs to be assigned to the arc line to assume the fluid domain is infinitely large and to avoid any reflection from the edge

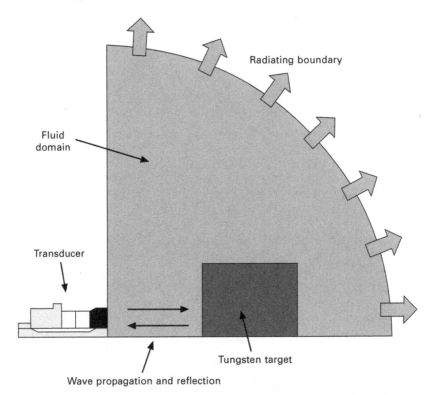

Radiating boundary

Fluid
domain

Transducer

Tungsten target

Wave propagation and reflection

6.5 A Langevin transducer sending and receiving acoustic signals
with a tungsten target through a fluid domain.

line. A tungsten target is placed 200 mm away from the transducer and its
backside is clamped along its thickness direction to observe the acoustic
wave reflection effect more clearly.

The transient simulation parameters for this example are shown in Fig. 6.6.
A 5 kV-peak pulse signal (500Vp/mm) is applied to the piezoelectric rings
for 40 μsec. Before deciding transient parameters such as time gap (Delta T),
it is always suggested to use either harmonic or modal analysis to find out a
fundamental or interested resonance frequency of the structure. For instance,
in this simulation example, the resonance frequency of the transducer is 32.9
kHz which corresponds to 30 μsec. Therefore, a time gap smaller than that
length is needed to observe any behavior related with the resonance mode.
Generally, a time gap of 1/10 smaller than the resonance cycle is suggested,
so 3 μsec was used in this example. PARA1 (θ parameter) of 2 was used
since it is the smallest integer number that is larger than 1.366.

The thickness direction point stress analysis results on the tungsten target
surface toward the transducer side are shown in Fig. 6.7. Since the sound
velocity in water is ~1 490 m/s and the distance between the transducer

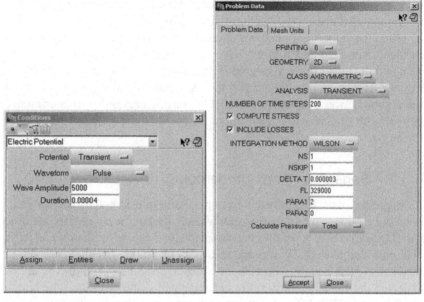

6.6 Transient simulation parameters used for the Langevin transducer example.

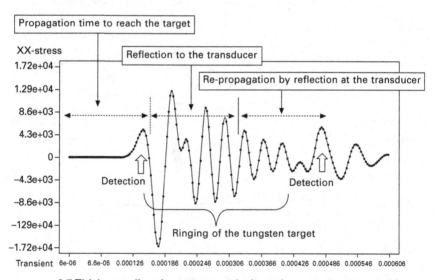

6.7 Thickness direction stress analysis at the tungsten target side.

and the target is 200 mm, the travel time of the acoustic wave will be 134 μsec and the simulation results show the same time until it detects the first wave advancing from the transducer. The tungsten target reflects some of the wave and starts ringing as it absorbs energy. The reflected wave travels back to the transducer and bounces again back to the tungsten target, which is denoted as the second detection point in Fig. 6.7.

When the same stress analysis is conducted on the transducer head mass surface, overshoot and ringing behaviors of the transducer can be clearly seen and the small reflected signal is detected after ~ 350 μsec as shown in Fig. 6.8. However, it is longer than the calculated round trip acoustic signal travel time between the transducer and the target. This is due to interference between the ringing wave from the transducer and the reflected wave from the target.

6.3.2   Sensor: ringing and damping

As suggested in the first transient example, harmonic or modal analysis needs to be done prior to the transient simulation to determine an appropriate time gap (Delta T). Table 6.1 shows the modal analysis results for the piezoelectric disk with diameter of 10 mm and thickness of 5 mm. The main resonance mode with 50% coupling coefficient is observed at 128 kHz, thus it can be expected the fundamental ringing behavior will occur with the time length of ~7.8 μsec (1/128 000). To detect such motion, a time gap that is smaller than 7 μsec is required. In this example, 1 μsec was used which will provide seven measurement points in showing one cycle of the resonance mode.

Figure 6.9 shows the transient analysis parameters used in this example. 50

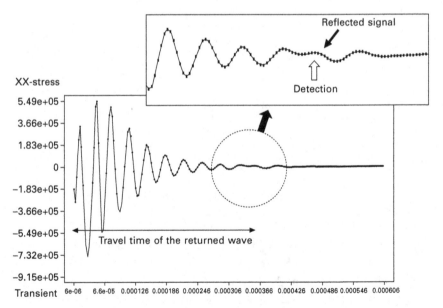

6.8 Longitudinal direction stress analysis at the transducer head mass surface.

Table 6.1 Modal analysis results of the piezoelectric disk

Mode	Resonance frequency (Hz)	Antiresonance frequency (Hz)	Coupling coefficient (%)
1	0	0	0
2	0	0	0
3	83 800	83 800	0
4	128 000	147 000	50
5	147 000	147 000	1
6	147 000	150 000	19
7	150 000	150 000	2
8	150 000	176 000	52
9	182 000	182 000	0
10	182 000	182 000	0

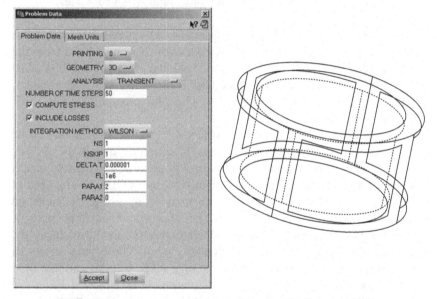

6.9 Transient parameters for the piezoelectric disk simulation.

points with 1 μsec time gap were simulated with θ parameter of 2. A pressure condition of 10 MPa was assigned on the top surface and the bottom surface was clamped to the thickness direction of the disk. In the current simulation conditions, the pressure condition does not have time domain information and it should be added through modification of the ATILA code file.

To modify the ATILA code file directly, GiD pre-processor information, such as dimensional information and boundary conditions, need to be converted into the ATILA codes. This can be done by using the 'Convert to ATI' function as shown in Fig. 6.10 and it generates a 'project.ati' file, which is the ATILA code, in the simulation file folder.

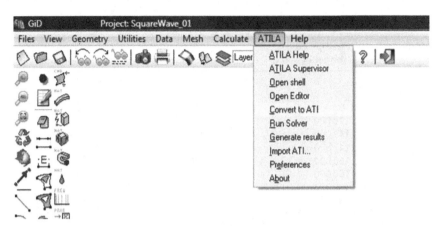

6.10 'Convert to ATI' function for generation ATILA code file.

Figure 6.11 shows a 'project.ati' file opened from WordPad of MS Windows. It shows various conditions in ATILA codes which were defined from the GiD preprocessor. Under the 'Excitation' field, the pressure condition of 10 MPa can be found and the '0.000000e-000' is the time domain information. By changing this number to '-5.000000e-006', the pressure condition will be applied for 5 μsec.

After saving the changes to the 'project.ati' file, the simulation can be run manually as shown in Fig. 6.12 (a). 'Run Solver' makes the ATILA Supervisor run and the calculation window will pop up showing calculation processes. Once all the calculation is complete, the ATILA results need to be converted back to GiD compatible information by using the 'Generate results' function as shown in Fig. 6.12 (b). The combined three steps of 'Convert ATI', 'Run Solver' and 'Generate results' are identical as the 'Calculation' function under the 'Calculate' menu. These three stages of step-by-step processes are required to modify ATILA codes and add time domain information to the pressure or displacement condition.

Figure 6.13 shows point displacement analysis results along the thickness direction on the center of the top surface of the piezoelectric disk. More than 600 nm initial downward displacement is generated by the 5 μsec impulse shock with 10 MPa. The disk bounced back and started ringing. By calculating logarithmic decrement of the ringing behavior, damping ratio and quality factor can be obtained using the formulae below, where ζ is the damping ratio, δ is the logarithmic decrement, and Q is the quality factor.

$$\zeta = \frac{\delta}{\sqrt{(2\pi)^2 + \delta^2}} \text{ where } \delta = \ln \frac{x_1}{x_2} \qquad [6.1]$$

$$Q = \frac{1}{2\zeta} \qquad [6.2]$$

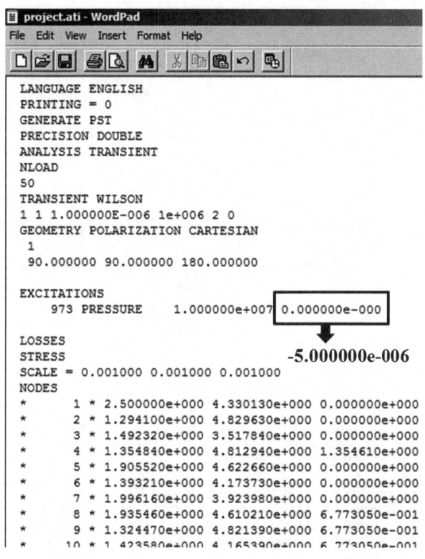

6.11 'project.ati' file modification to provide pulse time length.

The transient response with $\theta = 2$, in Fig. 6.13 (a), provided a damping ratio of 0.117 and quality of 4.3. Considering the quality factor of piezoelectric material (~70), the calculated quality factor is much smaller than the material property. This is partially due to the clamping condition on the bottom of the disk but another important factor is artificial damping by the θ parameter. In the Wilson-θ method, the simulation is stable as long as the θ parameter is larger than 1.366. As the θ parameter gets larger, artificial (mathematical) damping effect becomes more dominant. The clear difference between two

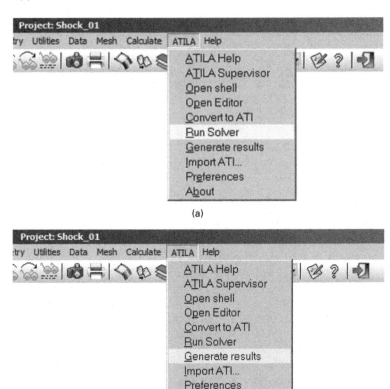

(a)

(b)

6.12 Manual calculation steps (a) 'Run Solver' for ATILA Supervisor calculation and (b) 'Generate results' for converting ATILA results into GiD compatible information.

different θ parameters of 2 and 1.4 are shown in Fig. 6.13. When θ is 1.4, clearly there is less damping effect and calculated damping ratio and Q in this case are 0.018 and 27.5, respectively. Therefore, the θ parameter needs to be tuned with the actual experimental case to improve preciseness of a simulation set.

6.3.3   Actuator: operation optimization with customized waveform

The last transient example will show how a user defined waveform can be integrated in ATILA transient simulation. When the bender actuator described in Fig. 6.3 is driven with a square input signal, the structure overshoots and starts ringing. It can be reduced by adjusting the rise and fall times of the signal to the natural resonance frequency of the structure[1]. However, default

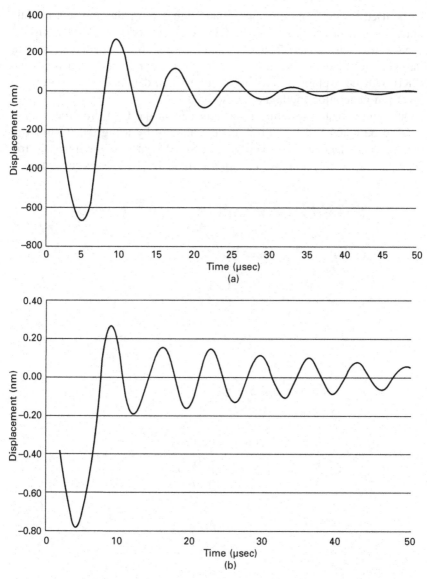

6.13 Transient displacement response of the piezoelectric disk under impulse shock pressure: (a) $\theta = 2$ and (b) $\theta = 1.4$.

waveforms provided by ATILA do not have such controllability. Alternatively, ATILA provides the function of user defined input signal operation. The input parameter can be electric potential, pressure, or displacement. Users can generate their own input signals as long as 1st and 2nd derivatives can be obtained from the input function.

As explained in the previous two examples, harmonic or modal analysis can be used for deciding the appropriate time gap for the transient module simulation. In this actuator case, the 1st resonance mode is at 200 Hz thus the time gap was selected as 250 μsec as shown in Fig. 6.14. The θ parameter of 2 has been selected and its relationship with other parameters such as NS and NSKIP will be explained in a later section when details of the customized waveform generation method are described.

Once the actuator structure is designed from the GiD pre-processor, it needs to be converted in ATILA code manually by using the 'Convert to ATI' function. During the GiD pre-processor design step, the input electric potential can be any number or condition, such as force 1V or external,

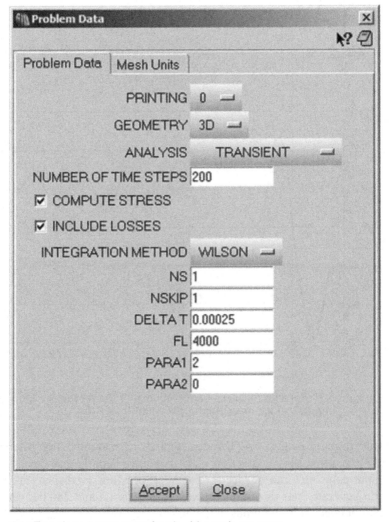

6.14 Transient parameters for the bimorph actuator.

since it will be replaced with a user-defined waveform later. The electric potential condition for the 1V case can be found from the 'project.ati' file under the 'Excitation' field, as shown in Fig. 6.15. It needs to be changed to 0.000000e+000 and by doing so ATILA will use a 'project.exc' file as the excitation condition.

The 'project.exc' file is the one that contains user defined waveform information and needs to be generated by a user, using Windows Notepad (or WordPad) and MS Excel (or any other program that provides mathematical calculation). The basic structure of the file has four columns as shown in Fig. 6.16. The first column is time and it needs to increase based on two series of numbers that are defined by the time gap (Delta T), NS, and $NSKIP$. The first set of series is 0, $\theta^* \Delta T$, $(1 + \theta)^* \Delta T$, $(2 + \theta)^* \Delta T$, $(3+ \theta)^* \Delta T$ ... and the second series is $NS^*\Delta T$, $2^*NS^*\Delta T$, $3^*NS^*\Delta T$, $4^*NS^* \Delta T$... where the number of step defined by $NSKIP$ is skipped. The 1st column is combining these two series of numbers and it is suggested to generate three times longer time than the targeted simulation period (Delta T × Number of Time Steps). Due to this complexity, $\theta = 2$, $NS = 1$, and $NSKIP = 1$ are suggested for simulation, except when artificial damping is critical.

```
LANGUAGE ENGLISH
PRINTING = 0
GENERATE PST
PRECISION DOUBLE
ANALYSIS TRANSIENT
NLOAD
200
TRANSIENT WILSON
1 1 2.500000E-004 4000 2 0
GEOMETRY POLARIZATION CARTESIAN
 1
 -180.000000 90.000000 180.000000

EXCITATIONS
    539 ELECPOT    1.000000e+000  0.000000e+000

                    0.000000e+000
LOSSES
STRESS
SCALE = 0.001000 0.001000 0.001000
NODES
*       1 * 5.000000e+000 6.666670e+000 2.000000e+000
*       2 * 0.000000e+000 6.666670e+000 2.000000e+000
*       3 * 0.000000e+000 6.666670e+000 0.000000e+000
```

6.15 Modification of 'project.ati' to declare existence of a user-defined waveform file 'project.exc'.

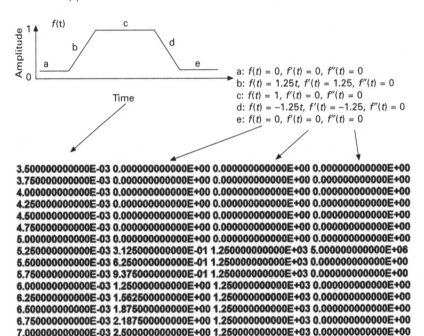

a: $f(t) = 0$, $f'(t) = 0$, $f''(t) = 0$
b: $f(t) = 1.25t$, $f'(t) = 1.25$, $f''(t) = 0$
c: $f(t) = 1$, $f'(t) = 0$, $f''(t) = 0$
d: $f(t) = -1.25t$, $f'(t) = -1.25$, $f''(t) = 0$
e: $f(t) = 0$, $f'(t) = 0$, $f''(t) = 0$

3.500000000000E-03 0.000000000000E+00 0.000000000000E+00 0.000000000000E+00
3.750000000000E-03 0.000000000000E+00 0.000000000000E+00 0.000000000000E+00
4.000000000000E-03 0.000000000000E+00 0.000000000000E+00 0.000000000000E+00
4.250000000000E-03 0.000000000000E+00 0.000000000000E+00 0.000000000000E+00
4.500000000000E-03 0.000000000000E+00 0.000000000000E+00 0.000000000000E+00
4.750000000000E-03 0.000000000000E+00 0.000000000000E+00 0.000000000000E+00
5.000000000000E-03 0.000000000000E+00 0.000000000000E+00 0.000000000000E+00
5.250000000000E-03 3.125000000000E-01 1.250000000000E+03 5.000000000000E+06
5.500000000000E-03 6.250000000000E-01 1.250000000000E+03 0.000000000000E+00
5.750000000000E-03 9.375000000000E-01 1.250000000000E+03 0.000000000000E+00
6.000000000000E-03 1.250000000000E+00 1.250000000000E+03 0.000000000000E+00
6.250000000000E-03 1.562500000000E+00 1.250000000000E+03 0.000000000000E+00
6.500000000000E-03 1.875000000000E+00 1.250000000000E+03 0.000000000000E+00
6.750000000000E-03 2.187500000000E+00 1.250000000000E+03 0.000000000000E+00
7.000000000000E-03 2.500000000000E+00 1.250000000000E+03 0.000000000000E+00

6.16 'project.exc' with the user-defined wave form information.

The second column is amplitude and it can be electric potential, pressure, or displacement. The third and fourth columns are corresponding to 1st and 2nd derivates of the function from the 1st (time) and 2nd (amplitude) columns. For instance, if displacement in the 2nd column is changing based on the time increment in the 1st column, the 3rd column will be velocity and the 4th column will be acceleration or deceleration.

A time gap of 250 μsec was used and electric potential in the 2nd column increased to 10 V with a rise time of 2 ms which was then maintained for 20 ms. And it decreased to zero over fall time of 2 ms. The rise and fall times were later adjusted to optimize the actuator performance. The 3rd and 4th columns correspond to the 1st and 2nd derivative values for the function as shown in Fig. 6.16. This file needs to be saved in HTML format to remove the column format from MS Excel. Using the 'Save as' function, the file can be stored in the simulation folder with the name 'project.htm'.

When the 'project.htm' is executed, a web browser can open it as a pure series of numbers without any column format. The numbers can be easily copied to a blank Windows Notepad by using the 'Ctrl-A', 'Ctrl-C' and 'Ctrl-V', short keys. This file can then be saved as 'project.exc' in the simulation folder, using the 'Save As' function of Windows Notepad.

Figure 6.17 shows an input signal and output displacement results of the bender actuator when the rise time is 2 ms. In this case, there is almost 50%

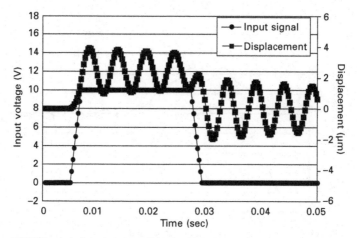

6.17 User-defined wave with rise/fall time of 2 ms and displacement response of the actuator.

overshoot and it is followed by continuous ringing. A similar behavior is again observed when the signal goes back to zero with the same fall time of 2 ms. Therefore, the operation condition needs to be adjusted to obtain precise controllability for the actuator.

Figure 6.18 (a) shows the time domain displacement change of the actuator when the rise time is 8 ms. It shows that just slowing the rise time and fall time cannot solve the problem. From harmonic and modal analyses, we know the resonance frequency and it can be used to minimize overshoot and ringing. Figure 6.18 (b) shows the response of the actuator when the rise and fall times are matching with one cycle of the resonance frequency. Apparently, undesired overshoot and displacement fluctuation were reduced and the operation of the actuator was stabilized.

6.4   Conclusion and future trends

The time domain analysis capability of ATILA can provide a variety of information, such as acoustic wave propagation, reflection, damping effect, overshoot, and ringing behaviors, which are valuable for piezoelectric devices design. The basic transient module function enables the simple application of transient electric potential to a device which might be useful in underwater or non-destructive test simulations as shown in the first example. With small modifications of the ATILA code file to provide the duration of excitation condition, the transient analysis can be extended to external pressure and displacement conditions. It will allow the simulation of accelerometers, force sensors, and energy harvesting devices with an impulse energy source. ATILA also allows users to build their own waveforms, which greatly enhances

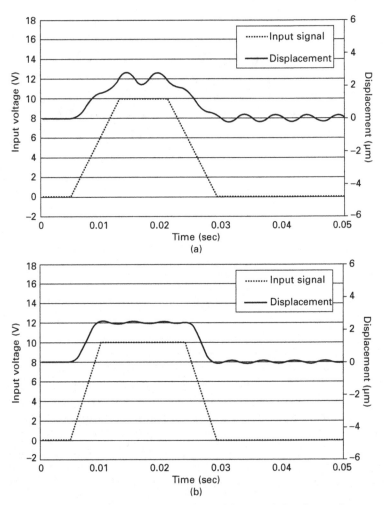

6.18 Excitation condition optimization with user-defined waveform modifications (a) rise time 8 ms and (b) 5 ms.

the freedom of the time domain simulation. Any shape of excitation signal can be applied as long as the 1st and 2nd derivatives of the function can be calculated. For appropriate use of the transient module, it is recommended to combine it with other analysis modules such as modal and harmonic. The time gap between simulation points especially, needs to be correctly decided to simulate a structure correctly.

6.5   Reference

1.   K. Uchino and J. R. Giniewicz (2003), *Micromechatronics*, Chapter 5 Drive/control techniques for piezoelectric actuators, New York, Marcel Dekker, Inc., ISBN 0-8247-4109-9.

7

Designing ultrasonic motors (USM) with ATILA

S-J. YOON, Korea Institute of Science and Technology, Korea

DOI: 10.1533/9780857096319.2.155

Abstract: Piezoelectric ultrasonic motors offer many advantages such as high retention being very controllable, high torque at low speed, light weight, simple structure and no electromagnetic field induction compared with the conventional electromagnetic motors. These advantages have helped to expand the application fields where precise position control and rotational/linear motions can be utilized. One of the most remarkable features of the compact ultrasonic motor is that it has higher design flexibility compared with that of the conventional electromagnetic motors whose efficiency significantly decreases with miniaturization. In order to build a novel ultrasonic motor for a specific purpose, it is essential to examine the structural design and the electrical and mechanical properties prior to preparing a real motor. The ATILA simulation tool offers useful information related to the performance for a designed piezoelectric ultrasonic motor. A real motor can therefore easily be manufactured with minimized trial and error. In this chapter, two types of tiny motors are presented, including the process of ATILA simulation and the fabrication of ultrasonic piezoelectric motors.

Key words: ATILA simulation, ultrasonic piezoelectric motor, actuator, resonance frequency, electromechanical property, dynamic property.

7.1 Introduction

The ultrasonic piezoelectric motor comprising piezoelectric actuators and mechanical components can be constructed utilizing various piezoelectric resonant modes and mechanical forces, i.e. a tiny disk type using an inertia force or a rectangular plate one using a frictional force, etc. In addition to this diversity, it has the following advantages compared with conventional motors:

- stable operation with proper velocity and torque, which is suited for direct drive without any gears for reduction of speed or converting mechanisms for changing operating directions
- quick response and excellent controllability of starting, stopping and reversing
- small size and light weight, and
- absence of any electronic disturbances.

Various kinds of the piezoelectric ultrasonic linear motors, using a traveling wave or an impact force, have been proposed and their applications have been studied intensively. The piezoelectric ultrasonic linear motors using a traveling wave have also been designed based on the combination of two different vibration modes where the transverse and longitudinal modes are combined to achieve an elliptical motion on the surface of the contact point. The performance of these ultrasonic motors can be optimized utilizing the ATILA simulation offering some results in association with the piezoelectric resonance frequency and displacement. It is therefore very important to examine the performance of a designed motor in advance. The ATILA simulation effectively provides answers for whether an operating principle of designed structure is right, what the optimal resonance frequency is, and what the final dynamic and electrical properties are. In this chapter, I present how effectively ATILA works for two different types of ultrasonic motors.

7.2   Procedure for finite element method (FEM) analysis – ATILA

This chapter introduces the structure, operating principle, and modeling of the piezoelectric ultrasonic linear motor. In recent years, computer simulations have become an important tool in electromechanical transducer design [1–5]. A balanced combination of computer simulations and experimental work leads to design concepts which are more efficient in quality and time. The main reasons for its use are that the finite element method (FEM) is very helpful for an analysis of mechanical structures with different geometry and materials, and it is very useful for studying the coupling effect between the actuator and test structure. Many finite element analysis (FEA) software packages are commercially available, including ANSYS, PZFLEX, and ATILA [6]. ATILA is especially designed for piezoelectric devices, which take into account the coupling between the transducer mechanical structure and the surrounding medium [7–11]. In modeling piezoelectric actuators, two approaches are usually used. A FEA of the actuator is very important for designing a novel miniature ultrasonic linear motor, because it will be able to offer us some information such as possible driving frequency and performance of the motor. To make the analysis clear, before the analysis of the transducer, we shall review the construction of the proposed motor. A flow chart of typical procedures for FEM analysis is displayed in Fig. 7.1. For modeling of the piezoelectric linear motors, the first step is to define the dimension of the piezoelectric ceramics. It is a very important procedure because piezoelectric ceramics must generate the radial vibration at the low electric field.

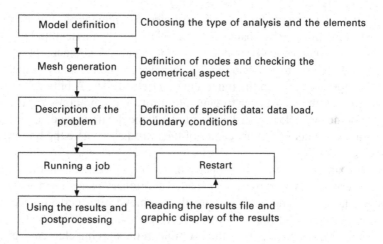

7.1 Flow chart of typical implementation procedures for FEM analysis.

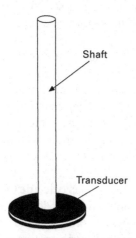

7.2 The structure of a tiny ultrasonic linear motor.

7.3   Tiny ultrasonic motor (USM)

7.3.1   Design and concept

The basic configuration of the piezoelectric ultrasonic motor is shown in Fig. 7.2. The motor is composed of two components:

1. elastic body and shaft
2. piezoelectric ceramic disks and shaft.

The transducer is made of two active piezoelectric disks poled in its thickness direction and a metal disk (elastic plate), which has the same bimorph structure

(Fig. 7.3). Two separate disks of piezoelectric element are metallized and poled in the thickness expansion mode. They are then assembled in a + − + − stack and mechanically bonded. A thin metal disk is placed between the two piezoelectric disks. The outer electrodes are connected together and a field is applied between the inner and outer electrodes. A bimorph structure was used as the transducer to generate ultrasonic vibrations. As the radial mode of the piezoelectric disk converted into the flexural mode, up-and-down motion was generated at the center of the transducer where the bimorph was placed. [12–17]

The parasitic vibration happens and brings degradation of operation characteristics if the transducer is loaded at ordinary places such as the PCB, metal plate, etc. The shaft is crucial to achieve high performance of the motors. The mass of the shaft must be lighter than that of the transducer. If the shaft mass is heavier than the transducer, the moving element can create a non-uniformity movement by distortion of the shaft. The shaft is loaded on the center of the transducer. A moving element is fixed on the shaft on the center of the transducer. The moving element, is compressed to a surface of the shaft by rubber tube. The moving element must have a sufficient weight for a high friction factor.

The phenomenon of piezoelectricity, as a solid-state method for converting electrical signals into mechanical motion, generates kinetic energy which is the force for operating a motor. In particular we have found that the motor can be operated simply by the of laws of physics. The operating principle of the motor is explained by the characteristics of piezoelectricity and Newton's first law. In other words, the motor exploits the vibration modes of piezoelectric ceramics, the inertia principle and the contact force of the friction.

Generally speaking, the two piezoelectric elements, piezoelectric motor and piezoelectric transducer, can work in either longitudinal mode or transverse mode with a corresponding resonant frequency. According to the different vibration modes and mechanical structure, piezoelectric motors could be

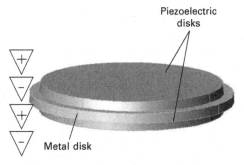

7.3 Configuration of the transducer.

classified into two main categories: thickness mode and radial mode. [13–16] In this study, piezoelectric ceramics are designed to have a radial resonance mode whose operation frequency is dependent on the ratio of thickness and diameter. By applying an electrical potential to the piezoelectric transducer, mechanical deformation is induced in the piezoelectric ceramics designed by the radial mode generating rule as shown in Fig. 7.4. The operation principle using the radial mode of piezoelectric ceramics is described below

This sawtooth electrical potential has two kinds of acceleration: linearly rising acceleration and suddenly falling acceleration. When electrical potential linearly increases with time, the linearly rising acceleration is defined as a_r. As the saw tooth electrical potential decreases suddenly with time, the suddenly falling acceleration is defined as a_f.

$$a_f \rangle a_r \qquad [7.1]$$

With saw tooth electrical potential being applied, this motor operates under two kind forces: inertia and frictional force.

$$F_{g1} = ma_r \qquad [7.2]$$

$$f_s \rangle ma_r \qquad [7.3]$$

$$F_{g2} = ma_f \qquad [7.4]$$

$$f_s \langle ma_f \qquad [7.5]$$

The explanation of the operating behavior of the motor in detail is as shown in Fig. 7.5. The moving element locates at the position 'a' at the beginning

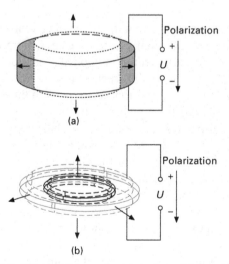

7.4 Elongation and contraction of (a) the piezoelectric ceramic (b) transducer when a electrical potential is applied.

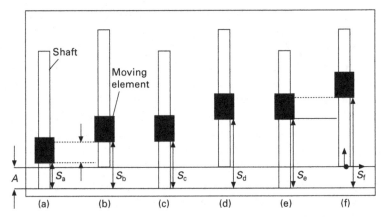

7.5 Schematic illustration of the movement of a moving element which is loaded with the shaft.

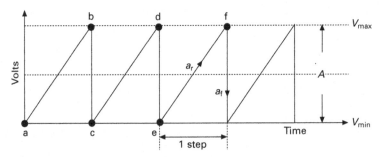

7.6 Schematic of sawtooth electrical potential.

of the motion. When electrical potential is not applied, which is in position 'a' in Fig. 7.6, the moving element is initially at a distance S_a from the left end of the shaft. When the electrical potential is applied from zero to the maximum electrical potential, i.e., the 'a'–'b' region in Fig. 7.6, the shaft and the moving element together move position 'a' to 'b' with the distance 'A' smoothly and linearly. As the electrical potential 'b'–'c', which suddenly falls to the minimum electrical potential, is applied, the shaft moves to the bottom on a distance 'A', region 'b'–'c'. At this time, the moving element remains motionless because of its inertia, and the shaft is slipped by the electrical potential. If the electrical potential applied from the minimum electrical potential to the maximum electrical potential, which is linearly rising to maximum electrical potential, 'c'–'d' region, the shaft moves on a distance 'A' together with the moving element as shown in Fig. 7.5 (c) – (d) According to Fig. 7.5 the position 'd'–'e' region has the same movement as position 'b'–'c' and the position 'e'–'f' region has the same movement as position 'c'–'d'. Figure 7.5 states that the moving element continuously goes from the bottom to top repeating this kind of the motion. Having changed a slope direction of the saw tooth electrical potential, we shall receive a change of direction of the moving element. The proposed motor realizes our described principle of inertia and the contact force of the friction.

When a saw tooth driving pulse having a calm leading edge and an abrupt trailing edge is applied to the piezoelectric element by the voltage-applying device, the piezoelectric element expands to shift to its thickness direction calmly at the calm leading edge of the driving pulse, and the driving shaft fixed to the transducer calmly shifts to an axial direction. At this time, the moving element which is frictionally coupled with the driving shaft moves together with the driving shaft due to the frictional force. In order to move the moving element in an opposite direction, the saw tooth waveform to be applied to the piezoelectric element is changed and a driving pulse composed of an abrupt leading edge and a calm trailing edge is applied to the piezoelectric element, so that the movement can be achieved by an opposite function to the above one.

7.3.2   Finite element analysis of tiny ultrasonic linear motor

Based on the flow chart as shown in Fig. 7.1, typical FEM analysis is demonstrated as shown in Figs 7.7–7.11. The material properties of a piezoelectric motor designed for FEM analysis are given in Table 7.1. Figures 7.7 and 7.9 show the boundary conditions of the piezoelectric ceramic. One side of the piezoelectric ceramic is connected to a ground and a voltage potential is applied to the opposite side of the piezoelectric ceramic as shown in Fig. 7.10. Considering the dimension of the piezoelectric ceramic, it must be poled in its thickness direction to generate the radial vibration. In order to follow the operating principle, when the piezoelectric ceramic is driven by electrical potential, the piezoelectric ceramic must generate the radial vibration modes which are periodical extension and contraction on the radius direction of the piezoelectric ceramic disk. Now, the model is finished and is ready to be meshed. The mesh will be a generated volume mesh in order to achieve greater accuracy. By selecting a sufficient volume mesh,

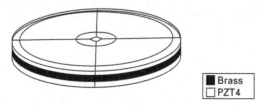

Brass
PZT4

7.7 Material condition of transducer.

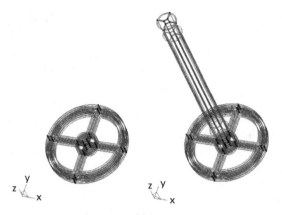

7.8 Drawing of a tiny USM.

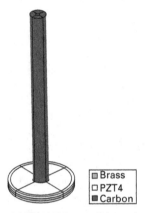

□ Brass
□ PZT4
■ Carbon

7.9 Material condition of a tiny USM.

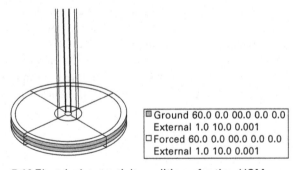

□ Ground 60.0 0.0 00.0 0.0 0.0
External 1.0 10.0 0.001
□ Forced 60.0 0.0 00.0 0.0 0.0
External 1.0 10.0 0.001

7.10 Electrical potential condition of a tiny USM.

the elements will be analyzed without meshing error. Figure 7.11 shows the 3D mesh of the piezoelectric ceramic disk. The result of harmonic analysis for the motor is shown in Fig. 7.12. Based on the simulation result, the

7.11 Mesh generation of a tiny USM.

Table 7.1 Physical properties of the motor's elements used for modeling

Elements	Young's Modulus (GPa)	Density (kG/m³)	Poisson's ratio
Elastic material (brass)	92	8270	0.33
Shaft material (carbon)	64	2230	0.2

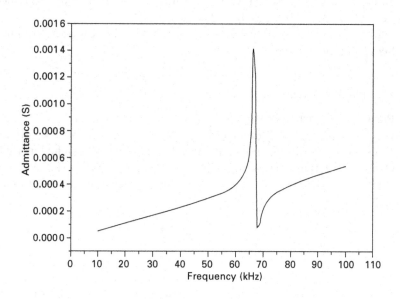

7.12 Admittance curves of a tiny USM.

motor can be operated near the frequency of 65.8 kHz. The distribution of displacement towards the moving direction of axis at the input frequency of 65.8 kHz is presented in Plate VII (between pages 194 and 195) as the results of the harmonic analysis. These results show that the simulated motor designed by ATILA effectively releases the up and down movement.

Geometry/drawing and material assignment

Problem – TULA USM
Brass elastic material – 5.5 mm ∅ × 0.2 mm t
PZT 4 – 5.5 mm
Shaft – 1.31 mm ∅ × 15mm

Geometry/drawing

Geometry → Create → points → 0,0
Utilities → Copy → second point → (0.2,0) (–0.2,0) (0,0.2) (0,–0.2)
Geometry → Create → Line → Join of all points respectively
Utilities → Copy → second point → (0.655,0) (–0.655,0) (0, 0.655) (0, –0.655) (2.5, 0) (–2.5, 0) (0,2.5) (0, –2.5) (2.75,0) (–2.75,0) (0,2.75) (0, –2.75)
Geometry → Create → Line → Join of all points respectively
Geometry → Create → NURBS surfaces → Automatic → number of sides 4
Utilities → Copy → Entities type: Surfaces → Do extrude: Volumes → Second point (0,0,0.185) (0,0,0.2) (0,0,0.185)
Utilities → Copy → Entities type: Surfaces → Do extrude: Volumes → Second point (0,0,15)

Material assignment

Piezoelectric materials
Data → Materials → Piezoelectric → PZT4 → Assign → Pick volumes
Click Draw → All materials → Check the material of assigned as PZT4.
Data → Materials → Elastic → brass → Assign → Pick volume
Click Draw → All materials → Check the Material are assigned as PZT4 and Brass.

Boundary conditions

Polarization/Local Axes

Data → Conditions → Volumes → Geometry → Polarization (Cartesian) → Define Polarization (P1) (0,0,0.2) direction.

Choose 3 polarization (Local-Axes P1) → Choose the PZT all three volumes → Finish.

Potential

Data → Conditions → Surfaces → Electric Potential → Ground → Assign the top surface of the PZT.
Data → Conditions → Forced Potential 20.0 with phase 0 → Assign the bottom surface of the PZT.

Meshing

Meshing → Structured → Surfaces → Select all volumes → Then cancel the further process.
Meshing → Structured → Lines → Enter number to divide line → Choose for the lines → Generate.
View Animation-vibration Mode at a particular frequency
View results → Default Analysis/Step → Harmonic-Magnitude → Set a Frequency
(Peak Point: 65.8 kHz for Resonance Mode).
Set Deformation → Displacement

Parameter other than displacement

Set Results View → View results → Contour Fill → Electric Potential or Von Mises Stress
After setting both "results view" and "Deformation" → Click to see the Animation.

7.3.3   Fabrication of a tiny ultrasonic linear motor

A piezoelectric ceramic material used in a motor's transducer needs to have the following features: high piezoelectric coupling constant (k_{ij}), high mechanical quality factor (Q_m) and low loss factor ($\tan\delta$). Therefore, KP14 (Kyoungwon Ferrite Co. Ltd) was used as the piezoelectric ceramic material for the transducer. Uniformly electroded piezoelectric ceramics poled in their thickness directions were bonded to a metal disk (brass) using adhesive epoxy. The performance and reliability of the piezoelectric motor depend heavily on the mechanical, electrical and chemical properties of the bonding layers between each layer. Therefore, the characteristics of the bonding layer and its effect on the motor performance must be considered. In this experiment, in order to control the bonding layer with uniformity and thickness, we used an ultrasonic welding machine which had controllable temperature and vibration intensity. From this experimental procedure, we can obtain the uniform thickness layer. To perform the operation of the motor, the shaft is located on the center of the transducer exactly. If the alignment of the shaft deviates from center of the transducer, it will generate undesirable vibrations which have negative influence on the motor operation. To solve this problem, we were using the optimum designed aligner which can minimize the alignment error of the shaft. Finally the prototype miniature piezoelectric ultrasonic linear motors were fabricated as shown in Fig. 7.13. Table 7.2 shows the specification of a tiny USM.

7.4   Butterfly-shaped ultrasonic linear motor

7.4.1   Design and concept

In recent years, micro industries and consumer devices such as mobile phones, PDAs, and micro-positioners, that are required to be very thin as well as having very low energy consumption and manufacturing cost, called for linear motors with an extremely low profile. Although many of the proposed piezoelectric transducers for ultrasonic linear motors could achieve large

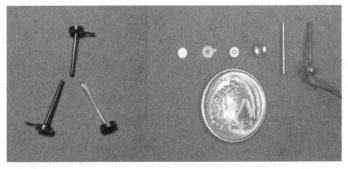

7.13 Components of a tiny USM.

Table 7.2 Specification of tiny USM

TULA35			
Size	Φ4 × 0.4	Stroke	3~11 mm
Speed	20 mm/s	Force	20 g·f
TULA50			
Size	Φ5.5 × 0.5	Stroke	3~20 mm
Speed	40 mm/s	Force	50 g·f
TULA70			
Size	Φ7.6 × 1.0	Stroke	3~30 mm
Speed	50 mm/s	Force	100 g·f

forces and high torques even with a small volume of <1000 mm³, it was difficult to install inside thin electronic devices due to the absence of a low profile [15–17] and also, most of proposed piezoelectric motors could not achieve the required layer structures due to their unique operating principles and structures. Considering the operating principle of a piezoelectric motor, a low profile motor can be designed when the surface of the piezoelectric ceramic and the moving axis become parallel.

The basic configuration of the piezoelectric ultrasonic motor is shown in Figure 7.14(a) The motor is composed of four components; elastic plate, supporter, piezoelectric plates. The transducer is made of two active piezoelectric plates, poled in its thickness direction and a metal plate, which is the samé as a unimorph structure. Figure 7.14(b) They are then assembled in a + – stack and mechanically bonded. The transducer has been design to have a flexural vibration mode, which is generated by the

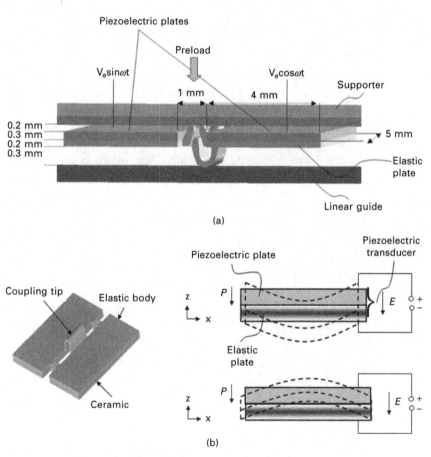

7.14 (a) Configuration of butterfly-shaped USM (b) operating principle of piezoelectric transducer.

piezoelectric ceramic and metal joint plate. The piezoelectric transducer is simply composed of an elastic plate including two piezoelectric ceramic plates. The center of the elastic plate connecting both the wings was bent to make a tip for a point contact to a linear guide. The tip acts on transferring the mechanical energy formed by the piezoelectric vibration to the linear guide. The piezoelectric ceramics were poled in the thickness direction and then firmly affixed on both the wings of the elastic plate using an epoxy. The vibration of the piezoelectric ceramics was excited by applying two harmonic oscillations with a phase difference of $\pi/2$. It is expected that the elliptical trajectory on the tip can be generated by superposing two resonance modes of piezoelectric ceramics such as the longitudinal and transverse modes as reported elsewhere [8]. First of all, behavior of the piezoelectric transducer was investigated to find the most suitable supporting method to a frame, minimizing the interference against piezoelectric vibrations.

7.4.2   Finite element analysis of butterfly-shaped ultrasonic linear motor

The structure of a butterfly-shaped ultrasonic linear motor for modeling is shown in Fig. 7.15. Brass is used for a common ground electrode and both the electrodes deposited on the piezoelectric ceramic surface are used for the applications of electric potentials. The piezoelectric ceramics are poled in thickness direction prior to joining the elastic element. The FEM analysis procedure for the butterfly-shaped ultrasonic linear motor is presented as below.

Geometry/drawing and material assignment

Problem – Butterfly-shaped USM
Brass elastic material – 5 by 8, t = 0.2 mm
PZT 4 – 4 by 8, t = 0.2

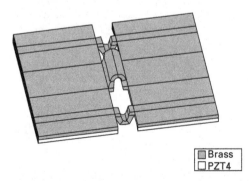

Brass
PZT4

7.15 The structure of butterfly-shaped USM.

Geometry/drawing

Create two 'fixed leg'
Geometry → Create → points → 0,0 3,0
Create line
Utilities → copy → Second point Y 2 → Do extrude line → select point
0,0 3,0
Utilities → copy → Entities type – line → → Do extrude – Surface → Y-1,
0.5, 1.5, 2, 1.5, 1, 0.5, 1
Create leg 1
Geometry → points → (4.25, 0.2, 1.5) (4.25, 0.2, 1) (4.75, 0.2, 1.5) (4.75,
0.2, 1.0) (4.31, 0, 1) (4.31, 0, 1.5) (4.69, 0, 1) (4.69, 0, 1.5) (4.4, –0.3, 1)
(4.4, –0.3, 1.5) (4.6, –0.3, 1) (4.6, –0.3, 1.5) (4.25, –0.5, 1) (4.25, –0.5, 1.5)
(4.75, –0.5, 1) (4.75, –0.5, 1.5)
Geometry → Create → Line → join of all points respectively
Geometry → Create → NURBS surfaces → Automatic → number of sides
4
Geometry → Create → Volume → Automatic 6-sided volumes
Create leg 2
Geometry → points → (4.25, 6.5, 0.2) (4.25, 7.0, 0.2) (4.75, 6.5, 0.2) (4.75,
7.0, 0.2) (4.31, 6.5, 0) (4.31, 7, 0) (4.69, 6.5, 0) (4.69, 7, 0) (4.4, 6.5, –0.3)
(4.4, 7, –0.3) (4.69, 6.5, 0.0) (4.69, 7, 0) (4.4, 6.5, –0.3) (4.4, 7, –0.3) (4.6,
6.5, –0.3) (4.6, 7, –0.3) (4.25, 6.5, –0.5) (4.25, 7, –0.5) (4.75, 6.5, –0.5)
(4.75, 7, –0.5)
Geometry → Create → Line → join of all points respectively
Geometry → Create → NURBS surfaces → Automatic → number of sides
4
Geometry → Create → Volume → Automatic 6-sided volumes
Create Tip
Geometry → points → (4.5, 3, 1) (4.5, 5, 1) (4.5, 3, 0.8) (4.5, 5, 0.8) (4.3,
3, 0.6) (4.3, 5, 0.6) (4.7, 3, 0.6) (4.7, 5, 0.6) (4.1, 3, 0.6) (4.1, 5, 0.6) (4.9,
3, 0.6) (4.9, 5, 0.6) (4.27, 3, 0.2) (4.27, 5, 0.2) (4.73, 3, 0.2) (4.73, 5, 0.2)
(4.25, 3, 0) (4.25, 5, 0) (4.75, 3, 0) (4.75, 5, 0)
Geometry → Create → Line → join of all points respectively
Geometry → Create → NURBS surfaces → Automatic → number of sides
4
Geometry → Create → Volume → Automatic 6-sided volumes

Material assignment

Piezoelectric materials
Piezoelectric ceramic material properties using ATILA are shown in Fig.
7.16.

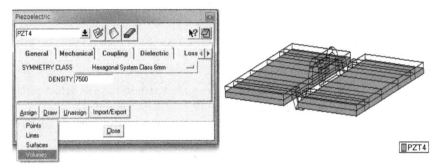

7.16 Material condition of PZT layer.

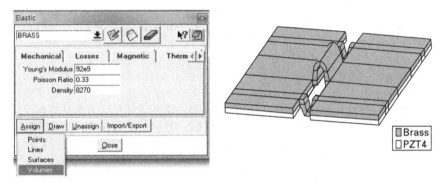

7.17 Material condition of a tiny motor.

Data → Materials → Piezoelectric → PZT4 → Assign → Pick volumes
Click Draw → All materials → Check the material of assigned as PZT4

Elastic materials
The material properties of the elastic element using ATILA are assigned
and shown in Fig. 7.17.

Data → Materials → Piezoelectric → Brass → Assign → Pick volumes
Click Draw → All materials → Check the material of assigned as Brass
and PZT4

Boundary conditions

Problem – butterfly USM
Brass elastic material – 5 by 8, t = 0.2 mm
PZT 4 – 4 by 8, t = 0.2

Polarization/Local Axes

Data → Conditions → Volumes → Geometry → Polarization (Cartesian) → Define Polarization (P1) (0,0,0.2) direction.
Choose 3 polarization (Local-Axes P1) → Choose the PZT all three volumes → Finish.

Potential

The boundary conditions of electrical potentials for butterfly USMs using ATILA are assigned as shown in Fig. 7.18.
Data → Conditions → Surfaces → Electric Potential → Ground → Assign the top two surfaces of the PZT.
Data → Conditions → Forced Potential 20.0 with phase 0 → Assign the bottom right-side surface
Data → Conditions → Forced Potential 20.0 with phase 90 → Assign the bottom left-side surface
This is how sine and cosine are applied on PZT plates.

Displacement condition

The boundary conditions of displacement for butterfly USMs using ATILA are assigned as shown in Fig. 7.19.
Data → Conditions → Surfaces → Displacement → X,Y, and Z displacement → Clamped → Assign the PZT Leg bottom surfaces. To check assignment → Draw → All conditions → Include local axes.

Meshing

The assignment of mesh for butterfly USMs is shown in Fig. 7.20.

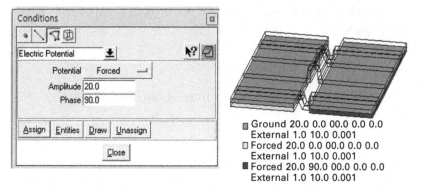

7.18 Electrical potential condition of butterfly USM.

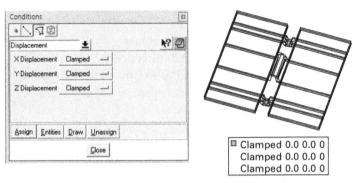

7.19 Displacement condition of butterfly USM.

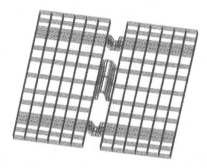

7.20 Mesh generation of butterfly USM.

Mapped Mesh

Meshing → Structured → Volume → Select all volumes → Then Cancel the further process.
Meshing → Structured → Line → Enter number to divide line → Generate
Problem Type
Data → Problem data → 3D, Harmonic, Click both Compute Stress and Include Losses

Frequency

Data → Problem data → Harmonic → Interval (20,000-150,000 Hz)

Calculation

Calculate → Calculate window → Start
Post Process/View results
Click to open the post calculation domain.

Click Admittance/Impedance result
Admittance Peak Points: X Hz and X Hz → This peak corresponds to the
First and Second resonance modes.

An admittance plot of the butterfly piezoelectric linear motor based on the
results of modal analysis is presented in Fig. 7.21. Longitudinal and transverse
vibrations are detected according to frequency change. The vibration shapes
and the frequencies of the motor are illustrated in Plate VIII (between pages
194 and 195) when electric signals with phase difference of $\pi/2$ are applied
to each piezoelectric layer. Linear motions can be finally generated when
superposition of two different vibration modes is effectively excited at a
certain frequency.

View animation – vibration mode at particular frequency
View results → Default analysis/Step → Harmonic-magnitude → Set a
Frequency
Double Click loading frequency: 61 kHz Harmonic case → Click ok (single-
click and watt for a while)
Set Deformation → Displacement
View results → Deformation → Displacement.
Parameter other than displacement
Set results view → View results → Contour fill → Electric Potential or von
Mises stress.
After setting both "Results view" and "Deformation" → Click to see the
Animation.

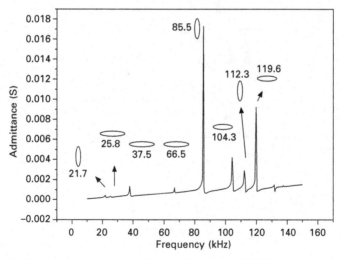

7.21 Admittance curves of butterfly-shaped USM.

When this motor is driven at an input frequency of 75 kHz corresponding to the intermediate frequency between the two resonances, superposed elliptical motions can be detected on the tip of the motor as shown in Plate IX (between pages 194 and 195). These elliptical motions finally compel the motor to move linearly.

7.4.3   Fabrication of butterfly-shaped ultrasonic linear motor

Based on the simulated results, actual piezoelectric motors were manufactured. Two protrusions heading for the opposite direction of the contact point tip were also built to fix the piezoelectric transducer to a supporter using epoxy. Figure 7.22 shows the components of the motor. A schematic of the butterfly linear motor is shown in Fig. 7.23. The center of the elastic plate connecting both the wings is bent to make a tip for a point contact to a linear guide.

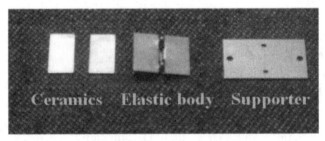

7.22 Components of butterfly-shaped USM.

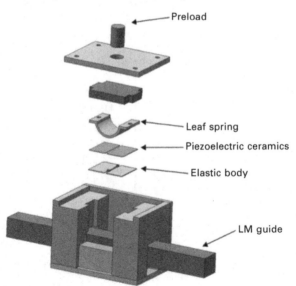

7.23 Schematic of butterfly-shaped USM.

7.5   Conclusions

The goals of this research were the development of a high performance miniature piezoelectric ultrasonic linear motor and evaluation of the characteristics of the motor operating in flexural mode. From this chapter, the results can be summarized as follows: the radial vibration of the piezoelectric ceramic disk is converted into flexural vibration through the transducer. This research was aimed at optimizing the piezoelectric motor design and constructive parameters. The length of the shaft, the diameter of the shaft and the thickness of the elastic material on the motor were experimented with so that their frictional and resonance conditions matched the moving element of the motor. ATILA finite element analysis software was used extensively to optimize and understand the behavior of the transducers used in the motors. Resonance frequencies, vibration modes, admittance, admittance spectra, and displacements in the Cartesian coordinate were calculated. The proposed motors were fabricated with various transducer ranges in size 4 ϕ, 5.5 ϕ and 7.6 ϕ mm in diameter. Using these conditions, when the modified motor had the forces 20, 50 and 100 g·f, the velocity of 20, 40 and 50 mm/sec were achieved, respectively. The advantage of the modified motor is its thin design, which makes it suitable for installation in a camera as an automatic focusing device. It is expected to be utilized for miniature mobile device application and medical applications. A novel piezoelectric linear motor with a low profile has been proposed and its characteristics have been investigated. The butterfly-shaped piezoelectric transducer has successfully generated an elliptical motion on the connecting tip. The superposition of the longitudinal and transverse vibrations led to efficient motor behavior. A butterfly-shaped motor with a very low profile of ~1mm was successfully driven with the resonance frequency superposed with the longitudinal and transverse vibration mode. A manufactured butterfly motor with a very low profile of ~1mm has been successfully driven, presenting the following dynamic properties: a maximum velocity of 88 mm/s and a thrust force of 162 g at the intermediate frequency range between two different resonance frequencies. In particular, the butterfly configuration can be easily realized using conventional metal–ceramic bonding technologies with a very low manufacturing cost. It can clearly be seen that the suggested motor in this chapter can be candidate for slim electronic devices. Ultrasonic piezoelectric motors with different operating principles and structures have been successfully designed and manufactured using ATILA and providing not only mechanical FEA but also the optimization of piezoelectric actuators. In particular, the electrical and dynamic properties of the designed motors could be easily explored as functions of various sizes and harmonic resonance frequencies through the ATILA simulation. This approach is very useful to understand the operating principles and expections of the final dynamic behavior.

7.6   References

1. P. D. Atherton and K. Uchino, 'New developments on piezo motors and mechanisms', *Actuator 98, 6th International Conference on New Acturators*, Bremen, Germany, 164–169, 1998.
2. ATILA, a 3D FEM Software for piezoelectric and magnetostrictive structures, Magsoft(US), 1998.
3. Y. Bar-Cohen, X. Bao and W. Grandia, 'Rotary ultrasonic motors actuated by traveling flexural waves', *Proceedings of the Smart Structure and Materials*, San Diego, CA, 1–5 March 1998.
4. M. Bexell and S. Johansson, 'Characteristic of a piezoelectric miniature motor', *Actuator 96, 5th International Conference on New Actuators*, Bremen, Germany, 173–176 1996.
5. M. Brissaud, 'Characterization of piezoceramics', *IEEE Trans. Ultrason. Ferroelect. Freq. Cont.* 38, 603–617, 1991.
6. W. Brener, G. Haddad, H. Detter, G. Popovic, A. Vujanic and N. Delic, 'The measurement of minimotors and micromotors torque-characteristic using miniaturized cable brake', *Microsystem Technologies*, 68–71, 1997.
7. J. Zhang, A.-C. Hladky-Hennion, W. J. Hughes and R. E. Newnham, 'Modeling and underwater characterization of cymbal transducers and arrays', *IEEE UFFC*, Vol. 48, No. 2, 560–568, 2001.
8. S.-H. Park, J. Agraz, S. Tuncdemir, Y.-D. Kim, R. Eitel, C. Randall and K. Uchino, 'Delta-shaped piezoelectric ultrasonic motor for 2-dimensional positioning', *Jpn. J. Appl. Phys.* 47, 313–318, 2008.
9. A.-C. Hladky-Hennion, 'Finite element analysis of the propagation of acoustic waves in waveguides', *Journal of Sound and Vibration*, 192(2), 119–136, 1996.
10. A.-C. Hladky-Hennion and P. Langlet, 'Finite element analysis of the propagation of acoustic waves along waveguides immersed in water', *Journal of Sound and Vibration*, 200(4), 519–530, 1997.
11. A.-C. Hladky-Hennion, P. Langlet and R. Bossut, 'Finite element modeling of radiating waves in immersed wedges', *Journal of Sound and Vibration*, 212(2), 265–274, 1998.
12. S.-J. Yoon and H.-P. Ko, Novel piezoelectric linear ultrasonic motor based on shaking beam, in *18th International Congress on Acoustics*, Kyoto, Japan, April 4, 2004.
13. H.-P. Ko, S. Kim, C.-Y. Kang, H.-J. Kim, S.-J. Yoon, 'Optimization of a piezoelectric linear motor in terms of the contact parameters', *Mater. Chem. Phys.* 90, 322–326, 2005.
14. H.-P. Ko, S. Kim, J.-S. Kim, H.-J. Kim, S.-J. Yoon, 'Wear and dynamic properties of piezoelectric ultrasonic motor with frictional materials coated stator', *Mater. Chem. Phys.* 90, 391–395, 2005.
15. T. Hemsel, M. Mracek, J. Twiefel, P. Vasilijev, 'Prezoelectric linear motor concepts based on coupling of longitudinal vibrations', *Ultrasonics*, 44, 591, 2006.
16. H.-P. Ko, S. Kim, S. N. Borodinas, P. E. Vasiljev, C.-Y. Kang, S.-J. Yoon, 'A novel tiny ultrasonic linear motor using the radial mode of a bimorph', *Sens. Actuator A* 125, 477, 2006.
17. W.-H. Lee, D.-S. Baek, C.-Y. Kang B.-K. Ju, S.-J. Yoon, 'Butterfly-shaped ultra slim piezoelectric ultrasonic linear motor', *Sens. Actuator A* 168, 127–130, 2011.

8
Piezocomposite applications of ATILA

A-C. HLADKY-HENNION, ISEN Lille, France

DOI: 10.1533/9780857096319.2.177

Abstract: Periodic structures have attracted considerable interest over the past three decades. Thus, passive structures with 1D or 2D periodicity are in standard use in underwater acoustics. Moreover doubly periodic active structures, such as 1–3 piezocomposite materials made of parallel piezoelectric bars embedded in a passive matrix, are also of great interest for mine hunting, underwater or medical ultrasonic imaging. In this chapter, a brief presentation of passive and active periodic structures is described. Then, the generic model developed for periodic studies is presented for the particular case of a 1–3 piezocomposite. The periodic structure is immersed in a fluid and the transmission and reflection coefficients are calculated. The test example discussed at the end of the chapter is devoted to an actual Alberich coating and an actual 1–3 piezocomposite for which previous experimental results are available.

Key words: periodic structures, compliant tube panel, Alberich anechoic coating, 1–3 piezocomposites, transmitting voltage response (TVR), free field voltage sensitivity (FFVS).

8.1   Introduction

In underwater acoustics, passive periodic structures with 1D or 2D periodicity are now in standard use. 1D periodicity corresponds, for example, to compliant tube gratings used to increase the level and directivity of low frequency sources or to isolate hydrophone arrays from structure-borne noise (Brigham 1977, Radlinski 1982, Hennion 1990). 2D periodicity can be associated with low frequency non reflecting or non transmitting multilayered coatings, called Alberich coatings, in which one or several layers contain doubly periodic inclusions, such as spherical or cylindrical cavities (Fig. 8.1), to enhance energy absorption via resonance effect (Lane 1981, Gaunaurd 1985, Hladky-Hennion 1991). Moreover, active periodic materials have also been developed by combining piezoelectric ceramics with passive polymers. Superior properties have been achieved in these composites by taking advantage of the most profitable properties of each of the constituents (Gururaja 1985, Smith 1984, Hladky-Hennion 1993), and a great variety of structures have been made, each characterized by the connectivity between their two phases. Among these materials, composites made of piezoceramic rods embedded in an epoxy matrix (Fig. 8.2) with a regular periodicity (1–3 connectivity) is a main constituent for sonic or ultrasonic transducer applications because

177

they offer improved electromechanical properties and the possibility to tailor these properties to optimize system performances (Gururaja 1985).

In order to explain the physical behavior of the passive periodic structures and to aid in their design, several authors have developed accurate mathematical models which have provided results in nice agreement with measured values. Multiple scattering approach (Brigham 1977) and wave guide approach (Radlinski 1982) have been used for the study of circular cylinders gratings and elongated tubes gratings respectively. For 1–3 piezocomposites, a simple analytical model considering thickness mode oscillations has been established, that is valid when the lateral spatial scale of the composite is fine enough for this composite (Smith 1984). The designer's possibilities related to the modeling of periodic structures are greatly broadened by using numerical methods, which allow the description of:

- any geometry
- anisotropy or piezoelectricity of the constitutive materials
- internal losses
- frequency dependence of the material properties
- specific electric boundary conditions, and
- normal or oblique incidence of the impinging wave.

This chapter presents a global 3D mathematical model, relying upon the ATILA finite element code, which has been developed to analyze the scattering or the radiation of plane acoustic waves from 1D or 2D immersed passive or active periodic structures at any incidence. The model requires a mesh of only one unit cell of the periodic structure, including a small part of the surrounding fluid domain. This simple approach is possible due to the use of classical Bloch type relations, the effects of the remaining fluid domain being accounted for by matching the pressure field in the finite element mesh with simple plane wave expansions of the incoming and outgoing waves. After an outline of the method, the chapter describes the results obtained for an Alberich coating (Fig. 8.1) and a 1–3 piezocomposite (Fig. 8.2). Comparison of the finite element results with measurements demonstrates that the finite element approach is accurate and well suited to describe the behavior of periodic structures.

8.2   General formulation

The generic model developed for periodic studies is presented for the particular case of a 1–3 piezocomposite. Its extension to any other doubly periodic active structure is straightforward. A 1–3 piezocomposite forms a doubly periodic network (Fig. 8.2). It is supposed to be coupled to semi-infinite fluid domains on both sides, infinite and doubly periodic in the x and y directions, its plane being normal to the z direction.

8.1 Picture of an Alberich anechoic coating with a doubly periodic array of cylindrical holes.

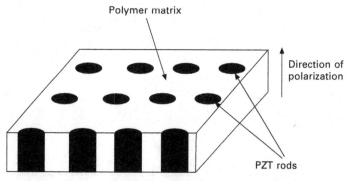

8.2 Schematic description of a 1–3 piezocomposite made of PZT rods embedded in a polymer matrix.

An active structure can be used as an emitter and radiates acoustic waves on both sides or solely on one side, which is then designed as the 'front' side. It can also be used as a receiver which scatters acoustic waves on both sides (reflected and transmitted waves) or solely on the front side (reflected waves only). In the second case, there is an incident plane wave impinging on the structure and coming from the front half space. In the case of passive structures, it is clearly evident that only the second case has to be considered. Moreover, for active structures and in the standard case in which all the piezoelectric elements are electrically connected in parallel, only a plane acoustic wave propagating along the z-axis can be emitted or detected. It is generally the case for 1–3 piezocomposite plates which are fully electroded on both sides. However, other electrical excitations or connections can be applied to enforce specific phase shifts between the piezoelectric elements. Then, plane waves, the propagation directions of which are oblique with respect to the z-axis, can be emitted or detected.

For sake of simplicity, the equations are presented without taking into account the electrical effects; the equations for an active periodic structure can be found in reference (Hladky-Hennion 1993). For modeling purposes, the whole domain is split into three successive regions by two planes which are parallel to the structure plane, the S+ and S− surfaces (Fig. 8.3). The first and the third regions are semi-infinite fluid domains. The second region includes the periodic structure and a small part of the surrounding fluid domain. The S+ and S− surfaces, parallel to the xOy plane, limit the finite element mesh and represent, respectively, the boundary between Regions

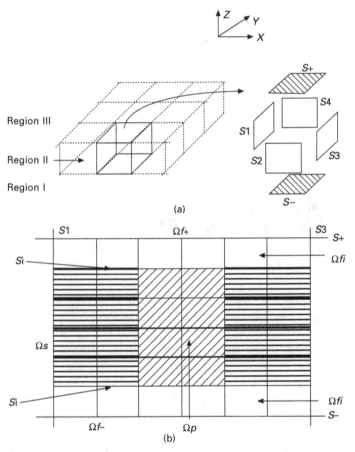

(a)

(b)

8.3 Schematic description of a doubly periodic structure used to define the S−, S+, S1, S2, S3 and S4 planes and finite element mesh of the cross section of the unit cell in the xOz plane.

I and II and the boundary between Regions II and III. The unit cell, which is $2d_1$ wide in the x direction, and $2d_2$ wide in the y direction, is limited by the $S1$ and $S3$ planes, parallel to the yOz plane, and the $S2$ and $S4$ planes, parallel to the xOz plane.

Because the structure is assumed to extend from $-\infty$ to $+\infty$ in the x and y directions and to be periodic, any space function F (pressure, displacement, electrical potential, etc.) has to satisfy the relation:

$$F(x + 2d_1, y + 2d_2, z) = F(x, y, z)\, e^{j2d_1 k_1 \sin\theta\cos\varphi}\, e^{j2d_2 k_1 \sin\theta\sin\varphi}$$

$$= F(x,y,z) e^{j\gamma_1} e^{j\gamma_2} \qquad [8.1]$$

where k_1 is the wave-number in Region I, θ is the angle between vector k_1 and the Oz axis, ϕ is the angle between the projection of vector k_1 in the xOy plane and the Ox axis. If the two fluid domains on both sides of the structure are different, the phase factor remains the same thanks to Snell-Descartes relations. Moreover, due to equation [8.1] and to the time independent wave equation, the total pressure in Regions I and II can be expanded in the form:

$$p^+(x,y,z) = \sum_{n,m=-\infty}^{+\infty} T_{nm}^p e^{jk_{nm3}z} e^{j\alpha_n x} e^{j\beta_m y} \qquad [8.2]$$

$$p^-(x,y,z) = p_i(x,y,z) + \sum_{n,m=-\infty}^{+\infty} R_{nm}^p e^{-jk_{nm1}z} e^{j\alpha_n x} e^{j\beta_m y}$$

where

$$p_i(x, y, z) = P_i e^{jk_1(x\sin\theta\cos\varphi + y\sin\theta\sin\varphi + z\cos\theta)} \qquad [8.3]$$

and

$$\alpha_n = \frac{n\pi}{d_1} + \frac{\gamma_1}{2d_1},\ \beta_m = \frac{m\pi}{d_2} + \frac{\gamma_2}{2d_2},\ k_{nm1}^2 = k_1^2 - \alpha_n^2 - \beta_m^2,\ k_{nm3}^2 = k_3^2 - \alpha_n^2 - \beta_m^2$$

$$[8.4]$$

In these equations, k_3 is the wave-number in Region III. p_i is the incident wave if it exists. Equation [8.2] represents a doubly infinite series of waves radiated or scattered by the structure. The R_{nm}^p and T_{nm}^p terms correspond respectively to the front and back Regions I and III and must be determined. In these expansions, elementary waves are either evanescent or propagating, depending on the sign of k_{nm1}^2 and k_{nm3}^2. In the same way, the pressure normal gradient can be expanded as a series of propagating and evanescent waves.

Due to the use of classical Bloch type relations between displacement, pressure or electrical potential values at points which are separated by the spatial period, only one unit cell of Region II is meshed with finite elements, including a small part of the surrounding fluid domain. If a steady-state harmonic analysis is considered, the complete system of equations is written as:

$$
\begin{bmatrix}
[K_{uu}] - \omega^2 [M] & [K_{u\phi}] & -[L] \\
[K_{u\phi}]^T & [K_{\phi\phi}] & [0] \\
-[L]^T & [0] & \dfrac{[H] - \omega^2 [M_1]}{\rho^2 c^2 \omega^2}
\end{bmatrix}
\begin{bmatrix}
U \\
\Phi \\
P
\end{bmatrix}
= -
\begin{bmatrix}
F \\
Q_p \\
\dfrac{\psi}{\rho\omega^2}
\end{bmatrix}
\qquad [8.5]
$$

where $[H]$ and $[M_1]$ are the fluid compressibility and consistent mass matrix, Ψ contains the nodal values of the pressure normal gradient on the fluid domain boundaries $S-$ and $S+$. Other terms in equation [8.5] are classical finite element terms and have been previously defined. This system can take into account damping in the materials through the use of complex elastic, piezoelectric and dielectric constants, depending or not upon the frequency.

8.2.1   Introduction of the periodic boundary conditions

The phase relation (equation [8.1]) between nodal values associated with the $S1$ and $S3$ planes on the one hand, and with the $S2$ and $S4$ planes on the other hand, are incorporated in the left hand side matrix of equation [8.5], defining the boundary conditions between adjacent cells. The phase relation is applied to the displacement, pressure and electrical potential on these planes. The resulting matrix is complex but hermitian. In terms of the finite element method, this operation is a static condensation of the degrees of freedom belonging to the $S3$ and $S4$ planes.

8.2.2   Introduction of the acoustic boundary conditions

To couple the remaining fluid domains, above the $S+$ surface and below the $S-$ surface, the pressure field described by the finite element interpolation is matched with the plane wave expansions of the incoming and outgoing waves. The formalism is described in Hennion (1990) and equations are not reproduced here. Writing the continuity equations introduces matrix relations between the nodal values of the pressure normal derivative and the nodal values of the pressure on the $S-$ and $S+$ surfaces, which are then incorporated into system (equation [8.5]). Instead of a matching with the plane wave expansions, a finite element method-boundary element method (FEM-BEM) coupling can also be used to take into account the fluid domains above and below the periodic structure (Wilm 2003).

8.2.3   Introduction of the electric boundary conditions

Then, in practical cases, the general system of equation [8.5] has to be modified, depending upon the electrical boundary conditions and the type of application. Thus, in the simple case of passive structure, the second line and the second column of equation [8.5] have been deleted. The resulting system provides the displacement field and the pressure field in the whole unit cell, which allows the computation of the transmission and reflection coefficients. In the case of an active structure, the electrical potential is first split into two parts, one corresponding to the applied electrical potential which is the same for all the nodes of the hot electrode, the other for the electrical potential nodal values for all the inner nodes. The reference potential is assumed to be zero (grounded electrode). Then, two cases can be briefly examined:

1.   In the first case, the transmitting voltage response (TVR) of the structure is determined, which is the ratio of the far-field acoustic pressure amplitude (plane wave amplitude) to the voltage amplitude applied across the electrical input terminals. In that case, no incident pressure is applied.
2.   In the second case, the free field voltage sensitivity (FFVS) is determined, which is the ratio of the output open circuit voltage amplitude to the free field acoustic pressure amplitude of the undisturbed incident plane wave. In that case, an incident pressure is prescribed.

8.3   Transmission coefficient of an Alberich coating

The Alberich coating described in Fig. 8.1 has been modeled and its acoustical behavior analyzed. The panel is 4 cm thick. The cylindrical inclusions, which are 2 cm high and whose diameter is 1.5 cm, are arranged as a doubly periodic structure. The grating spacing is 5 cm. The panel is made of polyurethane, the physical properties of which depend on both temperature and frequency. These have been obtained from master curves provided by the manufacturer, and updated parameter values have been used for the computation at each frequency. The mesh is presented in Fig. 8.4. It satisfies the $\lambda/4$ convergence criterion for frequencies lower than 17 kHz.

Figure 8.5 compares the finite element results with measurements, when the grating is excited by a plane wave at normal incidence. The overall agreement is good. The displacement field of the elementary cell is displayed in Fig. 8.6 at the resonance frequency, in the xOz plane. The amplitude is normalized. The resonance displacement field is a combination of a radial motion of the hole wall and a small deformation of the cover layer (Lane 1981, Gaunaurd 1985). Nevertheless, the absorption mechanism is complex because the losses in the polyurethane introduce an important phase shift

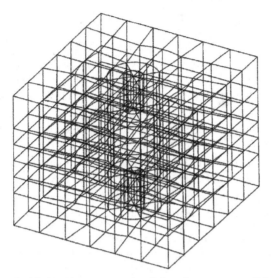

8.4 Finite element mesh of the elementary cell for the Alberich anechoic coating. The center part is the air cavity.

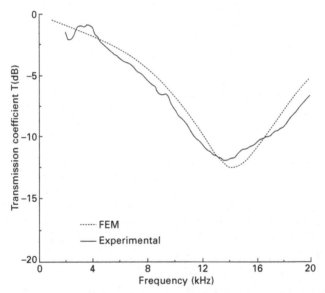

8.5 Frequency variations of the transmission coefficient of the Alberich anechoic coating measured (full line) and calculated by FEM (dotted line).

for the displacement across the thickness. Thus, it seems that simple models can only provide a first insight in such a case and that numerical modeling is required. Moreover, Fig. 8.6 shows that shear effects are large.

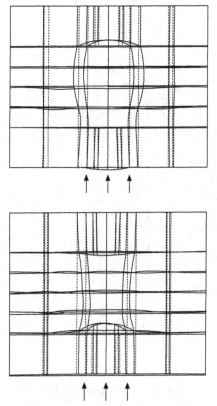

8.6 Displacement field of the elementary cell of the Alberich anechoic coating, at 16 kHz in the *xOz* plane at two different moments separated by $\frac{1}{4}$ of the period. The dashed lines correspond to the rest position (Reprinted with permission from A.C. Hladky-Hennion and J.N. Decarpigny (1991), *J. Acoust. Soc. Am.*, **90**, 3356–3367. Copyright 1991, Acoustical Society of America).

8.4   1–3 piezocomposite

The test example discussed in this section is devoted to an actual 1–3 piezocomposite for which previous experimental results are available (Gururaja 1985). The sample corresponds to a 20 percent Navy Type II piezoelectric ceramic composite in Spurrs epoxy. The epoxy properties are $\rho = 1\,100$ kg/ m^3, $c_l = 2\,200$ m/s and $c_t = 1\,000$ m/s; the loss angles for the longitudinal and transverse wave velocities being, respectively, 0.03 and 0.10. The rod diameter is 0.45 mm, the periodicity is 0.90 mm and the thickness is 0.66 mm (sample 200). The transducer is air backed.

Figure 8.7 presents the finite element mesh of the unit cell, where the cylindrical part corresponds to the piezoelectric bar embedded in epoxy. Figure 8.8 presents the variations of the FFVS versus frequency, calculated

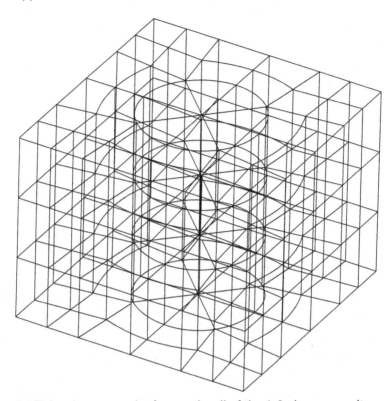

8.7 Finite element mesh of one unit cell of the 1–3 piezocomposite.

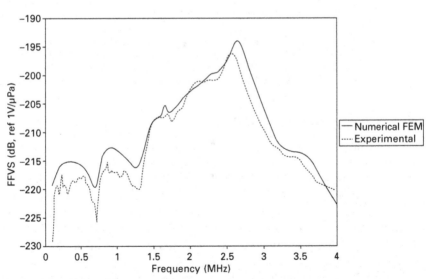

8.8 Frequency variations of the free field voltage sensitivity (FFVS) for the 1–3 piezocomposite measured (dotted line) and calculated by FEM (solid line).

with the finite element method and measured. The agreement is good between the curves and the discrepancy is attributed to uncertainties on the material losses. On the one hand, in the lower part of the curve, the FFVS minima correspond to the first lateral resonance modes which are associated with standing waves in the epoxy and are related to the piezoceramic rod periodicity. These modes are due to the classical Bragg scattering of laterally propagating shear waves, with polarization parallel to the rods. Their frequencies are independent of thickness. Figure 8.9(a) presents the corresponding displacement field of the unit cell in the diagonal plane at 0.7 MHz. On the other hand, the maximum of the curve corresponds to the excitation of the thickness mode of the piezoceramic rods. Figure 8.9(b) presents the corresponding displacement field of the unit cell at 2.6 MHz. It demonstrates that the sensitivity maximum corresponds to the excitation of the thickness mode of the piezoceramic rods. The in-air antiresonance frequency of this mode being 3.27 MHz, the shift due to water loading is close to 20%.

Figure 8.10 compares the frequency variations of the TVR, measured and computed with the finite element method. It also shows quite good agreement. The maximum of the response at 2.0 MHz corresponds to the excitation of the thickness mode of the piezoceramic rods, the in air resonance frequency of which is 2.92 MHz, thus displaying a 29% shift due to water loading.

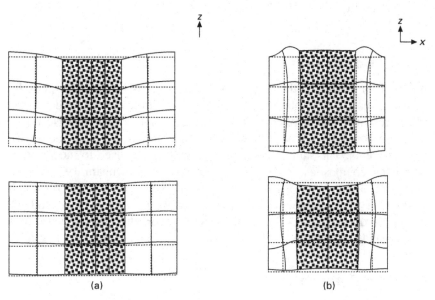

(a)   (b)

8.9 Real and imaginary parts of the displacement field for the 1–3 piezocomposite at: (a) 0.7 MHz in the diagonal plane and (b) 2.6 MHz in the *xOz* plane. Dashed lines correspond to the rest position and the displacement amplitude is arbitrary.

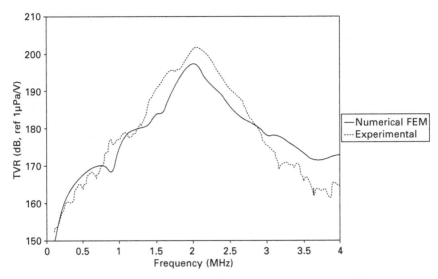

8.10 Frequency variations of the transmitting voltage response (TVR), measured (dotted line) and calculated by FEM (solid line).

This example clearly demonstrates that the finite element approach described here constitutes an accurate tool for the analysis of the behavior of 1–3 piezocomposites, and further, can be used as guidance for optimization purposes.

8.5   Conclusion

A model for predicting the behavior of immersed passive or active periodic structures has been implemented in the ATILA finite element code. It has been presented and applied to the analysis of Alberich coatings and of 1–3 piezocomposites. The results of the model are in nice agreement with measurements. The same numerical approach can be used to model other promising composites, with other connectivities (Newnham 1978), or to improve 1–3 piezocomposites or with material with improved properties such as single crystals. Another approach to the previous problem is the study of the wave propagation in periodic materials that gives other characteristics such as passbands or stopbands. This extension is the goal of the next chapter.

8.6   References

G.A. Brigham, J.J. Libuha and R.P. Radlinski (1977), 'Analysis of scattering from large planar gratings of compliant cylindrical shells', *J. Acoust. Soc. Am.* **61**, 48–59.

G.C. Gaunaurd (1985), 'Comments on "Absorption mechanisms for waterborne sound in Alberich anechoic layers"', *Ultrasonics* **23**(2), 90–91.

T.R. Gururaja, W.A Schulze, L.E. Cross and R.E. Newnham (1985), 'Piezoelectric composite materials for ultrasonic transducer applications. Part II: evaluation of ultrasonic medical applications', *IEEE Trans. Sonics Ultrason.* **SU–32**, 499–513.

A.C. Hennion, R. Bossut, J.N. Decarpigny and C. Audoly (1990), 'Analysis of the scattering of a plane acoustic wave by a periodic structure using the finite element method: application to compliant tube gratings', *J. Acoust. Soc. Am.* **87**, 1861–1870.

A.C. Hladky-Hennion and J.N. Decarpigny (1991), 'Analysis of the scattering of a plane acoustic wave by a doubly periodic structure using the finite element method: application to Alberich anechoic coatings', *J. Acoust. Soc. Am.* **90**, 3356–3367.

A.C. Hladky-Hennion and J.N. Decarpigny (1993), 'Finite element modeling of active periodic structures: application to 1–3 piezocomposites', *J. Acoust. Soc. Am.* **94**(2), 621–635.

R. Lane (1981), 'Absorption mechanisms for waterborne sound in Alberich anechoic layers', *Ultrasonics* **19**(1), 28–30.

R.E. Newnham, D.P. Skinner and L.E. Cross (1978), 'Connectivity and piezoelectric-pyroelectric composites', *Mat. Res. Bull.* **13**, 525–536.

R.P. Radlinski and M.M. Simon (1982), 'Scattering by multiple gratings of compliant tubes', *J. Acoust. Soc. Am.* **72**, 607–614.

W.A. Smith, A.A. Shaulov and B.M. Singer (1984), 'Properties of composite piezoelectric materials for ultrasonic transducers'. In: *Proc. IEEE Ultrasonics Symposium*, pp. 539–544.

M. Wilm, S. Ballandras, A. Reinhardt, V. Laude, R. Armanti, W. Daniau, F. Lanterai, J.F. Gelly and O. Burat (2003), 'A 3-D mixed finite element/boundary element model for the simulation of periodic ultrasound transducers radiating in layered media'. *In: IEEE Ultrasonics Symposium*, pp. 1654–1657.

9

Phononic crystal (PC) applications of ATILA

A-C. HLADKY-HENNION, ISEN Lille, France

DOI: 10.1533/9780857096319.2.190

Abstract: Phononic crystals (PCs) are usually defined as artificial materials made of periodic arrangement of scatterers embedded in a matrix. The band structure of PCs may present under certain conditions absolute band gaps: they display frequency ranges in which waves cannot propagate. This fact is analogous to photonic band gaps for electromagnetic waves. Therefore, such systems can be applied as noise and vibration isolation, acoustic wave guiding, acoustic filters, etc. Moreover, band structures of PCs may exhibit dispersion curves with a negative slope, inducing negative refraction phenomenon. In this chapter, the general formalism is first presented. It is applied in the second part to a phononic crystal inducing filtering application and in the last section, negative refraction of elastic waves is presented for focusing application.

Key words: phononic crystals, pass band and stop band, guiding applications, negative refraction.

9.1   Introduction

The propagation of elastic waves in periodic composite media, such as phononic crystals, has attracted a great deal of interest for the last two decades (Vasseur 1997, Yang 2002). Phononic crystals (PCs) are 2D or 3D periodic arrangements of inclusions in a matrix. They may exhibit absolute band gaps where the propagation of elastic waves is forbidden in all directions. These band gaps arise under certain conditions of contrast in density and elastic properties, composition, geometry of the array of inclusions, and inclusion shape. When the periodicity of a PC is broken, it is possible to create highly localized defects within the acoustic band gap, which are analogous to localized modes in photonic crystals and to localized impurity states in semiconductors. Extended defects such as rows of different inclusions in the phononic lattice have been shown to guide elastic waves within the crystal band gap. Defect modes can then lead to functionalities such as filtering and multiplexing (Khelif 2005).

Moreover, band structures of PCs may exhibit dispersion curves with a negative slope, i.e., the wave vector and the group-velocity vector associated with an acoustic wave point in opposite directions. This property is typical of a left-handed material and implies a negative index of refraction in the Snell–Descartes law (Yang 2004, Page 2003). Using negative-index PCs,

190

flat superlenses able to focus elastic waves with a resolution lower than the diffraction limit have been realized (Sukhovich 2008, Sukhovich 2009). Such superlenses have potential applications in the fields of medical imaging or ultrasonic beam-based therapy.

In this chapter, the next section presents the general formulation in the case of a 2D PC. Then, two examples are presented. The first one concerns piezoelectric PC plates for waveguiding applications, the second one concerns negative refraction of longitudinal waves in the case of a triangular lattice of steel rods in an epoxy matrix.

9.2   General formulation

To present the model, a doubly periodic structure is considered. The array can be square, rectangular, and triangular or more generally can have an oblique symmetry (Fig. 9.1). For the sake of simplicity, the square array is presented in this chapter. The periodic structure contains two or more different phases, and consists, for instance, in a periodic array of holes in a solid matrix or a periodic array of cylindrical rods or tubes in a solid matrix. The structure is supposed to be infinite and periodic in the $x0y$ plane and is infinite and uniform in the third direction, thus the problem is bidimensional, depending only on the x and y coordinates using plane strain conditions. The whole domain is split into successive cells (Fig. 9.2). Due to the periodicity of the structure, the $A1$ and $A2$ lines, parallel to the y axis, and the $B1$ and $B2$ lines, parallel to the x axis, limit the unit cell, which is $2d_1$ wide in the x direction and $2d_2$ wide in the y direction. In Fig. 9.2, corners are marked by letter C.

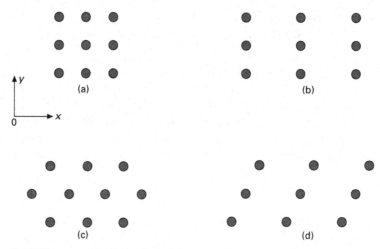

9.1 Different periodic lattices (a) square (b) rectangular (c) triangular or centered hexagonal and (d) oblique.

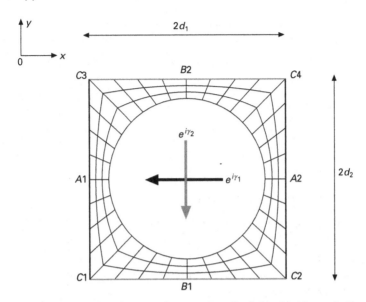

9.2 Schematic description of one unit cell of the doubly periodic structure, used to define the *A1, A2, B1* and *B2* lines, the *C1, C2, C3,* and *C4* corners, and the phase relation between the lines.

Then the structure is excited by a plane, monochromatic wave, the direction of incidence of which is marked by an angle θ with respect to the positive y axis. The incident wave is characterized by a real wave vector $\vec{k}$, the modulus of which is the wave number k. Because the structure is assumed to extend from $-\infty$ to $+\infty$ in the x and y directions and to be periodic, any space function F (pressure, displacement, electrical potential, etc.) has to satisfy the classical Bloch relation:

$$F(x + 2d_1, y + 2d_2) = F(x, y)\, e^{j2d_1 k \sin\theta} e^{j2d_2 k \cos\theta}$$

$$= F(x, y)\, e^{j\gamma_1} e^{j\gamma_2} \qquad [9.1]$$

Using the relation in equation [9.1] allows us to reduce the model to only one unit cell which can be meshed using finite elements (Fig. 9.2). Writing the relation in equation [9.1] between the displacement values for nodes separated by one period provides the boundary conditions between adjacent cells. Using, the finite element method, a modal analysis is considered and the whole system of equations is classically:

$$([K_{uu}] - \omega^2[M])U = F \qquad [9.2]$$

where the unknown is the vector of nodal values of the displacement U. $[K_{uu}]$ and $[M]$ are, respectively, the structure stiffness and coherent mass matrices. ω is the angular frequency. F contains the nodal values of the applied forces.

The application of the periodic boundary conditions implies that the phase relation in equation [9.1] between nodal values belonging to the $A1$ and $A2$ lines, on the one hand, to the $B1$ and $B2$ lines on the other hand, has to be incorporated in the matrix equation [9.2]. The unit cell is divided into nine parts: the four lines $A1$, $A2$, $B1$ and $B2$, the four corners $C1$, $C2$, $C3$ and $C4$ and the inner domain I. Displacement vector U and force vector F are then split into the corresponding nine parts. Due to the relation in equation [9.1], their components have to verify:

$$U_{A2} = e^{j\gamma_1}U_{A1}; \ U_{B2} = e^{j\gamma_2}U_{B1}; \ U_{C2} = e^{j\gamma_1}U_{C1};$$

$$U_{C3} = e^{j\gamma_2} U_{C1}; \ U_{C4} = e^{j\gamma_1+j\gamma_2} U_{C1} \tag{9.3}$$

Then owing to the equilibrium of interconnecting forces between two adjacent cells, the relation in equation (9.1) leads to analogous relations for the force vector. F_I, which corresponds to forces applied to inner nodes, is equal to zero. Defining the reduced vector U_R as a vector containing values of the displacement on the $A1$ and $B1$ lines, on the $C1$ corner and in the inner domain I, relations in equation [9.3] imply a simple matrix relation between U and U_R which can be written as:

$$U = [P_U]U_R = [P_U]\begin{bmatrix} U_{A1} \\ U_{B1} \\ U_{C1} \\ U_I \end{bmatrix} \tag{9.4}$$

In the same way, a matrix relation can be defined between the vector F and the reduced vector F_R:

$$F = [P_F]F_R = [P_F]\begin{bmatrix} F_{A1} \\ F_{B1} \\ F_{C1} \\ 0 \end{bmatrix} \tag{9.5}$$

Thus, the equation to be solved can be reduced to:

$$[P_U]^{*T}([K_{uu}] - \omega^2[M])[P_R]U_R = ([K_R] - \omega^2[M_R])U_R$$

$$= [P_U]^{*T}[P_F]F_R \tag{9.6}$$

Finally, the matrices $[K_R]$ and $[M_R]$ are divided following four parts, $A1$, $B1$, $C1$ and I and the resulting equation is :

$$([K_R] - \omega^2 [M_R]) \ U_R = 0 \tag{9.7}$$

A detailed expression of $[K_R]$ and $[M_R]$ is presented in Langlet (1995). For a given value of the wave number k, the phase shifts of equations [9.1] and

[9.3] are deduced and incorporated in the relations in equations [9.4] and [9.5]. The resolution of the system in equation [9.7] gives the corresponding eigen values ω, that are real because the reduced matrices $[K_R]$ and $[M_R]$ are hermitian.

The angular frequency ω is a periodical function of wave vector $\vec{k}$. Thus, the problem can be reduced to the first Brillouin zone (Brillouin 1953). The dispersion curves are built varying $\vec{k}$ on the first Brillouin zone for a given propagation direction. The whole diagram is deduced using symmetries.

9.3   Phononic crystals for guiding applications

Absolute band gaps may appear in the band structure of a phononic crystal plate composed of passive or piezoelectric materials. The existence of these absolute gaps depends strongly on the ratio of the plate thickness to the crystal periodicity with the largest gap occurring when this ratio is around 1. To obtain gaps at telecommunication frequencies of the order of gigahertz, the thickness of the plate should be of the order of micrometers. In this section, the properties of piezoelectric phononic crystal freestanding plates are reported. The introduction of rectilinear defects is also considered and it demonstrates the ability of the defect to guide acoustic waves with frequencies falling inside the forbidden band of the parent phononic crystal plate.

The phononic crystal considered in this section is composed of a square array of parallel cylindrical air inclusions holes of radius R drilled in a PZT5A piezoelectric matrix (Fig. 9.3). The cylindrical air inclusions are assumed parallel to the z axis. The filling factor f of inclusions is defined as $\pi R^2/a^2$, and is equal to 0.7 to ensure the existence of an absolute band gap in the band structure of the bulk phononic crystal. The lattice parameter a of the periodic array is equal to 0.77 μm in order to locate the band gap around 1.5 GHz, a common frequency in telecommunications. The thickness of the plate is denoted by h. Optimal conditions for gap formation in the plate

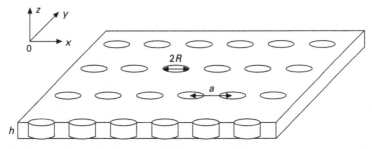

9.3 Phononic crystal plate of thickness *h*. The basic phononic crystal is composed of a square array of parallel cylindrical air inclusions (holes) of radius *R* drilled in a piezoelectric matrix. The lattice parameter is *a*.

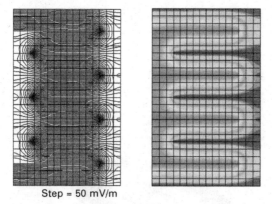

Step = 50 mV/m

Plate I Potential distribution around the internal electrode edges in an eight-layered multilayer actuator (2D simulation results).

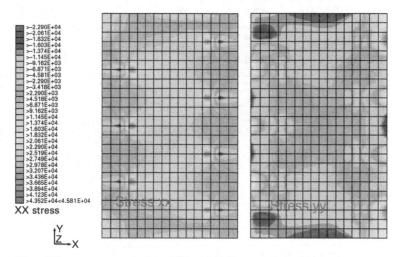

>−2.290E+04
>−2.061E+04
>−1.832E+04
>−1.603E+04
>−1.374E+04
>−1.145E+04
>−9.162E+03
>−6.871E+03
>−4.581E+03
>−2.290E+03
>−3.418E+03
>2.290E+03
>4.518E+03
>6.871E+03
>9.162E+03
>1.145E+04
>1.374E+04
>1.603E+04
>1.832E+04
>2.061E+04
>2.290E+04
>2.519E+04
>2.749E+04
>2.978E+04
>3.207E+04
>3.436E+04
>3.665E+04
>3.894E+04
>4.123E+04
>4.352E+04<4.581E+04

XX stress

Stress xx

Stress yy

Plate II Stress concentration (XX and YY) around the internal electrode edges (2D simulation results).

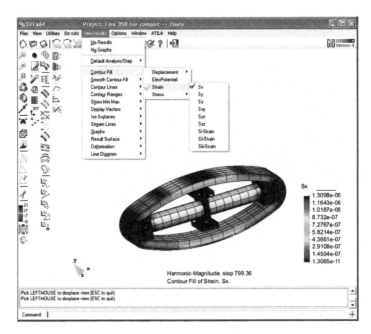

Plate III Contour fill of strain.

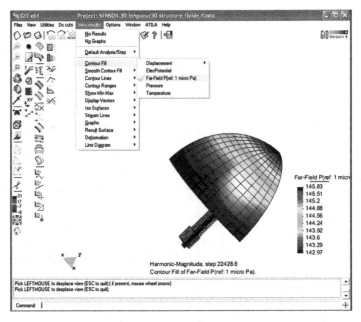

Plate IV Contour fill of far-field.

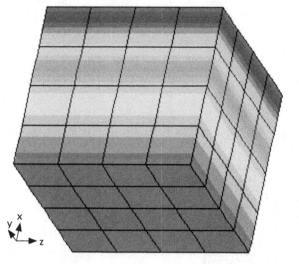
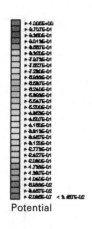

Potential

Plate V Potential profile in the cube.

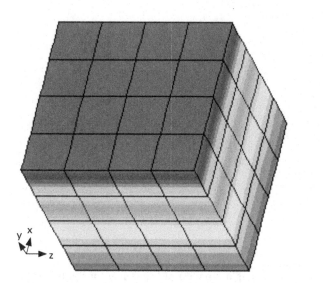
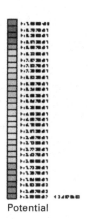

Potential

Plate VI Potential profile in the cube.

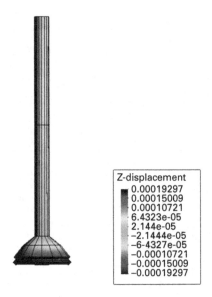

Z-displacement
0.00019297
0.00015009
0.00010721
6.4323e-05
2.144e-05
−2.1444e-05
−6.4327e-05
−0.00010721
−0.00015009
−0.00019297

Plate VII The first resonance mode of a tiny USM (65.8 kHz).

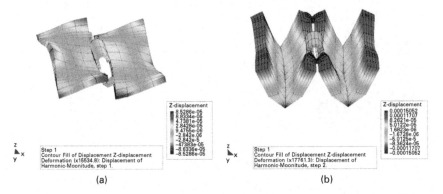

Plate VIII The transverse vibration mode 66 kHz (a) and longitudinal vibration mode 88 kHz (b) as a function of frequency for the butterfly-shaped USM.

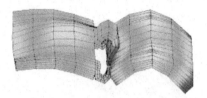

Z-displacement
8.3949e-07
6.5294e-07
4.6838e-07
2.7983e-07
9.387e-08
-9.3286e-08
-2.7984e-07
-4.564e-07
-6.5295e-07
-8.3949e-07

z
y x

Step 2
Contour Fill of Displacement Z-displacement
Deformation (x37255e.06): Displacement of Harmonic-Magnitude, step 2.

Plate IX Elliptical motion on the tip 76 kHz.

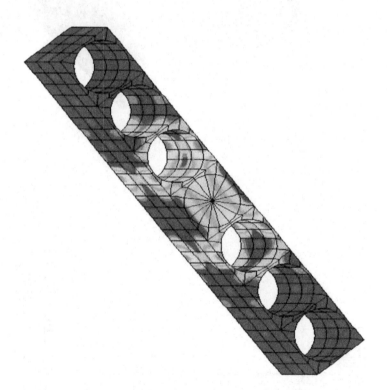

Plate X Modulus of the displacement field for the waveguide mode at 1.221 GHz and a wavenumber equal to 3.468 μm⁻¹. The red color corresponds to the maximum displacement and the blue color to the minimum.

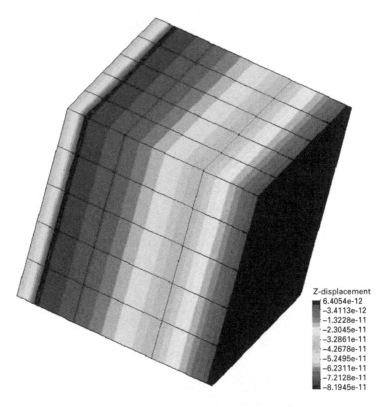

Z-displacement

6.4054e-12
−3.4113e-12
−1.3228e-11
−2.3045e-11
−3.2861e-11
−4.2678e-11
−5.2495e-11
−6.2311e-11
−7.2128e-11
−8.1945e-11

Plate XI Contour fill of the *Z* displacement at the resonance frequency.

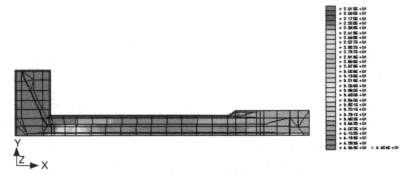

Plate XII Temperature profile from the finite element analysis (°C).

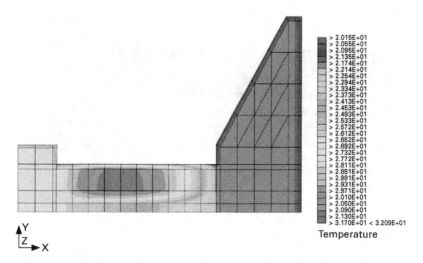

Plate XIII Temperature profile from the finite element analysis (°C).

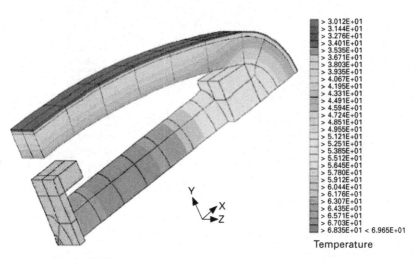

Plate XIV Temperature profile from the finite element analysis (°C).

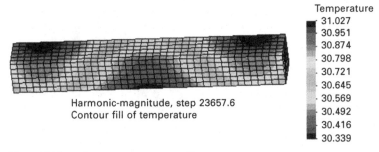

Temperature
31.027
30.951
30.874
30.798
30.721
30.645
30.569
30.492
30.416
30.339

Harmonic-magnitude, step 23657.6
Contour fill of temperature

Plate XV Steady temperature profile.

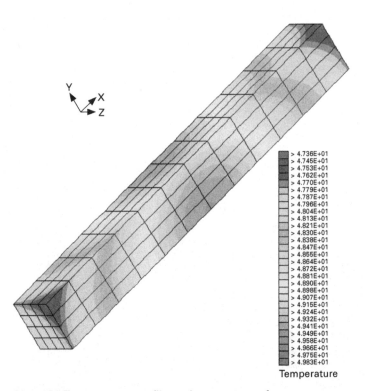

Plate XVI Temperature profile at the resonance frequency.

modes are obtained for h of the same order as a. Dispersion curves of the phononic crystal plate are calculated using a 3D unit cell: the structure is supposed to be of finite thickness along the z direction, infinite but periodic in the two other directions x and y. The band structures are rendered in terms of a frequency, function of the modulus of the wave vector, and are plotted along the principal directions of propagation of the 2D irreducible Brillouin zone ΓXM (Brillouin 1953).

Figure 9.4 gives the band structure of the phononic crystal plate described above, when $h = a$, where only propagation in the xOy plane is considered. An absolute band gap ranging from 1.1808 to 1.3072 GHz appears. In this band gap, waves are evanescent whatever the propagation direction is. The three lowest branches in the band structure, starting at the Γ point, respectively, correspond to the antisymmetric $A0$ Lamb mode, the shear horizontal mode, and the symmetric $S0$ Lamb mode.

The case of a rectilinear waveguide created inside the lead zirconate titanate PZT5A/air phononic crystal plate is then investigated. A supercell containing seven unit cells in the y direction is considered in the finite element calculations. The lattice parameter a and the thickness of the plate h are the same as for the perfect plate. Two systems are considered. In the first system, each of the seven unit cells contains an air hole. In the second system, the hole in the fourth unit cell is filled with PZT5A, thus constituting a linear waveguide in the x direction. Figure 9.5(a) and (b) show the band structure

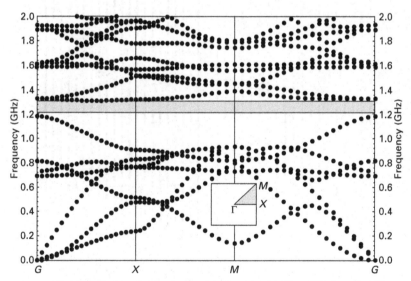

9.4 Elastic band structures calculated with the ATILA code. The phononic crystal plate of thickness $h = a = 0.77$ µm is made of a square array of holes drilled in a PZT5A piezoelectric matrix with a filling fraction of 0.7. The inset represents the Brillouin zone (Γ*XM*) of the square array.

of the phononic crystal plate and the plate with a waveguide, respectively. Only the ΓX path of the Brillouin zone is presented that corresponds to the direction of propagation of the elastic waves inside the waveguide. Without the linear waveguide (Fig. 9.5(a)), it exhibits many additional branches with respect to those in Fig. 9.4, resulting of the folding of the bands in the y direction due to the seven unit-cell periodicity in that direction. The band structure still shows the same forbidden band as the one displayed in Fig. 9.4. When a linear waveguide is introduced in the structure, guiding modes appear inside the band gap of the perfect phononic crystal plate (Fig. 9.5(b)). More specifically, the modulus of the displacement field for the waveguide mode having a frequency $f = 1.221$ GHz and a wave vector equal to 3.468 μm^{-1} is illustrated in plate X (between pages 194 and 195). It corresponds to a

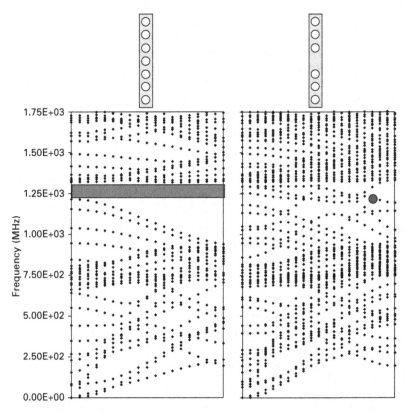

9.5 Band structure along the ΓX direction calculated with a supercell containing 1 × 7 unit cells, for (a) the perfect phononic crystal plate and (b) the phononic crystal plate containing a waveguide formed by filling the hole in the fourth unit cell. The inset shows the 1 × 7 supercell considered in each case. The two straight lines indicate the location of the guided mode analyzed in Plate X (between pages 194 and 195).

three quarter view of the 3D displacement field in the *xy* plane. It clearly shows that the acoustic displacement is concentrated within and in the close vicinity of the waveguide. The displacement field is very weak in the rest of the phononic crystal since the mode considered lies within the forbidden band of the phononic crystal plate.

The calculations presented in this section prove also that a linear defect in such a structure can guide plate mode. This study also suggests that other structural defects such as point defects, cavities, and various channels inserted inside the phononic crystal plate could also lead to the existence of vibrational modes inside the absolute stop bands. These defect modes could then be used to realize functional acoustic devices such as specific filters or demultiplexers (Khelif 2005).

9.4   Phononic crystals for negative refraction applications

Negative refraction is a refraction phenomenon where the refracted wave is propagating on the same side as the incident wave with respect to the normal to the interface. This phenomenon is 'abnormal' if we refer to the Snell–Descartes law. In that case, one can consider a negative index of refraction for the refraction medium. This property allows the design of flat lens, as illustrated in Fig. 9.6, with a view to focus acoustic waves

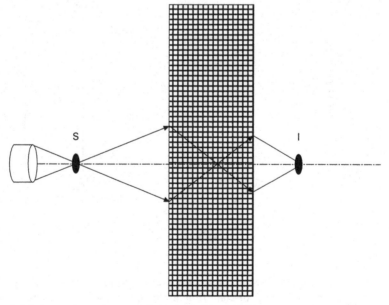

9.6 Schematic representation of the focalization using a material with a negative index of refraction. S = source, I = image.

where the production of real acoustic images from a point source is illustrated.

One can study negative refraction media by using PCs where dispersion curves exhibit branches with a negative slope, i.e., the wave vector and the group-velocity vector associated with an acoustic wave point in opposite directions. In that case, the index of refraction in the PC is negative. This is for instance the case for a triangular lattice (spacing = 2.84 mm) of steel rods (diameter 2 mm) in epoxy, thus, the corresponding filling factor is equal to 0.45. The density of steel is 7800 kg/m³ and the longitudinal and transverse wave velocities are VL, s = 6180 m/s and VT, s = 3245 m/s, respectively. For the epoxy, the density is 1150 kg/m³; the longitudinal and transverse wave velocities are VL, e = 2440 m/s and VT, e = 1130 m/s, respectively.

Figure 9.7 presents the dispersion curve on the first Brillouin zone. A first branch with a negative slope is obtained in the lower part of the band

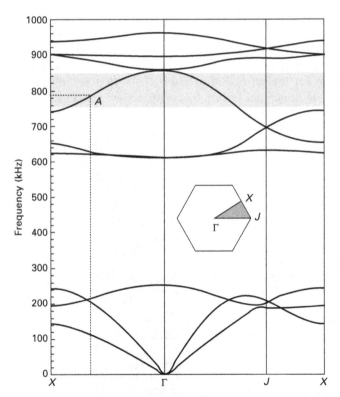

9.7 Elastic band structures for the 2D phononic crystal made of a triangular array of steel rods embedded in epoxy. The grey area corresponds to the frequency range in which a unique branch of negative refraction takes place.

structure but it is related to a mainly transverse mode, that is not easily excited (Hladky-Hennion 2008). Another branch with a negative slope appears in the frequency range 750 kHz–850 kHz; phase velocity and group velocity are of opposite signs. By drawing the displacement field for the negative branch, one can see that the corresponding mode is mainly longitudinal and symmetric with respect to the propagation direction, thus it can be easily excited and coupled to an external fluid domain. Moreover, the equifrequency contours (EFCs) are drawn in the frequency range of interest, i.e., the intersection of the 3D dispersion curves with a horizontal plane corresponding to a fixed frequency. Their shape is circular, thus the wave vector of the elastic wave and the group velocity are antiparallel whatever the propagation direction. This condition is required with the perspective of using the PC for focusing the waves (Sukhovich 2007). As the frequency increases, the radius of the EFC clearly decreases, as expected for left-handed materials.

Experiments on a prism shaped PC have been performed and have demonstrated that a negative angle of refraction is obtained that is in a good agreement with the numerical simulation (Croënne 2011).

In order to verify the coupling efficiency with an external fluid medium, a flat lens is designed based on the PC under study. A finite element simulation is performed to study accurately the ultrasonic field radiated from the PC. The lens is 9-cells thick and 41-cells wide in order to avoid edge effects. A plane wave is impinging the flat lens with an angle of incidence equal to 50° with respect to the normal of the lens. The frequency of the excitation frequency is 786 kHz. The characteristics of the external fluid medium are determined with a view to match the refractive index between the PC and the fluid at 786 kHz. Figure 9.8 shows the pressure field around the lens; the beam is negatively deviated but pressure levels before and after the flat lens are highly different, thus the matching of impedance between the PC and the external fluid medium has to be improved.

A similar flat lens containing 7-cells thick and 65-cells wide is used for the simulation of the focusing capability of the PC with a negative refraction index. This is an important goal for medical imaging devices. Once again, the characteristics of the external fluid medium are determined for matching the refractive index between the PC and the fluid at 786 kHz. In the simulation, losses in epoxy are taken into account thus the expected performances of the device are more precisely quantified. The excitation corresponds to a point source placed 3 mm below the lower interface. Once again, the refractive index between the PC and the fluid are matched at 786 kHz; the wave numbers inside and outside the crystal are the same in amplitude but they have opposite signs. Figure 9.9 presents the pressure field computed with ATILA. Due to impedance mismatch between the PC and the surrounding fluid and to the losses in epoxy, the level of the pressure is one hundred times lower in the top part of the figure. Nevertheless, focusing is well

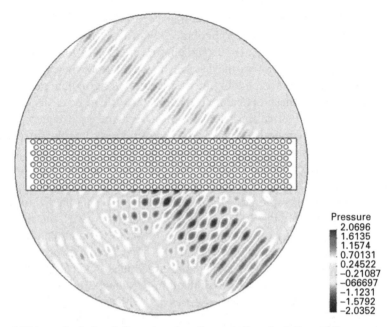

9.8 Numerical simulation showing the negative deviation of the beam, incident with an angle of 50° with respect to the normal to the PC lens.

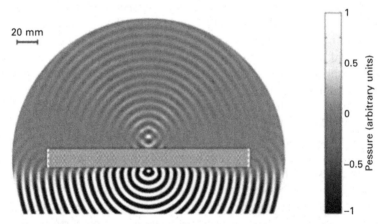

9.9 Simulated pressure field (normalized to source amplitude of 100) for a PC-made flat lens immersed in a fluid at 786 kHz. The fluid refractive index is matched to the PC index. A point source is located below the lens, 3 mm away from the bottom interface.

observed above the flat lens. The distance between the source and the image is approximately twice the thickness of the flat lens (Sukhovich 2007). More details on the image spot can be found in Croenne (2011). Figure 9.9 clearly shows that the negative refraction effects associated to the focusing of waves are evidenced. Therefore, the solid flat lens can be used for imaging systems in fluid environments.

9.5   Conclusion

A model for predicting the modes propagating in periodic structures has been implemented in the ATILA finite element code. With the help of the dispersion curves, pass bands as well as stop bands are determined and it allows the use of periodic structures for filtering applications. Using other characteristics of the dispersion curves such as a branch with a negative slope, acoustic or elastic waves can be negatively refracted and have applications for imaging purposes. These results allow us to go further in waves engineering by using tunable phononic crystals with the help of active (piezoelectric or magnetostrictive) materials, where the elasticity of these materials can be controlled by the application of an external field (magnetic or electric) (Robillard 2009). Moreover, gradient index phononic crystals (GRIN PCs) are of interest (Lin 2009); they are structures where the positions, the dimensions and/or the physical properties of the inclusions are gradually varying along the propagation direction of the incident wave. GRIN PCs have potential applications for self collimation, mirage, cloaking and super-bending of elastic waves.

9.6   References

L. Brillouin (1953), *Wave Propagation in Periodic Structures*, Dover, New-York.

C. Croenne, E.D. Manga, B. Morvan, A. Tinel, B. Dubus, J. Vasseur and A.-C. Hladky-Hennion (2011), 'Negative refraction of longitudinal waves in a two-dimensional solid-solid phononic crystal', *Phys. Rev. B* **83**, 054301.

A.C. Hladky-Hennion, J. Vasseur, B. Dubus, B. Djafari-Rouhani, D. Ekeom and B. Morvan (2008), 'Numerical analysis of negative refraction of transverse waves in an elastic material', *J. Appl. Phys.* **104**, 064906.

A. Khelif, A. Choujaa, S. Benchabane, B. Djafari-Rouhani and V. Laude (2005), 'Experimental study of guiding and filtering of acoustic waves in a two dimensional ultrasonic crystal', *Z. Kristallogr.* **220**, 836–840.

P. Langlet, A.-C. Hladky-Hennion and J.N. Decarpigny (1995), 'Analysis of the propagation of plane acoustic waves in passive periodic materials using the finite element method', *J. Acoust. Soc. Am.* **95**, 1792–2800.

S.C.S Lin, T.J. Huang, J.H. Sun, T.T. Wu (2009), 'Gradient-index phononic crystals', *Phys Rev. B* **79**, 094302.

J.H. Page, S. Yang, M.L. Cowan, Z. Liu, C.T. Chan and P. Sheng (2003), '3D phononic crystals'. In *Wave Scattering in Complex Media: From Theory to Applications*, edited by B.A. van Tiggelen and Sergey Skipetrov (Kluwer Academic Publishers: NATO Science Series, Amsterdam 2003), pp. 283–307.

J.F. Robillard, O. Boumatar, J.O. Vasseur, P.A. Deymier, M. Stippinger and A.C.

Hladky-Hennion (2009), 'Tunable magnetoelastic phononic crystals', *Appl. Phys. Lett.* **95**, 124104.

A. Sukhovich (2007), 'Wave phenomena in phononic crystals', PhD thesis, University of Manitoba.

A. Sukhovich, L.J. Jing, and J.H. Page (2008), 'Negative refraction and focusing of ultrasound in two-dimensional phononic crystals', *Phys. Rev. B* **77**, 014301.

A. Sukhovich, B. Merheb, K. Muralidharan, J.O. Vasseur, Y. Pennec, P.A. Deymier and J. H. Page (2009), 'Experimental and theoretical evidence for subwavelength imaging in phononic crystals', *Phys. Rev. Lett.* **102**, 154301.

J.O. Vasseur, B. Djafari-Rouhani, L. Dobrzynski and P.A. Deymier (1997), 'Acoustic band gaps in fibre composite materials of boron nitride structure', *J. Phys.: Condens. Matter* **9**, 7327.

S. Yang, J.H. Page, Z. Liu, M.L. Cowan, C.T. Chan and P. Sheng (2002), 'Ultrasound tunneling through 3D phononic crystals', *Phys. Rev. Lett.* **88**, 104301.

S. Yang, J.H. Page, Z. Liu, M.L. Cowan, C.T. Chan and P. Sheng (2004), 'Focusing of sound in a 3D phononic crystal', *Phys. Rev. Lett.* **93**, 024301.

10

Studying the behavior of piezoelectric single crystals for sonar using ATILA

A. LOUSSERT, ISEN Brest, France, J-C. DEBUS, ISEN Lille, France and G. VANDERBORCK, Thales Underwater System SAS, France

DOI: 10.1533/9780857096319.2.203

Abstract: For underwater applications and manufacture of sonar for autonomous underwater vehicles (AUV), large areas of piezoelectric materials with very good electromechanical properties are often needed. Piezoelectric single crystals (typically the compositions PMN-PT or PZN-PT[1]) are high-performance materials (high yields), but are difficult to manufacture in large areas while maintaining homogeneous properties. This study on the behavior of piezoelectric single crystals will be conducted with the use of a finite-element code (ATILA) which was developed at ISEN in collaboration with the French Ministry of Defense. The results confirm the good fit between the models and experimental results after a phase of optimization.

Key words: finite element model, smart material, single crystal, acoustic, ATILA.

10.1   Introduction

Single crystals have excellent piezoelectric properties. In this chapter, we will discuss the use of finite element code (ATILA) to model the behavior, and electrical and piezoelectric characteristics of single crystals.

For this, we will begin with a little reminder of the history of single crystals and their uses in different fields of industry or army, and then we will discuss the issue of consistency between an analytical model needed to validate this new module of computer code. This will require the construction of a 3D model based on an existing module and on which many experiments have been performed.

We used a multiparameter study to test a large number of cases that were tested in parallel for validation. A curves adjustment step between the analytical model and experiments is needed to precisely tune the behavior of these, sometimes, very complex simulations. Indeed, although we have the manufacturer's specifications on the different values of the piezoelectric tensor, we know that the smallest difference in these values can cause an important error on the form or magnitude of the complex impedance.

203

The modeling results will be compared with those from our experiments and enable us to verify the very good agreement between the two series.

10.2   State of the art single crystal technology

10.2.1 Manufacturing methods and physical properties

A single crystal is a periodic and regular arrangement of atoms. There are forms that naturally appear in piezoelectric materials like quartz or tourmaline. They were also used in the first generation of applications, before the development of ceramics.

Ferroelectric crystals can have a domain structure. We distinguish the monodomain and polydomain single crystals by one or more polarization directions coexisting in the crystal. In a crystallographic description, the crystals are not strictly polydomain single crystals but twinned crystals; however, we will continue to discuss the single crystal.

The highest known piezoelectric coefficients are obtained for polydomain single crystals. In practice, they have drawbacks that limit their use in many devices: cost, availability, etc. These materials have a good ability to convert mechanical energy into electrical energy (and vice versa), low dielectric loss and stability characteristics under the influence of external constraints such as the electric field, temperature and mechanical stress[2]. Actuators and sensors are a class of devices that use piezoelectric materials as active elements in medical imaging (ultrasound) and velocimetry. In addition, sonar modems are essential in the domain of underwater communications where it is necessary to increase performance in this difficult and complex channel[3].

The single crystal corresponds in terms of characteristic coefficients for the material to a large coupling coefficient for the lateral mode (k_{31}) and longitudinal mode (k_{33}), and a high piezoelectric coefficient. The variation is also as small as possible and without hysteresis of constant frequency (N_{31} or N_{33}) during a heat cycle and of their piezoelectric coefficient (d_{33} and d_{31}) under the action of mechanical stress.

So far materials like ferroelectric ceramic type zircono-lead titanate (PZT) have been doped to obtain higher performance. Generally, they have a k_{31} of about 30% and a k_{33} of about 65%, and a mechanical 'quality' factor surge well above 500 (no units). As for their characteristics, they remain reasonably stable when subjected to the thermal, mechanical or electrical excitations.

In the late 1980s, there was renewed interest in single crystals where previously ceramics had been preferred because they were easier to manufacture in large quantities, less fragile and less expensive. However, the results obtained on these crystals in terms of piezoelectric characteristics (k_{33} greater than 90%, k_{31} above 80%, d_{33} higher than 2 000 pC/N and d_{31} higher than 1000 pC/N) are expected to result in a significant gain in performance for many transducers and sensors. Since then, important research programs have started in the United States, Japan and China.

The research activity in this area remains important to integrate single-crystal transducers, using both their ability for electromechanical conversion and their electro-optical or acousto-optical effects.

10.2.2 History

Ferroelectric and piezoelectric phenomena were discovered long ago. Indeed, the Indians of Ceylon had already observed the piezoelectric phenomenon unknowingly before the French mineralogist Abbé René Just Haüy managed to observe the electrical phenomenon resulting from the action of mechanical pressure on certain crystalline materials in 1817. The theoretical and experimental studies of this phenomenon was made later by the brothers Pierre and Jacques Curie, who are credited with the discovery and proof of 'direct piezoelectric effect' and its relationship to crystal symmetries. 'The inverse piezoelectric effect' was suggested by the theoretical physicist Lippmann in 1881 and confirmed experimentally by the Curie brothers in the same year. 'The inverse piezoelectric effect' manifests itself in the mechanical deformation of a material under an electric field. Industrial applications appeared especially during the First World War (between 1916 and 1917): the ultrasonic wave generator for underwater measurement and detection by Langevin and the control of radio frequencies in the fluctuations in using quartz by Cady. Today, different applications are used in the telephones, automobiles, aeronautics, etc. Technological advances will make their appearance in the form of barium titanate ceramic ($BaTiO_3$) and zircono-lead titanate (PZT) thanks to the first piezoelectric materials. It was not until the twentieth century that the Voigt tensor behavior of piezoelectric materials was introduced. Today, thanks to advances in research and easy communication between researchers, new materials in the form of single crystals have been produced for their excellent dielectric and piezoelectric properties.

10.2.3 The piezoelectric effect

Piezoelectricity and ferroelectricity

Piezoelectricity manifests itself by a polarization of the cell with the appearance of a dipole moment $\mu = q \times d$ where q = electric charge of the dipole and d = distance between centroids. The appearance of polarization in a material is due to the influence of mechanical stress. This is the result of an interaction between electrical and elastic properties of a material. Indeed, the application of mechanical stress on a material shows a bias and is called 'the direct piezoelectric effect' (Fig. 10.1). This effect is reversible and corresponds to

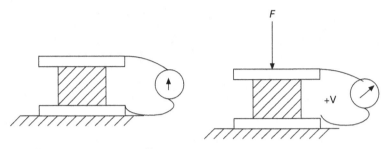

10.1 Direct piezoelectric effect.

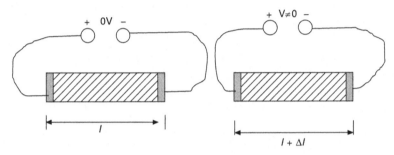

10.2 Reverse piezoelectric effect.

a deformation of the material by applying an external electric field termed 'the reverse piezoelectric effect' (Fig. 10.2).

Piezoelectricity is the subject of numerous applications. From the gas lighter to the crystal oscillator in our watches and countless electronic systems, through to the transmitting and receiving devices used in military and medical systems based on piezoelectricity; all these products have invaded our daily lives.

Quartz oscillators

Quartz oscillators, such as the one presented in Fig. 10.3 can provide a time base in many systems. In many of these, the oscillation frequency used was 32 768 Hz divided by two fifteen times; we obtained a frequency of 1 Hz (a period of oscillation per second) which is well suited for example, for a watch (Fig. 10.3).

To produce piezoelectric ceramics, a powder is agglomerated into a mold, thereby obtaining the desired geometry for the macroscopic sample. Each grain has, at first, a field-aligned ferroelectric random (situation corresponding to Fig. 10.4(a)). This does not provide satisfactory physical properties. Therefore a sintering process (poling) must be applied to the material; this is achieved by heating the pressed powder without reaching the melting point of the

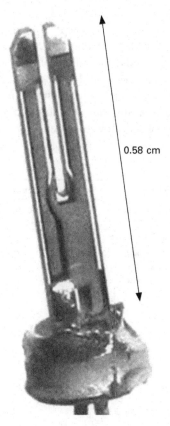

10.3 Quartz oscillators.

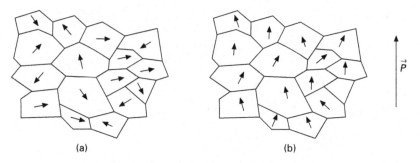

10.4 Polarization of a ferroelectric material.

material while applying a strong electric field across the material. This has, to some extent, the effect of aligning the polarization of the areas that are imposed by the external electric field. From this, we obtain the situation in Fig. 10.4(b).

The different types of polarization

There are different types of polarization. A dielectric medium includes carrying charges and free carriers which can move under the influence of an electric field. The phenomenon of polarization can be regarded as resulting from displacement of charged carriers compared to their equilibrium position under the influence of an electric field. Table 10.1 summarizes the three resonant modes that can be observed in the case of a hollow tube cell.

Table 10.1 The three resonant modes

Sample (P = polar; S = stress)		Dimensions		Measured constances	
		I.R.E.	Usual	Piezo electric and dielectric	Mechanical
Plate		$l < L/5$	$L = 15$ mm $L = 3$ mm	k_{33} d_{33} g_{33} ε^T_{33} e^5_{33}	s^D_{33} s^E_{33} Q_{33}
Lateral		$l < L/3$ $e < L/5$	$L = 25$ $l = 5$ $e = 5$	k_{31} d_{31} g_{31}	s^D_{11} s^E_{11} Q_{31}
Width		$L \gg e$	$L \gg e$	k_1 e_{33} h_{33} ε^5_{33}	c^D_{33} c^E_{33} Q_1
Shear		$L > 8e$	$L = 10$ mm $l = 5$ mm $e = 1$ mm	k_{15} d_{15} g_{15} ε^T_{11} ε^5_{11}	c^D_{55} c^E_{55} s^D_{55} s^E_{55} Q_{15}

10.3   Modeling the behavior of single crystal materials using ATILA software

In this chapter, a module is defined to quickly calculate very complex 3D piezoelectric sensors. With this new module, it is now possible to calculate this type of structure in reasonable time and then allow this complex multiparametric study.

10.3.1 Description and validation of a model

For this module (Fig. 10.5), called VDB8b and built by Thales Sophia-Antipolis, many experiments have been carried out to be defined as reference for our finite element modeling. The model defined in our study is a 3D structure with 20 single crystal transducers (2 mm high and 0.9×0.9 mm^2 in section). Copper strips connect the transducers 5 by 5 at the same potential.

The addition of a backing is essential to maintain a share of the transducers in the desired mechanical configuration and also to have a sufficient decoupling to emit in a special direction. This backing has a slightly larger section than the entire antenna and is 2 mm thick. The transducer's impedance and admittance of the module based on 'PMN23PTMod' single crystals have been checked. This file serves as a reference source in the rest of the document.

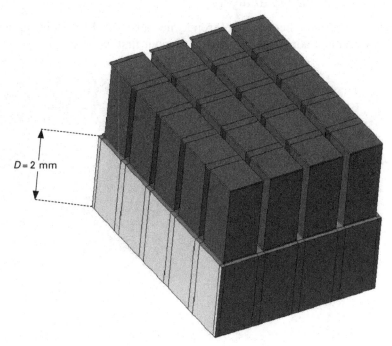

$D = 2$ mm

10.5 Module of a single crystal material.

10.4   The experiment

10.4.1 Description of the model

Several mock-up transducers have been designed and tested both in air (Fig. 10.6) and in water (Fig. 10.7).

Electric impedance, admittance, transmitted voltage response have been measured and compared.

10.4.2 Results

Tests in air

In Fig. 10.8 we can see a plot of the admittance (conductance) in air versus frequency.

Tests in water

Figure 10.9 shows the same transducers measured in water.

10.5   Analysis of results

10.5.1 *In vacuo* analysis

A comparison between reference module (VDB8b) admittance and experimental admittance (VDB81) was our first work. Figure 10.10 shows

10.6 Mock-up transducer tested in air.

10.7 Mock-up transducer tested in water.

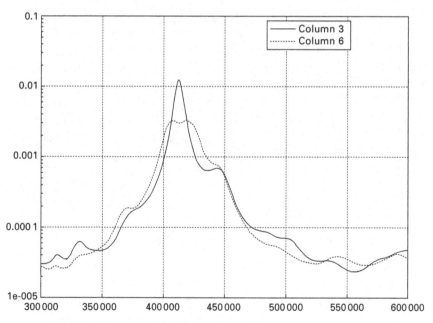

10.8 Conductance for columns 3 and 6.

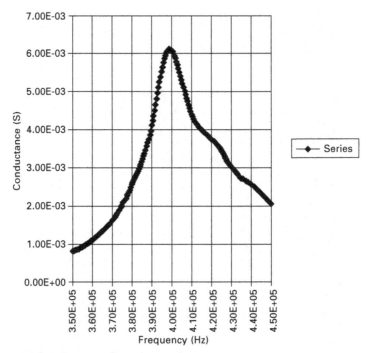

10.9 Conductance for columns 5.

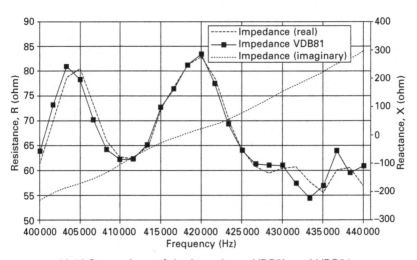

10.10 Comparison of the impedance VDB8b and VDB81.

that this comparison permitted us to quickly detect the resonant frequency. The impedance curve is added for better comprehension for all data users (Fig. 10.11). After optimization of material properties and, in particular, in active elements (single crystals), a very good agreement is shown between modeled data and experimental results.

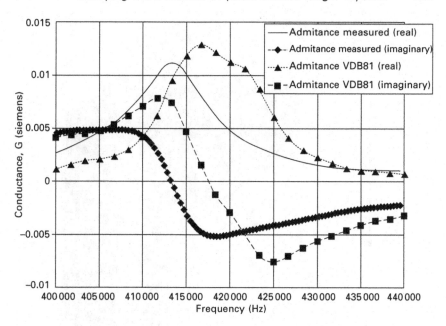

10.11 Comparison of the admittance VDB8b and VDB81.

The resonant frequency of this module is located in the vicinity of 417 kHz. The frequency corresponding to the minimum of the real impedance (resistance) is slightly lower than the resonant frequency of the module in Fig. 10.10. This is quite normal. The slight modification of the impedance is only visible near the resonance where the behaviors are more sensitive to disturbance.

Modification of the elongation of the backing to 6 mm: VDB8e

The file was then edited with the aim of extending up the backing to 6 mm (Fig. 10.12) in order to test the effect of increasing the mass of the back module on its proper functioning in the vicinity of resonance. Then macro-elements were added (VDB8e) and if one is to respect the rules of modeling[4], the minimum width of the final elements will not be touched. This amounts to almost a three-fold increase of the number of elements to calculate.

The evolution of the admittance and impedance as a function of the elongation of the backing is compared in Figs 10.13 and 10.14. There is no evolution of the admittance by raising the number of 3D elements of the module. This would seem to mean that the backing is already playing its full part *in vacuo* from a thickness of 2 mm.

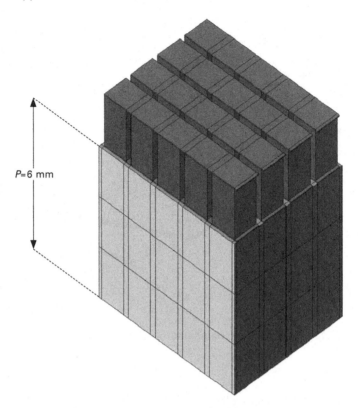

10.12 Modification of the backing (VDB8e).

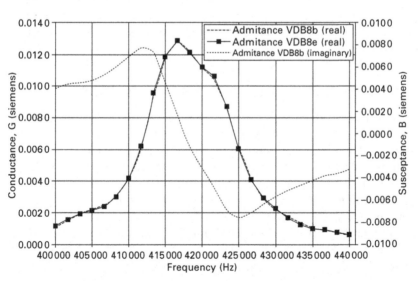

10.13 Comparison of the admittance VDB8b and VDB8e.

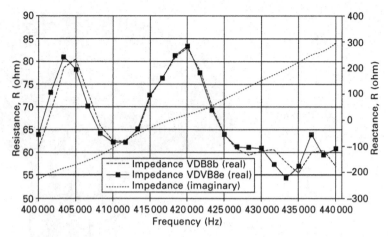

10.14 Comparison of the impedance VDB8b and VDB8e.

10.5.2 In water analysis

Module with a backing of 8 mm in water: VDB10

For this model, a sphere of fluid was added on the front panel of the module (Fig. 10.15). Considering the symmetry, only one eighth of a sphere was needed. On the following lines, the evolution of the admittance and impedance according to the addition of fluid was observed. There is a significant evolution of the admittance: the resonant frequency was modified from 417 kHz to 395 kHz. Nevertheless, this downward shift of the resonance frequency is quite normal because of the higher charge due to fluid on the front panel of the transducer (Figs 10.16 to 10.19).

Structure with another material: VDB9e

Now, in comparison with the reference module VDB8b, the single crystal material is modified to VDB9e. It is necessary to make a verification of the impedance and admittance of the transducer module based on single crystals Pb (Zn1/3Nb2/3) O3-(6-7)% PbTiO3. This change is based on an article describing the characteristics of this crystal[5]. Below, the evolution of the admittance and impedance according to the modified material is compared. There is no evolution of the admittance by modifying the single crystal material of the module (Figs 10.20 and 10.21). This would seem to mean that the material:

- is either the same type as the PMN23PTMod, or
- has only very moderate changes of the module characteristic versus piezoelectric ceramics.

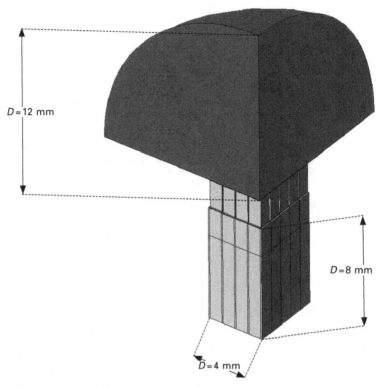

10.15 Description of the fluid model: VDB10.

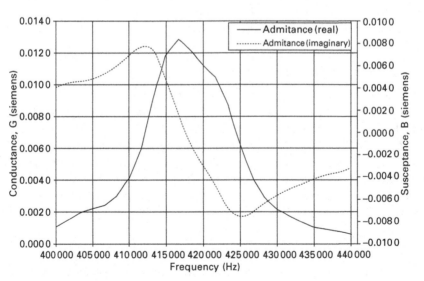

10.16 Admittance of VDB8b.

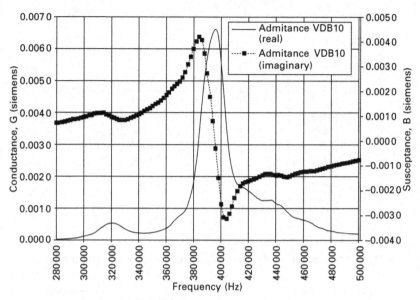

10.17 Admittance of VDB10.

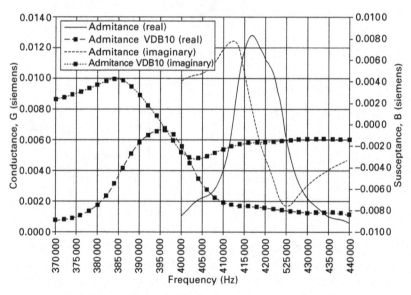

10.18 Comparison of the admittance VDB8b and VDB10.

10.6   The analytic model

This section presents the modeling of a single crystal plate radiating in an infinite water column. The electrical and mechanical behavior of a sample crystal plate will be defined from a judicious combination of the fundamental

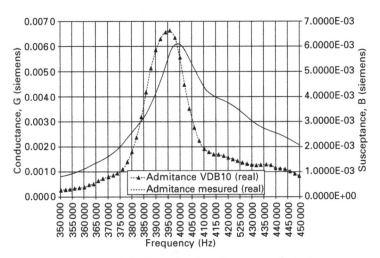

10.19 Comparison of the measured and computed admittance.

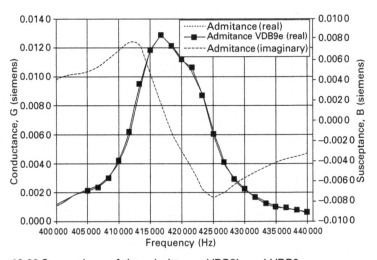

10.20 Comparison of the admittance VDB8b and VDB9e.

equations of solid state physics applied to the case of piezoelectric materials (laws of motion and constitutive equations of piezoelectricity, in the first place). Characteristic quantities of the sample (spatial amplitude, temporal displacement field and resonant frequency associated with each mode of deformation) will be obtained.

10.6.1 The analytical solution

The PMN-30PT single crystal plate is laterally clamped and is surmounted by an infinite water column (Fig. 10.22). This electrical excited plate radiates a

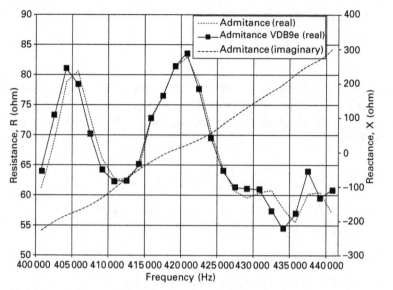

10.21 Comparison of the impedance VDB8b and VDB9e.

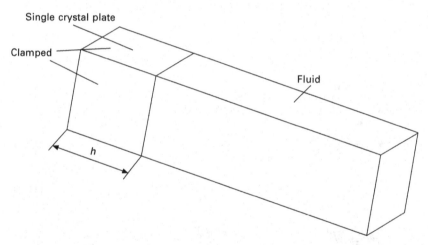

10.22 Single crystal plate in water column.

plane wave into the fluid. It has a thickness 'h'; the electric field is parallel to the longitudinal axis. It is assumed that simple harmonic longitudinal waves propagating along the z-direction have a complex displacement given by:

$$u^*_z = A^* \sin kz + B^* \cos kz$$
$$= (A^R + jA^I) \sin kz + (B^R + jB^I) \cos kz \qquad [10.1]$$

where $k = \dfrac{\omega}{C_s}$ $\qquad [10.2]$

and the speed of sound in the single crystal is defined as:

$$C_s = \frac{1}{\sqrt{\rho_s S_{33}^D}}$$ [10.3]

where S_{33}^D is the elastic compliance at electric charge constant and ρ_s is the mass density of the single crystal.

When the fringing effects are neglected, the electric displacement is defined as[6]:

$$D_1 = 0, D_2 = 0 \text{ and } \frac{\partial D_3^*}{\partial z} = 0$$ [10.4]

Therefore, D_3 is a constant. The piezoelectric equations are:

$$T_3^* = C_{33}^D S_3^* + h_{33} D_3^*$$ [10.5a]

$$E_3^* = - h_{33} S_3^* + \beta_{33}^T D_3^*$$ [10.5b]

For the plate, the boundary condition at each end is:

at $z = 0$, $T_3^*(0) = 0$ and at $z = h$, $T_3^*(t) = p^*(h)$; the fluid pressure is defined as:

$$p(z) = p^R(z) + jP^I(z)$$ [10.6]

Assuming that:

$$D_3^* = D_0^* e^{j\omega t}$$ [10.7]

then the values of A^* and B^* are determined as:

$$A^R = \frac{h_{33}}{kC_{33}^D} D_0^R$$ [10.8]

$$A^I = \frac{h_{33}}{kC_{33}^D} D_0^I$$ [10.9]

$$B^R = - \frac{p^R(h) + h_{33}(1 - \cos kh)D_0^R}{kC_{33}^D \sin kh}$$ [10.10]

$$B^I = - \frac{p^I(h) + h_{33}(1 - \cos kh)D_0^I}{kC_{33}^D \sin kh}$$ [10.11]

The potential difference between the electrodes is:

$$V = - \int_0^L E_3^* dx$$ [10.12]

Using Eq. [10.5b], the electric displacement is:

$$D_0^R = \frac{V - \dfrac{h_{33}(1 - \cos kh)p^R(h)}{kC_{33}^D \sin kh}}{\dfrac{h_{33}^2\left(\sin kh + \tan \dfrac{kh}{2}(1 - \cos kh)\right)}{kC_{33}^D} - \beta_{33}^S h} \qquad [10.13]$$

$$D_0^I = \frac{-\dfrac{h_{33}(1 - \cos kh)p^I(h)}{kC_{33}^D \sin kh}}{\dfrac{h_{33}^2\left(\sin kh + \tan \dfrac{kh}{2}(1 - \cos kh)\right)}{kC_{33}^D} - \beta_{33}^S h} \qquad [10.14]$$

At $z = h$ the fluid pressure is given as[7]:

$$p^R(h) = -\alpha(vX_a \sin kh - Y_a \cos kh)V \qquad [10.15]$$

$$p^I(h) = -\alpha(X_a \cos kh - vY_a \cos kh)V \qquad [10.16]$$

where

$$v = \frac{\rho_s C_s}{\rho_f C_f} \qquad [10.17]$$

ρ_f is the fluid mass density and C_f is the speed of sound in the fluid.

$$\alpha = \frac{h_{33}(\cos kh - 1)}{\omega A(\cos^2 kh + v^2 \sin^2 kh)} \qquad [10.18]$$

A is the area of the plate, X_a and Y_a are the real and imaginary parts of the admittance. The impedance of the structure is defined as:

$$Z = \frac{1}{jC_0\omega}\left(1 - j\frac{k_t^2}{kh}\frac{2v(1 - \cos kh) - j \sin kh}{\cos kh + jv \sin kh}\right) \qquad [10.19]$$

Then, the real part (reactance R) and the imaginary part (reactance X) of the impedance are defined as:

$$R = -\frac{1}{C_0\omega}\frac{k_t^2}{kh}\frac{2v(1 - \cos kh)\cos kh - v \sin kh^2}{\cos kh^2 + v^2 \sin kh^2} \qquad [10.20]$$

$$X = -\frac{1}{C_0\omega}\left(1 - \frac{k_t^2}{kh}\frac{\sin kh \cos kh + 2v^2(1 - \cos kh)\sin kh}{\cos kh^2 + v^2 \sin kh^2}\right) \qquad [10.21]$$

The conductance X_a and the susceptance Y_a are can be written as:

$$X_a = \frac{R}{R^2 + X^2} \qquad [10.22]$$

$$Y_a = -\frac{X}{R^2 + X^2} \qquad \text{[10.23]}$$

10.6.2 Application

Geometry of the model

The plate consists of a PMN-30PT single crystal with a square area 1 mm by 1 mm and a 1 mm thickness. It is laterally clamped (Fig. 10.23). The height of the water column is 3 mm.

Validation

Figure 10.24 shows the mesh of the plate defined by a $5 \times 5 \times 5$ 3D solid elements and the mesh of the fluid is defined by $5 \times 5 \times 10$ 3D fluid elements.

Harmonic analysis

The analytical results of the plate for a 1 V harmonic excitation have been compared with the numerical results. In plate XI (between pages 194 and 195) displaying the contour fill of the real part of the Z displacement at the

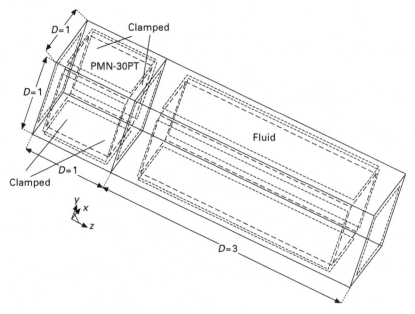

10.23 Geometry of the model.

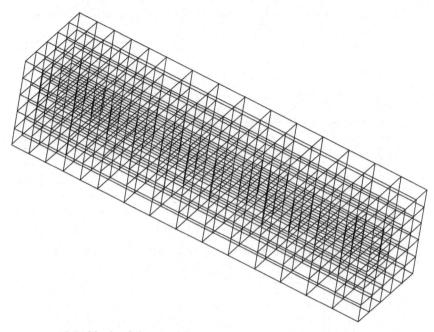

10.24 Mesh of the model.

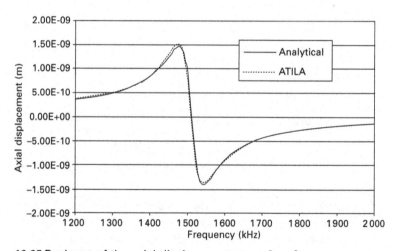

10.25 Real part of the axial displacement at $z = 0$ vs frequency.

resonance frequency (1.509 MHz), the longitudinal waves radiate plane waves into the fluid. Figures 10.25 to 10.28 display, respectively, the real and imaginary parts of the axial displacement versus frequency comparing the analytical Eq. [10.1] and numerical results at $z = 0$ and $Z = h$. The results obtained for the axial displacements show very good agreement.

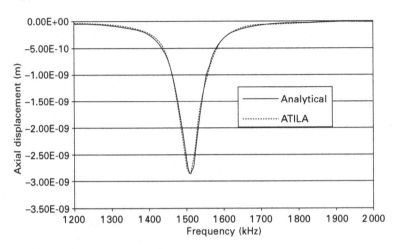

10.26 Imaginary part of the axial displacement at $z = 0$ vs frequency.

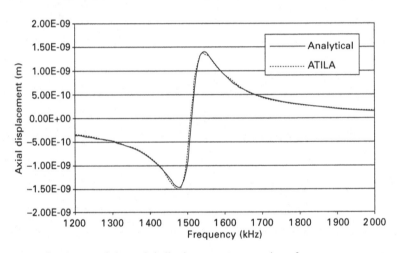

10.27 Real part of the axial displacement at $z = h$ vs frequency.

Figure 10.29 and 10.30 show the real and imaginary part of the electrical displacement versus frequency comparing the analytical (Eqs [10.13] and [10.14]) and numerical results with very good agreement.

The real and imaginary parts of the pressure at the fluid-structure interface versus frequency are displayed in Figs 10.31 and 10.32; the comparison between the analytical (Eqs [10.15] and [10.16]) and numerical results is very good.

Figures 10.33 to 10.36 show, respectively, the real and imaginary parts of the impedance and admittance versus frequency comparing the analytical (Eqs [10.20] to [10.23]) and numerical results. The results obtained show very good agreement.

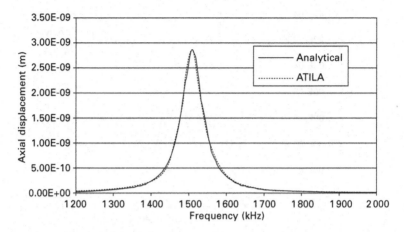

10.28 Imaginary part of the axial displacement at $z = h$ vs frequency.

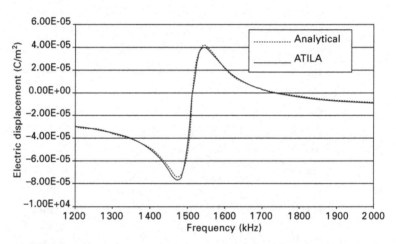

10.29 Real part of the electrical displacement vs frequency vs frequency.

10.7   Conclusion

In this chapter, the use of finite element code (ATILA) to model the behavior as well as electrical and piezoelectric characteristics of a single crystal plate has been shown. The issue of consistency between an analytical model required for the validation of this new module of computer code was discussed. Moreover design and simulation of a 3D model based on an existing module have been made and numerous experiments have been realized in parallel.

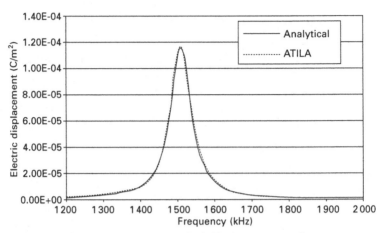

10.30 Imaginary part of the electrical displacement vs frequency.

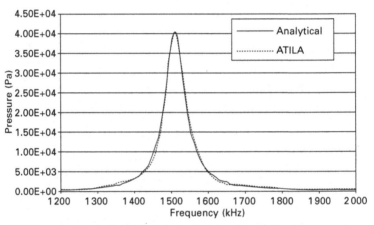

10.31 Imaginary part of the pressure at $z = h$ vs frequency.

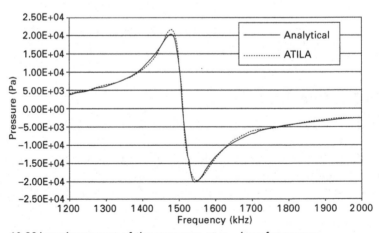

10.32 Imaginary part of the pressure at $z = h$ vs frequency.

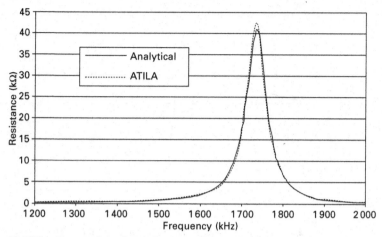

10.33 Real part of the impedance vs frequency.

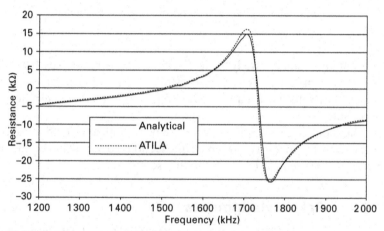

10.34 Imaginary part of the impedance vs frequency.

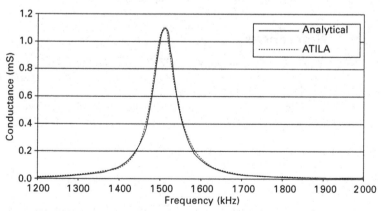

10.35 Real part of the admittance vs frequency.

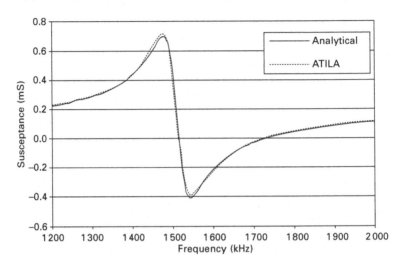

10.36 Imaginary part of the admittance vs frequency.

A multiparameter study to test a large number of cases for validation has been conducted. A curve adjustment step between analytical model and experiments has been necessary to precisely tune the behavior of these simulations.

The modeling results have therefore been compared with those from the experiments previously presented in Section 10.4 and have validated the very good agreement between the two series.

10.8   Acknowledgments

The authors would like to thank French Ministry of Defense (DGA) and Thales Underwater Systems for their support.

10.9   References

1.   Ritter, T., *et al.*, 2000, 'Single crystal PZN/PT-polymer composites for ultrasound transducer applications'. *IEEE Transactions on Ultrasonics, Ferroelectrics and Frequency Control*, 47, 792–800. 0885-3010.
2.   Kuwata, J., Uchino, K., Nomura, S., 1982, 'Dielectric and piezoelectric properties of $0.91Pb(Zn1/3Nb2/3)O3-0.09PbTiO3$'. *Japanese Journal of Applied Physics*, 121, 1298–1302.
3.   Bouvet P. J., Loussert A., 2000, 'Capacity analysis of underwater acoustic MIMO communications'. *IEEE Oceans '10*, Sydney, Australia.
4.   Mestouri, H., Loussert, A., Keryer, G., 2008, 'Multiparameters finite element modelling of transducers arrays'. *IEEE Acoustics '08*. 1003–1008.
5.   Jin, J., Rajan, K. K., Lim, L. C., 2006, 'Properties of Single Domain Pb(Zn1/3Nb2/3)

O3-(6-7)%PbTiO3 Single Crystal'. *Japanese Journal of Applied Physics*, 45(11), 8744–8747.

6.   Wilson, O. B., 1988, *An Introduction to the Theory and Design of Sonar Transducers*. Los Altos: Peninsula Publishing.

7.   Carton, J.L., Debus, J.C., Decarpigny, J.N., 1982, Contrat DCAN-Toulon (GERDSM). T.SM. S.80.48.826.329.T.

11

Thermal analysis in piezoelectric and magnetostrictive materials using ATILA

J-C. DEBUS, ISEN Lille, France

DOI: 10.1533/9780857096319.2.230

Abstract: In this chapter, a coupled electromechanical thermal analysis is presented. For a steady-state solution, the thermal behaviour is weakly coupled to the electromechanical response. A simple model, a tonpilz, a doubled-ended and a flextensional transducer serve as validation of the numerical model compared to the analytical models. The transient thermal analysis is developed and the temperature and dissipated power distribution are obtained at each step. The validation concerns piezoelectric ring transducers driven at high power levels under continuous sine-wave drive. The aim of the second section of this chapter is to present heat generation in a magnetostrictive transducer. The development of heat generation is defined with two validations. The first example consists of a cylinder in vacuum, the second example shows the temperature behaviour of a Janus transducer; the results are compared with an analytical model and measurements.

Key words: piezoelectric ceramics, magnetostrictive material, thermal analysis, finite-element, transducers.

11.1   Introduction

Traditionally, designers of sonar transducers strive to optimize the balance in energy storage between electrical limits (e.g., arcing, depolarization) and mechanical limits (e.g. fracture, fatigue, non-linear response)[1-3]. The thermal impact can be neglected in transducer design where low duty-cycles are employed, but thermal limits become a critical issue for designing high-power long duty cycle applications. Pushing a design to its thermal limits can lead to increased losses, ceramic depoling or thermal runaway. The thermal limit is dependent on both material losses and the heat transfer design of the transducer.

Recently, the actuator community[3] has investigated high-power large amplitude vibration response and found thermal stability issues in piezoceramics due to shifts in resonance frequencies, hysteresis in admittance and a decrease in the mechanical quality factor, Q.

Developments made previously in the finite element code ATILA allow for heat generation in the transducers[4]. In the ATILA code, losses in active and passive materials can be taken into account by using physical constants. The dissipated power for each element and for the whole structure can be

230

obtained[5,6], then a thermal analysis by heat transfer and including conduction and convection gives the temperature in the transducer. These results are obtained for a harmonic analysis; it is also important to obtain these results for a transient analysis. This analysis is the aim of the chapter.

11.2   Heat generation in piezoelectric materials

11.2.1 Material losses and dissipated power

The sources of heating for a transducer are mainly due to losses in materials, both active and passive, as well as the mechanical assembly of the design. Mechanical sources such as friction and contact surfaces must be addressed in the quality of manufacture. The temperature rise in a design will impact the efficiency of the transducer and the generated heat must be transferred away from the active materials. In passive materials especially, such as polymers, the transition from glass to rubbery phase impacts significantly on the physical properties. Although controllable in the design or selection of the polymer, the temperature at which transition occurs must be avoided.

For a piezoelectric material, the stress and strain tensors and electric field and electric displacement vectors are coupled through constitutive relations. Choosing strain and electric displacements as independent variables, the relations are written as:

$$\{S^*\} = [s^{E^*}]\{T^*\} + [d^*]^T\{E^*\}$$
$$\{D^*\} = [d^*]\{T^*\} + [\varepsilon^{T^*}]\{E^*\} \tag{11.1}$$

where the symbol * denotes a complex quantity.

The material coefficients are written as complex quantities to define losses as negative phase[5,7]:

$$[s^{E^*}] = \lfloor s^{E^r}\rfloor - j\lfloor s^{E^i}\rfloor$$
$$[d^*] = [d^r] - j[d^i] \tag{11.2}$$
$$[\varepsilon^{T^*}] = [\varepsilon^{T^r}] - j[\varepsilon^{T^i}]$$

Material loss factors are directly measured from electric displacement, D versus electric field, E for dielectric, mechanical strain, S versus stress, T for elastic and mechanical strain, versus electric field for piezoelectric losses, respectively. The dissipated power density is defined by Holland[5] as:

$$p_d = \frac{1}{2}\omega I_m(\{E^*\}^T\{\overline{D^*}\} + \{T^*\}^T\{\overline{S^*}\}) \tag{11.3}$$

where ω is the angular frequency, I_m denotes the imaginary component and defines the conjugate value. The dissipated power may be written as:

$$p_d = \frac{1}{2} \omega (\{E^i\}^T \{D^r\} - \{E^r\}^T \{D^i\} + \{T^r\}^T \{S^r\} - \{T^r\}^T \{S^i\})$$

[11.4]

11.3   Implementation of ATILA for the thermal analysis of piezoelectric materials

11.3.1 Steady-state problems for heat transfer

For a steady-state solution, the thermal behaviour is weakly coupled to the electromechanical response. The method thus takes advantage of the order of magnitude which is greater than the time constant for thermal effects compared to the mechanical behaviour. A two-step analysis is performed whereby the electromechanical behaviour is first computed, and the resulting dissipated power is then applied as a heat generator to determine the resulting temperature of the system.

The heat source term is entered into the equation for heat transfer using the heat equation as:

$$\frac{\partial}{\partial x}\left(k_{xx} \frac{\partial T}{\partial x}\right) + \frac{\partial}{\partial y}\left(k_{yy} \frac{\partial T}{\partial y}\right) + \frac{\partial}{\partial z}\left(k_{zz} \frac{\partial T}{\partial z}\right) + Q = 0 \qquad [11.5]$$

where T denotes temperature (°C), k_{xx}, k_{yy}, k_{zz} are the conductivity coefficients (W/m/°C) along x, y, z, respectively, and Q is the heat generated (W/m^3) within the body including the dissipated power from material losses. Q is positive if the heat is put into the body.

The boundary conditions associated with Eq. [11.5] can be expressed in two different forms. If the temperature is known along a part of the boundary then

$$T = T_s \qquad [11.6]$$

where T_S is the boundary temperature at the surface S. If heat is gained or lost at the boundary Γ due to convection, $h(T - T_\infty)$, or a heat flux, q, then

$$k_{xx} \frac{\partial T}{\partial x} \ell_x + k_{yy} \frac{\partial T}{\partial y} \ell_y + k_{zz} \frac{\partial T}{\partial z} \ell_z + q + h(T - T_\infty) = 0 \qquad [11.7]$$

where h is the convective thermal film coefficient (W/m^2/°C), q is the heat flux (W/m^2), T_∞ is the ambient temperature of the surrounding medium.

It is implemented in ATILA using the so-called weak formulation as[4]:

$$\sum_e ([k_T^e]\{T^e\}) = \sum_e (\{Q^e\} - \{q^e\} - [k_h^e]\{T^e\} + \{k_{T_\infty}^e\}) \qquad [11.8]$$

where:

$$[k_T^e] = \int_{D^e} [B^e]^T [C^e][B^e]dD^e \quad \text{is the conductivity matrix}$$

$$[k_h^e] = \int_{\Gamma^e} h[N^e]^T [N^e]d\Gamma^e \quad \text{is the convection matrix}$$

$$\{k_{T_\infty}^e\} = \int_{\Gamma^e} hT_\infty \lfloor N^e \rfloor d\Gamma^e \quad \text{is the convection vector}$$

$$\{q^e\} = \int_{\Gamma^e} q \lfloor N^e \rfloor d\Gamma^e \quad \text{is the thermal flux vector}$$

and $\{Q^e\} = -\int_{D^e} \lfloor N^e \rfloor p_d^e dD^e$ is the thermal load vector including the dissipated power from material losses.

The dissipated power density (Eq. [11.4]) provides the internal heat generation. It is calculated for each element from:

$$p_d^e = \frac{1}{2}\omega\left(\{u^r \; \Phi^r\}^T \begin{bmatrix} k_{uu}^i & k_{u\Phi}^i \\ k_{\Phi u}^i & k_{\Phi\Phi}^i \end{bmatrix} \begin{Bmatrix} u^r \\ \Phi^r \end{Bmatrix} + \{u^i \; \Phi^i\}^T \begin{bmatrix} k_{uu}^i & k_{u\Phi}^i \\ k_{\Phi u}^i & k_{\Phi\Phi}^i \end{bmatrix} \begin{Bmatrix} u^i \\ \Phi^i \end{Bmatrix} \right)$$

[11.9]

11.3.2 Transient analysis method

The inclusion of time variable effects can be made directly from Eq. [11.5] where the right term of the equation is the rate of heat increase in domain D

$$\frac{\partial}{\partial x}\left(k_{xx} \frac{\partial T}{\partial x} \right) + \frac{\partial}{\partial y}\left(k_{yy} \frac{\partial T}{\partial y} \right) + \frac{\partial}{\partial z}\left(k_{zz} \frac{\partial T}{\partial z} \right) + Q = \rho s_h \frac{\partial T}{\partial t} \quad [11.10]$$

ρ is the density and s_h is the specific heat coefficient (J/kg/°C).

With the weak formulation, the system of equations to solve the transient thermal problem can be written in the following form:

$$[C]\{\dot{T}\} + [K]\{T\} = \{Q(t)\} \quad [11.11]$$

where

$[C] = \sum_e \int_{D^e} \rho s_h [N^e]^T [N^e]dD^e$ is the specific heat mass matrix with the specific heat coefficient s_h and ρ the density

$[K] = \sum_e ([k_T^e] + [k_h^e])$ is the thermal conduction and convection (stiffness) matrix and $\{Q(t)\} = \sum_{e} (\{Q^e(t)\} - \{q^e\} + \{k^e_{T_\infty}\})$ is the total thermal loading.

This vector is assumed constant and it is obtained from the harmonic analysis at one frequency. It will be denoted $\{Q_0\}$,

and $\{\dot{T}\} = \left\{\dfrac{dT}{dt}\right\}$ denotes the first time derivative.

In direct integration, Eq. [11.11] is integrated using a numerical step-by-step procedure. Instead of trying to satisfy this equation at any time t, it is aimed at satisfying this one only at discrete time intervals apart from Δt. By applying the method of weighted residuals over a time interval Δt, the following solution to Eq. [11.11] is obtained[8]:

$$T_{t+1} = ([C] + \theta \Delta t[K])^{-1}([C] - (1 - \theta)\,\Delta t[K])T_t + \Delta t\{Q(t)\} \quad [11.12]$$

where T_t is the temperature at time t. The θ parameter takes the following values depending on the selected weighting method:

- $\theta = 0$ Euler
- $\theta = \frac{1}{2}$ Crank–Nicolson
- $\theta = \frac{2}{3}$ Galerkin
- $\theta = 1$ back difference

The combination of this method within a transient analysis with ATILA can be done in the following way, for each time step:

- $Q(t)$ is calculated from the ATILA transient analysis for the piezoelectric system.
- $T(t + 1)$ is computed from Eq. [11.12]

11.3.3 Piezoelectric cylinder

Harmonic analysis

An analytical formulation was developed to validate the dissipated power calculation in ATILA and thermal analysis. The geometry consists of a PZT4 piezoelectric cylinder having a length of 30 mm and a radius of 10 mm (Fig. 11.1). The dynamic excitation is provided electrically to the cylinder using two electrodes located at the two ends. The axial axis is the poled direction.

To validate this analysis, a 1D model is considered (Fig. 11.2). The only significant stress is along the cylinder axis parallel to the electric field, the z-direction[6].

Therefore the constitutive equations for a piezoelectric material [Eq. 11.1] can be simplified to:

$$S_3^*(z) = s_{33}^{E^*} T_3(z) + d_{33}^* E_3^*(z)$$
$$D_3^*(z) = d_{33}^* T_3^*(z) + \varepsilon_{33}^{T^*} E_3^*(z) \qquad [11.13]$$

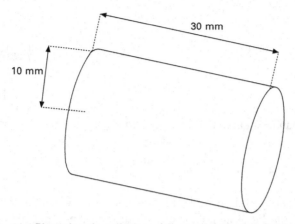

11.1 Piezoelectric cylinder with parallel electric field.

11.2 1D piezoelectric modelling.

This system of equations expresses S_3, E_3 in relation to T_3 and D_3. It can also be inverted to obtain:

$$T_3^*(z) = \frac{1}{s_{33}^{E^*}} S_3^*(z) - \frac{d_{33}^*}{s_{33}^{E^*}} E_3^*(z)$$

$$D_3^*(z) = \frac{d_{33}^*}{s_{33}^{E^*}} S_3(z) + \left(\varepsilon_{33}^{T^*} - \frac{d_{33}^{2^*}}{s_{33}^{E^*}} \right) E_3^*(z) \qquad [11.14]$$

This set of equations can also be written as:

$$T_3^* = c_{eq}^* S_3^* - e_{eq}^* E_3^*$$

$$D_3^* = e_{eq}^* S_3 + \varepsilon_{eq}^s E_3^* \qquad [11.15]$$

where:

$$c_{eq}^* = \frac{1}{s_{33}^{E^*}}, e_{eq}^* = \frac{d_{33}^*}{s_{33}^{E^*}}, \varepsilon_{eq}^s = \varepsilon_{33}^{T^*} - \frac{d_{33}^{2^*}}{s_{33}^{E^*}} \qquad [11.16]$$

If the mechanical, piezoelectric and dielectric losses are defined, respectively, as:

$$s_{33}^{E^*} = (1 - j \tan\theta')s_{33}^E, d_{33}^* = (1 - j \tan \phi')d_{33}, \varepsilon_{33}^{T^*} = (1 - j \tan\delta')\varepsilon_{33}^T$$

$$[11.17]$$

Eq. [11.16] becomes:

$$c_{eq}^* = \frac{(1 + j \tan \phi')}{s_{33}^E}, \ e_{eq}^* = \frac{d_{33}^*(1 - j \tan\theta'')}{s_{33}^{E^*}}, \ \varepsilon_{eq}^* = \varepsilon_{eq}^s(1 - j \tan\delta'')$$

[11.18]

where $\tan\theta'' = \tan\theta' - \tan\phi$, $\tan\delta'' = \dfrac{\varepsilon_{eq}^{s^r}}{\varepsilon_{eq}^{s^i}}$ and $\varepsilon_{eq}^{s^i}$

$$= \varepsilon_{33}^T \tan\delta' + \frac{d_{33}(\tan\theta'' - \tan\theta')}{s_{33}^E}$$

In case of a static analysis, linear displacement and electric field distributions along the z-axis can be assumed. The axial displacement and the electric potential, $u(z)$ and $\phi(z)$ respectively, can be expressed as:

$$u(z) = \left(1 - \frac{z}{\ell}\right) u_0 + \frac{z}{\ell} u_1$$

$$\phi(z) = \left(1 - \frac{z}{\ell}\right) \phi_0 + \frac{z}{\ell} \phi_1$$

[11.19]

where ℓ is the length of the cylinder and u_1 and ϕ_1, and u_2 and ϕ_2 are the displacements and electric potential at $z = 0$ and $z = 1$, respectively.

The axial strain and the electric field can be then calculated as:

$$S_3 = \frac{du(z)}{dz} = \frac{u_1 - u_0}{\ell}$$

$$E_3 = -\frac{d\Phi(z)}{dz} = \frac{\Phi_0 - \Phi_1}{\ell}$$

[11.20]

Replacing Eq. [11.20] into Eq. [11.15] results in a system of equations where u_2, u_1, ϕ_2, ϕ_1 are unknown as:

$$\begin{Bmatrix} F_1^* \\ F_2^* \\ -q_1^* \\ -q_2^* \end{Bmatrix} = \frac{A}{\ell} \begin{bmatrix} c_{eq}^* & -c_{eq}^* & -e_{eq}^* & e_{eq}^* \\ -c_{eq}^* & c_{eq}^* & e_{eq}^* & -e_{eq}^* \\ e_{eq}^* & -e_{eq}^* & \varepsilon_{eq}^{S^*} & -\varepsilon_{eq}^{S^*} \\ -e_{eq}^* & e_{eq}^* & -\varepsilon_{eq}^{S^*} & \varepsilon_{eq}^{S^*} \end{bmatrix} \begin{Bmatrix} u_1^* \\ u_2^* \\ \Phi_1^* \\ \Phi_2^* \end{Bmatrix}$$

[11.21]

where q_1 and F_1, and q_2 and F_2 are respectively the electric charges and the mechanical forces at $z = 0$ and $z = 1$, and A the cross-sectional area. If $u_1 = 0$ and $\phi_1 = 0$ and no mechanical force is applied to the two ends of the cylinder, Eq. [11.21] becomes:

$$\begin{bmatrix} c^*_{eq} & -e^*_{eq} \\ e^*_{eq} & \varepsilon^s_{eq} \end{bmatrix} \begin{Bmatrix} u^*_2 \\ \Phi_2 \end{Bmatrix} = \frac{\ell}{A} \begin{Bmatrix} 0 \\ -q^*_2 \end{Bmatrix}$$ [11.22]

To extend this model to a dynamic analysis, it is necessary to include the inertia effect and consider that the axial displacement does not vary linearly along the z-axis but as a sinusoid. The dynamic mass m_d for a harmonic analysis where the displacement has a sinusoidal shape, is related to the static unit mass m_0 by

$$m_d = \frac{\ell}{\pi}(\pi - 2)m_0$$ [11.23]

and Eq. [11.22] becomes:

$$\begin{bmatrix} \dfrac{m_d \ell}{A} & 0 \\ 0 & 0 \end{bmatrix} \begin{Bmatrix} \ddot{u}^*_2 \\ \ddot{\Phi}^*_2 \end{Bmatrix} + \begin{bmatrix} c^*_{eq} & e^*_{eq} \\ e^*_{eq} & -\varepsilon^s_{eq} \end{bmatrix} \begin{Bmatrix} u^*_2 \\ \Phi^*_2 \end{Bmatrix} = \frac{\ell}{A} \begin{Bmatrix} 0 \\ q^*_2 \end{Bmatrix}$$ [11.24]

The first equation of system of Eq. [11.24] is defined as:

$$\frac{m_d \ell}{A} \ddot{u}^*_2 + c^*_{eq} u^*_2 + e^*_{eq} \Phi^*_2 = 0$$ [11.25]

The real and imaginary parts of the displacement of the cylinder at $z = l$ can be written as a function of ϕ_2:

$$u^r_2 = -\frac{c^r_{eq} - \omega^2 \dfrac{m_d \ell}{A}}{\left(c^r_{eq} - \omega^2 \dfrac{m_d \ell}{A}\right)^2 + c^{i2}_{eq}} e^r_{eq} \Phi^r_2$$

$$u_2 i - \frac{c^i_{eq}}{c_{eq} - \omega^2 \dfrac{m_d \ell}{A}} u^r_2$$ [11.26]

and from Eq. [11.9] the dissipated power can then be expressed as:

$$P_{ana} = \frac{1}{2} \frac{A}{\ell} \omega (c^i_{eq}(u^r_2 + u^i_2) + \varepsilon^i_{eq}\Phi^r_2)$$ [11.27]

Analytical results are compared with ATILA modelling results in Figs 11.3 to 11.5 for a PZT-4 piezoelectric cylinder at 25°C where $\phi_2 = 1\,000$ V; the losses values are 0.02. The ATILA finite element mesh consists of an eight-noded, axisymmetrical, quadrilateral, piezoelectric element. Figures 11.3 and 11.4 display, respectively, the real and the imaginary parts of the

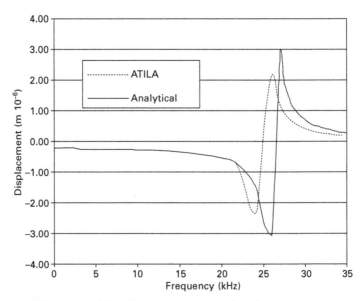

11.3 Real part of the displacement at z = l vs frequency.

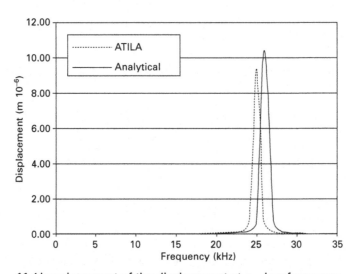

11.4 Imaginary part of the displacement at z = l vs frequency.

displacement at z = l, whereas Fig. 11.5 displays the total dissipated power versus the frequency. These figures show a relatively good agreement between the analytical and finite element modelling.

The resonance and anti-resonance frequencies for this cylinder are calculated considering that no losses take place in the material and dataset material parameters of the PZT4 at 25°C are 24 995 Hz and 28 784 Hz, respectively.

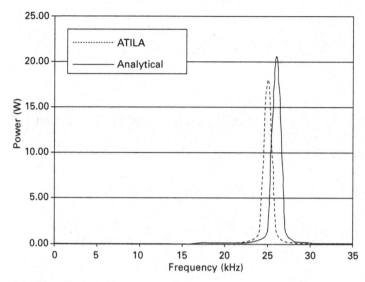

11.5 The dissipated power vs frequency.

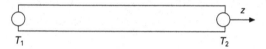

11.6 1D thermal modelling.

At the resonance frequency, the dissipated power is found to be more than 20 W. This high value can be estimated by the square of electric voltage to the global impedance that becomes small around the resonance frequency. This would suggest the use of the anti-resonance frequency instead of the resonance frequency to avoid thermal limits[2,3].

Thermal analysis

To validate the thermal analysis, the piezoelectric cylinder is defined with one element using ID linear interpolation (Fig. 11.6).

The interpolating polynomial for the ID element is

$$T(z) = N_1(z)T_1 + N_2(z)T_2 \qquad [11.28]$$

where $N_1(z) = \left(1 - \dfrac{z}{\ell}\right)$ and $N_2(z) = \dfrac{z}{\ell}$; the element has a length ℓ.

For a steady thermal analysis with one element, Eq. [11.9] becomes

$$([K_T] + [K_{h1}] + [K_{h2}])\{T\} = \{K_{T\infty 1}\} + \{K_{T\infty 2}\} + \{Q\} \qquad [11.29]$$

where

$$[K_T] = \frac{Ak_{zz}}{\ell} \begin{bmatrix} 1 & -1 \\ -1 & 1 \end{bmatrix}$$ is the conductivity matrix; A is the cross-section

area

$$[K_{h1}] = \frac{Ph\ell}{6} \begin{bmatrix} 2 & 1 \\ 1 & 2 \end{bmatrix}$$ is the convection matrix for element; P is the

perimeter

$$[K_{h2}] = hA \begin{bmatrix} 0 & 0 \\ 0 & 1 \end{bmatrix}$$ is the convection matrix at node 2

$$\{k_{T\infty1}\} = \frac{hT_\infty P\ell}{2} \begin{Bmatrix} 1 \\ 1 \end{Bmatrix}$$ is the convection vector for the element

$$\{k_{T\infty2}\} = \frac{hT_\infty A}{2} \begin{Bmatrix} 1 \\ 1 \end{Bmatrix}$$ is the convection vector at node 2

$$\{Q\} = \frac{p_d A\ell}{2} \begin{Bmatrix} 1 \\ 1 \end{Bmatrix}$$ is the thermal load vector; p_d is the dissipated power

density

The numerical values used are:

$k_{xx} = 2$ W/m/°C, $S_h = 858$ J/kg/°C, $h = 10$ W/m²/°C, $d = 2 \ 10^{-2}$ m, $\ell = 3$ 10^{-2} m and the frequency used is $20\,000$ Hz; from Eq. [11.27], the power dissipated is $8.34 \ 10^{-2}$ W. With these values, Eq. [11.29] is

$$\begin{Bmatrix} 0.433 & -0.283 \\ -0.283 & 0.483 \end{Bmatrix} \begin{Bmatrix} T_1 \\ T_2 \end{Bmatrix} = \begin{Bmatrix} 7.17 \\ 8.17 \end{Bmatrix} \qquad [11.30]$$

The results are $T_1 = 44.75$ °C and $T_2 = 43.14$ °C

To compare this model with an ATILA model, the finite element mesh (Fig 11.7) consists of one conduction element (eight-node quadrilateral) and two convection elements (three nodes). All these elements are axisymmetrical with a symmetry plane at the origin. A harmonic analysis has been performed with a voltage of $1\,000$ V at a frequency of $20\,000$ Hz. Figure 11.8 displays the cylinder temperature profile. The temperatures at both ends are 44.47 °C and 42.25 °C, respectively. A good agreement is observed between the simple model and the ATILA model.

For a transient thermal analysis with one element, Eq. [11.11] becomes:

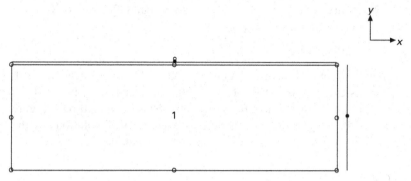

11.7 Mesh of the piezoelectric cylinder.

Temperature

11.8 Steady temperature profile.

$$[C]\{\dot{T}\} + ([K_T] + [K_{h1}] + [K_{h2}])\{T\} = \{K_{T\infty1}\} + \{K_{T\infty2}\} + \{Q\}$$

[11.31]

where

$[C] = \dfrac{\rho s_h A \ell}{6}\begin{bmatrix} 2 & 1 \\ 1 & 2 \end{bmatrix}$ is the specific heat-mass matrix with the specific heat

coefficient s_h. This value is 858 J/kg/°C, then Eq. [11.31] becomes:

$$0.02145\begin{bmatrix} 2 & 1 \\ 1 & 2 \end{bmatrix}\begin{Bmatrix} \dot{T_1} \\ \dot{T_2} \end{Bmatrix} + \begin{bmatrix} 0.433 & -0.283 \\ -0.283 & 0.483 \end{bmatrix}\begin{Bmatrix} T_1 \\ T_2 \end{Bmatrix} = \begin{Bmatrix} 7.06 \\ 8.06 \end{Bmatrix}$$

[11.32]

To obtain a simple solution, one only considers the value of the cylinder end. For the homogeneous solution of the differential equation, Eq. [11.32] becomes:

$$\frac{dT_2}{dt} + 1.564T_2 = 0$$

[11.33]

With the boundary conditions: $T_2 = 20$ °C at $t = 0$ and $T_2 = 43.14$ °C at $t = \infty$, the analytical solution of Eq. [11.33] is:

$$T_2 = (20{-}43.14)e^{-1.564t} + 43.14 \qquad [11.34]$$

To compare this model with an ATILA model, the finite element mesh is the same as the one used for the steady thermal analysis. This analysis corresponds to Eq. [11.12] where $\theta = 1/2$ (Crank–Nicholson method[8]). Figure 11.9 displays the temperature versus time for the analytical solution and the ATILA model. A good agreement is observed between the two results.

11.3.4 Piezoelecric transducers

The first application concerns a tonpilz transducer defined on Fig. 11.10. This transducer is composed of one stack of 78 X51 ceramics pre-stressed by a steel rod (steel 2) between an aluminium end-mass and a tail-mass made of steel. The surface in contact with the external medium is covered in rubber for protection against seawater. The power dissipated in operation is 10 W. The table in Fig. 11.11 compares temperatures computed from the analytical and 2D numerical model. Analytical results have been obtained with electrical circuit equivalent[9]. The temperature profile is shown in Plate XII (between pages 194 and 195).

The following application is a double-ended longitudinal vibrator composed of two stacks of 26 PZT4 ceramics pre-stressed by a steel rod between an aluminium end-mass and a central tail-mass made of cupronickel (Fig. 11.12)

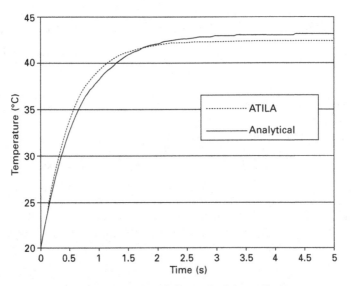

11.9 Transient temperature of the end of the cylinder.

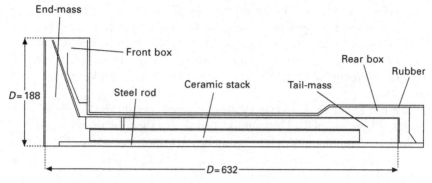

11.10 The tonpilz transducer.

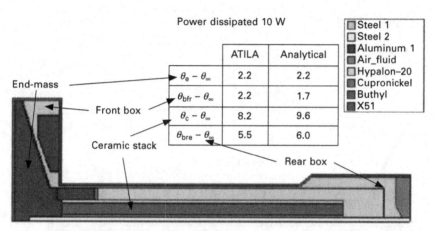

11.11 Temperature (°C) – comparison of analytical and FEA (ATILA).

Power dissipated 10 W

	ATILA	Analytical
$\theta_e - \theta_\infty$	2.2	2.2
$\theta_{bfr} - \theta_\infty$	2.2	1.7
$\theta_c - \theta_\infty$	8.2	9.6
$\theta_{bre} - \theta_\infty$	5.5	6.0

Steel 1
Steel 2
Aluminum 1
Air_fluid
Hypalon–20
Cupronickel
Buthyl
X51

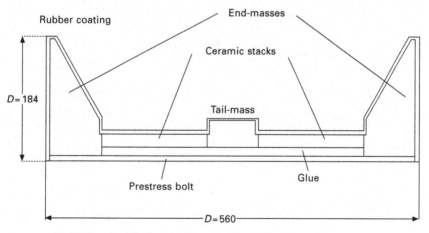

11.12 The doubled-ended longitudinal vibrator.

The surface in contact with the external medium is covered in rubber. The power dissipated in operation is 10 W. The table in Fig. 11.13 compares temperatures computed from the analytical and 2D numerical model. These results prove that a good agreement is found between analytical and numerical results. The temperature profile is shown in Plate XIII (between pages 194 and 195).

The last example is a class IV flextensional transducer. It is built with a thick elliptical shell of fibreglass. Inside the shell, at its midplane, 12 piezoelectric motors are tightly inserted. Each motor consists of 28 PZT4 ceramics mounted between steel-made central and end pieces. The external surface of the shell is covered in rubber (Fig. 11.14). The power dissipated in operation is 5 W. The table in Fig. 11.15 compares temperatures computed

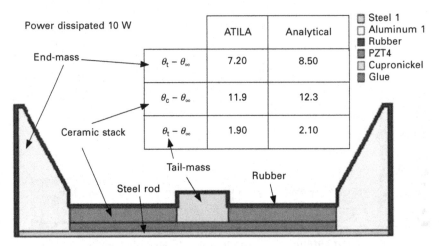

Power dissipated 10 W

	ATILA	Analytical
$\theta_t - \theta_\infty$	7.20	8.50
$\theta_c - \theta_\infty$	11.9	12.3
$\theta_t - \theta_\infty$	1.90	2.10

Legend: ☐ Steel 1 · ☐ Aluminum 1 · ■ Rubber · ■ PZT4 · ☐ Cupronickel · ▨ Glue

End-mass · Ceramic stack · Tail-mass · Rubber · Steel rod

11.13 Temperature-comparison of analytical and FEA (ATILA) (°C).

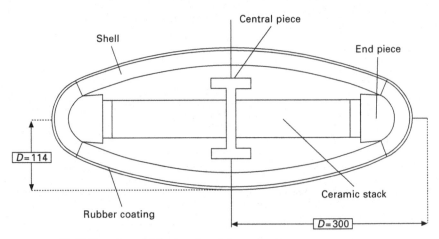

Shell · Central piece · End piece · $D=114$ · Rubber coating · Ceramic stack · $D=300$

11.14 The class IV flextensional transducer.

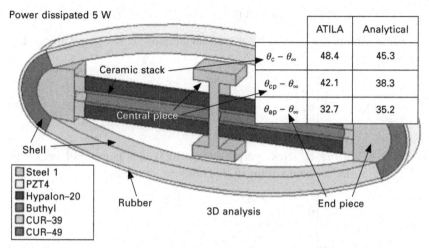

	ATILA	Analytical
$\theta_c - \theta_\infty$	48.4	45.3
$\theta_{cp} - \theta_\infty$	42.1	38.3
$\theta_{ep} - \theta_\infty$	32.7	35.2

11.15 Temperature-comparison of analytical and FEA (ATILA) (°C).

from the analytical and 3D numerical model. These results prove that a good agreement is found between analytical and numerical results. The 3D temperature profile is shown in Plate XIV (between pages 194 and 195).

11.4   Strains and stresses in piezoelectric materials caused by thermal effects

11.4.1 Initial thermal strain

Initial strains, that is strains which are independent of stress, may be due to many causes. In this case, temperature changes will result in an initial strain vector. The temperature field produces strains which are a function of the temperature distribution. It is assumed that the coefficient of the thermal expansion is independent of temperature. If such strains are denoted by $\{S_0\}$ then the stresses will be caused by the difference between the actual and thermal strains. Thus, the relationship between stresses and strains will be of the form:

$$\{\tau\} = [C^E](\{S\} - \{S_0\}) \qquad [11.35]$$

where $[C^E]$ is the rigidity matrix at constant field and the initial $\{S_0\}$ is defined as:

$$\{S_0\} = \lfloor S_{xx0} S_{yy0}\, S_{zz0} S_{xy0}\, S_{xz0} S_{zx0} \rfloor^T \qquad [11.36]$$

For a piezoelectric material in an element subject to a temperature rise T^e with coefficients of thermal expansion $\alpha_x,\ \alpha_y\ \alpha_z$ the initial strain can be written as:

$$\{S_0\} = T^e \lfloor \alpha_x \ \alpha_y \ \alpha_z \ 0 \ 0 \ 0 \rfloor^T \qquad [11.37]$$

No shear strains are caused by a thermal dilatation. For plane stress, Eq. [11.37] becomes:

$$\{S_0\} = T^e \begin{Bmatrix} \alpha_x \\ \alpha_y \\ 0 \end{Bmatrix} \qquad [11.38]$$

In plane strain the τ_{zz} stress perpendicular to the xy plane will be a new value, the initial thermal strains in this case are given by:

$$\{S_0\} = T^e \begin{Bmatrix} \alpha_x - \alpha_z \dfrac{S_{13}^E}{S_{33}^E} \\ \alpha_y - \alpha_z \dfrac{S_{13}^E}{S_{33}^E} \\ 0 \end{Bmatrix} \qquad [11.39]$$

Then, in axisymmetrical stress analysis, Eq. [11.37] becomes:

$$\{S_0\} = T^e \lfloor \alpha_r \ \alpha_z \ \alpha_\theta \ 0 \ 0 \ 0 \rfloor^T \qquad [11.40]$$

11.4.2 Equivalent nodal forces

The displacement field is defined as:

$$u^e = [N^e]\{U^e\} \qquad [11.41]$$

where u^e is the displacement field in one element, $\{U^e\}$ is the nodal displacement vector and $\{N^e\}$ is the shape function matrix.

The strain vector is defined by this relation:

$$\{S^e\} = [B^e]\{U^e\} \qquad [11.42]$$

where $[B^e]$ is obtained from the derivatives of the shape functions.
The nodal force vector due to initial strain can be obtained using the so-called weak formulation as[8]:

$$\{f^e\} = \int_{D^e} [B^e]^T [C^E]\{S_0^e\} dD^e \qquad [11.43]$$

11.4.3 Thermal stress

The stresses due to the thermal forces are computed from a static analysis from this equation:

$$\begin{bmatrix} [K_{uu}] & [K_{u\Phi}] \\ [K_{u\Phi}]^T & [K_{\Phi\Phi}] \end{bmatrix} \begin{Bmatrix} U \\ \Phi \end{Bmatrix} = \begin{Bmatrix} F \\ 0 \end{Bmatrix}$$ [11.44]

where $[K_{uu}]$, $[K_{u\Phi}]$, $[K_{\Phi\Phi}]$, are, respectively, the stiffness, piezoelectric and dielectric matrices, $\{U\}$ and $\{\Phi\}$ are, respectively, the displacement nodal values vectors and the electrical potential. The force vector is obtained from Eq. [11.43] as:

$$\{F\} = \sum_e \{f^e\}$$ [11.45]

Then, for each node 'i', the stress vector is obtained from Eq. [11.35] as:

$$\{\tau^i\} = [C^E](\{S^i\} - \{S_0^i\})$$ [11.46]

11.4.4 ATILA analysis for thermal stress

To compute thermal stress from a transient analysis in the ATILA code, a three-step analysis is performed.

Harmonic analysis

The electromechanical behaviour is applied to the structure, with a harmonic analysis (Eq. [11.47]), the resulting dissipated power is obtained from Eq. [11.48] where 'r' and 'i' denote, respectively, the real and imaginary parts of components.

$$\begin{bmatrix} [K_{uu}^*] - \omega^2[M] & [K_{u\Phi}^*] \\ [K_{u\Phi}^*]^T & [K_{\Phi\Phi}^*] \end{bmatrix} \begin{Bmatrix} U^* \\ \phi^* \end{Bmatrix} = \begin{Bmatrix} F^* \\ -q^* \end{Bmatrix}$$ [11.47]

$$p_d^e = \frac{1}{2} \omega \left(\{u^r \ \Phi^r\}^T \begin{bmatrix} k_{uu}^i & k_{u\Phi}^i \\ k_{\Phi u}^i & k_{\Phi\Phi}^i \end{bmatrix} \begin{Bmatrix} u^r \\ \Phi^r \end{Bmatrix} + \{u^i \ \Phi^i\}^T \begin{bmatrix} k_{uu}^i & k_{u\Phi}^i \\ k_{\Phi u}^i & k_{\Phi\Phi}^i \end{bmatrix} \begin{Bmatrix} u^i \\ \Phi^i \end{Bmatrix} \right)$$ [11.48]

Transient analysis

The second step consists of the thermal transient response of the structure. The system of equations to solve the transient thermal problem can be written in the following form:

$$[C]\{\dot{T}\} + [K]\{T\} = \{Q(t)\}$$ [11.49]

where

$[C] = \sum_e \int_{D^e} s_h [N^e]^T [N^e] dD^e$ is the specific heat (mass) matrix with the specific heat coefficient s_h, $[K] = \sum_e ([k_T^e] + [k_h^e])$ is the thermal conduction and convection (stiffness) matrix and $\{Q(t)\} = \sum_e (\{Q^e(t)\} - \{q^e\} + \{k_{T_\infty}^e\})$ represents the total thermal loading. This vector is assumed constant and is obtained from the harmonic analysis at one frequency. It will be denoted $\{Q_0\}$ and $\{\dot{T}\} = \left\{ \dfrac{dT}{dt} \right\}$ denotes the first time derivative

where:

$[k_T^e] = \int_{D^e} [B^e]^T [C^e][B^e] dD^e$ is the conductivity matrix

$[k_h^e] = \int_{\Gamma^e} h[N^e]^T [N^e] d\Gamma^e$ is the convection matrix

$\{k_{T_\infty}^e\} = \int_{\Gamma^e} hT_\infty \lfloor N^e \rfloor d\Gamma^e$ is the convection vector

$\{q^e\} = \int_{\Gamma^e} q\lfloor N^e \rfloor d\Gamma^e$ is the thermal flux vector

and $\{Q^e\} = -\int_{D^e} \lfloor N^e \rfloor p_d^e dD^e$ is the thermal load vector including the dissipated power from material losses.

In direct integration, Eq. [11.11] is integrated using a numerical step-by-step procedure. Instead of trying to satisfy this equation at any time t, it is aimed at satisfying this one only at discrete time intervals Δt apart. By applying the method of weighted residuals over a time interval Δt, the following solution to Eq. [11.11] is obtained[8]

$$T_{t+1} = ([C] + \theta \Delta t[K])^{-1}([C] - (1 - \theta)\Delta t[K])T_t + \Delta t\{Q_0\} \qquad [11.12]$$

where T_t is the temperature at time t.

The θ parameter takes the following values depending on the selected weighting method:

$\theta = 0$ Euler
$\theta = {}^1/_2$ Crank–Nicolson
$\theta = {}^2/_3$ Galerkin
$\theta = 1$ back difference

The combination of this method within a transient analysis with ATILA can be carried out in the following way, for each time step:

- Q_0 is calculated from the ATILA harmonic analysis for the piezoelectric system.
- T_{t+1} is computed from Eq. [11.12].

Stress analysis

At each time step 't', for temperature $T^e(t)$, a static analysis is performed from this equation:

$$\begin{bmatrix} [K_{uu}] & [K_{u\Phi}] \\ [K_{u\Phi}]^T & [K_{\Phi\Phi}] \end{bmatrix} \begin{Bmatrix} U(t) \\ \Phi(t) \end{Bmatrix} = \begin{Bmatrix} F(t) \\ 0 \end{Bmatrix}$$

[11.50]

where

$$\{F(t)\} = \sum_e \{f^e(t)\}$$

[11.51]

and

$$\{f^e(t)\} = \int_{D^e} [B^e]^T [C^E] \{S_0^e(t)\} dD^e$$

[11.52]

where

$$\{S_0^e(t)\} = (T^e(t) - T_\infty) \lfloor \alpha_x \ \alpha_y \ \alpha_z \ 0 \ 0 \ 0 \rfloor^T$$

[11.53]

and T_∞ is the ambient temperature

Then the stresses for each node are obtained from Eq. [11.46]

$$\{\tau^i\} = [C^E](\{S^i\} - \{S_0^i\})$$

[11.54]

where the strain vector $\{S^i\}$ is obtained from the displacement vector $\{U\}$ (Eq. [11.50]). The thermal stresses can be added to harmonic stresses due to the displacement vector obtained from Eq. [11.46].

11.5   Numerical validation of the model

11.5.1 Description of the model

An analytical formulation is used to validate the dissipated power calculation in ATILA as well as the thermal analysis with stresses. The geometry consists of a PZT-4 piezoelectric cylinder having a length of 25 mm, an outer diameter of 60 mm and an inner diameter of 50 mm (Fig. 11.16). The dynamic excitation is provided electrically to the cylinder using two electrodes located at the outer and inner surfaces. Figure 11.10 shows the configuration of a radially poled, 31-mode piezoelectric cylinder.

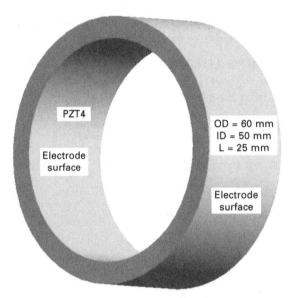

11.16 Piezoelectric cylinder radially poled.

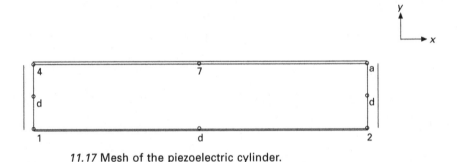

11.17 Mesh of the piezoelectric cylinder.

11.5.2 Numerical model

To validate this development, a finite element mesh (Fig. 11.17) consists of one conduction element (eight-node quadrilateral) and four convection elements (three nodes). All these elements are axisymmetrical. A harmonic analysis has been performed with a voltage of 1 500 V at a frequency of 5 000 Hz. The thermal conductivity kc is equal to 2.1 W/m/°C, the in-air convection film coefficient is equal to 10 W/m²/°C and the losses are 0.0032.

The analytical results are issued from the methods of Berlincourt[10] and Camp[11] for a ring with the assumption that the width and thickness of the ring are small compared to its circumference.

If simple harmonic excitation is assumed, a solution for the steady state displacement is[12]:

$$u_r = \frac{2\pi t L d_{31}}{j\omega S_{11}^E} \frac{1}{Z_m} E_0 e^{j\omega t} \qquad [11.55]$$

where the mechanical impedance is:

$$Z_m = j\left(\omega M - \frac{1}{\omega C_m}\right) \qquad [11.56]$$

M is the mass of the cylinder given by $M = 2\pi\rho t L$, ρ is the density, t is the thickness, L is the length, a is the mean radius of the cylinder, ω is the pulsation, $E_3 = E_0 e^{j\omega t}$ the sinusoidal electric field, S_{11}^E is the circumferential elastic compliance at field constant and the mechanical compliance C_m is:

$$\frac{1}{C_m} = \frac{2\pi t L}{a S_{11}^E} \qquad [11.57]$$

The mechanical resonance frequency is given by:

$$f_r = \frac{1}{2\pi}\sqrt{\frac{1}{a^2 \rho S_{11}^E}} \qquad [11.58]$$

the electromechanical coupling coefficient for this mode is given by:

$$k_{31} = \sqrt{\frac{d_{31}^2}{S_{11}^E \varepsilon_{33}^T}} \qquad [11.59]$$

and the circumferential stress is given by

$$T_{\theta\theta} = \frac{u_r}{a S_{11}^E} - \frac{d_{31} E_3}{S_{11}^E} \qquad [11.60]$$

The comparison of analytical results and modeling results are shown in Table 11.1. A good agreement is observed between the analytical model and the ATILA model. From the energy balance (heat flow) equation for a solid material[13,14], the internal heat source in watts/volume is given by:

$$Q = \omega E^e \varepsilon_{33}^T \tan \delta' \qquad [11.61]$$

where the electric field may be written as $V/2a$; V is the rms voltage across the electrodes, $2a$ is the wall thickness of the ceramic cylinder and ε_{33}^T is the dielectric permittivity at constant strain and $\tan \delta$, is the loss.

The steady-state temperature is given by:

$$T^{ss} = \frac{Q V_c}{A_c}\left(\frac{a}{k_c} + \frac{1}{h}\right) + T_0 \qquad [11.62]$$

where V_c is the total volume of ceramic, A_c is the total surface area (including inner diameter (ID), outer diameter (OD), and end surfaces), k_c is the thermal

Table 11.1 Comparison of analytical and FEA (ATILA) electromechanical results

	f_r (Hz)	k_{31} (%)	u_r (m)	$T_{\theta\theta}$ (N/m^2)
Analytical	18 929	32.7	1.0908E-06	2.250E+05
ATILA	19 210	31.0	1.0877E-06	2.156E+05

Table 11.2 Comparison of analytical and FEA (ATILA) thermal results

	Q (W/m^3)	P (W)	T^{ss} (°C)	u_{re} (m)	u_{ri} (m)
Analytical	5.204E+04	1.124	30.8	1.32E-06	1.10E-06
ATILA		1.124	31.0	1.36E-06	1.17E-06

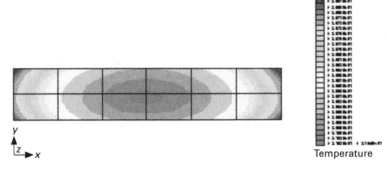

Temperature

11.18 Temperature profile through the cylinder (°C).

conductivity, h is the in-air convection film coefficient, a is one-half the thickness of the ceramic cylinder and T_0 is the ambient temperature.

If the electric field effect is negligible, the radial thermal displacement is given by:

$$u_r = \alpha_r(T^{ss} - T_0)r \qquad [11.63]$$

where α_r is the radial thermal expansion coefficient (4.0×10^{-06}), and r is a radial co-ordinate.

In Table 11.2, P is the dissipated power, $P = Q*V_c$. The comparison of analytical results and modelling results are shown in Table 11.2. A good agreement is observed between the analytical model and the ATILA model. The temperature profile is shown in Fig. 11.18.

If the electric field effect is negligible, the axial dilatation is given by:

$$\Delta L_T = \alpha_r(T^{ss} - T_0)L \qquad [11.64]$$

If the cylinder is fixed at both ends, the axial stress is given by:

$$T_{xx} = -\frac{\Delta L_T}{LS_{11}^E}$$ [11.65]

The comparison of analytical results and modelling results are shown in Table 11.3. A difference is observed between the analytical model and the ATILA model due to the electric field effect. The axial stress profile is shown on Fig. 11.19.

For a transient analysis, Fig. 11.20 displays the axial thermal stress versus time. On the same figure, the axial harmonic stress is combined with the axial thermal stress.

11.6 Experimental validation of the model

In the previous section, the transient thermal analysis has been developed and the temperature and dissipated power distribution have been obtained at each step. In this section, a validation of transient thermal computation is presented. The validation concerns piezoelectric ring transducers driven at high power levels under continuous sine-wave drive. The transducers consist of several piezoelectric ceramic cylinders of three sizes that are coated with a polymeric insulator as a water barrier[15]. The testing in-air of uncoated and coated ceramic cylinders has been performed to determine the temperature-versus-time profile for different drive levels.

Table 11.3 Comparison of analytical and FEA (ATILA) thermal stresses

	ΔL_T(m)	T_{xx} (N/m²)
Analytical	1.10E-06	−4.47E+06
ATILA	1.14E-06	−4.37E+06

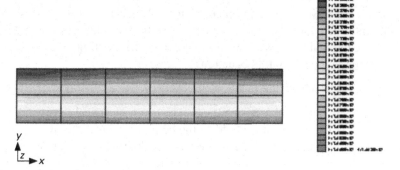

11.19 Axial stress profile of the cylinder.

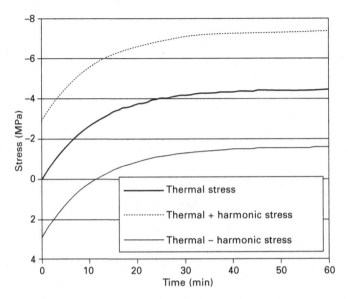

11.20 Axial stress of the cylinder vs time.

11.6.1 Analytical model

The energy balance equation for a solid material is[13]:

$$\frac{\partial T}{\partial t} = \frac{k}{\rho S_h} \nabla^2 T + \frac{Q}{\rho S_h} \qquad [11.66]$$

where T is the temperature (°C), t is the time (sec), ρ is the density (kg/m^3), S_h is the specific heat coefficient (J/kg/°C), k is the thermal conductivity (W/m/°C) and Q is the internal heat generation (W/m^3). At solid–liquid interfaces where convection is important, the heat flux (W) is defined as:

$$q = Ah(T - T_\infty) \qquad [11.67]$$

where h is the convection film coefficient (W/m^2/°C), T is the temperature at the interface, and T_∞ is the temperature in the fluid far from the interface.

The internal sources are the results of dielectric heating in the piezoelectric material as given by this equation[16]:

$$Q = \omega E^2 \varepsilon^T \tan \delta_e \qquad [11.68]$$

where ω is the angular frequency, $\tan \delta_e$ is the electrical dissipation factor, $E = V/t$ is the rms electric field in the ceramic (where V is the rms voltage across the electrodes, and t is the wall thickness of the ceramic cylinder) and $\varepsilon^T = K^T \varepsilon_0$ (where K^T is the dielectric constant and ε_0 is the dielectric constant of the vacuum).

Model for an uncoated cylinder

For a 31-mode piezoelectric uncoated cylinder, Fig. 11.21 shows the basic configuration of the radially poled cylinder. For steady state, the energy balance (Eq. [11.66]) may be written as:

$$k \frac{\partial^2 T}{\partial x^2} + Q = 0 \qquad [11.69]$$

The expression of an approximate steady-state temperature at the ceramic wall outer surface is obtained from Eq. [11.69] as:

$$T^{ss} = \frac{QV_c}{A_c}\left(\frac{a}{k_c} + \frac{1}{h}\right) + T_0 \qquad [11.70]$$

where V_c is the total volume, A_c is the total surface area (including inner diameter (ID), outer diameter (OD), and end surfaces), k_c is the thermal conductivity, a is one-half the wall thickness of the ceramic cylinder and T_0 is the initial temperature.

The approximate time-dependent model can be obtained from Eq. [11.66][13] as:

$$\frac{\partial \overline{T}}{\partial t} = \frac{Q}{\rho S_h} - \frac{hA_c}{\rho S_{hc} V_c}(\overline{T} - T_\infty) \qquad [11.71]$$

The solution to Eq. [11.71] is given by:

$$\overline{T} = (T_{ss} - T_0)(1 - e^{-t/\tau}) + T_0 \qquad [11.72]$$

where τ the time constant to reach steady state is defined as:

$$\tau = \frac{\rho S_{hc} V_c}{hA_c} \qquad [11.73]$$

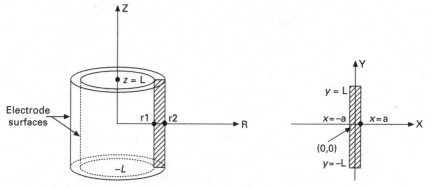

11.21 Radially poled piezoelectric ceramic cylinder.

With Eq. [11.70], the approximate time-dependent temperature can be expressed as:

$$T(t) = \frac{QV_c}{A_c}\left(\frac{a}{k_c} + \frac{1}{h}\right)(1 - e^{-t/\tau}) + T_0 \qquad [11.74]$$

The finite element solution with the ATILA model is shown on Fig. 11.22; the agreement between models is good (Fig. 11.23).

Model for a coated cylinder

The case where a ceramic cylinder is encased in a protective polymer coating is studied in this section. The ceramic and the coating are assumed as lumped parameters. A linear temperature profile in the polymer is assumed. The thermal energy balance equation for the coated ceramic is written as[13]:

$$\rho_c S_{hc} V_c \frac{\partial T_a}{\partial t} = QV_c - k_p A_c \frac{(T_a - T_b)}{d} \qquad [11.75]$$

where d is the thickness of the coating, T_a is the temperature at the ceramic/

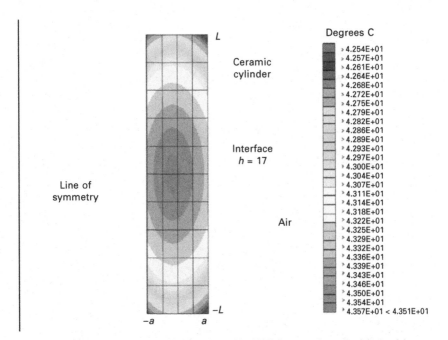

11.22 Axisymmetrical FE model for PZT-8 ceramic cylinder 2 with dimensions of OD = 1.826 inches, ID = 1.45 inches, and length = 0.807 inch at steady state, driven at 1000 Vrms (inputs to model: f = 10kHz, H = 17, K^T = 1100, T_0 = 23 °C, dissipation = 0.0065, k_c = 2.1, S_{hc} = 420, ρ_c = 7600).

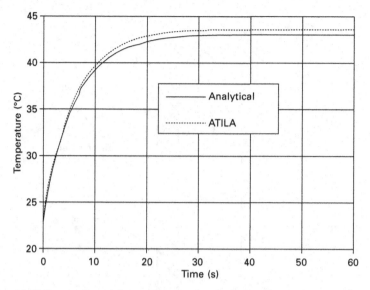

11.23 Comparison of approximate analytical and axisymmetrical FE model solutions for uncoated PZT-8 ceramic cylinder with dimensions of OD = 1.826 inches, ID = 1.45 inches and length = 0.807 inch (T_0 = 23 °C).

polymer coating interface and T_b is the temperature at the polymer coating/ fluid interface (Fig. 11.24).

From Eq. [11.75], the steady-state temperature can be found by integrating with respect to time and applying the boundary condition at the interface. This approximate solution is defined as:

$$T_a^{ss} = \left(\frac{1}{h} + \frac{d}{k_p}\right)\frac{QV_c}{A_c} + T_0 \qquad [11.76]$$

The approximate time-dependent temperature for a coated cylinder can be written as:

$$T_a = \frac{Q}{\tau_s \rho_c S_{hc}}(1 - e^{-\lambda_2 t}) + T_0 \qquad [11.77]$$

where:

$$\tau_s = \frac{\varepsilon_2}{\varepsilon_1} \qquad [11.78]$$

$$\lambda_2 = \frac{1}{2}\,\varepsilon_1\left(1 - \sqrt{1 - 4\frac{\varepsilon_2}{\varepsilon_1^2}}\right) \qquad [11.79]$$

with $\varepsilon_1 = 2\tau_c + \tau_p + \tau_h,\ \varepsilon2 = \tau_c\tau_h,\ \varepsilon_3 = \tau_p + \tau_h$ \qquad [11.80]

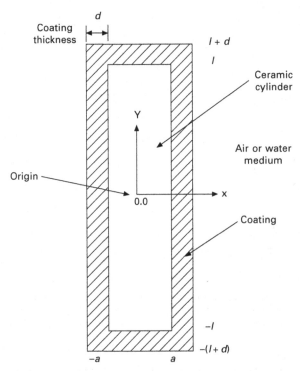

11.24 Epoxy/coated ceramic cylinder layout.

and $\quad \tau_c = \dfrac{k_p A_c}{d\rho_c S_{hc} V_c}, \tau_p = \dfrac{k_p A_p}{d\rho_p S_{hp} V_p}, \tau_h = \dfrac{2h A_p}{\rho_p S_{hp} V_p}$ [11.81]

The piezoceramic material and polymer coating material are represented by the subscripts c and p, respectively. The Vs and As are the volumes and areas, respectively, of the ceramic and coating (only the area exposed to the fluid in the case of the coating).

Figure 11.25 compares the simplified model (Eq. [11.77]) with the FE model. The temperature profile with the FE model is shown in Fig. 11.26.

11.6.2 Experimental validation

Bare cylinder in air

The first test consists of bare cylinders in air. Three cylinders with different dimensions (Table 11.4) and properties (Table 11.5) have been modelled. The values of the film coefficient h are shown on Table 11.7 on page 264. Each cylinder has been driven at three voltage levels – 500, 750 and 1 000 Vrms or 707.1, 1 060.7 and 1 414.2 V for the FEA models.

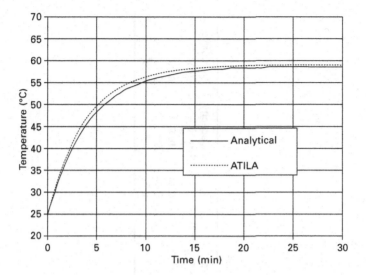

11.25 Comparison of approximate analytical and axisymmetrical FE model solutions for coated PZT-8 ceramic cylinder 3 with dimensions of OD = 1.054 inches, ID = 0.791 inch, and length = 0.807 inch (T_0 = 25 °C).

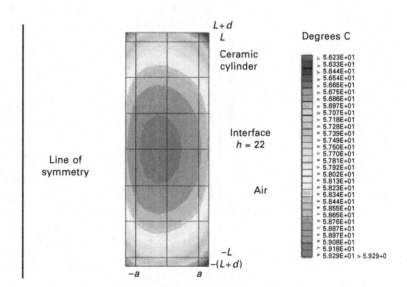

11.26 Axisymmetrical FE model for coated PZT-8 ceramic cylinder 3 with dimensions of OD = 1.054 inches, ID = 0.791 inch, and length = 0.527 inch at steady state, driven at 1000 Vrms (inputs to model: f = 10kHz, H = 17, K^T = 1100, T_0 = 25 °C, dissipation = 0.01, k_c = 2.1, S_{hc} = 420, ρ_c = 7600).

Table 11.4 Piezoelectric ceramic cylinder dimensions and measured small signal properties

Cylinder no.	OD (in./cm)	ID (in./cm)	Length (in./cm)	Material	Resonant frequency (kHz)	k_{eff}	Capacity (nF)	Dissipation ($\tan\delta_e$)
1	2.546/6.467	2.160/5.486	0.964/2.449	PZT-4 (Type I)	17.2	0.34	10.8	0.0032
2	1.826/4.638	1.454/3.693	0.807/2.050	PZT-8 (Type III)	26.2	0.33	5.5	0.0026
3	1.054/2.677	0.791/2.009	0.527/1.339	PZT-8 (Type III)	47.1	0.32	2.5	0.0034

Table 11.5 Piezoelectric ceramic material properties[16,17]

Property	PZT-4 (Navy Type I)	PZT-8 (Navy Type III)
Density ρ (kg/m^3)	7600	7600
Curie temperature (°C)	≥300	≥300
Heat capacity C_c (J/kg °C)	420	420
Thermal conductivity k_c (K/m °C)	2.1	2.1
Dielectric constant K^T ($\varepsilon^T/\varepsilon_0$)	1300	1000–1100
Dissipation factor (tan δ) large signal (4 kVrm/cm)	0.04	0.01

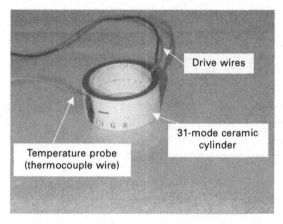

11.27 Uncoated ceramic 31-mode cylinder with thermocouple wire expoxied[2].

Table 11.6 FE model results

Cylinder no.	Resonant frequency (kHz)	K_{eff}
1	17.4	0.31
2	26.3	0.27
3	46.9	0.27

For comparison, the temperature was measured by a thermocouple attached to the outer radius of the cylinder at the mid-point of the length (Fig. 11.27)[13]. The resonant frequencies and the coupling coefficient obtained by FE models are shown on Table 11.6. Figures 11.28 to 11.30 compare the simplified model (Eq. [11.74]), the FE model and the measured values. The results are quite good; a slight difference exists between the simplified or FE model and the measurement due to the value of the heat capacity of the PZT-8 ceramic.

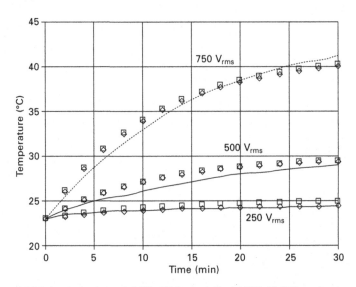

11.28 Analytical model (◊), FEA-modelled (ATILA) (□) and measured (__) uncoated cylinder 1 in-air at 5 kHz.

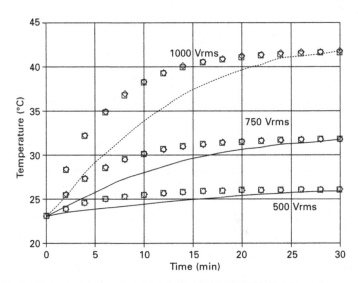

11.29 Analytical model (◊), FEA-modelled (ATILA) (□) and measured (__) uncoated cylinder 2 in-air at 10 kHz.

Coated cylinder in air

The same three cylinders with an epoxy have been modelled. The applied epoxy has a relatively high thermal conductivity ($k \approx 1$) and high heat capacity ($C \approx 1400$), but a low electrical conductivity. The density is 1 830

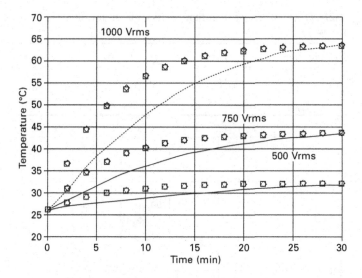

11.30 Analytical model (◊), FEA-modelled (ATILA) (□) and measured
(__) uncoated cylinder 3 in-air at 10 kHz.

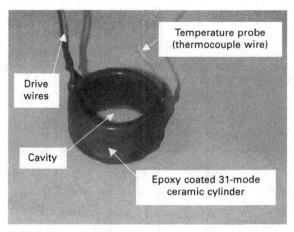

11.31 Epoxy coated, 31-mode cylinder with thermocouple[15].

kg/m^3 and the sound speed is 2 000 m/s. Figure 11.31 shows a representative coated cylinder[15].The values of h assumed in the model were the same as those used for the bare cylinders (Table 11.7). The results (Figs 11.32 to 11.34) are relatively good; a difference exists between the simplified or FE model and the measurement due to the value of the heat capacity of the PZT-8 ceramic.

Table 11.7 In-air convection film coefficients (h) for different ceramic cylinders

Cylinder no.	5 kHz	10 kHz	15 kHz
1	10	–	–
2	–	17	22
3	–	22	30

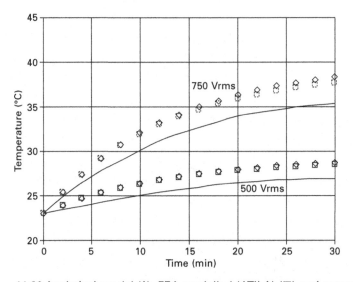

11.32 Analytical model (◊), FEA-modelled (ATILA) (□) and measured (__) coated cylinder 1 in-air at 5 kHz.

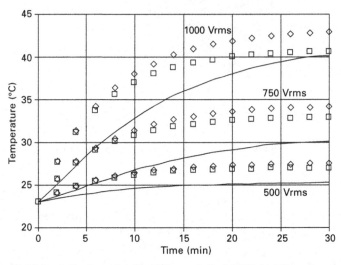

11.33 Analytical model (◊), FEA-modelled (ATILA) (□) and measured (__) coated cylinder 2 in-air at 10 kHz.

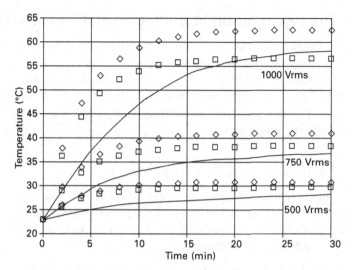

11.34 Analytical model (◊), FEA-modelled (ATILA) (□) and measured (_) coated cylinder 3 in-air at 10 kHz.

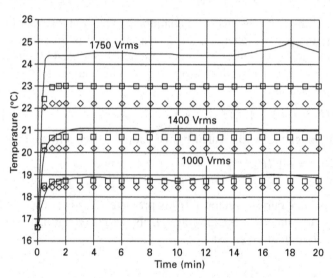

11.35 Analytical model (◊), FEA-modelled (ATILA) (□) and measured (_) in-water cylinder 2 with epoxy coating at 26 kHz (ring resonance).

Coated cylinder in water

The modelling result for cylinder 2 is shown on Fig. 11.35 with a film coefficient of 1 350 W/m². The results are quite good at the two voltage levels (1 000 Vrms and 1 400 Vrms); the quick flatness of temperature is evident for the different voltage drive levels for the analytical, FEA-modelled and measured cylinder.

11.7   Heat generation in magnetostrictive materials

The use of magnetostrictive projectors makes the heating problem critical. Several heat sources must be considered: the Joule effect in the excitation coil, the mechanical and magnetic losses in the magnetostrictve material and the eddy currents in the magnetostrictive rod and the other metallic parts. The aim of this section is the development of the heat generation in a magnetostrictive transducer.

11.7.1 Material losses and dissipated power

For a magnetostrictive material, the stress $\{T\}$ and $\{S\}$ straintensors and magnetic field $\{H\}$ and magnetic induction $\{B\}$ vectors are coupled through constitutive relations. Choosing strain and magnetic field as independent variables, the relations are written as[18]:

$$\{S\} = [s^H]\{T\} + [d]^T\{H\}$$
$$\{B\} = [d]\{T\} + [\mu^T]^T\{H\} \qquad [11.82]$$

where $[s^H]$ is the constant magnetic compliance tensor at constant magnetic field, $[d]$ is the piezomagnetic strain tensor and $[\mu^T]$ is the constant stress magnetic permeability tensor. The magnetic field is induced by sets of coils, each set being supplied by an electric current. The total magnetic field $\{H\}$ can be expressed as:

$$\{H\} = \{H_s\} + \{H_r\} \qquad [11.83]$$

$\{H_s\}$ is the magnetic field created by the source currents in vacuum:

$$\{H_s\} = + [^0H^s]\,\{I^s\} \qquad [11.84]$$

where
$\{I^s\}$ is the source current vector. $[^0H^s]$ is pre-determined for each coil using the Bio-Savart numerical integration. $[H_r]$ is the non-rotational component of the magnetic field given as:

$$\{H_r\} = -\left\{\frac{\partial \Phi_M}{\partial x}\right\} \qquad [11.85]$$

where $\{\Phi_M\}$ is the magnetic potential vector. The material coefficients are written as complex quantities to define losses as negative phase angles:

$$[s^H] = [s^{H^r}] - j[s^{H^i}]$$
$$[d] = [d^r] - j[d^i] \qquad [11.86]$$
$$[\mu^T] = [\mu^{T^r}] - j[\mu^{T^i}]$$

The dissipated power density is defined as:

$$P_d = \frac{1}{2} \omega I_m (\{B\}^T \{H^*\} + \{T\}^T \{S^*\})$$ [11.87]

where ω is the angular frequency, $\{H^*\}$, $\{S^*\}$ are, respectively, the conjugate of the magnetic induction and the strain vector at the circular frequency ω. I_m is the imaginary part of the value. The dissipated power may be reduced to an expression written in engineering notation in terms of the electric field and stress by substituting Eq. [11.82] for Eq. [11.87]:

$$P_d = \frac{1}{2} \omega I_m (\{H^r\}^T [d^*]\{T^*\} + \{H^r\}^T [\mu^{T^*}]\{H^*\}$$

$$+ \{T^r\}^T [s^{H^*}]\{T^*\} + \{T^r\}^T [d^*]^T \{H^*\})$$ [11.88]

The first and the last terms express the dissipated power density from the magnetic induction and the mechanical stress coupling, the second term is a purely magnetic dissipation whereas the third term is a purely mechanical dissipation.

The heat generation density, q_J, obtained by the Joule effect in the coil is defined, for the coil volume, as:

$$q_J = \frac{RI^2}{V}$$ [11.89]

where R is the coil resistance, I is the current in the coil and V is the coil volume. For a harmonic analysis, the magnetic excitation currents are data (nine currents max); R and V are obtained by the harmonic analysis.

11.7.2 Implementation of ATILA for the thermal analysis of magnetostrictive materials

Steady problems for heat transfer

For a steady-state solution, the thermal behaviour is weakly coupled to the electromechanical response. The method thus takes advantage of the order of magnitude which is greater than the time constant for thermal effects compared to the mechanical behaviour. A two-step analysis is performed whereby the electromechanical behaviour is first computed, and the resulting dissipated power is then applied as a heat generator to determine the resulting temperature of the system. The heat source term is entered into the equation for heat transfer using the heat equation as:

$$\frac{\partial}{\partial x}\left(k_{xx} \frac{\partial T}{\partial x}\right) + \frac{\partial}{\partial y}\left(k_{yy} \frac{\partial T}{\partial y}\right) + \frac{\partial}{\partial z}\left(k_{zz} \frac{\partial T}{\partial z}\right) + P_d^T = 0$$ [11.90]

where T denotes temperature (°C), k_{xx}, k_{yy}, k_{zz} are the conductivity coefficients (W/m/°C) along x, y, z, respectively, P_d^T is the heat generated (W/m³) within the body including the dissipated power from material losses and the heat generation density from the Joule effect. This value is positive if the heat is put into the body.

The boundary conditions associated with Eq. [11.90] can be expressed in two different forms. If the temperature is known along a part of the boundary then

$$T = T_S \qquad [11.91]$$

where T_S is the boundary temperature at the surface S. If heat is gained or lost at the boundary Γ due to convection, $h(T - T_\infty)$, or a heat flux, q, then

$$k_{xx} \frac{\partial T}{\partial x} \ell_x + k_{yy} \frac{\partial T}{\partial y} \ell_y + k_{zz} \frac{\partial T}{\partial z} \ell_z + q + h(T - T_\infty) = 0 \qquad [11.92]$$

where h is the convective thermal film coefficient (W/m²/°C), q is the heat flux (W/m²) and T_∞ is the ambient temperature of the surrounding medium.

A coupled magneto-mechanical thermal analysis was implemented in the ATILA finite element code to allow for computation of heat generation in transducers. The finite element formulation is:

$$\sum_e ([k_T^e]\{T^e\}) = \sum_e (\{Q^e\} + \{Q_J^e\} - \{q^e\} - [k_h^e]\{T^e\} + \{k_{T_\infty}^e\}) \qquad [11.93]$$

where:

$$[k_T^e] = \int_{D^e} [B^e]^T [C^e][B^e] dD^e \quad \text{is the conductivity matrix} \qquad [11.94]$$

$$[k_h^e] = \int_{\Gamma^e} h[N^e]^T [N^e] d\Gamma^e \quad \text{is the convection matrix} \qquad [11.95]$$

$$\{k_{T_\infty}^e\} = \int_{\Gamma^e} hT_\infty \lfloor N^e \rfloor d\Gamma^e \quad \text{is the convection vector} \qquad [11.96]$$

$$[q^e] = \int_{\Gamma^e} q \lfloor N^e \rfloor d\Gamma^e \quad \text{is the thermal flux vector} \qquad [11.97]$$

$$\{Q^e\} = -\int_{D^e} \lfloor N^e \rfloor p_d^e dD^e \quad \text{is the thermal load vector}$$

including the dissipated power from material losses $\qquad [11.98]$

and $\{Q_J^e\} = -\int_{D_J^e} [N_J^e] q_J^e dD_J^e$ is the thermal load

vector obtained by the Joule effect. $\qquad [11.99]$

11.7.3 Thermal load formulation

Thermal load from material losses

The dissipated power density (Eq. [11.88]) provides the internal heat generation. It is calculated first for each piezomagnetic element (HEXA20M, PRIS15M, PYRA13M, TETR10M, QUAD08M, TRIA06M) from:

$$
p_d^e = \frac{1}{2}\,\omega \left(\{\tilde{u}^r \ \tilde{\Phi}_M^r \ \tilde{I}^{S^r}\}^T
\begin{bmatrix}
[k_{uu}^i] & [k_{u\Phi}^i] & [k_{uI}^i] \\
[k_{u\Phi}^i]^T & [k_{\Phi\Phi}^i] & [k_{\Phi I}^i] \\
[k_{uI}^i]^T & [k_{\Phi I}^i]^T & [k_{II}^i]
\end{bmatrix}
\begin{Bmatrix}
\tilde{u}^r \\
\tilde{\Phi}_M^r \\
\tilde{I}^{S^r}
\end{Bmatrix}
\right.
$$

$$
\left.
+ \{\tilde{u}^i \ \tilde{\Phi}_M^i \ \tilde{I}^{S^i}\}^T
\begin{bmatrix}
[k_{uu}^i] & [k_{u\Phi}^i] & [k_{uI}^i] \\
[k_{u\Phi}^i]^T & [k_{\Phi\Phi}^i] & [k_{\Phi I}^i] \\
[k_{uI}^i]^T & [k_{\Phi I}^i]^T & [k_{II}^i]
\end{bmatrix}
\begin{Bmatrix}
\tilde{u}^i \\
\tilde{\Phi}_M^i \\
\tilde{I}^{S^i}
\end{Bmatrix}
\right) \qquad [11.100]
$$

It is also calculated for each magnetic element (HEXA20G, PRIS15G, PYRA13G, TETR10G, QUAD08G, TRIA06G) from:

$$
p_d^e = \frac{1}{2}\,\omega \left(\{\tilde{\Phi}_M^r \ \tilde{I}^{S^r}\}^T
\begin{bmatrix}
[k_{\Phi\Phi}^i] & [k_{\Phi I}^i] \\
[k_{\Phi I}^i]^T & [k_{II}^i]
\end{bmatrix}
\begin{Bmatrix}
\tilde{\Phi}_M^r \\
\tilde{I}^{S^r}
\end{Bmatrix}
\right.
$$

$$
\left.
+ \{\tilde{\Phi}_M^i \ \tilde{I}^{S^i}\}^T
\begin{bmatrix}
[k_{\Phi\Phi}^i] & [k_{\Phi I}^i] \\
[k_{\Phi I}^i]^T & [k_{II}^i]
\end{bmatrix}
\begin{Bmatrix}
\tilde{\Phi}_M^i \\
\tilde{I}^{S^{ir}}
\end{Bmatrix}
\right) \qquad [11.101]
$$

where $\tilde{u}^r, \tilde{u}^i, \tilde{\Phi}_M^r, \tilde{\Phi}_M^i, \tilde{I}^{S^r}, \tilde{I}^{S^i}$, are the real and imaginary parts of, respectively, the nodal displacement, magnetic potential and source current vectors:

$$
[k_{uu}^i] = \int_{D_E} [B]^T [c^{H^i}][B]dD \ \text{ is the stiffness matrix} \qquad [11.102]
$$

$$
[k_{u\Phi}^i] = \int_{D_{ME}} [B]^T [c^{s^i}][B]dD \ \text{ is the piezomagnetic}
$$
coupling matrix $\qquad\qquad\qquad\qquad\qquad\qquad\qquad$ [11.103]

$$
[k_{\Phi\Phi}^i] = -\int_{D_M} [B]^T [\mu^{s^i}][B]dD \ \text{ is the magnetic stiffness}
$$
matrix $\qquad\qquad\qquad\qquad\qquad\qquad\qquad\qquad\qquad$ [11.104]

$$
[k_{uI}^i] = -\int_{D_{ME}} [B]^T [e^i][N]\, dD \ [^0 H^S] \ \text{ is the source-}
$$
structure coupling matrix $\qquad\qquad\qquad\qquad\qquad\qquad$ [11.105]

$$[k_{\Phi I}^{i}] = -\int_{D_M} [B]^{T}[\mu^{s^i}][N]\, dD\, [^0H^S]$$ is the source-

magnetization coupling matrix   [11.106]

$$[k_{II}^{i}] = -[^0H^S]^{T}\int_{D_M} [N]^{T}[\mu^{s^i}][N]\, dD\, [^0H^S]$$ is the

inductance matrix in vacuum   [11.107]

$[c^H] = [s^H]^{-1}$ is the constant magnetic elastic tensor

at constant magnetic field   [11.108]

$[e] = [d][s^H]^{-1}$ is the piezomagnetic stress tensor   [11.109]

and $[\mu^s] = [\mu^T] - [d][s^H]^{-1}[d]^T$ is the constant

strain magnetic permeability tensor.   [11.110]

Thermal load from the Joule effect

The heat generation density, q_J, obtained by the Joule effect in the coil can be defined for three types of inducers. The first type of inducer (Fig. 11.36) consists of a cylindrical inducer with a circular section and a thin thickness. Due to the thin thickness, it is modelled by three-node axisymmetrical isoparametric elements – LINE03CL (Fig. 11.37). It must be attached to the outer surface of a magnetostrictive element.

The second type of inducer is a cylindrical inducer with a circular section (Fig. 11.38); it is modelled by 2D axisymmetrical elements – QUAD08CL,TRIA06CL (Fig. 11.39) and by 2D axisymmetrical magnetic elements – QUAD08G,TRIA06G.

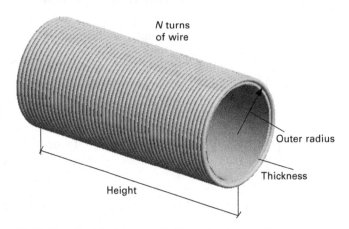

11.36 1D cylindrical inducer with a circular section.

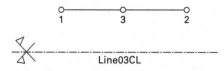

11.37 1D inducer element.

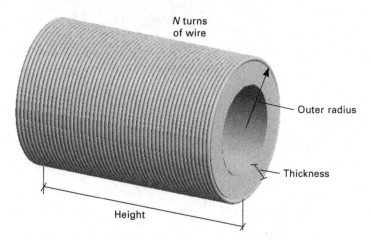

11.38 2D cylindrical inducer with a circular section.

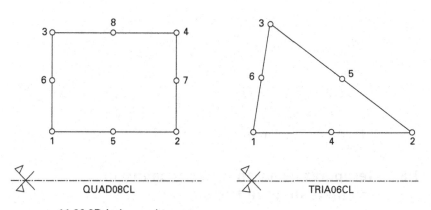

11.39 2D inducer element.

The last type of inducer is a cylindrical inducer with a rectangular section (Fig. 11.40); it is modelled by 3D elements – HEXA20CL, PRISM15CL, TETRA10CL, PYRA13CL (Fig. 11.41) and by 3D magnetic elements – HEXA20G, PRISM15G, TETRA10G, PYRA13G.

For this type of inducer, the heat generation density, q_J is computed from Eq. [11.89], the thermal load vector is then obtained from Eq. [11.99].

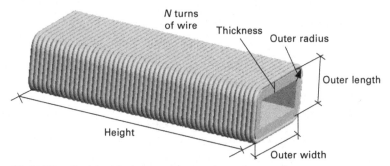

11.40 3D cylindrical inducer with a rectangular section.

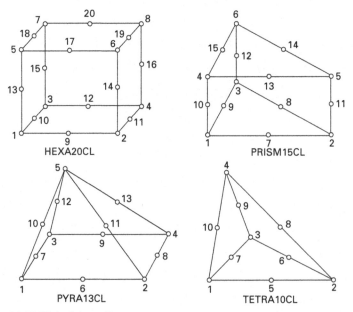

11.41 3D inducer element.

11.8   Temperature in an internal cavity in a magnetostrictive transducer

The aim of this section is to validate the development of the heat generation in a magnetostrictive transducer. Many transducers have cavities in which the temperature is unknown. So a variational formulation has been developed to take the internal cavities into account. In this report, 1D and 2D isoparametric elements are presented with a validation. Then the development of heat generation is defined with three validations. The first example consists of a cylinder in vacuum, the second example shows the temperature behaviour of a Janus transducer, the results are compared with an analytical model and measurements.

11.8.1 Variational formulation

For a steady problem, the equation for heat transfer using the heat equation is:

$$\frac{\partial}{\partial}\left(k_{xx}\frac{\partial T}{\partial x}\right) + \frac{\partial}{\partial}\left(k_{yy}\frac{\partial T}{\partial y}\right) + \frac{\partial}{\partial}\left(k_{zz}\frac{\partial T}{\partial z}\right) + P_d + h(T - T_\infty)$$
$$+ h'(T - T_{ci}) = 0 \qquad [11.111]$$

where T denotes the temperature, T_∞ is the temperature of the external medium and T_{ci} is the temperature of the internal cavity. k_{xx}, k_{yy}, k_{zz} are the conductivity coefficients along x, y, z, respectively, h the convective thermal film coefficient, h' the convective thermal film coefficient in the cavity and P_d is the heat source.

A variational formulation of the above problem is:

$$\chi = \int_D \frac{1}{2}\left(k_{xx}\left(\frac{\partial T}{\partial x}\right)^2 + k_{yy}\left(\frac{\partial T}{\partial y}\right)^2 + k_{zz}\left(\frac{\partial T}{\partial z}\right)^2 - 2QT\right)dD + \int_{\Gamma_1} qT\,dS_1$$
$$+ \frac{1}{2}\int_{\Gamma_2} h(T - T_\infty)^2 d\Gamma_2 + \frac{1}{2}\int_{\Gamma_3} h'(T - T_{ci})^2 d\Gamma_3$$

$$[11.112]$$

where Q is the heat generation rate, q is the heat flux prescribed on the Γ_1 boundary, Γ_2 is the boundary of heat transfer and Γ_3 is the cavity boundary.

It is implemented in ATILA using the so-called weak formulation as:

$$\sum_e ([k_T^e]\{T^e\}) = \sum_e (\{Q^e\} - \{q^e\} - [k_h^e]\{T^e\} + \{k_{T_\infty}^e\})$$
$$+ \sum_{\acute{e}} (T_{ci}\lfloor k_{h_{ci}}^{e'}\rfloor^T - T_{ci}k_{ci}^{e'}) - (\lfloor k_{h_{ci}}^{e'}\rfloor + [k_h^{e'}])\{T^{e'}\}$$

$$[11.113]$$

where:

$$[k_T^e] = \int_{D^e} [B^e]^T [C^e]\lfloor B^e \rfloor dD^e \text{ is the conductivity matrix} \quad [11.114]$$

$$[k_h^e] = \int_{\Gamma_2^e} h^e \lfloor N^e \rfloor^T \lfloor N^e \rfloor d\Gamma^e \text{ is the convection matrix} \quad [11.115]$$

$$\{k_{T_\infty}^e\} = \int_{\Gamma_2^e} h^e T_\infty \lfloor N^e \rfloor^T d\Gamma^e \text{ is the convection vector} \quad [11.116]$$

$$\{q^e\} = \int_{\Gamma_1^e} q\lfloor N^e \rfloor^T d\Gamma^e \text{ is the thermal flux vector} \qquad [11.117]$$

$$\{Q^e\} = -\int_{D^e} p_d^e \lfloor N^e \rfloor^T dD^e \text{ is the thermal load vector including}$$

the dissipated power from material losses   [11.118]

$$[k_h^{e'}] = \int_{\Gamma_3^{e'}} h'^{e'} \lfloor N^e \rfloor^T \lfloor N^e \rfloor d\Gamma_3^e \text{ is the convection}$$

matrix in the cavity   [11.119]

$$\lfloor k_{h_{ci}}^{e'} \rfloor^T = -\int_{\Gamma_3^{e'}} h'^{e'} \lfloor N^e \rfloor^T d\Gamma_3^{e'} \text{ is the convection}$$

vector in the cavity   [11.120]

and $k_{ci}^{e'} = \int_{\Gamma_3^{e'}} h'^{e'} d\Gamma_3^{e'}$ is the convection coefficient in the

cavity   [11.121]

Then matrix Eq. [11.112] can be written as:

$$\begin{bmatrix} [K_{Th}] & \{K_{hci}\} \\ \{K_{hci}\}^T & K_{ci} \end{bmatrix} \begin{Bmatrix} \{T\} \\ T_{ci} \end{Bmatrix} = \begin{Bmatrix} \{F\} \\ 0 \end{Bmatrix} \qquad [11.122]$$

where:

$$[K_{Th}] = \sum_e ([k_T^e] + [k_h^e]) + \sum_{e'} [k_h^{e'}] \qquad [11.123]$$

$$[K_{hci}] = \sum_{e'} \{k_{hci}^{e'}\} \qquad [11.124]$$

$$K_{ci} = \sum_{e'} k_{ci}^{e'} \qquad [11.125]$$

$$\{F\} = \sum_e (\{Q^e\} + \{q^e\} + \{k_{T_\infty}^e\}) \qquad [11.126]$$

11.8.2 Validation

Description of the model

The validation for the computation of the internal cavity temperature consists of an axisymmetrical model transducer (Fig. 11.42). The PZT cylinder has a length of 30 mm and a radius of 10 mm. The dynamic excitation is provided electrically to the cylinder using two electrodes located at the ends of the cylinder. This cylinder is axially poled. It is between a steel end-mass and a tail-mass made of aluminium.

Results

Figure 11.43 shows the steady-state ATILA FEA model temperature profile through a section of the model driven at 1 000 V rms. The inernal cavity temperature is 24.05 °C. In this case the total heat flux in the cavity is zero.

11.8.3 Applications

Magnetostrictive cylinder: 2D analysis

The first validation consits of half a terfenol cylinder (Fig. 11.44) having a length of 25 mm and a radius of 3.25 mm. This cylinder is surrounded by a vacuum defined by a cylinder having a length of 50 mm and a radius of 16.3 mm. The dynamic excitation is provided to the cylinder by a coil driven at 1 A.

Figure 11.45 shows the steady-state ATILA FEA model temperature profile through a section of the model driven at 10 kHz

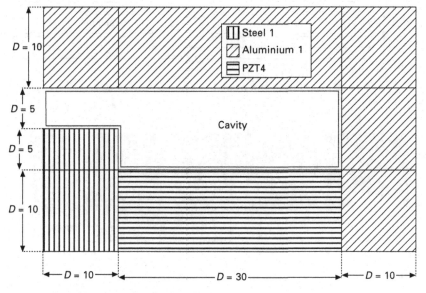

11.42 Description of the example.

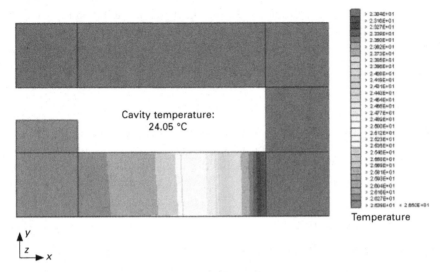

11.43 Steady temperature profile.

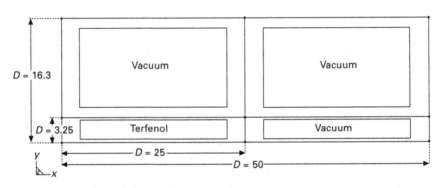

11.44 Description of the model.

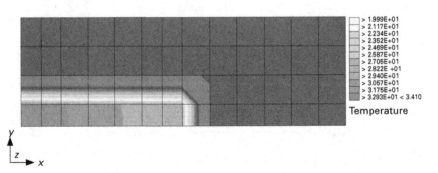

11.45 Steady temperature profile.

Magnetostrictive Janus transducer: 2D analysis

In this example, a magnetostrictive Janus transducer is defined in Fig. 11.46. The electrical power in operation is 25 W corresponding to a current excitation of 32.5 A at 350 Hz. The deformed shape of this transducer is defined in Fig. 11.47.

The steady temperature profile of the Janus transducer is shown in Fig. 11.48. The temperature has been measured in three locations (Fig. 11.48).

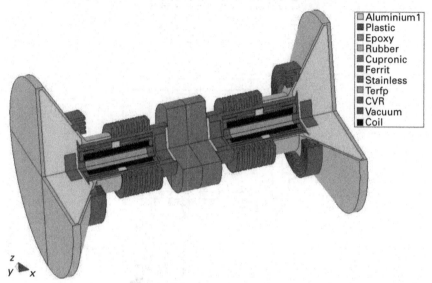

11.46 Definition of materials of a magnetostrictive Janus transducer.

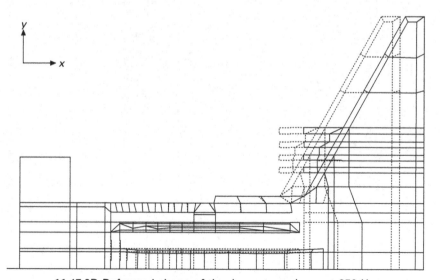

11.47 2D Deformed shape of the Janus transducer at 350 Hz.

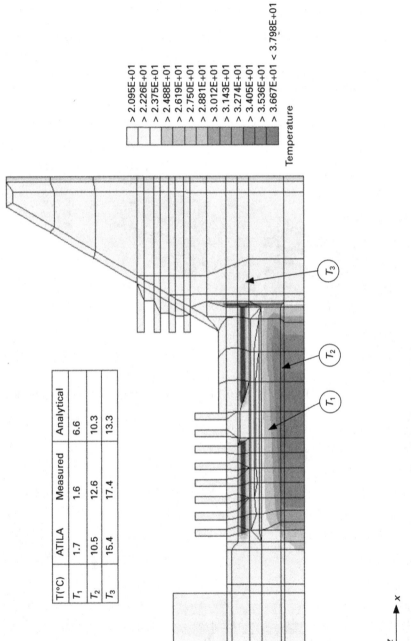

T(°C)	ATILA	Measured	Analytical
T_1	1.7	1.6	6.6
T_2	10.5	12.6	10.3
T_3	15.4	17.4	13.3

> 2.095E+01
> 2.226E+01
> 2.375E+01
> 2.488E+01
> 2.619E+01
> 2.750E+01
> 2.881E+01
> 3.012E+01
> 3.143E+01
> 3.274E+01
> 3.405E+01
> 3.536E+01
> 3.667E+01 < 3.798E+01

Temperature

11.48 Steady temperature profile of the Janus transducer.

The table in Fig. 11.48 compares temperatures computed from the ATILA model, the analytical model[19] and measurements. These results prove that a good agreement is found between results. Figure 11.49 displays the dissipated power for each material.

11.9   Conclusion

A coupled electromechanical thermal analysis has been presented in this chapter. For a steady-state solution or transient analysis, the thermal behaviour is coupled to the electromechanical response. A three-step analysis is performed. The electromechanical behaviour is first computed from a harmonic analysis. The resulting dissipated power is then applied as a heat generator to determine the resulting temperature of the device for a steady-state or transient analysis. At each time step, a stress analysis is obtained in the device.

However, traditional transmitting materials, such as PZT-8, exhibit some non-linearity in stress and temperature, but predicting performance under high stress and higher temperatures can be achieved by taking advantage of the weak coupling. To predict the performance of these devices by considering the highly non-linear behaviour with a fully non-linear solution is the aim of future developments.

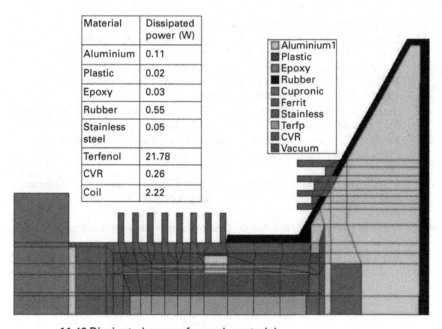

Material	Dissipated power (W)
Aluminium	0.11
Plastic	0.02
Epoxy	0.03
Rubber	0.55
Stainless steel	0.05
Terfenol	21.78
CVR	0.26
Coil	2.22

11.49 Dissipated power for each material.

11.10   References

1. Woollett R.S., 'Power limitations of sonic transducers', *IEEE Trans. Sonics, Ultrason.* SU-15(4), 218–229, Oct. 1968.
2. Butler S.C., Montgomery R., 'Thermal analysis of high drive transducer elements', *J. Acoust. Soc. Am.* 105, 1121, Mar. 1999.
3. Priya S., Viehland D., *et al.*, 'High-power resonant measurements of piezoelectric materials: Importance of elastic nonlinearities', *J. Appl. Phys.* 90, 1469–1479, Aug. 2001.
4. Debus J.C., 'Latest developments in ATILA: Thermal computations', *Proceedings Second Annual ATILA Workshop in US*, Baltimore, May 17, 2001.
5. Holland R., 'Representation of dielectric, elastic and piezoelectric losses by complex coefficients', *IEEE Trans. Sonics Ultrason.* SU-14(1), 18–20, Jan. 1967.
6. Debus J.C., Pascal Mosbah P., Blottman III J.B., 'Thermal behaviour modelling of high power active devices using the ATILA finite element code', *CanSmart Meeting International Workshop Smart Materials & Structures*, Montreal, pp. 43–52, Oct. 2005.
7. Uchino K., Hirose S., 'Loss mechanisms in piezoelectrics: How to measure different losses separately', *IEEE Trans. Ultrason. Ferroelect. Freq. Contr.* 48(1), 307–321, Jan. 2001.
8. Zienkiewicz O.C., Taylor R.L., *The Finite Element Method, Vol. 1*, 5th edn, Butterworth-Heinemann, Oxford, 2000.
9. Dubus B., Boucher D., 'An analytical evaluation of the heating of low-frequency sonar projectors', *J. Acoust. Soc. Am.* 95, 1983–1990, 1994.
10. Berlincourt D.A., Curran D.R., Jaffe H., 'Piezoelectric and piezomagnetic materials and their function in transducers', Chapter 3, *Physical Acoustics*, Vol. 1A, Warren P. Mason (ed.) Academic Press, New York, 1964.
11. Camp L., *Underwater Acoustics*, Wiley, New York, 1970.
12. Wilson O.B., *An Introduction to the Theory and Design of Sonar Transducers*, Peninsula Publishing, Los Altos, CA, 1988.
13. White F.M., *Heat and Mass Transfer*, Addison-Wesley, Reading, MA, 1988.
14. Hooker W., 'Properties of PZT-based piezoelectric ceramics between –150 and 250 °C', NASA/CR-1998-208708, 1998.
15. Butler S.C., Blottman J.B., Montgomery R.E., 'A Thermal Analysis of High-Drive Ring Transducer Elements', NUWC-NPT Technical Report 11, 467, 2005.
16. *Piezoelectric Ceramics Catalog*, Channel Industries Inc., Santa Barbara, CA.
17. *Piezoelectric Technology Data for Designers Catalog*, Morgan Matroc Inc., Bedford, OH.
18. Claeyssen F., 'Conception et réalisation de transducteurs sonar basse fréquence à base d'alliages magnétostrictifs terres rares-fer', PhD. dissertation, INSA-Lyon, France, 1984.
19. Dubus B.P. Bigotte P., Boucher D., 'Thermal limit analysis of low-frequency, high power sonar projectors', *European Conference on Underwater Acoustics*, Elsevier Applied Science, 623–626, 1992.

12

Modelling the damping of piezoelectric structures with ATILA

J-C. DEBUS, ISEN Lille, France

DOI: 10.1533/9780857096319.2.281

Abstract: The damping of a structure can be obtained by a transfer of the vibratory energy into thermal energy (dissipation in an electrical resistance). The transfer is carried out by using piezoelectric materials (PZT piezoelectric plate) and is improved by charging the piezoelectric material by an electrical circuit. This chapter describes finite element-electric circuit matrices created in the ATILA code. First, analytical models have been developed for the damping of a piezoelectric cylinder and a cantilever beam with a PZT plate; the results are compared with the numerical values (ATILA). Then, the damping of a cantilever beam charged by an electrical circuit is measured at the end of the beam using a laser vibrometer and compared with the numerical results. Finally, the vibrations damping is studied on a large aluminium plate; experimental and numerical results are compared.

Key words: finite elements, heat transfer, vibration damping, piezoelectric material, negative capacitance, magnetostrictive material, high-power transducers.

12.1   Introduction

The damping of a structure can be obtained by a transfer of the vibratory energy into thermal energy (dissipation in an electrical resistance). The transfer is carried out by using piezoelectric materials (PZT piezoelectric plate) and it is improved by charging the piezoelectric material with an electrical network such as a passive dipole with a simple resistance, a resistance and an inductance or a resonant shunt network[1], a special circuit with a synchronized switching damping[2, 3] and an active dipole with a negative capacitance[4].

This chapter presents a coupled simulation finite element method for piezoelectric material charged by an electrical circuit. First, the finite element–electric circuit element matrices have been created in ATILA[2]. Linear electric circuit components, such as resistor, inductor and capacitor are considered for harmonic analysis.

An analytical model has been developed for a piezoelectric cylinder with several electric networks and has been compared with numerical results with the ATILA code. This damping is performed on a cantilever beam with a PZT plate. An analytical model has been developed for the damping of the cantilever beam charged by several electrical circuits and compared with numerical results.

281

Finally, vibrations damping is studied on a large aluminium plate (0.85m ×
0.78m × 2 mm). The device is presented and the position of the piezoelectric
transformers is determined for an optimization of the damping. The semi-
active damping method based on a negative capacitance circuit is briefly
recalled. Finally, experiments have been performed and the vibration velocity
as well as the reduction of the noise transmitted and compared with ATILA
code numerical results

12.2   Circuit coupled simulation method

For an harmonic analysis, the matrix equation for a piezoelectric transducer
is defined as:

$$
\begin{bmatrix} [K_{uu}^*]-\omega^2[M] & [K_{uv}^*] \\ [K_{uv}^*] & [K_{vv}^*] \end{bmatrix} \begin{bmatrix} \underline{U}^* \\ \underline{V}^* \end{bmatrix} = \begin{bmatrix} \underline{0} \\ -\underline{q}^* \end{bmatrix}
\tag{12.1}
$$

where $\lfloor K_{uu}^* \rfloor$ and $\lfloor K_{vv}^* \rfloor$ are, respectively, the complex rigidity and dielectric
matrices, $\lfloor K_{uv} \rfloor$ is the real piezoelectric matrix, $\underline{U}^*$ and $\underline{V}^*$ are, respectively,
the complex vectors of nodal values of the displacement field and electrical
potential, q^* is the complex vector of the nodal values of the electrical
charges. The input current is the time derivative of q as:

$$
I^* = \frac{dq^*}{dt} = j\omega q^*
\tag{12.2}
$$

In the case where an electric network is associated with a piezoelectric
transducer (Fig. 12.1) where h_{pz} and A are, respectively, the high and the
cross area, equation [12.1] has different values.

12.2.1 Elementary components

Resistor

For a resistor, equation [12.2] is defined as:

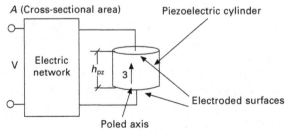

12.1 Piezoelectric transducer system with an electric network[5].

$$q^{R*} = \frac{I^*}{j\omega} = \frac{V^*}{j\omega R} = -j \frac{1}{\omega R} V^*$$ [12.3]

where R is the value of the resistor.

The finite element resistor (Fig. 12.2) can be defined as:

$$-j \frac{1}{\omega R} \begin{bmatrix} 1 & -1 \\ -1 & 1 \end{bmatrix} \begin{Bmatrix} V_1^* \\ V_2^* \end{Bmatrix} = \begin{Bmatrix} q_1^{R*} \\ q_2^{R*} \end{Bmatrix} = j \frac{1}{\omega} [k_{vv}^*]_R \{q^{R*}\}$$ [12.4]

This matrix is a complex matrix and it will be added to the imaginary part of the dielectric matrix of equation [12.1].

Inductor

For an inductor (see Fig. 12.4), the electric potential is defined as:

$$V^* = L \frac{dI^*}{dt}$$ [12.5]

where L is the value of the inductor.

Then, equation [12.2] becomes as:

$$q^{L*} = -\frac{V^*}{L\omega^2} = AD_3^*$$ [12.6]

where the electric displacement D_3^* is defined as

$$D_3^* = d_{31}^* T_1^* + \varepsilon_{33}^{T*} E_3^*$$ [12.7]

The finite element inductor (Fig. 12.3) can be defined as:

$$-\frac{1}{\omega^2 L} \begin{bmatrix} 1 & -1 \\ -1 & 1 \end{bmatrix} \begin{Bmatrix} V_1^* \\ V_2^* \end{Bmatrix} = \begin{Bmatrix} q_1^{L*} \\ q_2^{L*} \end{Bmatrix} = \frac{1}{\omega^2} [k_{vv}^*]_L \{q^{L*}\}$$ [12.8]

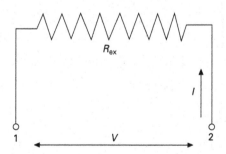

12.2 Finite element resistor.

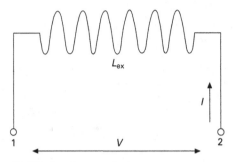

12.3 Finite element inductor.

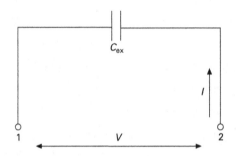

12.4 Finite element capacitor.

This real matrix depends upon to the square of the pulsation ω and it will be added to the real part of the dielectric matrix of equation [12.1].

Capacitor

For a capacitor, the electric charge is defined as:

$$q^C = CV \tag{12.9}$$

where C is the value of the capacitor.

The finite element capacitor (Fig. 12.4) can be defined as:

$$C \begin{bmatrix} 1 & -1 \\ -1 & 1 \end{bmatrix} \begin{Bmatrix} V_1 \\ V_2 \end{Bmatrix} = \begin{Bmatrix} q_1^C \\ q_2^C \end{Bmatrix} = [k_{vv}]_C \{q^C\} \tag{12.10}$$

12.2.2 Electric network

Resistor and capacitor in parallel

For the electric network with a resistor and a capacitor in parallel (Fig. 12.5), the current is defined as:

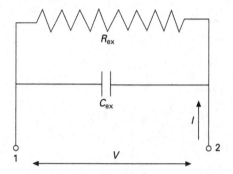

12.5 Finite element resistor and capacitor in parallel.

$$I^* = \left(\frac{1}{R_{ex}} + jC_{ex}\omega \right) V^*$$ [12.11]

With equation [12.7], the electrical displacement can be written as

$$D_3^* = \frac{V^*}{j\omega^2 A} \left(\frac{1}{R_{ex}} + jC_{ex}\omega \right) = d_{33}T_3^* + \varepsilon_{33}^{T*} E_3^*$$ [12.12]

$$0 = d_{33}T_3^* - \left(\varepsilon_{33}^{T*} + C_{ex} \frac{h_{pz}}{A} - \frac{h_{pz}}{Aj\omega R_{ex}} \right) \frac{V^*}{h_{pz}} = d_{33}T_3^* - \overline{\varepsilon_{33}^{T*}} \frac{V^*}{h_{pz}}$$

  [12.13]

A new dielectric coefficient is obtained as:

$$\overline{\varepsilon_{33}^{T*}} = \varepsilon_{33}^{T} \left(1 + C_{ex} \frac{h_{pz}}{A\varepsilon_{33}^{T}} - j \left(\tan\theta' + \frac{h_{pz}}{R_{ex}\omega A\varepsilon_{33}^{T}} \right) \right)$$ [12.14]

where $\tan\theta'$ is the dielectric loss.

With this new value, a real and imaginary part of the dielectric matrix $[k_{vv}^*]_{RCp}$ can be obtained.

Resistor and inductor in parallel

For an electric network with a resistor and an inductor in parallel (Fig. 12.6), the current in the inductor and the resistor are respectively defined as:

$$I_1^* = \frac{V^*}{jL_{ex}\omega}$$ [12.15]

$$I_2^* = \frac{V^*}{R_{ex}}$$ [12.16]

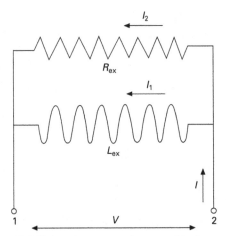

12.6 Finite element resistor and inductor in parallel.

Then the total in the circuit is:

$$I^* = I_1^* + I_2^* = \left(\frac{1}{jL_{ex}\omega} + \frac{1}{R_{ex}}\right)V^* = j\omega A D_3^* \qquad [12.17]$$

The electric displacement is written as:

$$D_3^* = \frac{V^*}{j\omega A}\left(\frac{1}{jL_{ex}\omega} + \frac{1}{R_{ex}}\right) = \frac{V^*}{A}\left(-\frac{1}{L_{ex}\omega^2} - \frac{j}{R_{ex}}\right) \qquad [12.18]$$

The dielectric coefficient becomes:

$$\overline{\varepsilon_{33}^{T*}} = \varepsilon_{33}^T\left(1 - \frac{h_{pz}}{L_{ex}\omega^2 A\varepsilon_{33}^T} - j\left(\tan\theta' + \frac{h_{pz}}{R_{ex}\omega A\varepsilon_{33}^T}\right)\right) \qquad [12.19]$$

Resistor, inductor and capacitor in parallel

For this last network (Fig. 12.7), the current in the capacitor is:

$$I_3^* = jC_{er}\omega \qquad [12.20]$$

With equation [12.7], the electrical displacement can be written as:

$$D_3^* = \frac{V^*}{j\omega A}\left(\frac{1}{jL_{ex}\omega} + \frac{1}{R_{ex}} + jC_{ex}\omega\right) = \frac{V^*}{A}\left(-\frac{1}{L_{ex}\omega^2} + C_{ex} - \frac{j}{R_{ex}}\right)$$

$$[12.21]$$

A new dielectric coefficient can be obtained as:

$$\overline{\varepsilon_{33}^{T*}} = \varepsilon_{33}^T\left(1 + \left(C_{ex} - \frac{1}{L_{ex}\omega^2}\right)\frac{h_{pz}}{A\varepsilon_{33}^T} - j\left(\tan\theta' + \frac{h_{pz}}{R_{ex}\omega A\varepsilon_{33}^T}\right)\right) \quad [12.22]$$

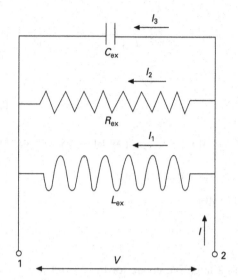

12.7 Finite element resistor, inductor and capacitor in series.

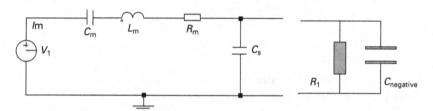

12.8 Equivalent circuit of a piezoelectric device.

12.3   Semi-active damping method

A structure with piezoelectric elements can be represented by an electric equivalent circuit (Fig. 12.8)[5] with a motional capacitance C_m, an inductor L_m, a resistor R_m and blocked capacitance of C_s. V_1 as the equivalent acoustic source. Here, the motional current I_m is proportional to the vibrating velocity. The resistance R_{ex} and the capacitance $C_{negative}$ are the external shunt impedance.

The maximal dissipation is obtained for a resistor according to this relation:

$$R_{ex} = \frac{1}{2\pi f_r (C_s + C_{negative})} \qquad [12.23]$$

where ω_r is the resonant pulsation.

Then, the vibrating velocity damping is expressed by the following relation where Q is the quality factor and k is the coupling factor:

$$\left[\frac{Im_{\text{with}}}{Im_{\text{without}}}\right]_{\text{dB}} = -20\log_{10}\left[1 + \frac{Q\,k^2}{2\,(1-k^2)}\frac{C_{\text{s}}}{(C_{\text{s}} + C_{\text{negative}})}\right] \qquad [12.24]$$

where

$$C_{\text{s}} = \varepsilon_{33}^{\text{s}}\frac{A}{h_{\text{pz}}} \qquad [12.25]$$

k must be the largest possible and $C_{\text{s}} + C_{\text{negative}}$ must be as near as possible to zero.

The external electrical network can be defined as:

Damping with an external resistor

$$R_{\text{ex}}(0) = \frac{1}{2\pi f_{\text{r}}C_{\text{s}}} \qquad [12.26]$$

Damping with a resistor and a negative capacitor in parallel

$$R_{\text{ex}}(C) = \frac{1}{2\pi f_{\text{r}}(C_{\text{ex}} + C_{\text{s}})} = \frac{1}{2\pi f_{\text{r}}C_{\text{s}}(1-\beta)} \qquad [12.27]$$

where

$$C_{\text{ex}} = -\beta C_{\text{s}} \qquad [12.28]$$

with β as a coefficient, the value must be fixed between 0 and 1.

Damping with a resistor and an inductor

$$L_{\text{ex}} = \frac{1}{(2\pi f_{\text{r}})^2 C_{\text{s}}} \qquad [12.29]$$

$$R_{\text{ex}}(L) = \sqrt{\frac{l_{\text{m}}}{C_{\text{s}}}} \qquad [12.30]$$

Damping with a resistor, a negative capacitor and an inductor

$$L_{\text{ex}} = \frac{1}{(2\pi f_{\text{r}})^2(C_{\text{s}} + C_{\text{ex}})} \qquad [12.31]$$

$$R_{\text{ex}}(L) = \sqrt{\frac{l_{\text{m}}}{(C_{\text{s}} + C_{\text{ex}})}} \qquad [12.32]$$

The new dielectric coefficient can be written as:

$$\overline{\varepsilon_{33}^{\text{T}*}} = \varepsilon_{33}^{\text{T}}(\overline{R} - j\overline{T}) \qquad [12.33]$$

For the different external shunts, the values of the real and imaginary parts of this complex coefficient are given in Table 12.1

Table 12.1 $\overline{R}$ and $\overline{T}$ values versus electrical network

	R	L	C	RC	RL	RLC
$\overline{R}$	1	$1-\left(\dfrac{f_r}{f}\right)^2$	$1-\beta\dfrac{\varepsilon^s_{33}}{\varepsilon^T_{33}}$	$1-\beta\dfrac{\varepsilon^s_{33}}{\varepsilon^T_{33}}$	$1-\left(\dfrac{f_r}{f}\right)^2$	$1-2\beta\dfrac{\varepsilon^s_{33}}{\varepsilon^T_{33}}$
$\overline{T}$	$\tan\theta'+\dfrac{\varepsilon^s_{33}}{\varepsilon^T_{33}}\dfrac{f_r}{f}$	$\tan\theta'$	$\tan\theta'$	$\tan\theta'+\dfrac{\varepsilon^s_{33}}{\varepsilon^T_{33}}\dfrac{f_r}{f}$	$\tan\theta'+\dfrac{\varepsilon^s_{33}}{\varepsilon^T_{33}}\dfrac{f_r}{f}\sqrt{\dfrac{k^2}{1-k^2}}$	$\tan\theta'+\dfrac{\varepsilon^s_{33}}{\varepsilon^T_{33}}\dfrac{f_r}{f}\sqrt{\dfrac{k^2}{1-k^2}}$

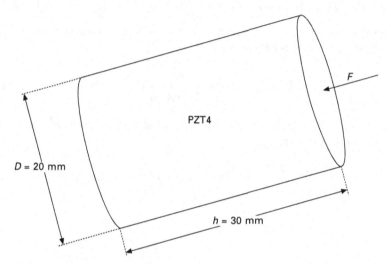

12.9 Piezoelectric cylinder.

12.4   Applications

12.4.1 Damping of a piezoelectric cylinder: an analytical solution

The first example concerns the damping of a piezoelectric cylinder by some electric circuit. The geometry consists of a PZT4 piezoelectric cylinder having a length of 30 mm and a diameter of 20 mm (Fig. 12.9). The dynamic excitation is provided to the cylinder using a force F located at one end. The axial axis is the poled direction (3-axis). The constitutive equations for a piezoelectric material can be simplified to:

$$S_3 = S^E_{33}T_3 + d_{33}E_3$$

$$D_3 = d_{33}T_3 + \varepsilon^T_{33}E_3 \qquad [12.34]$$

where T_3 is the axial stress = F/A, S_3 is the axial strain, E_3 is the electric field, D_3 is the electric displacement, S^E_{33} is the axial elastic compliance constant at constant E, ε^T_{33} is the axial dielectric constant at constant E, d_{33}

is the axial piezoelectric strain constant and F is the applied force on the cross-sectional area A.

The electric charge is defined as:

$$q = AD_3 \tag{12.35}$$

Taking into account losses, equation [12.34] is written as:

$$S_3^* = S_{33}^{E*}T_3 + d_{33}E_3^*$$
$$D_3^* = d_{33}T_3 + \varepsilon_{33}^{T*}E_3^* \tag{12.36}$$

For a resistor R_{ex} as an electric network (Fig. 12.1) the new axial dielectric constant at constant E can be defined as:

$$\overline{\varepsilon_{33}^{T*}} = \varepsilon_{33}^{T}\left(1 - j\left(\tan\theta' + \frac{h_{pz}}{R_{ex}\omega A\varepsilon_{33}^{T}}\right)\right) = \varepsilon_{33}^{T}(\overline{R} - j\overline{T}) \tag{12.37}$$

For an inductor L_{ex}, a capacitor C_{ex} and a $R_{ex}C_{ex}$-circuit, this constant becomes, respectively:

$$\overline{\varepsilon_{33}^{T*}} = \varepsilon_{33}^{T}\left(1 - \frac{h_{pz}}{L_{ex}\omega^2 A\varepsilon_{33}^{T}} - j\tan\theta'\right) = \varepsilon_{33}^{T}(\overline{R} - j\overline{T}) \tag{12.38}$$

$$\overline{\varepsilon_{33}^{T*}} = \varepsilon_{33}^{T}\left(1 + C_{ex}\frac{h_{pz}}{A\varepsilon_{33}^{T}} - j\tan\theta'\right) = \varepsilon_{33}^{T}(\overline{R} - j\overline{T}) \tag{12.39}$$

$$\overline{\varepsilon_{33}^{T*}} = \varepsilon_{33}^{T}\left(1 + C_{ex}\frac{h_{pz}}{A\varepsilon_{33}^{T}} - j\left(\tan\theta' + \frac{h_{pz}}{R_{ex}\omega A\varepsilon_{33}^{T}}\right)\right) = \varepsilon_{33}^{T}(\overline{R} - j\overline{T})$$
$$\tag{12.40}$$

From the first equation of [12.36] and equation [12.18], one obtains:

$$S_3^* = \left(S_{33}^{E*} - \frac{d_{33}^2}{\varepsilon_{33}^{T*}}\right)T_3 = \left(S_{33}^{E*} - \frac{d_{33}^2}{\varepsilon_{33}^{T*}}\right)\frac{F}{A} \tag{12.41}$$

The axial displacement of the cylinder can be written as:

$$u_3^* = \left(S_{33}^{E*} - \frac{d_{33}^2}{\varepsilon_{33}^{T*}}\right)\frac{h_{pz}}{A}F = u_3^{R} + ju_3^{I} = (K^{R} + jK^{I})F \tag{12.42}$$

where

$$K^{R} = \frac{A}{h_{pz}}\left(\frac{\overline{R}(S_{33}^{E}(\overline{R} - \tan\phi'\overline{T}) - d_{33}^2/\varepsilon_{33}^{T}) + \overline{T}(\tan\phi'\overline{R} + \overline{T})S_{33}^{E}}{(S_{33}^{E}(\overline{R} - \tan\phi'\overline{T}) - d_{33}^2/\varepsilon_{33}^{T})^2 + ((\tan\phi'\overline{R} + \overline{T})S_{33}^{E})^2}\right)$$
$$\tag{12.43}$$

$$K^I = \frac{A}{h_{pz}} \left(\frac{-\bar{T}(S_{33}^E(\bar{R} - \tan\phi'\bar{T}) - d_{33}^2/\varepsilon_{33}^T) + \bar{R}(\tan\phi'\bar{R} + \bar{T})S_{33}^E}{(S_{33}^E(\bar{R} - \tan\phi'\bar{T}) - d_{33}^2/\varepsilon_{33}^T)^2 + ((\tan\phi'\bar{R} + \bar{T})S_{33}^E)^2} \right)$$

[12.44]

From equation [12.1], for an harmonic analysis, the axial displacement can be written as:

$$u_3^R = \frac{F}{K^R + \dfrac{K^{I2}}{K^R - \omega^2 M_d} - \omega^2 M_d}$$

[12.45]

$$u_3^I = -\frac{K^I}{K^R - \omega^2 M_d}$$

[12.46]

where the dynamic mass is defined as $M_d = \rho A h_{pz}(2/\pi)^2$ and ρ is the density.

For the application, the values of the R_{ex}, L_{ex} and C_{ex} are defined[1] as

$$R_{ex} = \frac{1}{0.2C_s\omega_r}, C = -0.8C_s \text{ and } L = \frac{1}{C_T\omega_r^2}$$

where $C_S = \varepsilon_{33}^S \dfrac{A}{h_{pz}}$, $C_T = \varepsilon_{33}^T \dfrac{A}{h_{pz}}$ and ω_r is the pulsation of the resonance.

Figure 12.10 compares the axial displacement with losses obtained from analytical and numerical results. Figures 12.11 to 12.13 display the axial displacement with damping obtained from analytical and numerical results. The results are quite good.

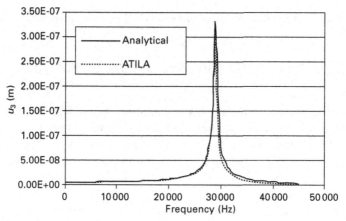

12.10 Axial displacement with no damping vs frequency.

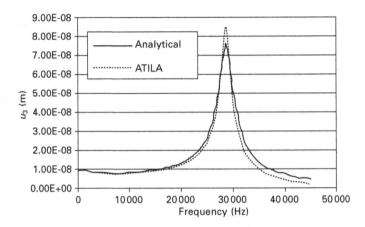

12.11 Axial displacement with R damping vs frequency.

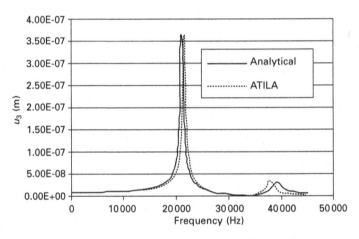

12.12 Axial displacement with L damping vs frequency.

12.4.2 Damping of a cantilever beam: an analytical solution

The second application concerns a cantilever beam with a piezoelectric patch (Fig. 12.14). The analytical and numerical results are compared. The damping is carried out by using piezoelectric material (PZT piezoelectric plates) and it is improved by charging the piezoelectric materials with an electric circuit. The position of the ceramics is determined for the damping of the first mode of the beam.

From the moment area method and the electric network damping, the deflection of the beam at the free end can be written as:

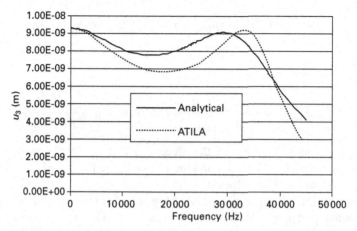

12.13 Axial displacement with RC damping vs frequency.

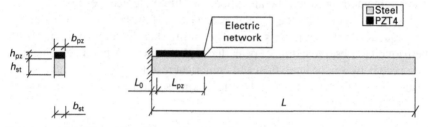

12.14 Piezoelectric patch with a firing circuitry.

$$v_{EC}^* = \frac{P}{M}(\underline{C} - j\underline{D})^2(1 + j\alpha_{pz})^2(R + jT) \qquad [12.47]$$

where

$$P = L_{pz}\left(L - L_0 - \frac{L_{pz}}{2}\right)p_0 d_{31}^2 b_{pz}\left(h_{st} - Y_G + \frac{h_{pz}}{2}\right)^2$$

$$h_{pz}\left(\frac{(L - L_0)^2}{2} - \frac{2}{3}(L - L_0)L_{pz} + \frac{L_{pz}^2}{3}\right)$$

$$\bar{M} = S_{11}^{E^2}(1 + \alpha_{pz}^2)^2(\underline{C}^2 + \underline{D}^2)^2\varepsilon_{33}^T(\bar{R}^2 + \bar{T}^2)$$

p_0 is the distributed load on the beam.

The real and imaginary parts of the deflection of the beam are given by these relations:

$$v_{EC}^R = \frac{P}{M}(\underline{C}^2 - \underline{D}^2)((\bar{R} - \alpha_{pz}^2\bar{R} - 2\bar{T}\alpha_{pz}) + 2\underline{C}\underline{D}(2\alpha_{pz}\bar{R} + \bar{T}(1 - \alpha_{pz}^2))$$

$$[12.48]$$

$$v_{EC}^1 = \frac{P}{M}(\underline{C}^2 - \underline{D}^2)((2R\alpha_{pz} + \bar{T}(1 - \alpha_{pz}^2)) - 2\underline{C}\underline{D}(\bar{R}(1 - \alpha_{pz}^2) - 2\bar{T}\alpha_{pz})$$

[12.49]

where

$$\underline{C} = E_{st}I_{stII} + \frac{I_{pz}}{S_{11}^E(1 - \alpha_{pz}^2)} \quad \text{and} \quad \underline{D} = \alpha_{st}E_{st}I_{stII} + \frac{\alpha_{pz}I_{pz}}{S_{11}^E(1 + \alpha_{pz}^2)}$$

E_{st} is the Young modulus of the steel, I_{stII} and I_{pz} are, respectively, the moment of inertia of the beam and the piezoelectric patch and α_{st} is the steel dissipation factor. The values of R and T are defined in Table 12.2.

The cantilever beam is described in Fig. 12.15. This beam has a harmonic distributed load $p_0 = 1$ Pa. With no electrical network damping, the analytical and numerical results are shown in Fig. 12.16. Figure 12.17 displays the deflection of the end of the beam vs the frequency. These figures show a good agreement between the analytical and finite element results.

Figure 12.18 displays the deflection of the end of the beam for a L-damping vs frequency. The damping is very efficient. In this figure, a zoom has been performed to observe a double peak due to the inducer. A good agreement is observed between the analytical and numerical results. Figures 12.19 to 12.21 display the deflection of the end of the beam vs frequency for, respectively, a C, a RC and a RL damping.

Table 12.2 $\bar{R}$ and $\bar{T}$ values versus electrical network

R	L	C	RC	RL
$\bar{R}$ 1	$1 - \dfrac{h_{pz}}{L\omega^2 A\varepsilon_{33}^T}$	$1 - C\dfrac{h_{pz}}{A\varepsilon_{33}^T}$	$1 + C\dfrac{h_{pz}}{A\varepsilon_{33}^T}$	$1 - \dfrac{L\omega^2}{(L\omega^2)^2 + (\omega R)^2}\dfrac{h_{pz}}{A\varepsilon_{33}^T}$
$\bar{T}$ $\tan\theta' + \dfrac{h_{pz}}{R\omega A\varepsilon_{33}^T}$	$\tan\theta'$	$\tan\theta'$	$\tan\theta' + \dfrac{h_{pz}}{R\omega A\varepsilon_{33}^T}$	$\tan\theta' + \dfrac{\omega R}{(L\omega^2)^2 + (\omega R)^2}\dfrac{h_{pz}}{A\varepsilon_{33}^T}$

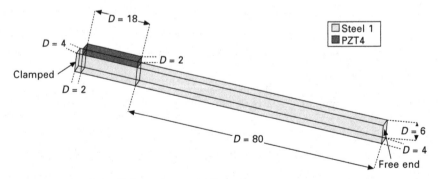

12.15 Description of the cantilever beam.

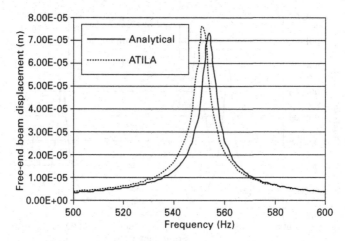

12.16 Deflection of the end of the beam – no damping.

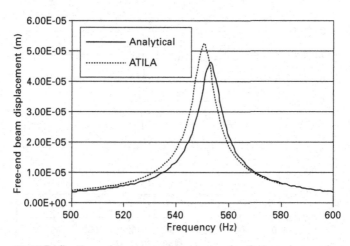

12.17 Deflection of the end of the beam for R damping vs frequency.

12.4.3 Damping of a cantilever beam: an experimental analysis[5]

This other application also concerns an aluminium cantilever beam (Fig. 12.22); the material for the damping is a PZ27 piezoelectric plate. The experimental and numerical results are compared. The dimensions of the beam are resumed in Fig. 12.23.

The over plate is used for the damping mode and the under plate is used for the excitation (Fig. 12.24). The damping is improved by charging the over piezoelectric plate with an electrical circuit. Experiments have been performed to adjust the different circuits on the beam. The vibrating velocity

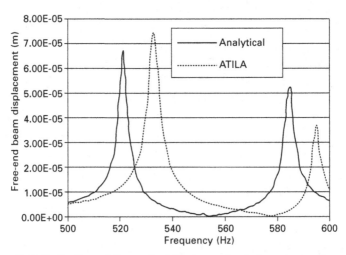

12.18 Deflection of the end of the beam for L damping vs frequency.

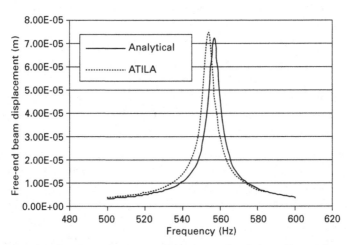

12.19 Deflection of the end of the beam for C damping vs frequency.

is measured at the end of the beam with the help of a laser vibrometer. The results for the first resonant frequency are shown in Table 12.3.

The displacement of the end of the beam vs frequency without an electric circuit is shown in Fig. 12.25. The experimental results are very close to the numerical results. Figures 12.26 to 12.29 compare the deflection of the end of the beam vs frequency for, respectively, a R, L, RC and a RLC circuit with the experimental results. The used values for R and L are, respectively, 82 Ωk, 120.23 H; for the RC circuit the values of R and C are, respectively, 188 Ωk and –8.19 nF. For the last circuit (RLC) the values are, respectively, $R = 1 \text{M}\Omega$, $L = 242$ H and $C = -8.19$ nF.

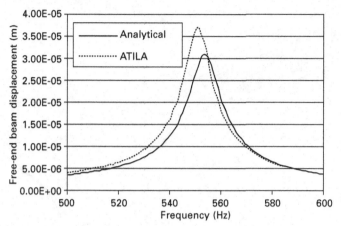

12.20 Deflection of the end of the beam for RC damping vs frequency.

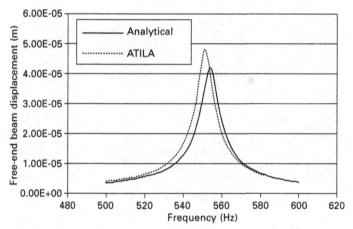

12.21 Deflection of the end of the beam for RL damping vs frequency.

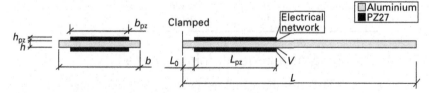

12.22 Description of the experimental cantilever beam.

Figures 12.30 and 12.31 display, respectively, the damping due to the different electric circuits both for numerical and experimental results. The experimental and numerical results are very close. The best damping is obtained with a RLC circuit.

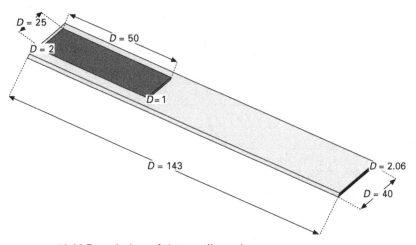

12.23 Description of the cantilever beam.

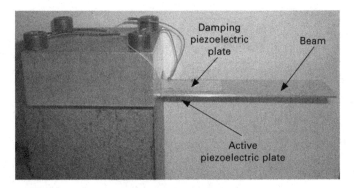

12.24 Beam with piezoelectric plates.

Table 12.3 First resonant frequency of the beam

	f_r (Hz)	k (%)
Experimental	118	0.120
Numerical	119	0.119

12.4.4 Damping of a large aluminum plate[6]

The last example concerns the damping of a large aluminium plate (0.85m × 0.78m × 2 mm) (Fig. 12.32). The damping is carried out by using piezoelectric materials (PZT piezoelectric plates – E–C and macro fibre composite MFC) and it is improved by charging the piezoelectric materials by an electrical circuit having a negative capacitance impedance. The optimal position and the geometry of the ceramics are determined using an analytical method and a numerical method with the help of the ATILA finite element code.

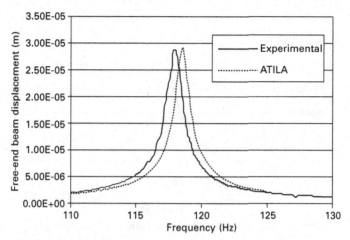

12.25 Deflection of the end of the beam – no damping.

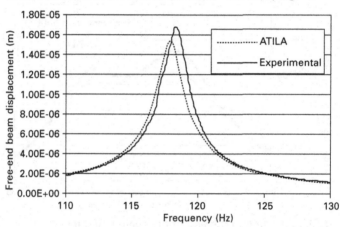

12.26 Deflection of the end of the beam – R damping.

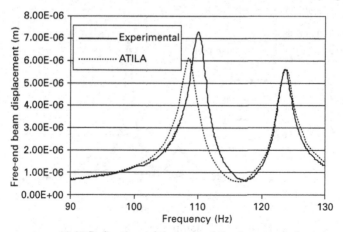

12.27 Deflection of the end of the beam – L damping.

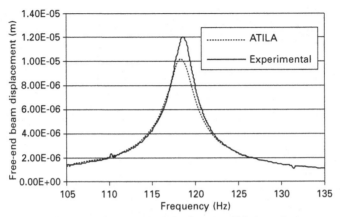

12.28 Deflection of the end of the beam – RC damping.

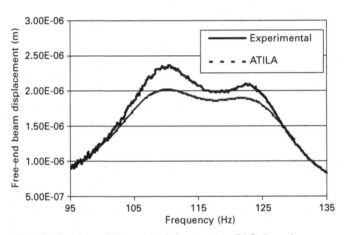

12.29 Deflection of the end of the beam – RLC damping.

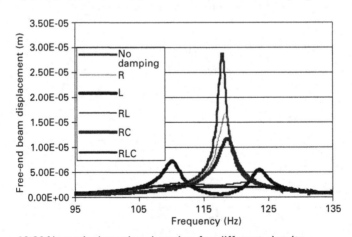

12.30 Numerical results: damping for different circuits.

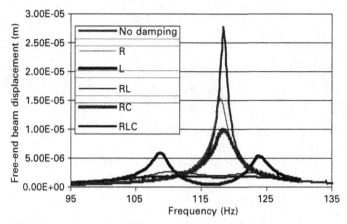

12.31 Experimental results-damping for different circuits.

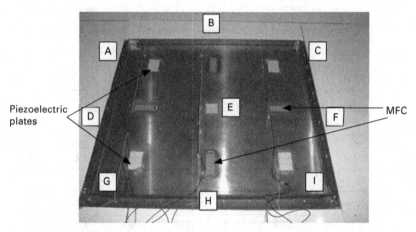

12.32 Plate with the piezoelectric transducers.

The central transducer (E) is used for the damping of mode (3, 3), whereas the transducers at the corners (A, C, G, I) are used for all modes (3, 1), (1, 3) and (3, 3)(Fig. 12.33). Experiments have been performed in the laboratory to adjust the different circuits on the free plate with the frame. The vibrating velocity is measured at the centre of the plate with the help of a laser vibrometer. Table 12.4 displays the quality factor, the coupling coefficient and the damping for experimental and numerical results. For damping, the results are quite good due to the boundary conditions, and the applied pressure on the plate is non-uniform.

Figure 12.34 displays the displacements along the *y*-axis of the plate u_z (no-damping) and u_z (RC damping) at 69.1 Hz frequency. In Fig. 12.35,

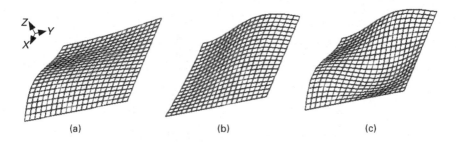

(a)   (b)   (c)

12.33 Modal analysis of a quarter of the plate: a-mode (3,1): 69.1 Hz, b-mode (1,3): 79.7 Hz, c-mode (3, 3): 133 Hz.

Table 12.4 Damping of modes (3, 1), (1, 3) and (3, 3) with different active circuits

	Mode (3,1)		Mode (1,3)		Mode (3,3)	
	Experiment	Numerical	Experiment	Numerical	Experiment	Numerical
Frequency (Hz)	64.0	69.1	75.5	79.7	126	133
Q	177	179	199	185	128	180

Position	Capacity (nF)	Coupling coefficient (%)				
E	35.9	4.5	3.8	3.5	3.9	3.8	4.1
ACGI	214.8	4.7	5.1	4.2	4.2	8.4	10.4

Position	Capacity (nF)	Resistor with negative capacity (kOhm)				
E	35.9	346	342	293	296	176	177
ACGI	214.8	57.9	54.1	49.0	46.9	29.5	28.0

Position	Damping (dB)					
E	5.6	7.4	4.1	7.2	3.3	7.4
ACGI	5.90	12.8	5.50	12.9	10.3	25.6

these displacements are normalized; they have the same shape. At 133 Hz frequency, one can see a high damping (Fig. 12.36) and a difference between the shapes of displacement without damping and RC damping (Fig. 12.37).

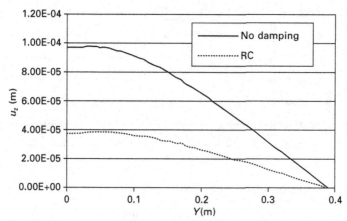

12.34 Displacement along the *y*-axis (RC damping at 69.1 Hz).

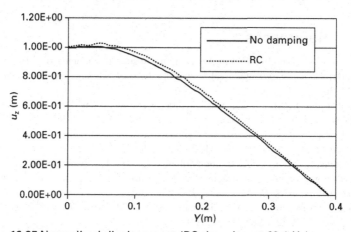

12.35 Normalized displacement (RC damping at 69.1 Hz).

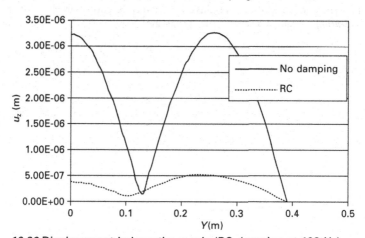

12.36 Displacement belong the *x*-axis (RC damping at 133 Hz).

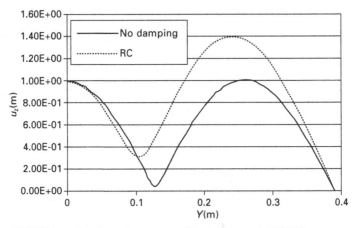

12.37 Normalized displacement (RC damping at 133 Hz).

12.5   References

1.   Hagood N. W. and Von Flotow A., 'Damping of structural vibrations with piezoelectric materials and passive electrical networks', *Journal of Sound and Vibration*, 146(2), 243–268, 1991.
2.   Hollkamp J. J., 'Multimodal passive vibration suppression with piezoelectric materials and resonant shunts', *J. Intell. Mater. Syst. Struct.* 549–57, 1994.
3.   Wu, S., 'Broadband piezoelectric shunts for passive structural vibration control', *Proceedings of SPIE 2001* 4331, 251–261, 2001.
4.   Behrens, S., Fleming, A. J. and Moheimani, S. O. R., 'New method for multiple-mode shunt damping of structural vibration using single piezoelectric transducer', *Proceedings of SPIE 2001* 4331, 239–250, 2001.
5.   Jacq M. and Vicente T., 'Amortissement semi-actif de vibration par capacité négative', *Rapport de Projet ISEN*, May 2009.
6.   Granger C. and Hladky-Hennion A. C., 'Damping of a large aluminium plate with piezoelectric materials and negative capacitance electrical circuits' *10th Cansmart Workshop*, Monréal, Canada, 10–11, October 2007.

13

Modelling the behaviour of single crystal devices with ATILA: the effect of temperature and stress on a single crystal bar, tonpilz and sphere submitted to a harmonic analysis

J-C. DEBUS, ISEN Lille, France

DOI: 10.1533/9780857096319.2.305

Abstract: Traditional transmitting materials, such as PZT-8, exhibit some non-linearity in stress and temperature, but predicting performance under high stress and higher temperatures can be achieved by taking advantage of the weak coupling. One needs to predict the performance of these devices by considering the highly non-linear behaviour with a fully non-linear solution procedure in the ATILA finite element software package. The aim of this chapter is to analyze the behaviour of simple devices submitted to a harmonic analysis. Analytical models are developed and compared with the numerical analysis via the ATILA code for several devices. ATILA does not have a non-linear solver yet. ATILA results are obtained with up-dated properties.

Key words: single crystal piezoelectric, thermal analysis, stress analysis, non-linearity, fluid-structure.

13.1 Introduction

Single crystal piezoelectric materials have much larger degrees of non-linearity in both stress and temperature. It is necessary to predict the performance of these devices by considering the highly non-linear behaviour with a fully non-linear solution procedure in the ATILA finite element software package. The analytical model will be developed and compared with the numerical analysis via the ATILA code for the harmonic analysis of several devices.

In the Section 13.4, for a longitudinal bar, an analytical solution taking losses into account, will be presented and compared with the ATILA code, the temperature will be determined and compared with a numerical solution. Then an iterative solution will be performed to take the variation of the single crystal properties into account depending on the temperature.

In Section 13.5, for a tonpilz transducer, an analytical model will be developed and compared with the ATILA code. The stress will also be determined and compared with a numerical solution. Then an iterative solution

305

will be performed to take the variation of the single crystal properties into account depending on the stress.

In Section 13.6, for the longitudinal bar, the analytical solution will be compared with the ATILA code. The temperature and the stress will also be determined and compared with a numerical solution. Then an iterative solution will be performed to take the variation of the single crystal properties into account depending on the temperature and the stress.

In Section 13.7, for a sphere in air and in water, analytical solutions have been compared with the ATILA code. The temperature and the stress will also be determined and compared with a numerical solution. Then an iterative solution will be performed to take the variation of the single crystal properties into account depending on the temperature and the stress. For each example, the ATILA results have been obtained with the updated single crystal properties.

13.2   Single crystal dependence

An expanding variety of single crystals has been developed for acoustical, optical, wireless communications and other applications. Materials used to fabricate single-crystal piezoelectric elements include lead magnesium niobate/lead titanate (PMN-PT), lead zirconate niobate/lead titanate (PZN-PT), lithium niobate ($LiNbO_3$), lithium niobate with dopants, lithium tetraborate ($Li_2B_4O_7$) and quartz. Barium titanate ($BaTiO_3$) is a potential non-lead source of piezoelectric crystals for low temperatures and room temperature applications. Single-crystal PMN-PT and PZN-PT elements exhibit[1-3] ten times the strain of comparable polycrystalline lead–zirconate–titanate elements (usable strain: 0.5% at 35 kV/cm). Crystals exhibit five times the strain energy density of conventional piezoceramics. The high electromechanical coupling of crystals[4-6] (>90%) increases the transducer bandwidth, resulting in greater sensitivity and acoustic power. However, new single crystal piezoelectrics that are being explored for compact, high power, and broadband SONAR transducers have much larger degrees of non-linearity in both stress and temperature.

13.2.1   Material properties

The single-crystal used in all the devices is a PMN-30PT[1]. The dielectric permittivity at constant stress coefficients matrix is defined as:

$$[\varepsilon^T] = \begin{bmatrix} 2.360\ 10^{-8} & 0 & 0 \\ 0 & 2.360\ 10^{-8} & 0 \\ 0 & 0 & 3.551\ 10^{-8} \end{bmatrix} (m/F)$$

The piezoelectric constant relating the strain to the electric field matrix is defined as:

$$[d] = \begin{bmatrix} 0 & 0 & 0 & 0 & 1.300\ 10^{-9} & 0 \\ 0 & 0 & 0 & 1.300\ 10^{-9} & 0 & 0 \\ -3.855\ 10^{-10} & -3.855\ 10^{-10} & 9.587\ 10^{-10} & 0 & 0 & 0 \end{bmatrix} \text{(C/N)}$$

and the elastic rigidity at constant electric field matrix is defined as:

$$[C^E] = \begin{bmatrix} 5.667\ 10^{10} & 2.930\ 10^{10} & 2.499\ 10^{10} & 0 & 0 & 0 \\ 2.930\ 10^{10} & 5.667\ 10^{10} & 2.499\ 10^{10} & 0 & 0 & 0 \\ 2.499\ 10^{10} & 2.499\ 10^{10} & 3.998\ 10^{10} & 0 & 0 & 0 \\ 0 & 0 & 0 & 1.368\ 10^{10} & 0 & 0 \\ 0 & 0 & 0 & 0 & 1.368\ 10^{10} & 0 \\ 0 & 0 & 0 & 0 & 0 & 1.3681\ 10^{10} \end{bmatrix} \text{(N/m}^2)$$

The mass density is $8\,000$ kg/m^3 and the elastic, electric and piezoelectric losses are respectively, $\tan\phi' = 0.002$, $\tan\delta' = 0.003$ and $\tan\theta' = 0.005$.

13.2.2 Temperature dependence

The temperature dependences of properties of single crystals are assumed to have a parabolic behaviour vs the temperature[7]. The temperature dependence of the dielectric permittivity constant ε_{33}^T, the piezoelectric constant d_{33}, the elastic rigidity constant C_{33}^E and the elastic compliance constant S_{33}^E are, respectively, defined as:

$$\varepsilon_{33}^T(\theta) = 2.7727\ 10^{-11}\theta^2 - 1.1091\ 10^{-09}\ \theta + 4.6581\ 10^{-08} \quad [13.1]$$

$$d_{33}(\theta) = 3.1113\ 10^{-13}\theta^2 - 1.2443\ 10^{-11}\ \theta + 4.0832\ 10^{-09} \quad [13.2]$$

$$C_{33}^E(\theta) = -1.8750\ 10^{+06}\theta^2 + 7.5000\ 10^{+07}\ \theta + 2.0250\ 10^{+10} \quad [13.3]$$

$$S_{33}^E(\theta) = 8.1639\ 10^{-15}\theta^2 - 3.2656\ 10^{-13}\ \theta + 4.2551\ 10^{-11} \quad [13.4]$$

Figures 13.1 to 13.4 present the temperature dependence corresponding to Eqs [13.1] to [13.4].

The temperature dependence of the dielectric impermeability β_{33}^T, the piezoelectric constant g_{33} and the elastic compliance S_{33}^D are, respectively, defined by these equations as:

$$\beta_{33}^T = \frac{1}{\varepsilon_{33}^T} \quad [13.5]$$

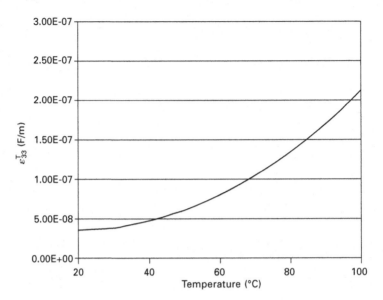

13.1 Temperature dependence of ε_{33}^{T}.

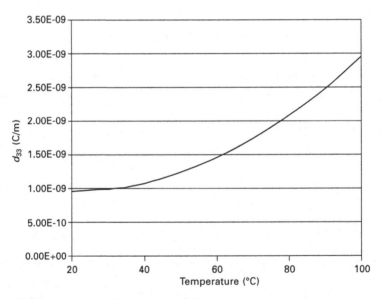

13.2 Temperature dependence of d_{33}.

$$g_{33} = \beta_{33}^{T} d_{33} \qquad\qquad [13.6]$$

$$S_{33}^{D} = S_{33}^{E} - \frac{d_{33}^{2}}{\varepsilon_{33}^{T}} \qquad\qquad [13.7]$$

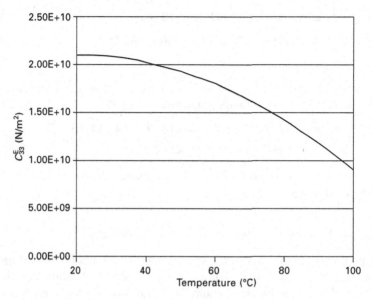

13.3 Temperature dependence of C_{33}^E.

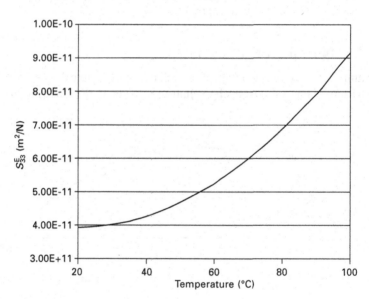

13.4 Temperature dependence of S_{33}^E.

13.2.3 Stress dependence[8]

The stress dependences of the piezoelectric constant d_{33}, the elastic compliance constant S_{33}^E, and the elastic compliance constant S_{33}^D are fitted using a parabolic function vs compressive stress T (MPa):

$$d_{33} = 958.75 + 17.235T - 0.72036T^2 \qquad\qquad [13.8]$$

$$S_{33}^E = 39.285 + 0.70661T + 0.0066186T^2 \qquad\qquad [13.9]$$

$$S_{33}^D = 15.525 + 0.59993T + 0.0143387T^2 \qquad\qquad [13.10]$$

The stress dependence of the piezoelectric constant g_{33} is fitted using a polynomial function vs compressive stress T (MPa):

$$g_{33} = 2.7015 \ 10^{-02} + 5.1050 \ 10^{-4}T - 1.0711 \ 10^{-04}T^2$$
$$+ 3.1697 \ 10^{-06}T^3 - 2.8433 \ 10^{-08}T^4 \qquad\qquad [13.11]$$

Figures 13.5 to 13.8 present the stress dependence corresponding to Eqs [13.8] to [13.11].

13.2.4 Stress and temperature dependence

To predict a device performance, the stress and temperature-dependent properties of the active materials are needed. In this study, the properties used are issued from the previous equations; no crossed dependence terms exist in these equations. As examples, Figs 13.9 and 13.10 present, respectively, the stress and temperature dependence of d_{33} and g_{33}.

13.3 Non-linear analysis

The aim of this study is to analyze the behaviour of simple devices submitted to a harmonic analysis. At each excitation frequency, the material properties

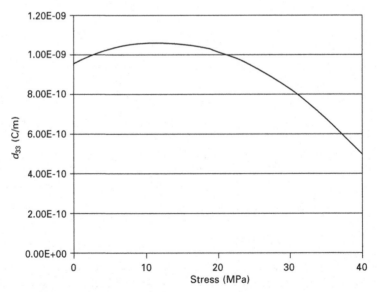

13.5 Stress dependence of d_3.

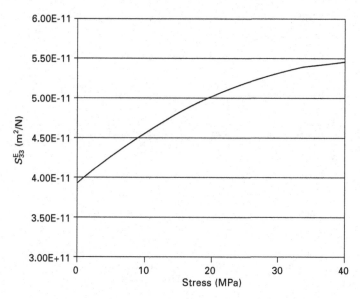

13.6 Stress dependence of S_{33}^E.

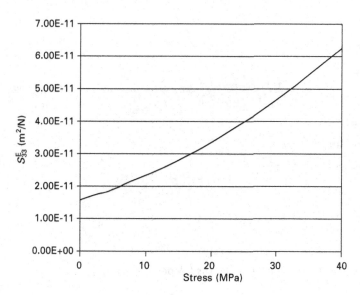

13.7 Stress dependence of S_{33}^D.

are defined for known stress and temperatures. From a harmonic analysis, new stress and temperatures are computed. These values are compared with the previous values. The process is stopped when the convergence is obtained. Figure 13.11 displays the flow-chart of the non-linear process. In this figure, and are the requested precisions to obtain the convergence.

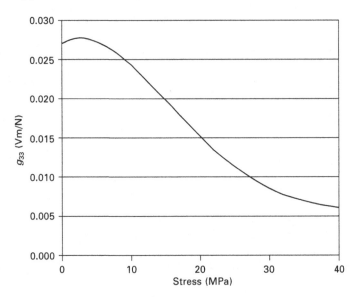

13.8 Stress dependence of g_{33}.

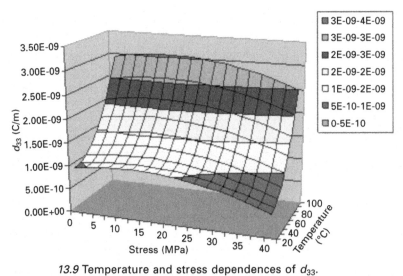

13.9 Temperature and stress dependences of d_{33}.

13.4   Harmonic analysis of a length expander bar with parallel field

13.4.1 Longitudinal displacement of the bar

The longitudinal bar has a length L, a width a and a thickness b (Fig. 13.12); the electric field is parallel to the longitudinal axis. It is assumed

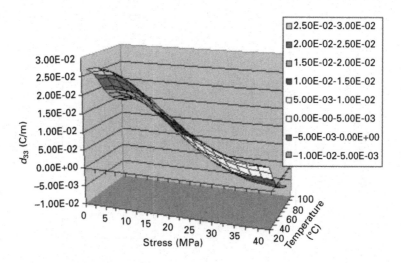

13.10 Temperature and stress dependences of g_{33}.

that simple harmonic longitudinal waves propagating along the x-direction have a displacement given by:

$$u_x^* = A^* \sin k^* x + B^* \cos k^* x \qquad [13.12]$$

where $\quad k^* = \dfrac{\omega}{C^{D^*}} \qquad [13.13]$

and

$$C^{D^*} = \dfrac{1}{\sqrt{\rho S_{33}^{D^*}}} \qquad [13.14]$$

It is assumed that the width and thickness of the bar are small compared to its length L and that the only significant stress is along the length of the bar. When the fringing effects are neglected, the electric displacement is defined as[9]:

$$D_1 = 0, D_2 = 0 \text{ and } \dfrac{\partial D_3}{\partial x} = 0 \qquad [13.15]$$

Therefore, D_3 is a constant. The piezoelectric equations are:

$$S_3^* = S_{33}^{D^*} T_3^* + g_{33}^* D \qquad [13.16a]$$

$$E_3^* = -g_{33}^* T_3^* + \beta_{33}^{T^*} D_3^* \qquad [13.16b]$$

For the unloaded bar, the applied forces are zero and the boundary condition at each end is

$T_3^* = 0$. Assuming that:

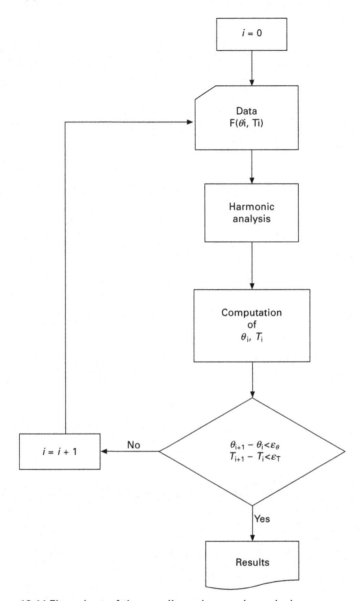

13.11 Flow-chart of the non-linear harmonic analysis.

$$D_3^* = D_0 e^{j\omega t} \tag{13.17}$$

Then the values of A^* and B^* are determined as:

$$A^* = \frac{g_{33}^* D_0^*}{k^*} \tag{13.18a}$$

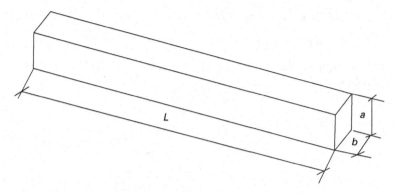

13.12 Length expanded bar with parallel electric field.

$$B^* = -\frac{g_{33}^* D_0^*}{k^*} \tan \frac{k^* L}{2} \qquad [13.18b]$$

From Eq. [13.16a] the stress can be written as:

$$T_3^* = \frac{S_{33}^{D^*}}{S_3^*} - \frac{g_{33}^*}{S_3^*} D_3^* \qquad [13.19]$$

Eq. [13.16b] becomes:

$$E_3^* = -\frac{g_{33}^*}{S_{33}^{D^*}} S_3^* + \left(\beta_{33}^{T^*} + \frac{g_{33}^{*2}}{S_{33}^{D^*}} \right) D_3^* \qquad [13.20]$$

The potential difference between the electrodes is:

$$V = -\int_0^L E_3^* dx \qquad [13.21]$$

Using Eq. [13.20], the electric displacement is:

$$D_3^* = \frac{S_{33}^{D^*}}{g_{33}^{*2}} \frac{V}{L} \frac{1}{\dfrac{\tan k^* L/2}{k^* L/2} - \left(\dfrac{\beta_{33}^{T^*} S_{33}^{D^*}}{g_{33}^{*2}} + 1 \right)} \qquad [13.22]$$

13.4.2 Determination of the losses

The complex parameters S^{E^*}, ε^{T^*} and d^* were introduced to account for the hysteresis losses associated with the elastic, electric and piezoelectric coupling energy as:

$$S^{E^*} = S^E (1 - j \tan \phi') \qquad [13.23a]$$

$$\varepsilon^{T^*} = \varepsilon^T(1 - j \tan \delta') \qquad\qquad [13.23b]$$

$$d^* = d(1 - j \tan \theta') \qquad\qquad [13.23c]$$

The relation for the elastic compliance at electric charge constant is defined as follows:

$$s_{33}^{D^*} = s_{33}^{E^*} - \frac{d_{33}^{*2}}{\varepsilon_{33}^{T^*}} \qquad\qquad [13.24]$$

$$s_{33}^{D^*} = s_{33}^E(1 - j \tan \phi') - \frac{d_{33}^2(1 - j \tan \delta')^2}{\varepsilon_{33}^T(1 - j \tan \theta')} \qquad\qquad [13.25]$$

Neglecting the loss coefficients at a higher order, Eq. [13.25] becomes[10]:

$$s_{33}^{D^*} = s_{33}^E - \frac{d_{33}^2}{\varepsilon_{33}^T} - j(s_{33}^E \tan \phi' - \frac{d_{33}^2(2 \tan \theta' - \tan \delta')}{\varepsilon_{33}^T} \qquad\qquad [13.26]$$

or

$$s_{33}^{D^*} = s_{33}^{D^R} - j s_{33}^{D^I} = s_{33}^D(1 - j \tan \phi'') \qquad\qquad [13.27]$$

where

$$\tan \phi'' = \frac{s_{33}^{D^R}}{s_{33}^{D^I}} \qquad\qquad [13.28]$$

and Eq. [13.14] becomes

$$C_D^* = \frac{1}{\sqrt{\rho s_{33}^{D^*}}} = \frac{1}{\sqrt{\rho s_{33}^D}} \frac{1}{\sqrt{1 - \tan \phi''}} = \frac{C_D}{(1 - j \tan \phi''/2)} \qquad\qquad [13.29]$$

and Eq. [13.13] can be written as:

$$k^* = \frac{\omega}{C_D}\left(1 - j \frac{\tan \phi''}{2}\right) \qquad\qquad [13.30]$$

The piezoelectric voltage constant coefficient g_{33}^* is defined by this relation:

$$g_{33}^* = \beta_{33}^{T^*} d_{33}^* = \frac{d_{33}^*}{\varepsilon_{33}^{T^*}} = \frac{d_{33}}{\varepsilon_{33}^T}\left(\frac{1 - j \tan \theta'}{1 - j \tan \delta'}\right) \qquad\qquad [13.31]$$

or

$$g_{33}^* = g^{33}(1 - j \tan \theta'') \qquad\qquad [13.32]$$

where

$$\tan \theta'' = \tan \theta' - \tan \delta' \qquad\qquad [13.33]$$

To obtain the value of D_3^*, the value of $k^*L/2$ is defined as:

$$\frac{k^*L}{2} = \frac{kL}{2}\left(1 - j\,\frac{\tan\delta''}{2}\right) = \alpha - j\beta \qquad [13.34]$$

where

$$\alpha = \frac{kL}{2} \qquad [13.35]$$

and

$$\beta = \frac{kL\tan\phi''}{4} \qquad [13.36]$$

The value of $\tan k^*L/2$ can be written as:

$$\tan\frac{k^*L}{2} = \tan(\alpha - j\beta) = \frac{\tan\alpha - \tan j\beta}{1 + \tan\alpha\tan j\beta} = \frac{\tan\alpha - j\tanh\beta}{1 + j\tan\alpha\tanh\beta}$$

$$\tan\frac{k^*L}{2} = C - jD \qquad [13.37]$$

where

$$C = \frac{\tan\alpha(1 - \tanh\beta^2)}{1 + (\tan\alpha\tanh\beta)^2} \qquad [13.38]$$

and

$$D = \frac{\tanh\beta(1 + \tan\alpha^2)}{1 + (\tan\alpha\tanh\beta)^2} \qquad [13.39]$$

Then, the electrical displacement can be written as:

$$D_3^* = \frac{S_{33}^D}{g_{33}^2}\frac{V}{L}\frac{\alpha^2 + \beta^2}{F^2 + G^2}[F + 2\gamma G - j(2\gamma F - G)] \qquad [13.40]$$

or

$$D_3^* = D_3^R + jD_3^I \qquad [13.41]$$

with

$$D_3^R = \frac{k}{g_{33}}E\frac{V}{L}(F + 2\gamma G) \qquad [13.42]$$

$$D_3^I = -\frac{k}{g_{33}}E\frac{V}{L}(2\gamma F - G) \qquad [13.43]$$

where

$$E = \frac{S_{33}^D}{kg_{33}} \frac{V}{L} \frac{\alpha^2 + \beta^2}{F^2 + G^2} \qquad [13.44]$$

$$F = \alpha C + \beta D - (\alpha^2 + \beta^2)\left(\frac{\beta_{33}^T S_{33}^D}{g_{33}^2} + 1\right) \qquad [13.45]$$

$$G = \alpha D - \beta C - (\alpha^2 + \beta^2)\frac{\beta_{33}^T S_{33}^D}{g_{33}^2}(2\gamma - \tan \delta') \qquad [13.46]$$

$$\lambda = \frac{\tan \phi''}{2} - \tan \theta'' \qquad [13.47]$$

From Eqs [13.18a] and [13.18b] the values of A^* and B^* are defined as:

$$A^* = \frac{VE}{L}(F + \gamma G + j(-\gamma F + G)) \qquad [13.48]$$

or

$$A^* = A^R + jA^I \qquad [13.49]$$

with

$$A^R = \frac{VE}{L}(F + \gamma G) \qquad [13.50]$$

$$A^I = \frac{VE}{L}(-\lambda F + G) \qquad [13.51]$$

and

$$B^* = -A^*(C - jD) \qquad [13.52]$$

or

$$B^* = B^R + jB^I \qquad [13.53]$$

with

$$B^R = -A^R C - A^I D \qquad [13.54]$$

$$B^I = A^R D - A^I C \qquad [13.55]$$

Then, the longitudinal displacement (Eq. [13.12]) becomes:

$$u_x^* = (A^R + jA^I)(\sin kx \cosh k'x - j \cos kx \sinh k'x)$$
$$+ (B^R + jB^I)(\cos kx \cosh k'x + j \sinh k'x \sin kx) \qquad [13.56]$$

where

$$k' = \frac{\tan\phi''}{2} k \tag{13.57}$$

or

$$u_x^* = u_x^R + ju_x^I$$

with

$$u_x^R = A^R \sin kx \cosh k'x + A^I \cos kx \sinh k'x$$
$$+ B^R \cos kx \cosh k'x - B^I \sin kx \sinh k'x \tag{13.58}$$
$$u_x^I = A^I \sin kx \cosh k'x + A^R \cos kx \sinh k'x$$
$$+ B^I \cos kx \cosh k'x - B^R \sin kx \sinh k'x \tag{13.59}$$

and

$$S_3^R = \frac{\partial u_x^R}{\partial x} \tag{13.60}$$

$$S_3^R = A^R (k \cos kx \cosh k'x + k' \sin kx \sinh k) + A^I(k' \cos$$
$$kx \cosh k'x - k \sin kx \sinh k'x) + B^R (k' \cos kx \sinh k'x - k$$
$$\sin kx \cosh k'x) - B^I(k \cos kx \sinh k'x + k' \sin kx \cosh k'x) \tag{13.61}$$

$$S_3^I = \frac{\partial u_x^I}{\partial x} \tag{13.62}$$

$$S_3^I = A^I (k \cos kx \cosh k'x + k' \sin kx \sinh k) - A^R(k' \cos$$
$$kx \cosh k'x - k \sin kx \sinh k'x) + B^I (k' \cos kx \sinh k'x - k$$
$$\sin kx \cosh k'x) + B^R(k \cos kx \sinh k'x + k' \sin kx \cosh k'x) \tag{13.63}$$

From Eq. [13.18a], we can define the stress T_3^*:

$$T_3^* = \frac{S_3^*}{S_{33}^{D*}} - \frac{g_{33}^*}{D_{33}^{D*}} D_3^* \tag{13.64}$$

or

$$T_3^* = T_3^R + jT_3^I \tag{13.65}$$

with

$$T_3^R = \frac{1}{S_{33}^D} [S_3^R - S_3^I \tan \phi'' - g_{33}(D_3^R - D_3^I (\tan\phi'' - \tan \theta''))] \tag{13.66}$$

$$T_3^I = \frac{1}{S_{33}^D} [S_3^I + S_3^R \tan \phi'' - g_{33}(D_3^I + D_3^R(\tan\phi'' - \tan \theta''))] \quad [13.67]$$

From Eq. [13.18b], we can define the field E_3^*:

$$E_3^* = - g_{33}^* T_3^* + \beta_{33}^{T^*} D_3^* = E_3^R + jE_3^I \qquad [13.68]$$

with

$$E_3^R = - g_{33}(T_3^R + T_3^I \tan \theta'') + \beta_{33}^T(D_3^R - D_3^I \tan \delta') \qquad [13.69]$$

$$E_3^I = - g_{33}(T_3^I - T_3^R \tan \theta'') + \beta_{33}^T(D_3^I + D_3^R \tan \delta') \qquad [13.70]$$

13.4.3 Application

Geometry of the simple model

The bar has a 10 mm × 10 mm square section and a 40 mm length (Fig. 13.13). At each extremity, one electrode is grounded and the other one has a potential. The material used is a PMN-30PT single crystal. Only a quarter has been modelled with two planes of symmetry, XOY and XOZ (Fig. 13.14). The validation has been performed with the ATILA code. The mesh of the numerical model is presented in Fig. 13.15.

Resonance and anti-resonance of the bar

For the numerical model, a modal analysis has been performed with the ATILA code to obtain the resonance, the anti-resonance and the coupling coefficient. A harmonic analysis with a tension excitation has permitted to obtain the resonance frequency and another harmonic analysis with a current

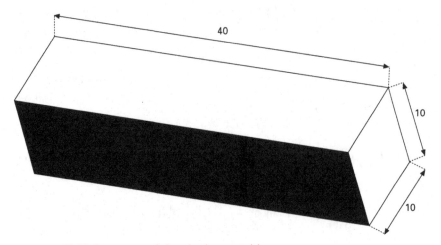

13.13 Geometry of the single crystal bar.

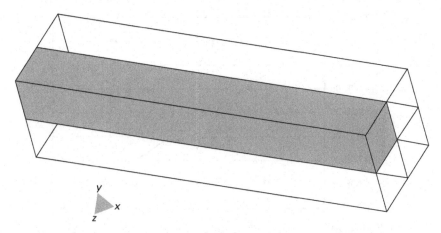

13.14 Geometry of the numerical model.

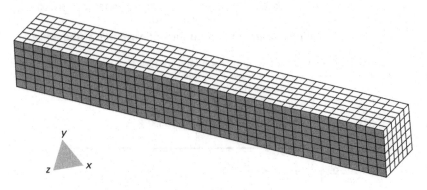

13.15 Mesh of the bar.

excitation has given the anti-resonance frequency when the real part of the electrical displacement becomes zero (Eq. [13.42]) (Fig. 13.16). Table 13.1 shows a good agreement between the analytical solution and finite element modelling.

Harmonic analysis of the bar

The analytical results of the bar for a 10 V harmonic voltage excitation have been compared with the numerical analysis. Figures 13.17 and 13.18 present, respectively, the real and imaginary parts of the longitudinal displacement, analytical results (Eqs [13.58] and [13.59]) vs numerical results.

In Figs 13.19 and 13.20, the real part and imaginary part of the strain obtained with, respectively, Eq. [13.61] and Eq. [13.63], are compared with the ATILA results. Then, the longitudinal stress has been compared (real and

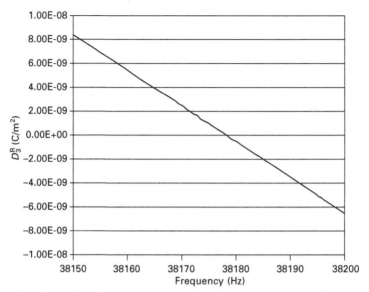

13.16 Electrical displacement around the anti-resonance frequency.

Table 13.1 Resonance and anti-resonance frequencies of the bar

	Analytical	ATILA
f_r (Hz)	23 765.8	23 657.6
f_a (Hz)	38 178.2	38 181.8
k (%)	78.2	78.3

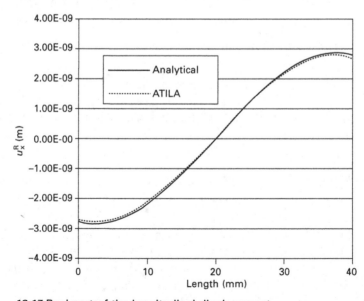

13.17 Real part of the longitudinal displacement.

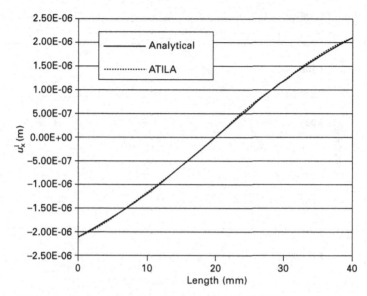

13.18 Imaginary part of the longitudinal displacement.

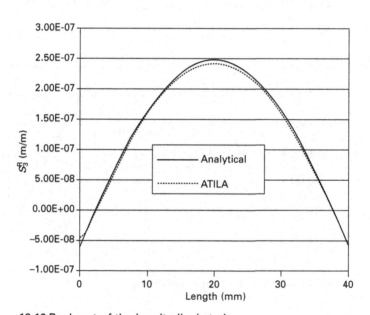

13.19 Real part of the longitudinal strain.

imaginary parts) from Eqs [13.66] and [13.67] with the numerical results (Figs 13.21 and 13.22). For all these results, the agreement between the analytical and numerical results is very good.

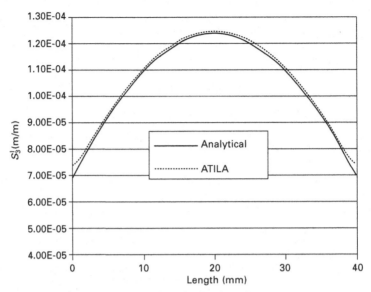

13.20 Imaginary part of the longitudinal strain.

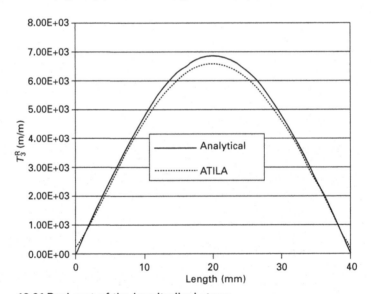

13.21 Real part of the longitudinal stress.

13.4.4 Dissipated power

The dissipated power density is defined by Holland[11] using the generalized Poynting's vector approach as:

$$P_d = \frac{1}{2}\,\omega I_m (\{E\}^T\{D^*\} + \{T\}^T\{S^*\})$$ [13.71]

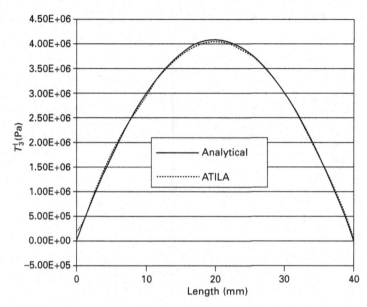

13.22 Imaginary part of the longitudinal stress.

where ω is the angular frequency and I_m denotes the imaginary component. The dissipated power may be reduced to an expression written in engineering notation in terms of the electric field and stress by substituting Eqs [13.16a] and [13.16b] into Eq. [13.71]:

$$P_d = \frac{1}{2} \omega I_m (\{E^r\}^T [d^*]\{T^*\} + \{E^r\}^T [\varepsilon^{T^*}]\{E^*\}$$

$$+ \{T^r\}^T [s^{E^*}]\{T^*\} + \{T^r\}^T [d^*]^T \{E^*\}) \qquad [13.72]$$

The first and the last terms express the dissipated power density from the electric field and the mechanical stress coupling, the second term is a purely electrical dissipation whereas the third term is a purely mechanical dissipation. Figure 13.23 compares the dissipated power vs frequency between the analytical and numerical results, this result is good.

13.4.5 Temperature due to the self-heating

Steady problem

For a steady-state solution, the thermal behaviour is weakly coupled to the electromechanical response. The heat source term is entered into the equation for heat transfer using the heat equation as:

$$\frac{\partial}{\partial x}\left(k_{xx}\frac{\partial T}{\partial x}\right) + \frac{\partial}{\partial y}\left(k_{yy}\frac{\partial T}{\partial y}\right) + \frac{\partial}{\partial z}\left(k_{zz}\frac{\partial T}{\partial z}\right) + Q = 0 \qquad [13.73]$$

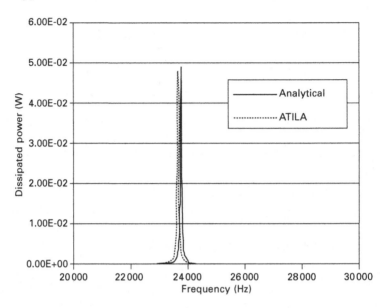

13.23 Dissipated power vs frequency.

where T denotes temperature (°C), k_{xx}, k_{yy}, k_{zz} are the conductivity coefficients (W/m/°C) along x, y, z, respectively, and Q is the heat generated (W/m³) within the body including the dissipated power from material losses. Q is positive if the heat is put into the body.

The boundary conditions associated with Eq. [13.73] can be expressed under two different forms. If the temperature is known along a part of the boundary then

$$T = T_S \qquad [13.74]$$

where T_S is the boundary temperature at surface S. If heat is gained or lost at boundary Γ due to convection, $h(T - T_\infty)$, or a heat flux, q, then

$$k_{xx} \frac{\partial T}{\partial x} \ell_x + k_{yy} \frac{\partial T}{\partial y} \ell_y + k_{zz} \frac{\partial T}{\partial z} \ell_z + q + h(T - T_\infty) = 0 \qquad [13.75]$$

where h the convective thermal film coefficient (W/m²/°C), q is the heat flux (W/m²), T_∞ is the ambient temperature of the surrounding medium.

One dimensional heat transfer

To validate the thermal analysis, the piezoelectric bar is defined with one element using one-dimensional linear interpolation (Fig. 13.24). The interpolating polynomial for the one-dimensional element is

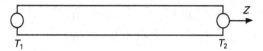

13.24 1D Thermal modelling.

$$T(z) = N_1(z)T_1 + N_2(z)T_2 \qquad [13.76]$$

where and $N_1(z) = \left(1 - \dfrac{z}{\ell}\right)$ and $N_2(z) = \dfrac{z}{\ell}$; the element has a length ℓ.

For a steady thermal analysis with one element, the finite element formulation is:

$$([K_T] + [K_{h1}] + [K_{h2}])\{T\} = \{K_{T\infty1}\} + \{K_{T\infty2}\} + \{Q\} \qquad [13.77]$$

where

$$[K_T] = \frac{Ak_{zz}}{\ell}\begin{bmatrix} 1 & -1 \\ -1 & 1 \end{bmatrix} \text{ is the conductivity matrix, } A \text{ is the cross-section area}$$

$$[K_{h1}] = \frac{Ph\ell}{6}\begin{bmatrix} 2 & 1 \\ 1 & 2 \end{bmatrix} \text{ is the convection matrix, } P \text{ is the perimeter}$$

$$[K_{h2}] = hA\begin{bmatrix} 0 & 0 \\ 0 & 1 \end{bmatrix} \text{ is the convection matrix at node 2}$$

$$\{k_{T\infty1}\} = \frac{hT_\infty P\ell}{2}\begin{Bmatrix} 1 \\ 1 \end{Bmatrix} \text{ is the convection vector}$$

$$\{k_{T\infty2}\} = \frac{hT_\infty A}{2}\begin{Bmatrix} 1 \\ 1 \end{Bmatrix} \text{ is the convection vector at node 2}$$

$$\{Q\} = \frac{p_d A\ell}{2}\begin{Bmatrix} 1 \\ 1 \end{Bmatrix} \text{ is the thermal load vector, } p_d \text{ is the dissipated power density}$$

The numerical values used are:

$$k_{xx} = 2 \text{ W/m/°C, } S_h = 858 \text{ J/kg/°C, } h = 10 \text{ W/m}^2\text{/°C, } T_\infty = 20°C$$

$$\ell = 0.04 \text{ m, } c = a/2 = 0.005 \text{ m,}$$

$$P = 4*c \text{ and } A = c^2$$

$$p_d = 4.894 \ 10^{-2} \text{ W at 23765.8 Hz resonance frequency}$$

With these values, Eq. [13.77] is:

$$\begin{Bmatrix} 2.83\ 10^{-03} & -25.83\ 10^{-04} \\ -25.83\ 10^{-04} & 2.83\ 10^{-03} \end{Bmatrix} \begin{Bmatrix} T_1 \\ T_2 \end{Bmatrix} = \begin{Bmatrix} 6.95\ 10^{-02} \\ 6.95\ 10^{-02} \end{Bmatrix} \qquad [13.78]$$

The results are $T_1 = 30.88\ °C$ and $T_2 = 30.88\ °C$

To compare this model with an ATILA model, a harmonic analysis has been performed at the resonance frequency of 23 657.6 Hz. Figure 13.25 presents the comparison between analytical and numerical temperatures. Plate XV (between pages 194 and 195) displays the cylinder temperature profile. A very good agreement is observed between the simple model and the ATILA model.

Temperature effect on the non-linear material behaviour of the bar

To study the non-linear material behaviour of the bar due to the temperature, the length expander bar with parallel field has been submitted to an excitation of 15 V. The material properties of the single crystal used correspond to an ambient temperature of 20 °C. At start, the resonance frequency is computed from a harmonic analysis. At each step of the harmonic analysis at the resonance frequency, from the updated properties of the single crystal, a new value of the temperature in the bar is obtained. Figures 13.26 and 13.27 sum up the iterative computation. The iteration is stopped when the convergence is obtained. This convergence is rapidly obtained. Table 13.2 displays the material properties of the single crystal at start and final steps

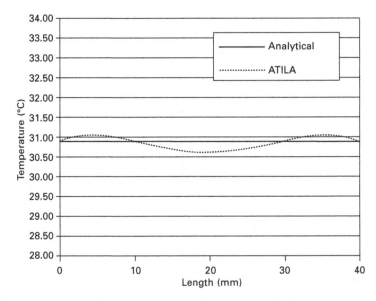

13.25 Temperature in the bar.

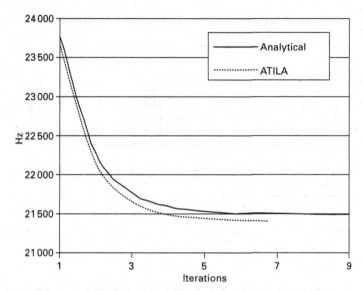

13.26 Resonance frequency iterative computation of the bar.

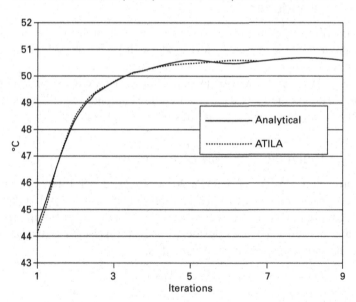

13.27 Temperature iterative computation of the bar at the resonance frequency.

of the computation. The comparison of the resonance frequency between analytical and numerical solution at the final step is shown in Table 13.3. The results show a good agreement between these values. plate XVI (between pages 194 and 195) displays the steady temperature profile at the resonance frequency obtained numerically.

Table 13.2 Comparison of the single crystal properties between the start and final computational steps

θ (°C)	20 (start)	45.15 (final)
S_{33}^E (m²/N)	3.9285 10⁻¹¹	4.4449 10⁻¹¹
d_{33} (C/N)	9.5875 10⁻¹⁰	1.1555 10⁻⁰⁹
ε_{33}^T (m/F)	3.5490 10⁻⁰⁸	5.3028 10⁻⁰⁸
S_{33}^D (m²/N)	1.3385 10⁻¹¹	1.9268 10⁻¹¹
g_{33} (Vm/N)	2.7015 10⁻⁰²	2.1790 10⁻⁰²

Table 13.3 Comparison of the resonance frequency between analytical and numerical analysis at the final step

	Analytical	ATILA	%
f_r (Hz)	22142	22039	0.47

13.5   Harmonic analysis of a single crystal tonpilz transducer

The aim of this section is to analyze a tonpilz transducer submitted to harmonic excitation. An analytical model will be developed and compared with an ATILA numerical solution. In the first part, a harmonic analysis taking the losses into account will be presented and compared with the numerical solution. Then in the second part, an iterative computation will be performed with the stress dependence properties of the single crystal.

13.5.1 Analytical solution of the tonpilz

This projector consists of a PMN-30PT driver, a beryllium head-mass, a brass tail-mass and a steel rod (Fig. 13.28). The electric field is parallel to the longitudinal axis. The driver is realized with one element and the head-mass and the tail-mass are considered as rigid masses. For the driver, the simple harmonic displacement assumed is:

$$u_D^*(x) = A_D^* \sin k_D^* x + B_D^* \cos k_D^* x \qquad [13.79]$$

And for the bolt, it is:

$$u_B^*(x) = A_B^* \sin k_B^* x + B_B^* \cos k_B^* x \qquad [13.80]$$

where

$$k_D^* = \frac{\omega}{c^{D^*}} \qquad [13.81]$$

and

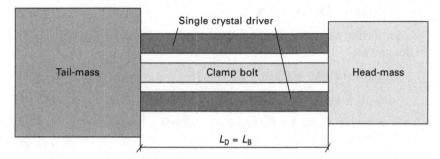

13.28 Tonpilz model.

$$k_B^* = \frac{\omega}{C^{B^*}} \qquad [13.82]$$

The underscript * means that all the values are complex.

The travelling speeds for longitudinal waves, respectively, for the driver and the bolt are:

$$C^{D^*} = \frac{1}{\sqrt{\rho_D S_{33}^{D^*}}} \qquad [13.83]$$

and

$$C^{B^*} = \sqrt{\frac{E_B^*}{\rho_B}} \qquad [13.84]$$

where ρ_D and ρ_B are, respectively, the mass density of the driver and of the bolt, S_{33}^D is of the elastic compliance at constant electric charge in the x direction and E_B is the Young modulus of the bolt.

It is assumed that the outer and inner diameters of the driver are small compared to its length and the only significant stress is along the length of the driver. Then, when fringing effects are neglected:

$$D_1^* = 0, D_2^{**} = 0 \text{ and } \frac{\partial D_3^*}{\partial x} = 0 \qquad [13.85]$$

The electrical displacement is constant. The deformation and the stress in the driver are:

$$S_3^*(x) = k_D(A_D^* \cos k_D x - B_D^* \sin k_D x) \qquad [13.86]$$

$$T_3^*(x) = T_D^* = \frac{S_3^*(x)}{S_{33}^{D^*}} - \frac{g_{33}^*}{S_{33}^{D^*}} D_3^*(x) \qquad [13.87]$$

The deformation and the stress in the bolt are:

$$S_B^*(x) = k_B^*(A_A^* \cos k_D^* x - B_B^* \sin k_B x) \qquad [13.88]$$

$$T_B^*(x) = E_B^* S_B^*(x) \tag{13.89}$$

The equilibrium and compatibility equations at $x = 0$ and $x = L_D$ (Fig. 13.29), are defined as:

at $x = 0$ $F_D^*(0) + F_B^*(0) + F_T^*(0) = 0$ [13.90]

$$u_D^*(0) = u_B^*(0) \tag{13.91}$$

at $x = L_D$ $F_D^*(L_D) + F_B^*(L_D) + F_T^*(L_D) = 0$ [13.92]

$$u_D^*(L_D) = u_B^*(L_D) \tag{13.93}$$

From these equations, the integration constants can be obtained as:

$$A_D^* - \frac{g_{33}^* D_3^{0^*}}{k_D^*} + \alpha_{BD}^* A_B^* = -\beta_D^* \frac{M_T}{M_D} B_D^*$$

$$B_B^* = B_D^*$$

$$A_B^* = \frac{A_D^* \sin \beta_D^* + B_D^*(\cos \beta_D^* - \cos \beta_B^*)}{\sin \beta_B^*}$$

$$A_D^* \cos \beta_D^* - B_D^* \sin \beta_D^* - \frac{g_{33}^* D_3^{0^*}}{k_D^*} + \alpha_{BD}^*(A_B^* \cos \beta_B^* - B_B^* \sin \beta_B^*)$$

$$= \beta_D^* \frac{M_H}{M_D}(A_D^* \sin \beta_D^* + B_D^* \cos \beta_D^*) \tag{13.94}$$

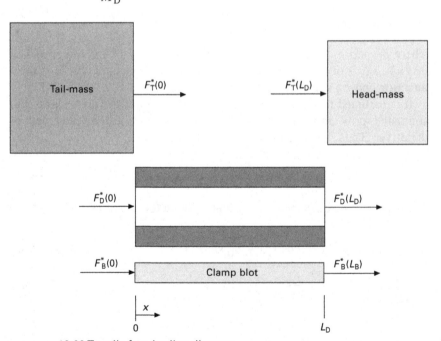

13.29 Tonpilz free bodies diagram.

where

$$\beta_B^* = k_B^* L_B \qquad\qquad [13.95]$$

$$\beta_D^* = k_D^* L_D \qquad\qquad [13.96]$$

$$\alpha_{BD}^* = \frac{M_B}{M_D} \frac{c_B^*}{c_D^*} \frac{L_D}{L_B} \qquad\qquad [13.97]$$

The longitudinal displacements are obtained from Eqs [13.79] and [13.80], the deformations from Eqs [13.86] and [13.88] and the stresses from Eqs [13.87] and [13.89].

13.5.2 Application

Geometry of the model

The tonpilz consists of a beryllium head-mass with a 30 mm diameter and a 15 mm height, of a brass tail-mass with a 30 mm diameter and a 20 mm height and a steel pre-stressed bolt with a 5 mm diameter and a 40 mm length. The driver consists of a PMN-30PT single crystal bar with a 6 mm inner diameter, a 12 mm outer diameter and a 40 mm height (Fig. 13.30)

Validation

This tonpilz being axisymmetrical, the mesh (Fig. 13.31) is a 2D mesh for an ATILA numerical analysis.

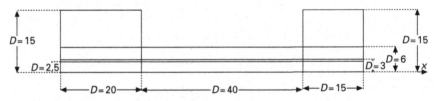

13.30 Tonpilz geometry.

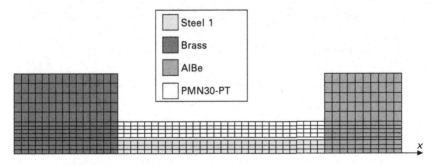

13.31 Tonpilz mesh.

Resonance and anti-resonance frequencies

To validate the analysis of the tonpilz, a modal analysis performed with the ATILA code gives the resonance and anti-resonance frequencies and the coupling coefficient. A first modelling has been carried out, assuming the head-mass and the tail-mass as elastic components. The second modelling assumes that the displacements of their end faces are constant. Then, in the last modelling, the head-mass and the tail-mass are considered as rigid bodies. Table 13.4 shows the results of the modal analysis. The agreement between the analytical and rigid mass numerical analysis is very good, so, these two models have been chosen for the following analysis.

Harmonic analysis

The analytical results of the tonpilz for a 1 V harmonic excitation have been compared with the numerical results. Figures 13.32 to 13.34 display,

Table 13.4 Comparison of a modal analysis results between analytical and numerical solutions

	ATILA			Analytical
	Free	Constant	Rigid masses	
f_r (Hz)	12237	13075	13182	13166
f_a (Hz)	15338	16616	16839	16896
k (%)	60.1	61.7	62.2	62.7

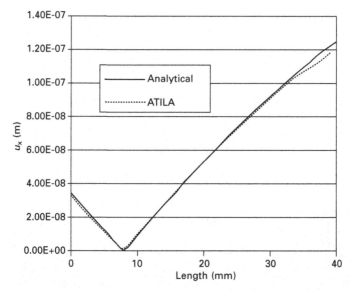

13.32 Axial displacement of the driver at the resonance frequency.

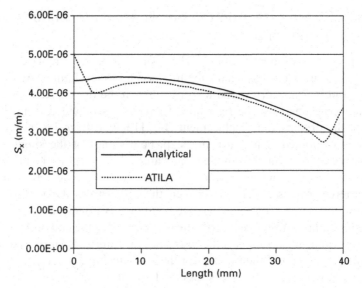

13.33 Axial deformation of the driver at the resonance frequency.

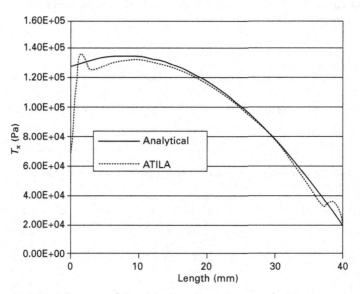

13.34 Axial stress of the driver at the resonance frequency.

respectively, the axial displacement modulus, the axial deformation and the axial stress at the resonance frequency comparing the analytical (Eqs [13.79], [13.86] and [13.87]) and numerical results. The results obtained for the axial displacement show a very good agreement. Therefore, for the deformation and the stress, at the end of the driver, a difference exists due to the head-mass and the tail-mass taken into account in the numerical model.

13.5.3 Stress effect on the non-linear material behaviour of the tonpilz

To study the non-linear material behaviour of a driver tonpilz due to the stress, the transducer has been submitted to an 1 V excitation. At start, the material properties correspond to zero stress in the driver. At each step of the harmonic analysis, the resonance frequency is obtained from the real part of the driver axial displacement (Eq. [13.79]); from Eq. [13.87], the stress is computed. The following step, new values of the single crystal properties are computed from the mean value of the stress in the driver. The iteration is stopped when the convergence is obtained. Table 13.5 displays the iterative process, giving at each step, the initial stress, the final stress and the new resonance frequency. The convergence is rapidly obtained. Table 13.6 shows the single crystal properties at start and at the end of the iterative process. Table 13.7 compares the resonance and anti-resonance frequencies obtained at the end of the process for the analytical and numerical solution. Figure 13.35 displays the axial stress modulus in the driver at the resonance frequency; the mean value stresses, respectively, for the analytical and numerical solution are 8.21 MPa and 8.19 MPa. The agreement between these values is very good.

Table 13.5 Stress iterative computation of the tonpilz at the resonance frequency

Iteration	Frequency (Hz)	T-start (MPa)	T-final (MPa)
1	12 166	0	10
2	12 765	10	8.20
3	12 789	8.20	8.21
4	12 789	8.21	8.21

Table 13.6 Comparison of the single crystal properties between start and final computational steps

Stress (Mpa)	0 (start)	8.21 (final)
S_{33}^E (m²/N)	$3.9285 \ 10^{-11}$	$4.4540 \ 10^{-11}$
d_{33} (C/N)	$9.5870 \ 10^{-10}$	$1.0517 \ 10^{-09}$
ε_{33}^T (m/F)	$3.5490 \ 10^{-08}$	$4.1064 \ 10^{-08}$
S_{33}^D (m²/N)	$1.3385 \ 10^{-11}$	$1.7606 \ 10^{-11}$
g_{33} (Vm/N)	$2.7015 \ 10^{-02}$	$2.5611 \ 10^{-02}$

Table 13.7 Comparison of the modal analysis results between analytical and numerical solutions at the final step

	Analytical	ATILA	%
f_r (Hz)	12 789	12 731	0.46
f_a (Hz)	15 221	15 155	0.44
k (%)	54.22	54.25	0.06

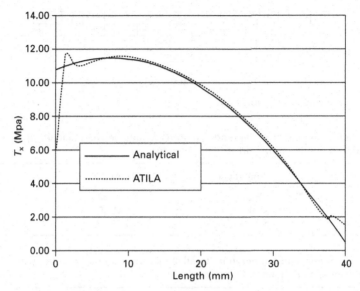

13.35 Axial stress of the driver at the resonance frequency.

13.6   Harmonic analysis of a single crystal bar with a bolt

The aim of this part is to analyze a device consisting of a single crystal bar with a pre-stressed bolt submitted to a harmonic excitation. The analytical model is the same as the previous model without the head-mass and the tail-mass. An iterative process will be realized taking into account the temperature and the stress effect on the material properties of the single crystal in the device.

13.6.1 Application

Model geometry

The device consists of a steel bolt with a 5 mm diameter and a 40 mm length. The driver consists of a PMN-30PT single crystal bar with a 6 mm inner diameter, a 12 mm outer diameter and a 40 mm height. This device having an axial symmetry, the mesh (Fig. 13.36) is a 2D mesh for an ATILA numerical analysis.

Validation

Resonance and anti-resonance frequencies

To validate this analysis of the tonpilz, a modal analysis performed with the ATILA code gives the resonance and anti-resonance frequencies and the

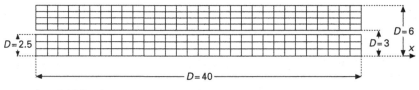

13.36 Device geometry.

Table 13.8 Comparison of the modal analysis results between analytical and numerical solutions of the driver with the bolt

	Analytical	ATILA	%
f_r (Hz)	35 280	35 087	0.55
f_a (Hz)	43 417	43 401	0.04
k (%)	58.28	58.86	0.99

Table 13.9 Stress and temperature iterative computation of the driver with the bolt at the resonance frequency

Iteration	Frequency (Hz)	T (Mpa)	θ (°C)	Frequency (Hz)
1		0	20	35 280
2	35 280	2.14	69	31 024
3	31 024	2.90	60.7	31 789
4	31 790	2.08	61.2	31 842
5	31 842	2.09	61.5	31 809
6	31 809	2.09	61.5	

coupling coefficient. Table 13.8 compares the values of the modal analysis between the analytical and numerical solution. The agreement between these results is very good.

Temperature and stress effect on the device

To study the non-linear material behaviour of a driver tonpilz due to the temperature and the stress, the device has been submitted to a 1 V excitation. At start, the material properties correspond to zero stress and an ambient temperature of 20 °C in the driver. At each step of the harmonic analysis, the resonance frequency is obtained and the temperature and the stress are computed. The following step, from the mean values of the temperature and the stress in the driver, new values of the single crystal properties are computed to determine the new resonance frequency. The iteration is stopped when the convergence is obtained for the temperature and the stress. Table 13.9 displays the iterative process, giving at each step, the resonance frequency, the stress and the temperature, then the new resonance frequency. The convergence is rapidly obtained. Table 13.10 shows the single crystal properties at start

Table 13.10 Comparison of the single crystal properties between start and final computational steps

θ (°C)	20	61.5
T (Mpa)	0	2.09
S_{33}^E (m²/N)	$3.9225\ 10^{-11}$	$5.4787\ 10^{-11}$
d_{33} (C/N)	$9.5875\ 10^{-10}$	$1.5275\ 10^{-09}$
ε_{33}^T (m/F)	$3.5490\ 10^{-08}$	$8.2200\ 10^{-08}$
S_{33}^D (m²/N)	$1.3385\ 10^{-11}$	$2.6403\ 10^{-11}$
g_{33} (Vm/N)	$2.7015\ 10^{-02}$	$1.8582\ 10^{-02}$

Table 13.11 Comparison of the modal analysis results between analytical and numerical solutions at the final step

	Analytical	ATILA	%
f_r (Hz)	31809	31645	0.52
f_a (Hz)	34899	34810	0.28
k (%)	41.14	41.66	1.25

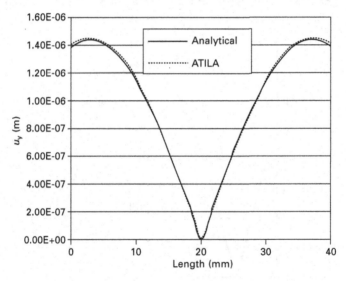

13.37 Axial displacement of the driver at the resonance frequency.

and at the end of the iterative process. Table 13.11 compares the resonance and anti-resonance frequencies obtained at the end of the process for the analytical and numerical solution. The mean value stresses, respectively, for the analytical and numerical solution are 2.09 and 2.04 MPa. Figures 13.37 to 13.40 display, respectively, the axial displacement modulus, the axial deformation modulus, the axial stress modulus and the real part of

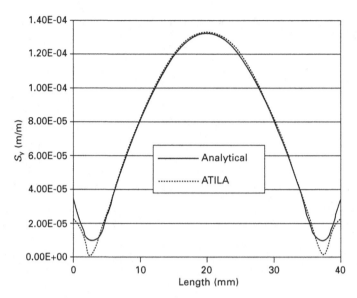

13.38 Axial deformation of the driver at the resonance frequency.

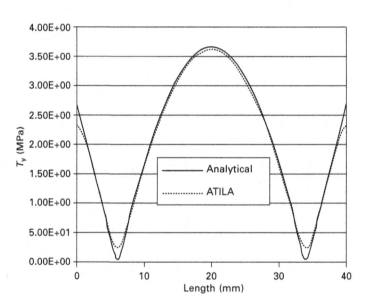

13.39 Axial stress of the driver at the resonance frequency.

the electric field at the resonance frequency comparing the analytical and numerical results. Fig. 13.41 shows the temperature along the driver. The agreement between these values is very good.

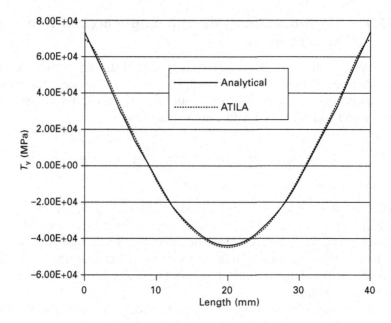

13.40 Electric field in the driver at the resonance frequency.

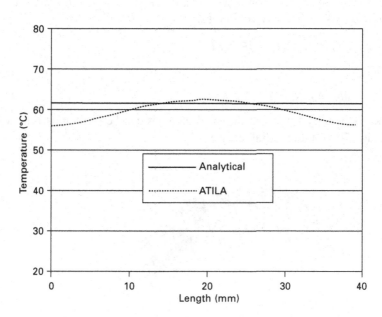

13.41 Temperature in the driver.

13.7   Harmonic analysis of a single crystal thin sphere in air

The aim of this part is to analyze a single crystal thin sphere having a harmonic excitation. This sphere will be submitted to stresses and a gradient of temperature. For the thin sphere in air, an analytical solution will be developed and compared with a numerical solution.

13.7.1 Analytical solution of the thin sphere

Equilibrium equation of the thin sphere

This thin shell spherical transducer has a wall thickness, $t << 2R_m$ with R_m, the mean radius (Fig. 13.42). A radial electric field, E_3, is applied between the electrode surfaces located on the inner and outer surfaces; the poling axis is radial. A circumferential stress is applied causing the expansion of the spherical wall in the radial direction. Due to the thin thickness, the radial stress is negligible.

On the shell element (Fig. 13.43), if the z axis is vertical, the coordinates are the spherical coordinates: θ is the longitudinal and ϕ is the complement to the latitude. Let ρ_c be the shell density, u_r its radial displacement, dF_1 its meridional force and dF_2 its hoop force[12].

The Newton's second law of motion of the shell element applied to the mass dm refers to the forces which are perpendicular to the middle of the shell (n axis). It may be written as:

$$dm\ddot{\vec{u}}_r = \sum d\vec{F}_i = d\vec{F}_1 + d\vec{F}_2 \qquad [13.98]$$

where

$$dm = \rho_c R_m d\theta R_m \sin\theta d\phi t \qquad [13.99]$$

The elementary forces on the shell element can be written as functions of T_1 and T_2 circumferential stresses:

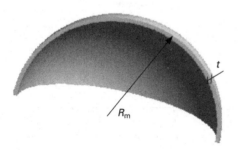

13.42 Shell model ($\frac{1}{4}$ of the shell).

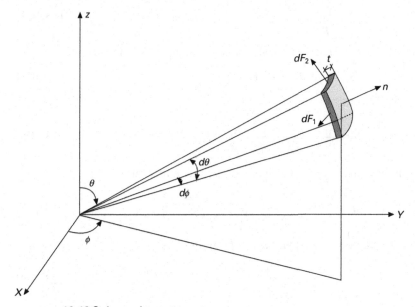

13.43 Sphere element.

$$dF_1 = -2T_1 \frac{d\phi}{2} \sin \theta t R_m d\theta \qquad [13.100]$$

$$dF_2 = -2T_2 \frac{d\theta}{2} \sin \theta t R_m d\phi \qquad [13.101]$$

or

$$\rho_c R_m \frac{\partial^2 u_r}{dt^2} = -(T_1 + T_2) \qquad [13.102]$$

Displacement, deformation and stress

If the independent variables are E and T, the constitutive equations are:

$$S_1 = S_{11}^E T_1 + S_{12}^E T_2 + d_{31} E_3$$
$$S_2 = S_{12}^E T_1 + S_{22}^E T_2 + d_{31} E_3$$
$$D_3 = d_{31} T_1 + d_{31} T_2 + \varepsilon_{33}^T E_3 \qquad [13.103]$$

Due to the spherical symmetry, the stresses and the deformations can be written as:

$$T_1 = T_2$$

$$S_1 = S_2 = \frac{u_r}{R} \tag{13.104}$$

From Eqs [13.103] and [13.104], the deformation S_1 is written as:

$$S_1 = (S_{11}^E + S_{12}^E)T_1 + d_{31}E_3 \tag{13.105}$$

Eq. [13.102] becomes:

$$\frac{\partial^2 u_r}{dt^2} = -\frac{2}{\rho_c R_m(S_{11}^E + S_{12}^E)}\left(\frac{u_r}{R} - d_{31}E_3\right) \tag{13.106}$$

In harmonic analysis with a pulsation ω, this equation is:

$$-\omega^2 u_r = -\frac{2}{\rho_c R_m(S_{11}^E + S_{12}^E)}\left(\frac{u_r}{R} - d_{31}E_3\right) \tag{13.107}$$

At the resonance, this equation can be written as:

$$\omega_r^2 = \frac{2}{\rho_c R_m^2(S_{11}^E + S_{12}^E)} \tag{13.108}$$

Then, the value of the resonance frequency is defined as:

$$f_r = \frac{1}{2\pi}\frac{1}{\sqrt{\rho_c R_m^2 S_c^E}} \tag{13.109}$$

where

$$S_c^E = \frac{(S_{11}^E + S_{12}^E)}{2} \tag{13.110}$$

From the electrical admittance, the coupling coefficient is:

$$k = \frac{d_{31}}{\sqrt{S_c^E \varepsilon_{33}^T}} \tag{13.111}$$

and the anti-resonance frequency can be obtained as:

$$f_e = \frac{f_r}{\sqrt{1 - k^2}} \tag{13.112}$$

From Eq. [13.107], the radial displacement can be written as:

$$u_r = \frac{-d_{31}V}{t\rho_c S_c^E(\omega_r^2 - \omega^2)}\frac{1}{R} \tag{13.113}$$

Taking the losses into account, the thin equation becomes:

$$u_r^* = \frac{-d_{31}^*V}{t\rho_c S_c^E{}^*(\omega_r^2 - \omega^2)}\frac{1}{R} \tag{13.114}$$

Respectively, the real and imaginary part of the radial displacements are:

$$u_r^R = -\frac{V}{t}\frac{R_m^2}{R}d_{31}\frac{(1+\tan\theta'\tan\phi')(1-(\omega/\omega_r)^2)+\tan\phi'(\tan\phi'-\tan\phi')}{(1-(\omega/\omega_r)^2)^2+\tan\phi'^2}$$

[13.115]

$$u_r^I = -\frac{V}{t}\frac{R_m^2}{R}d_{31}\frac{(\tan\phi'-\tan\theta')(1-(\omega/\omega_r)^2)-\tan\phi'(1+\tan\theta'\tan\phi')}{(1-(\omega/\omega_r)^2)^2+\tan\phi'^2}$$

[13.116]

From Eqs [13.104], taking the losses into account, the circumferential deformations are:

$$S_1^* = S_2^* = \frac{u_r^*}{R}$$

[13.117]

From Eqs [13.105] and [13.117], the real and imaginary part of the radial stress, respectively, can be written as:

$$T_1^R = \frac{S_1^R - d_{31}E_3(1+\tan\theta'\tan\phi') - S_1^I\tan\phi'}{S_{11}^E + S_{12}^E}$$

[13.118]

$$T_1^I = \frac{S_1^I + d_{31}E_3(\tan\theta'-\tan\phi') + S_1^R\tan\phi'}{S_{11}^E + S_{12}^E}$$

[13.119]

Electrical displacement, electric field

From Eq. [13.103], the electrical displacement is:

$$D_3^* = d_{31}^*(T_1^* + T_2^*) + \varepsilon_{33}^{T^*}E_3^*$$

[13.120]

From, Eqs [13.118] and [13.119], the real part and imaginary parts of the electrical displacement can be written as:

$$D_3^R = \frac{S_1^R - S_1^I\tan\theta'' - (S_{11}^D + S_{12}^D)(T_1^R + T_1^I\tan\phi'' + (T_1^R\tan\phi'' - T_1^I)\tan\theta'')}{g_{31}}$$

[13.121]

$$D_3^I = \frac{S_1^I + S_1^R\tan\theta'' - (S_{11}^D + S_{12}^D)(T_1^I - T_1^R\tan\phi'' - (T_1^R + T_1^I\tan\phi'')\tan\theta'')}{g_{31}}$$

[13.122]

From Eq. [13.120], with the complex values, the electric field is:

$$E_3^R = \frac{S_1^R - S_1^I \tan\theta'' - (S_{11}^E + S_{12}^E)(T_1^R + T_1^I \tan\phi' + (T_1^R \tan\phi' - T_1^I)\tan\theta'')}{d_{31}}$$

[13.123]

$$E_3^I = \frac{S_1^I + S_1^R \tan\theta'' - (S_{11}^E + S_{12}^E)(T_1^I - T_1^R \tan\phi' + (T_1^R + T_1^I \tan\phi')\tan\theta'')}{d_{31}}$$

[13.124]

Dissipated power

From Eq. [13.71], the dissipated power density of a piezolectric sphere can be written as:

$$p_d = \frac{\omega}{2}[E_3^I D_3^R - E_3^R D_3^I + 2(T_1^I S_1^R - T_1^R S_1^I)]$$

[13.125]

13.7.2 Application

Model geometry

The PMN-30PT single crystal sphere has an outer radius (R_e) 12.5 mm, an inner radius (R_i) 12 mm and a thickness of 0.5 mm (Fig. 13.44). Due to the spherical symmetry, the sphere is modelled with a 2D mesh. Figure 13.45 shows the mesh of a quarter of the sphere.

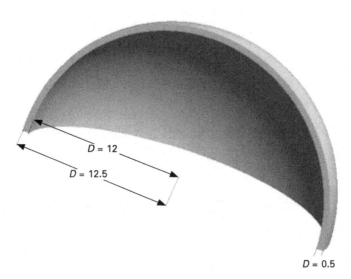

$D = 12$

$D = 12.5$

$D = 0.5$

13.44 Shell geometry.

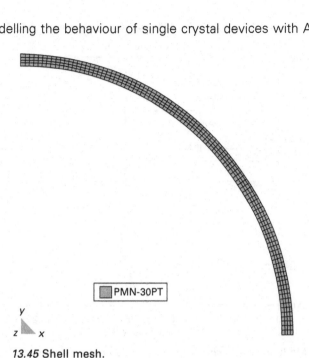

y

z   x

13.45 Shell mesh.

Table 13.12 Comparison of the modal analysis results between analytical and numerical solutions of the sphere

	Analytical	ATILA	%
f_r (Hz)	48 057.5	48 083.6	0.05
f_a (Hz)	65 227.2	65 224.2	0.00
k (%)	67.61	67.57	0.07

Validation

Resonance and anti-resonance frequencies

To validate this analytical solution of the sphere, a modal numerical analysis gives the resonance and anti-resonance frequencies and the coupling coefficient. Table 13.12 compares the values of the modal analysis between the analytical and numerical solution. The agreement between these results is very good.

Harmonic analysis

The analytical results of the sphere submitted to a 1 V harmonic excitation, 2000 V/m electric field, has been compared with the numerical results. Figures 13.46 to 13.48, display, respectively, the modulus of the radial displacement, the circumferential displacement and the circumferential stress vs frequency for the two analyses. The agreement between the analytical and numerical

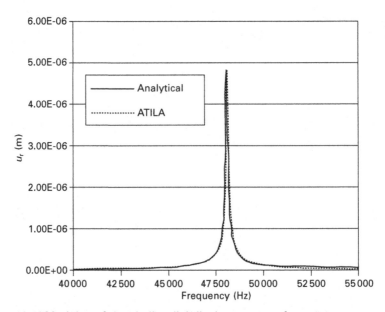

13.46 Modulus of the shell radial displacement vs frequency.

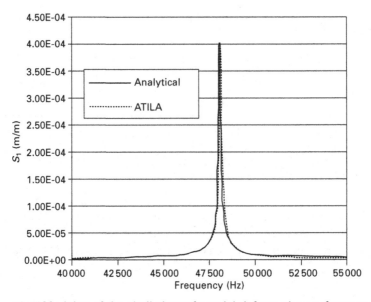

13.47 Modulus of the shell circumferential deformation vs frequency.

results is very good. Figures 13.49 to 13.51 show, respectively, at the resonance frequency, the modulus of radial displacement, the circumferential displacement and the circumferential stress along the thickness of the sphere. A slight difference is observed at the end of the shell.

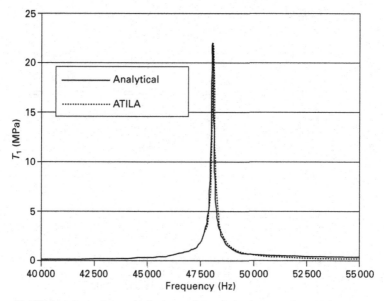

13.48 Modulus of the shell circumferential stress vs frequency.

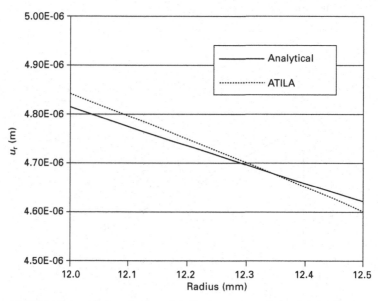

13.49 Modulus of the shell radial displacement along the thickness.

One dimensional heat transfer

To validate the thermal analysis, the shell is defined with a thermal element using a one-dimensional linear interpolation (Fig. 13.52). The interpolating polynomial for the one-dimensional element is

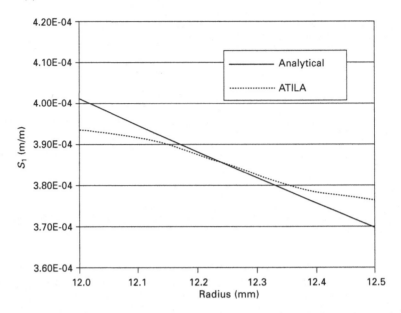

13.50 Modulus of the shell circumferential deformation along the thickness.

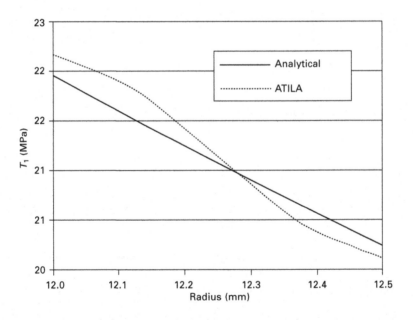

13.51 Modulus of the shell circumferential stress along the thickness.

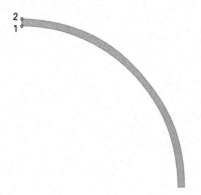

13.52 1D shell thermal model.

$$T(r) = N_1(r)T_1 + N_2(r)T_2 \qquad [13.126]$$

where

$$N_1(r) = \left(1 - \frac{r}{t}\right) \qquad [13.127]$$

$$N_2(r) = \frac{r}{t} \qquad [13.128]$$

For a steady thermal analysis with one element, the finite element formulation is:

$$([K_\mathrm{T}] + [K_\mathrm{h1}] + [K_\mathrm{h2}])\{T\} = \{K_{\mathrm{T}\infty 1}\} + \{K_{\mathrm{T}\infty 2}\} + \{Q\} \qquad [13.129]$$

where

$$[K_\mathrm{T}] = \frac{k(R_\mathrm{e}^3 - R_\mathrm{i}^3)}{3(R_\mathrm{e} - R_\mathrm{i})^2} \begin{bmatrix} 1 & -1 \\ -1 & 1 \end{bmatrix} \text{ is the conductivity matrix} \qquad [13.130]$$

$$[K_\mathrm{hRi}] = hS_\mathrm{i} \begin{bmatrix} 1 & 0 \\ 0 & 0 \end{bmatrix} \text{ is the convection matrix, } S_\mathrm{i} \text{ is the}$$

inner area at node 1 $\qquad [13.131]$

$$[K_\mathrm{hRe}] = hS_\mathrm{e} \begin{bmatrix} 0 & 0 \\ 0 & 1 \end{bmatrix} \text{ is the convection matrix, } S_\mathrm{e} \text{ is the}$$

outer area at node 2 $\qquad [13.132]$

$$\{k_{\mathrm{T}\infty\mathrm{Re}}\} = hT_\infty S_\mathrm{i} \begin{Bmatrix} 1 \\ 0 \end{Bmatrix} \text{ is the convection vector at node 1} \qquad [13.133]$$

$$\{k_{T\infty Re}\} = hT_\infty S_e \begin{Bmatrix} 0 \\ 1 \end{Bmatrix} \text{ is the convection vector at node 2} \quad [13.134]$$

$$\{Q\} = \frac{p_d V}{2} \begin{Bmatrix} 1 \\ 1 \end{Bmatrix} \text{ is the thermal load vector, } p_d \text{ is the}$$

$$\text{dissipated power density} \quad [13.135]$$

where

$$S_e = R_e^2$$

$$S_i = R_i^2$$

$$V = \frac{4}{3}\pi(R_e^3 - R_i^3)\frac{1}{4\pi}$$

The numerical values used are:

$R_i = 12$ mm, $R_e = 12{,}5$ mm, $k_{xx} = 2W/m/°C$,

$h = 10$ W/m^2/°C, $T_\infty = 20$ °C

$p_d = 4{,}9117\ 10^6$W/m^3 at 48057.5 Hz resonance frequency

With these values, Eq. [13.129] becomes:

$$\begin{bmatrix} 0.60177 & -0.60033 \\ -0.60033 & 0.60190 \end{bmatrix}\begin{Bmatrix} T_1 \\ T_2 \end{Bmatrix} = \begin{Bmatrix} 0.21309 \\ 0.21309 \end{Bmatrix} \quad [13.136]$$

The results are $T_1 = 141.95$ °C and $T_2 = 141.93$ °C.

To compare this model with an ATILA model, a harmonic analysis has been performed at the resonance frequency of 48 083.5 Hz. Figure 13.53 presents the comparison between analytical and numerical temperatures. A very good agreement is observed between the simple model and the ATILA model.

Temperature and stress effects on the non-linear material behaviour of the shell

To analyze the non-linear material behaviour of the shell due to the temperature and the stress, the shell has been submitted to an excitation of 0.5 V. The material properties of the single crystal used correspond to an ambient temperature of 20 °C and a zero stress. At each step of the harmonic analysis, the resonance frequency is obtained and the temperature and the stress are computed. The following step, from the mean values of the temperature and the stress in the shell, new values of the single crystal properties are computed to determine the new resonance frequency. The

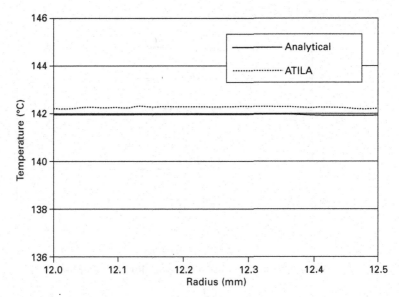

13.53 Shell temperature along the thickness.

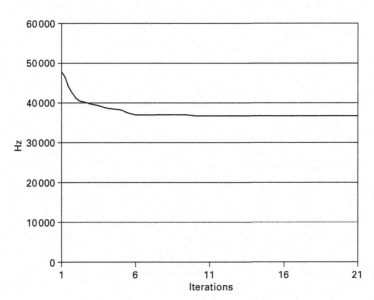

13.54 Resonance frequency iterative computation of the sphere in air.

iteration is stopped when the convergence is obtained for the temperature and the stress. Figures 13.54 to 13.56 summarize the iterative computation. The iteration is stopped when the convergence is obtained. The convergence is obtained after 21 iterations. Table 13.13 shows the single crystal properties at start and at the end of the iterative process.

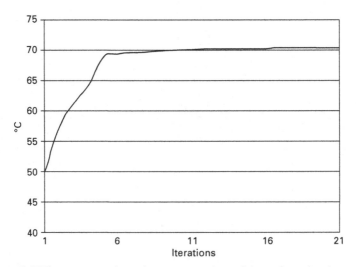

13.55 Temperature iterative computation of the sphere in air.

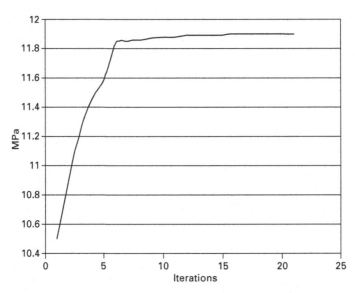

13.56 Stress iterative computation of the sphere in air.

13.8   Harmonic analysis of a single crystal thin shell in water: an analytical solution

13.8.1   Displacement and circumferential deformation

The analytical study of a piezoelectric shell in water can be obtained from the radial displacement defined as[13]:

Table 13.13 Comparison of the single crystal properties between start and final computational steps

θ (°C)	20	70.28
T (Mpa)	0	11.90
S_{33}^{E} (m²/N)	3.9285 10^{-11}	6.7186 10^{-11}
d_{33} (C/N)	9.5875 10^{-10}	1.8484 10^{-09}
ε_{33}^{T} (m/F)	3.5490 10^{-08}	1.5140 10^{-07}
S_{33}^{D} (m²/N)	1.3385 10^{-11}	4.4621 10^{-11}
g_{33} (Vm/N)	2.7015 10^{-02}	1.2208 10^{-02}

$$u_r^* = -\frac{N^*V}{j\omega(Z_m^* + Z_r^*)}$$ [13.137]

where Z_m^* and Z_r^* are, respectively, the mechanical and radiation impedance

$$Z_m^* = j\left(\omega m - \frac{1}{\omega e^*}\right)$$ [13.138]

$$Z_r^* = j\frac{4\pi\rho_f c_f k R_m^3}{1 + jkR_m}$$ [13.139]

ρ_f is the fluid mass density, $c_{f,}$ is the speed of the sound in the fluid and k is the wave number in the fluid. The mass of the shell is:

$$m = 4\pi R_m^2 \rho_c t$$ [13.140]

and

$$e^* = \frac{S_c^E(1 - j\tan\phi')}{4\pi t}$$ [13.141]

$$N^* = \frac{4\pi R_m d_{31}(1 - j\tan\theta')}{S_c^E(1 - j\tan\phi')}$$ [13.142]

The radiation impedance can be written as:

$$Z_r^* = R_r + j\omega M_r$$ [13.143]

where

$$M_f = 4\pi R_m^3 \rho_f$$ [13.144]

and

$$A = 4\pi R_m^2$$ [13.145]

The radiation resistance and the radiation mass are, respectively[14]:

$$R_r = \frac{\rho_f c_f A (kR_m)^2}{1 + (kR_m)^2} \qquad [13.146]$$

$$M_r = \frac{M_f}{1 + (kR_m)^2} \qquad [13.147]$$

From these equations, the real part and imaginary parts of the radial displacement are defined as:

$$u_{rm}^R = -\frac{d_{31} V R_m}{t} \left[\frac{(1 + \tan\phi' \tan\theta') X_1 + (\tan\phi' - \tan\theta') X_2}{(X_1^2 + X_2^2)(1 + \tan\phi'^2)} \right] \qquad [13.148]$$

$$u_{rm}^I = -\frac{d_{31} V R_m}{t} \left[\frac{(\tan\phi' - \tan\theta') X_1 - (1 + \tan\phi' \tan\theta') X_2}{(X_1^2 + X_2^2)(1 + \tan\phi'^2)} \right] \qquad [13.149]$$

where

$$X_1 = 1 - \left(\frac{\omega}{\omega_r}\right)^2 \left(1 + \frac{M_r}{m}\right) \qquad [13.150]$$

$$X_2 = \frac{\omega}{\omega_r^2} \frac{R_r}{m} + \tan\phi' \qquad [13.151]$$

ω' is obtained from Eq. [13.108].

Then, the real part and imaginary parts of the deformation are:

$$S_{1rm}^R = \frac{u_{rm}^R}{R_m} \qquad [13.152]$$

$$S_{1rm}^I = \frac{u_{rm}^I}{R_m} \qquad [13.153]$$

Fluid pressure

For the sphere in fluid[15], the dynamic equilibrium of a shell element (Fig. 13.43) can be written from Eq. [13.102] as:

$$\rho_c R_m \frac{\partial^2 u_r}{dt^2} = -(T_1 + T_2) - p_0^* \frac{R_e^2}{t R_m} \qquad [13.154]$$

where R_e is the outer radius of the shell, p_0^* is the pressure on the outer area of the shell, T_1 and T_2 are the stresses at the mean value of the radius R_m.

The value of the acoustic pressure in the fluid is obtained from the spherical wave equation[16]:

$$\Delta\psi(r)^* + k^2\psi(r)^* = 0 \tag{13.155}$$

where $\psi(r)$ is the speed flux defined as:

$$\psi(r)^* = \frac{p(r)^*}{j\rho_f\omega} \tag{13.156}$$

From Eq. [13.155], this flux is:

$$\psi(r)^* = \frac{4\pi R_e^2 v_0}{(1+jkR_e)} \frac{e^{-jk(r-R_e)}}{4\pi r} \tag{13.157}$$

Then, the acoustic fluid pressure is:

$$p(r)^* = j\frac{\rho_f\omega 4\pi R_e^2 e - jk(r-R_e)}{(1+jkR_e)4\pi r} \tag{13.158}$$

The real part and imaginary parts of the acoustic fluid pressure are:

$$p(r)^R = \frac{\rho_f\omega^2 R_m^2}{(1+(kR_e)^2 R_\infty)}(u_0^R\cos k(r-R_e) + u_0^I\sin k(r-R_e)$$
$$+ kR_e(u_0^I\cos k(r-R_e) - u_0^I\sin k(r-R_e))) \tag{13.159}$$

$$p(r)^I = \frac{\rho_f\omega^2 R_m^2}{(1+(kR_e)^2 R_\infty)}(u_0^I\cos k(r-R_e) - u_0^R\sin k(r-R_e)$$
$$- kR_e(u_0^R\cos k(r-R_e) + u_0^I\sin k(r-R_e))) \tag{13.160}$$

At the outer area of the shell, the pressure is defined as follows:

$$p_0^R = \frac{\rho_f\omega^2 R_m^2}{(1+(kR_e)^2 R_\infty)}(u_0^R + kR_eu_0^I) \tag{13.161}$$

$$p_0^I = \frac{\rho_f\omega^2 R_m^2}{(1+(kR_e)^2 R_\infty)}(u_0^I - kR_eu_0^R) \tag{13.162}$$

Stresses

From Eq. [13.154], the real part and imaginary parts of the circumferential stress are:

$$T_{1rm}^R = \frac{\omega^2\rho_c R_m}{2}u_{rm}^R + \frac{p^R R_e^2}{2tR_m} \tag{13.163}$$

$$T_{1rm}^{I} = \frac{\omega^2 \rho_c R_m}{2} u_{rm}^{I} + \frac{p^{I} R_e^2}{2t R_m} \qquad [13.164]$$

With the fluid, Eq. [13.105] can be written as:

$$S_1 = (S_{11}^{E} + S_{12}^{E})T_1 + S_{13}^{E}T_3 + d_{31}E_3 \qquad [13.165]$$

In this case, the real part and imaginary parts of the radial stress are:

$$T_3^{R} = \frac{S_1^{R} - d_{31}E_3(1 + \tan\theta'\tan\phi') - S_1^{I}\tan\phi' - (S_{11}^{E} + S_{12}^{E})T_1^{R}}{S_{13}^{E}}$$

$$[13.166]$$

$$T_3^{I} = \frac{S_1^{I} - d_{31}E_3(\tan\theta' - \tan\theta') + S_1^{R}\tan\phi' - (S_{11}^{E} + S_{12}^{E})T_1^{I}}{S_{13}^{E}} \quad [13.167]$$

Circumferential deformation

From the piezoelectric constitutive equations, the real and imaginary parts of the circumferential deformation become:

$$S_3^{R} = 2S_{13}^{E}(T_1^{R} + \tan\phi'T_1^{I}) + S_{33}^{E}(T_3^{R} + \tan\phi'T_3^{I}) + d_{33}E_3^{R} \qquad [13.168]$$

$$S_3^{I} = 2S_{13}^{E}(T_1^{I} - \tan\phi'T_1^{R}) + S_{33}^{E}(T_3^{I} - \tan\phi'T_3^{R}) - d_{33}\tan\theta'E_3^{R} \qquad [13.169]$$

Electrical displacement

When the shell is in water, the real and imaginary parts of the electrical displacement (Eq. [13.120] can be written as:

$$D_3^{R} = 2d_{31}(T_1^{R} + \tan\theta'T_1^{I}) + d_{33}(T_3^{R} + \tan\theta'T_3^{I}) + \varepsilon_{33}^{T}E_3^{R} \qquad [13.170]$$

$$D_3^{I} = 2d_{31}(T_1^{I} - \tan\theta'T_1^{R}) + d_{33}(T_3^{I} - \tan\theta'T_3^{R}) - \varepsilon_{33}^{T}\tan\delta'E_3^{R} \qquad [13.171]$$

Dissipated power density

In this case, the dissipated power density, from Eq. [13.71] can be written as:

$$p_d = \frac{\omega}{2}[E_3^{I}D_3^{R} - E_3^{R}D_3^{I} + 2(T_1^{I}S_1^{R} - T_1^{R}S_1^{I}) + T_3^{I}S_3^{R} - T_3^{R}S_3^{I}] \quad [13.172]$$

13.8.2 Application

Numerical model

To validate this analysis of the shell in water, the shell has been submitted to a harmonic excitation. To take into account the effects of the temperature and the stress on the behaviour of the single crystal material of the sphere, several data have been modified. The value of the excitation potential is 300 V, the value of the mechanical, dielectric and piezoelectric losses is 1%. Figure 13.57 shows the mesh of the shell in water. The radius of the non-reflecting boundary surface is 25 mm. The water temperature is 16 °C and the values of the film coefficient h_{water} is 1350 W/m²/°C.

Validation

Harmonic analysis

The analytical results of the sphere for a 300 V harmonic excitation, 6kV/cm electric field, has been compared with the numerical results. Figures 13.58 to 13.63 display, respectively, the real and imaginary parts of the radial displacement and of the circumferential deformation vs frequency for the two analyses. The agreement between the analytical and numerical results is very good.

Figures 13.64 and 13.65 display, vs frequency, respectively, the real and imaginary parts of the radial stress at the outer area of the shell and of the fluid pressure on the same area. A difference appears between these values

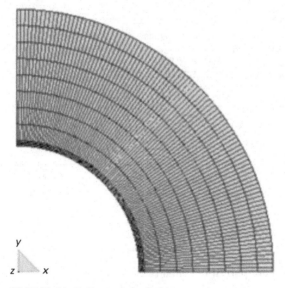

13.57 Fluid shell mesh in fluid.

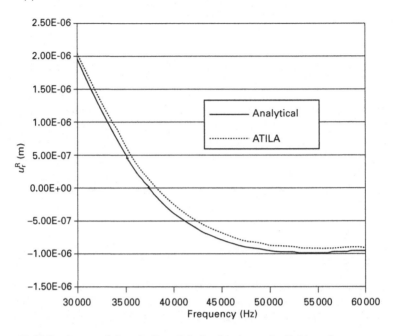

13.58 Real part of the shell radial displacement in fluid vs frequency.

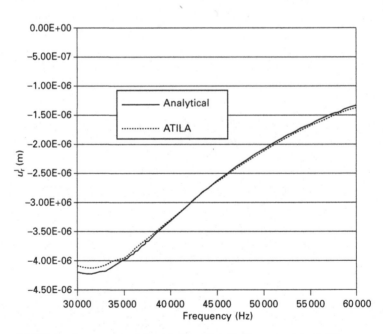

13.59 Imaginary part of the shell radial displacement in fluid vs frequency.

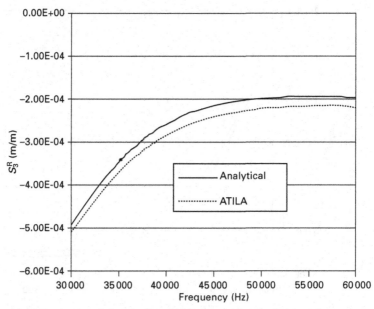

13.60 Real part of the shell radial deformation in fluid vs frequency.

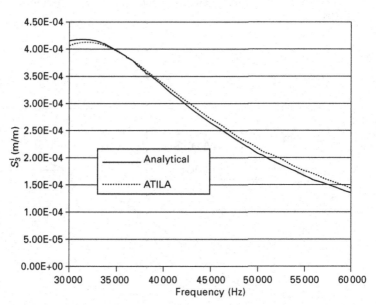

13.61 Imaginary part of the shell radial deformation in fluid vs frequency.

because, in the ATILA code, the stresses are computed from the nodes in a shell element. Figures 13.66 and 13.67 show, respectively, the real and imaginary parts of the circumferential stress vs frequency. Figures 13.68 to

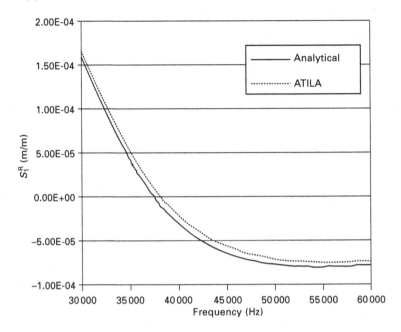

13.62 Real part of the shell circumferential deformation in fluid vs frequency.

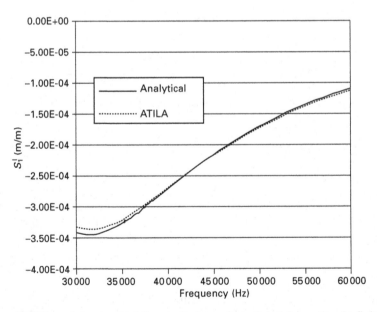

13.63 Imaginary part of the shell circumferential deformation in fluid vs frequency.

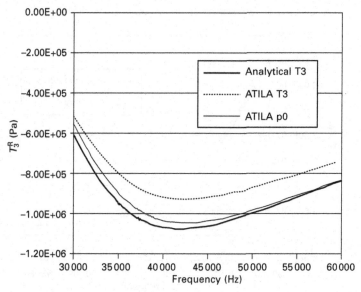

13.64 Real part of the shell radial stress in fluid vs frequency.

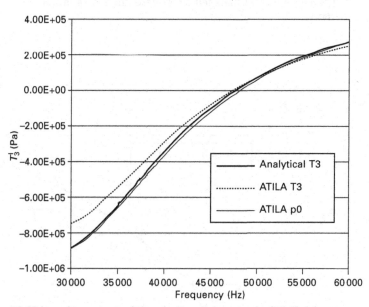

13.65 Imaginary part of the shell radial stress in fluid vs frequency.

13.71 display, respectively, the real and imaginary parts of the fluid pressure on the outer area of the shell and of the far field pressure. The transmitting voltage response is shown in Fig. 13.72. The agreement between the analytical and numerical results is very good.

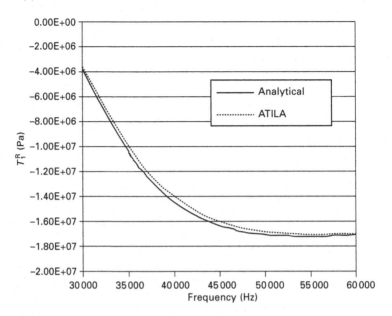

13.66 Real part of the shell circumferential stress in fluid vs frequency.

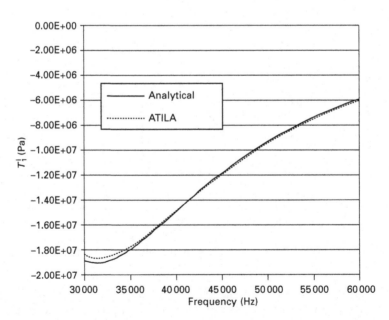

13.67 Imaginary part of the shell circumferential stress in fluid vs frequency.

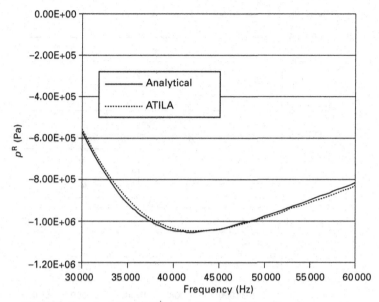

13.68 Real part of the shell pressure in fluid vs frequency.

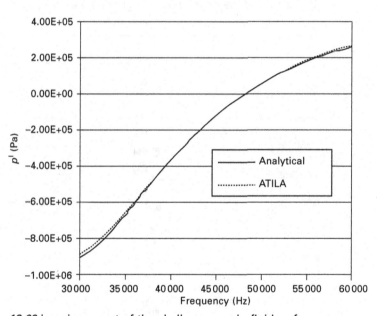

13.69 Imaginary part of the shell pressure in fluid vs frequency.

13.8.3 One dimensional heat transfer

To validate the thermal analysis, due to the spherical symmetry, the shell is defined with a one-dimensional thermal element (Fig. 13.73). Due to the

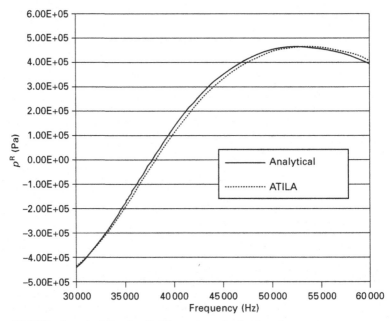

13.70 Real part of the far field pressure in fluid vs frequency.

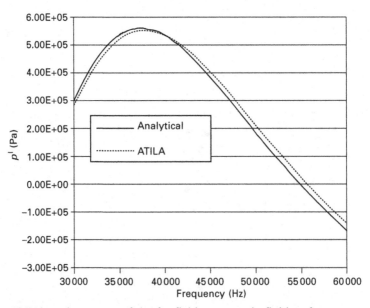

13.71 Imaginary part of the far field pressure in fluid vs frequency.

fluid, the temperature profile along the thickness is not linear. Assuming a parabolic temperature profile, the thermal element is a three-node finite element.

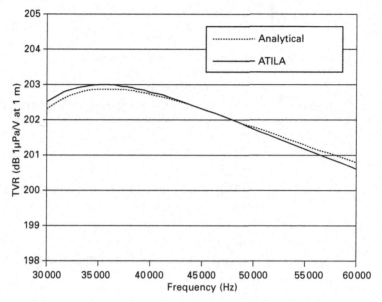

13.72 Shell transmitting voltage response (TVR).

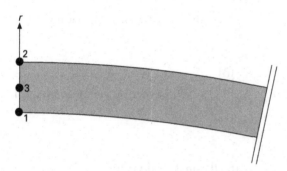

13.73 1D three-node shell thermal model.

The interpolating polynomial for the three-node element is

$$T(r) = N_1(r)T_1 + N_2(r)T_2 + N_3(r)T_3 \qquad [13.173]$$

where

$$N_3 = 4\frac{r}{t}\left(1 - \frac{r}{t}\right) \qquad [13.174]$$

$$N_1 = \left(1 - \frac{r}{t}\right) - \frac{N_3}{2} \qquad [13.175]$$

$$N_2 = \frac{r}{t} - \frac{N_3}{2} \qquad [13.176]$$

With this element, Eqs [13.130] to [13.136] become:

$$[K_T] = \frac{k(R_e^3 - R_i^3)}{3(R_e - R_i)^2} \frac{1}{3} \begin{bmatrix} 7 & -8 & 1 \\ -8 & 16 & -8 \\ 1 & -8 & 7 \end{bmatrix} \text{ is the conductivity matrix}$$

$$[13.177]$$

$$[K_{hRi}] = hS_i \begin{bmatrix} 1 & 0 & 0 \\ 0 & 0 & 0 \\ 0 & 0 & 0 \end{bmatrix} \text{ is the convection matrix at node 1 } [13.178]$$

$$[K_{hRe}] = h_{eau}S_e \begin{bmatrix} 0 & 0 & 0 \\ 0 & 0 & 0 \\ 0 & 0 & 1 \end{bmatrix} \text{ is the convection matrix at node 2}$$

$$[13.179]$$

$$\{k_{T\infty Ri}\} = hT_{air\infty}S_i \begin{Bmatrix} 1 \\ 0 \\ 0 \end{Bmatrix} \text{ is the convection vector at node 1 } [13.180]$$

$$\{k_{T\infty Re}\} = hT_{eau\infty}S_e \begin{Bmatrix} 0 \\ 0 \\ 1 \end{Bmatrix} \text{ is the convection vector at node 2} [13.181]$$

$$\{Q\} = \frac{p_d V}{6} \begin{Bmatrix} 1 \\ 4 \\ 1 \end{Bmatrix} \text{ is the thermal load vector} \qquad [13.182]$$

With the numerical values of the sphere in water, Eq. [13.129] becomes:

$$\begin{bmatrix} 1.612 & -1.601 & 0.200 \\ -1.601 & 3.202 & -1.601 \\ 0.200 & -1.601 & 1.402 \end{bmatrix} \begin{Bmatrix} T_1 \\ T_2 \\ T_3 \end{Bmatrix} = \begin{Bmatrix} 0.263 \\ 0.938 \\ 3.61 \end{Bmatrix} \qquad [13.183]$$

The results are $T_1 = 23.81°C$, $T_2 = 23.52 °C$ and $T_3 = 22.65 °C$.

Figure 13.74 shows a comparison between the temperatures obtained with a numerical analysis and with an analytical solution derived from a linear and quadratic temperature interpolation. A very good agreement is observed between the quadratic solution and the ATILA model.

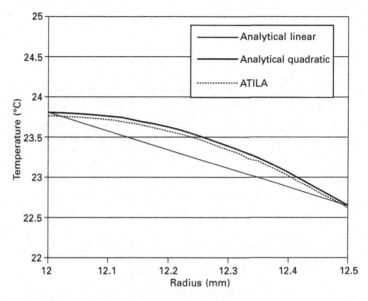

13.74 Shell temperature along the thickness.

13.8.4 Temperature and stress effects on the material behaviour of the shell in water

To analyze the non-linear material behaviour of the shell due to the temperature and the stress, this shell has been submitted to an excitation of 300V. The material properties of the single crystal used correspond to an ambient temperature of 20 °C and a zero stress. The excitation frequency, 42 000 Hz, used in this process is always the same because the transmitting voltage response for the shell is almost constant vs frequency. At each step of the harmonic analysis, the temperature and the stress are computed. The following step, from the mean values of the temperature and the stress in the shell, new values of the single crystal properties are computed to determine the new resonance frequency. The iteration is stopped when the convergence is obtained for the temperature and the stress. This process is the same for the analytical and numerical solution. Figures 13.75 to 13.76 sum up the iterative computation. The iteration is stopped when the convergence is obtained. The convergence is obtained rapidly. Table 13.14 shows the single crystal properties at the start and at the end of the iterative numerical process. Figures 13.77 and 13.78 display, respectively, the temperature and the circumferential stress along the thickness of the shell at the initial start and at the final step of the numerical process.

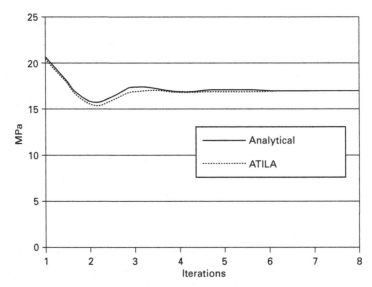

13.75 Temperature iterative computation of the sphere in water.

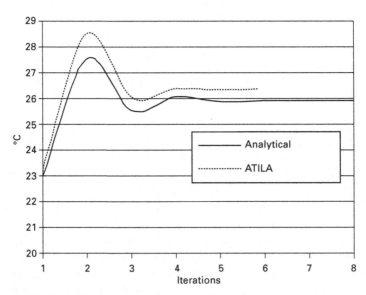

13.76 Stress iterative computation of the sphere in water.

13.9   Conclusion

The analytic models of these four devices have enabled us to know the effect of the temperature and the stress on the behaviour of the single crystal material. At each step of the non-linear harmonic analysis, the temperature

Table 13.14 Comparison of the single crystal properties between start and final computational steps

θ (°C)	20	70.28
T (MPa)	0	11.90
S_{33}^{E} (m²/N)	3.9285 10^{-11}	4.9227 10^{-11}
d_{33} (C/N)	9.5875 10^{-10}	1.0571 10^{-09}
ε_{33}^{T} (m/F)	3.5490 10^{-08}	6.0111 10^{-08}
S_{33}^{D} (m²/N)	1.3385 10^{-11}	3.0636 10^{-11}
g_{33} (Vm/N)	2.7015 10^{-02}	1.7586 10^{-02}

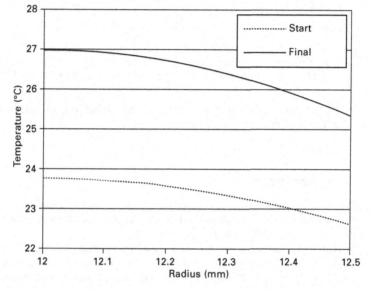

13.77 Shell temperature along the thickness at start and final step of the process.

and the stress are computed and the single crystal properties are updated. The iterative process is stopped when the convergence is obtained for these values. This process has been used for the analytical and numerical solution. These developments have been proposed to predict the performance of these devices considering the highly non-linear behaviour with a non-linear solution procedure. The ATILA solvers will also require updating to handle the constitutive relationships for single crystal materials. Further work will also be necessary to improve the structure of the code to boost the performance required to solve harmonic problems within a reasonable calculation time. Then, an updated version of ATILA with new solvers enabling significantly faster computing times will be proposed.

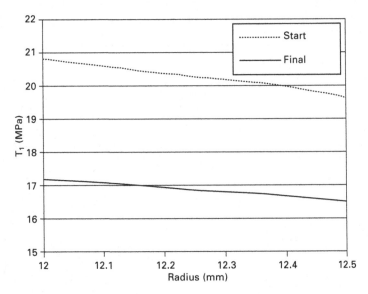

13.78 Circumferential stress along the thickness at start and final step of the process.

13.10   References

1.   J. Luo, W. Hackenberger, 'Development of relaxor piezoelectric single crystals for sonar and medical imaging transducers', *2009 US Navy Workshop on Acoustic Transduction Materials and Devices.*

2.   P. Han, 'Commercialization of large-sized PMN-PT based piezolectric crystals', *2009 US Navy Workshop on Acoustic Transduction Materials and Devices.*

3.   L.C. Lim, J. Jin, K.K. Rajan, 'PZN-PT single crystal underwater devices', *2009 US Navy Workshop on Acoustic Transduction Materials and Devices.*

4.   S.M. Lee, D.H. Kim, T.J. Kim, H.Y. Lee, 'Piezoelectric single crystals and single crystal-epoxy composites for energy harvesting applications', *59th ICAT/JTTAS Joint International Smart Actuator Symposium*, 2010.

5.   *APC International Ltd Products and Services.*

6.   *Morgan Matroc, Technical Ceramics.*

7.   A. Benayad, G. Sebald, B. Guiffard, L. Lebrun, D. Guyomar 'Temperature dependence of piezoelectric properties of PMN-PT and PZN-PT single crystals,' *J. Phys. IV France* 126, 53–57, 2005.

8.   L. Ching-Yu, 'Material characterization and modeling for piezoelectric actuation and power generation under high electromechanical driving levels', PhD thesis, MIT, June 2002.

9.   O. B. Wilson, *An Introduction to the Theory and Design of Sonar Transducers*, Peninsula Publishing, Los Altos, CA, 1988.

10. J. C. Debus, 'Outil de modélisation de transducteurs acoustiques à base de monocristaux piézoélectriques', *Marché* No. 2009 34 0034, DGA, December, 2010.

11.   R. Holland, 'Representation of dielectric, elastic and piezoelectric losses by complex coefficients', *IEEE* SU 14, 18, 1967.
12.   K. Anifrani, 'Contribution à l'étude de structures piézoélectrique à l'aide de la méthode des éléments finis', Thèse de Docteur en Physique, USTL Lille, Janvier 1988.
13.   B. Dubus, 'Analyse des limitations de puissance des transducteurs piézoélectriques', Thèse de Docteur en Sciences des Matériaux, USTL Lille, Septembre 1989.
14.   C. Sherman, J. L. Butler, *Transducers and Arrays for Underwater Sound*, Springer Sciences, New York, 2008.
15.   J. C. Debus, R. Bossut, 'Non-linear time domain of electrostrictve materials in a fluid domain using the finite element code ATILA', Report, NUWC, Contract number: N66604-98-M-5957.
16.   A. Pierce, *Acoustics: An Introduction to its Physical Principles and Applications*, Acoustical Society of America, Melville, 1991.

Index